T0323462

Pensions Imperilled

Pensions Imperilled

*The Political Economy of Private
Pensions Provision in the UK*

Craig Berry

OXFORD
UNIVERSITY PRESS

OXFORD

UNIVERSITY PRESS

Great Clarendon Street, Oxford, OX2 6DP,
United Kingdom

Oxford University Press is a department of the University of Oxford.
It furthers the University's objective of excellence in research, scholarship,
and education by publishing worldwide. Oxford is a registered trade mark of
Oxford University Press in the UK and in certain other countries

First Edition published in 2021

Impression: 1

Published in the United States of America by Oxford University Press
198 Madison Avenue, New York, NY 10016, United States of America

British Library Cataloguing in Publication Data
Data available

Library of Congress Control Number: 2020941923

ISBN 978–0–19–878283–4

DOI: 10.1093/oso/9780198782834.001.0001

Printed and bound in Great Britain by
Clays Ltd, Elcograf S.p.A.

Links to third party websites are provided by Oxford in good faith and
for information only. Oxford disclaims any responsibility for the materials
contained in any third party website referenced in this work.

Praise for Pensions Imperilled

This is an outstanding piece of scholarship and a really superb achievement. Craig Berry takes what most people mistakenly treat as the arcane subject matter of pensions policy and presents it as a thought-provoking page-turner. Anyone who is worried about getting old in the UK or about what it might take to embed more progressive economic alternatives will have to read this book, even if it is through their fingers.

Matthew Watson, Professor of Political Economy, University of Warwick

Pensions Imperilled employs a political economy perspective to explore how policy-making associated with wider social and economic change has presented challenges for financial security in retirement. It is up-to-date, accessible, and informative, considering emerging trends in pensions provision and their links to financialization and neoliberalism. It is key reading for those wanting to gain an in-depth understanding of how pensions policy and practice relates to the UK economy.

Liam Foster, Senior Lecturer in Social Policy and Social Work,
University of Sheffield

Utterly brilliant if very scary in its implications—not a book to have on your bedside table if you wish to sleep comfortably through the night. Highly original and depressingly persuasive, this is the most detailed and most troubling account we have of the impending pensions crisis. Its warnings need to be heeded.

Colin Hay, Professor of Political Sciences, Sciences Po Paris

Original and thorough, *Pensions Imperilled* provides a myth-busting analysis of pensions provision as a crucial element of British capitalist management, in comparative perspective. Presenting a unique treatment of temporality, and denouncing the inherent contradiction of an intergenerational collective arrangement that is increasingly premised on individualism and (further) financialization, Berry sounds the alarm for a UK pension crisis that has barely begun. A must-read for a multidisciplinary and truly inter-generational understanding of the perennial policy puzzles involving private pensions.

Giselle Datz, Associate Professor of Government and
International Affairs, Virginia Tech

In *Pensions Imperilled*, Craig Berry masterfully dispels the popular myths around population ageing and financial volatility that have legitimized the United Kingdom's far-reaching pension reforms for decades. Instead, Berry directs our attention to the pivotal role of statecraft—policy-makers' use of state power to create a political outcome consistent with their ideological views—as a catalyst behind the ongoing neoliberalization and financialization of the UK pension system. This book is essential reading for anyone alarmed by the rapidly disappearing promise of secure and adequate pensions for today's workforce.

Natascha van der Zwan, Assistant Professor in Public Administration,
Leiden University

Why does the UK find itself embroiled in a pension crisis? *Pensions Imperilled* draws on a wealth of research to show that the standard demographic arguments about ageing fall far short. Instead, Berry shows that changes in the UK's political economy, what is commonly referred to as 'financialization', led to policy changes that have made retirement security more precarious and individualized. *Pensions Imperilled* is a must read that rightly refocuses our attention onto political economy.

Michael A. McCarthy, Associate Professor of Sociology,
Marquette University

For May, my grandmother

Preface and Acknowledgements

I have been writing this book, albeit without realizing it, since Monday, 5 January 2009: my dad's fiftieth birthday, but also my first day in HM Treasury's pensions team. The one thing you quickly learn about the Treasury, and come to greatly appreciate, is just how incredibly smart everybody is. I learned a huge amount from my managers Ollie Entwistle, Paul Randle, and Darren Philp, and remain extremely grateful for their support during my brief time in the department. It was, and remains, the most important experience of my professional life. But as I got up to speed as quickly as I could about the mysterious world of pensions, it started to dawn upon me that something was quite wrong. I had joined the Treasury just as I was finishing off my PhD at the University of Sheffield on the role of globalization discourse in United Kingdom (UK) trade policy—nothing whatsoever to do with pensions policy—and came to realize that many of the forms of argument in favour of trade liberalization were also being used to justify pensions reform. The terminology was very different, but it became clear that, as dedicated as the then Labour government was to rectifying the 'underpensioned' problem, it was seeking to do so based on highly questionable assumptions about the ability of individuals—that is, citizen-workers, or citizen-worker-savers in this case—to provide for their own well-being, if only they were appropriately disciplined by competitive market dynamics.

Of course, the big questions around the 'neoliberal' drift in UK pensions policy were not my central concern at the Treasury. My day job centred on the implementation of the Financial Assistance Scheme (for members of insolvent pension schemes) and the administration of pensioner benefits. In the former task, I found myself part of the state machinery intimately involved in compensating for the failures of private pensions provision in the UK. In the latter, I confronted the early politics of post-crisis austerity, but simply lacked the headspace to connect what was happening to the state pension system, what was happening to private pensions, and what was happening to political-economic governance in the UK more generally. In 2010, craving this space, I took the opportunity to join a think-tank, the International Longevity Centre-UK (ILC-UK), so that I could ask some of the bigger questions about UK pensions (while still being able to pay the rent!). I had a great time at ILC-UK, particularly working with David Sinclair and Valentina Serra. I learned a lot about pensions from the wider ILC-UK community, particularly Jackie Wells, James Lloyd, Tom Boardman, and Lawrence Churchill, and I had more contact with the pensions minister, and the private pensions industry, than I had had as a Treasury civil servant. I also became part of the Pensions Research Network at the University of Westminster, organized by the late Orla Gough, a brilliant scholar from whom I learned a great deal about pensions provision.

My research at ILC-UK was always framed, however, by the issue of increasing longevity, and the notion that population ageing represented a crisis that required a radical reshaping of age-related welfare provision. I became extremely uncomfortable with the idea that increasing longevity was a huge problem for UK pensions provision. It felt like the problem was being defined in a way that *automatically* led to demands for the retrenchment of state provision, and a greater dependence for individuals on risky forms of private pensions saving. I endeavoured to develop progressive solutions, yet for a problem I was not convinced even existed, at least not in the way it was typically being framed in mainstream public debate.

After a short period freelancing, and lecturing on economic policy at the University of Warwick, I joined the Trades Union Congress (TUC) as Pensions Policy Officer. It was at this point, coming into contact with Nicola Smith, Nigel Stanley, Alice Hood, and the various trade union officials and pensions professionals that comprised the Trade Union Pension Specialists group, that I realized just how little I knew about pensions! One of the Treasury's endemic problems—which its leaders see as a strength—is its staggeringly limited institutional memory, owing to its rapid staff turnover rate. The trade union movement has no such problem. This has one or two of its own downsides, but the collective wisdom of trade union pensions officers such as Naomi Cooke, Phil McAvoy, Bryan Freake, and Neil Walsh, as well as actuaries Hilary Salt and Bryn Davies, was an invaluable resource in my role. I also came into contact with, and learned a great deal from, Doug Taylor and Dominic Lindley at Which?, Jane Vass at Age UK, and Gregg McClymont (then Labour's shadow pensions minister) and his adviser Andy Tarrant. I met Christine Berry (who was then at FairPensions, which became ShareAction) during this time too.

What did I learn about pensions provision while at the TUC? Above all, that there is nothing inevitable about the decline of traditional pensions provision in the UK. Indeed, while the prevailing narrative reads 'decline', the reality is 'struggle'. Nicola Smith—while she would often deny, preposterously, that she knew anything about pensions—schooled me in the messy world of distributional politics. Nigel Stanley was a treasure trove of good ideas about how to improve UK pensions—starting from where we are, not where we wish we were—and experience of why, alas, the best ideas rarely prevail. Much of the current book's account of the history of UK pensions provision is a regurgitation of knowledge I have picked up from people like Nigel, supplemented by the exemplary scholarship of academics such as Leslie Hannah, Hugh Pemberton, Howard Gospel, Paul Langley, Deborah Mabbett, John Macnicol, and Liam Foster. The outstanding work of Djuna Thurley at the House of Commons Library, and the journalism of Josephine Cumbo, have also been immensely helpful. Giselle Datz, Michael McCarthy, and Natascha van der Zwan have all produced work on pensions across the world which has shaped quite profoundly how I see pensions provision.

I would not claim that the labour movement, when it comes to pensions, has it all figured out. There are parts of this book my former colleagues will probably disagree with, although I would hope that the new understanding of pensions provision I offer helps to advance a progressive future for UK pensions which will greatly benefit all workers. Above all, while I caught the pensions bug at the Treasury, this book would have been inconceivable without my glorious eighteen months at Congress House—as well as those mentioned above, I owe a debt of gratitude to everyone I worked with at the TUC, especially Jennifer Mann, Helen Nadin, Janet Williamson, Duncan Weldon, Rob Holdsworth, and Anjum Klair. Frances O'Grady and Kay Carberry were inspirational leaders too. I also benefited from productive relationships with industry representatives at the National Association of Pension Funds (where I crossed paths with Darren Philp again), the Association of British Insurers and the Investment Management Association, as well as researchers at the Pensions Policy Institute, and indeed then pensions minister Steve Webb and his officials at the Department for Work and Pensions (Webb is mentioned a few more times than one might expect on my undergraduate course on economic policy-making!).

Of course, the book did not begin to materialize in any tangible, conscious sense until I returned to academia. I was, in truth, heartbroken to leave the TUC after such a short stint, but the prospect of raising my family in the North was too enticing. Luckily, I found (well, helped to build) another nurturing and comradely professional home at the University of Sheffield's Sheffield Political Economy Research Institute. In an important sense, it was my main research at Sheffield, on the post-crisis transformation of the British growth model, that helped me to find the final piece of the puzzle in terms of developing the book's argument. Benefiting from the invaluable tutelage of Tony Payne, and devouring Colin Hay's recent work on the financial crisis, I started to see how what I thought was happening to pensions provision in the UK was part of a much bigger story about what was happening to the economy more generally. Moreover, I realized that was what happening to pensions in a post-crisis environment was integral to how the pre-crisis growth model was able to reassert itself in the wake of the financial crisis— and so my expertise on pensions became part of the backbone of my research on economic policy. My time at Sheffield also afforded me the freedom to consider a new area of the pensions world, pension fund investments, which had been only tangentially relevant to my role at the TUC.

Overlapping, briefly, at Sheffield with Adam Leaver and Jo Grady was also extremely fortuitous. Both have added to my understanding of the world of pensions in various ways, and I hope the book serves as a platform for further collaboration. Liam Foster offered extremely helpful advice on parts of the book, and Scott Lavery was a top-notch colleague and collaborator too. And working with Kate Barker on the Industrial Strategy Commission (a whole other story…) was highly, if serendipitously, beneficial—with pensions being one of Kate's countless specialisms. The influence of Shiv Malik, Ben Little, and my friends at the Intergenerational Foundation (although they are chronically wrong about defined benefit pensions!) has also been important in this regard. I am grateful to Ben Rosamond for arranging for me to present the book at the Centre for European Politics at the University of Copenhagen in October 2019—and to Mark Blyth for arranging a similar visit to Brown University, although it was ultimately cancelled due to the COVID-19 pandemic. Parts of the book were also presented at the International Initiative for the Promotion of Political Economy conference in Lille (in person) and the Society for the Advancement of Socio-Economics conference in Amsterdam (virtually). Thanks to all who offered feedback on these occasions.

While conceived elsewhere, this book has been largely written at Manchester Metropolitan University (MMU), where I am part of a new research centre, known at the time of writing as Future Economies. I owe a huge thanks to all of my colleagues at MMU, particularly our leader Donna Lee. Donna's belief in me, and my research, at such a crucial moment in my career has been humbling. Richard Whittle in particular has extensive experience of various aspects of the pensions world, and I was pleasantly surprised to learn that my old friend and new colleague Rory Shand has also been dipping his toes in the pensions world. I have benefited from drawing upon Nick O'Donovan's expertise, and from the support of Adam Barber, who I first worked with on pension investments at Sheffield. Adam is now a valued friend and MMU colleague. I must also mention Sean McDaniel, who I have worked with on several projects, at both Sheffield and now

MMU. My work with Sean has helped me to develop my understanding of inter-generational relations (ditto Kate Alexander Shaw). Arianna Giovannini, Julie Froud, Katy Jones, and Tom Barker have been fantastic collaborators over the years too (albeit on projects which have distracted me from getting on with this one!) and I am delighted now to be working on various projects with John Evemy, Ed Yates, Sabaa Jahangir, Inga Rademacher, Daniel Bailey, and David Beel, as well as the Rethinking Economics team. My wonderful PhD student, Rebecca Weicht, has helped to sharpen my thinking on the welfare state (ditto my fellow supervisor Julia Rouse).

Thank you, also, to the team at Oxford University Press (OUP), especially Adam Swallow, Jenny King, and colleagues at SPi Global. Howard Gospel and Matthew Watson have been hugely helpful throughout the process too. Mat has actually been a constant presence in my stop-start academic career. I joined the civil service after my PhD in anticipation that a short pit-stop in the policy world—at the heart of government, no less—would enhance my academic career in the long run. This has, in the end, proved to be the case, but only because a handful of people, with Mat chief among them, went significantly beyond the call of duty in demonstrating that I had not been forgotten by academia—when at times it felt like I most definitely had been, both before and after I rejoined the ranks at Sheffield. I was delighted that OUP asked Mat to help with the book at the planning stage—it is immeasurably better as a result.

It goes without saying that nothing I do in my professional life is possible without the support of my family. My incredible wife Laura, and our perfect daughters Miriam and Sylvia, astound and inspire me every single day, and I hope I never lose sight of how lucky I am to live under the same roof as three such wonderful human beings. That I had a hand in rearing two of them is genuinely mind-boggling. Sylvia's health problems during the writing of this book have been a very unwelcome distraction, but her bravery in confronting them has been the best possible inspiration. I should add, Miriam has given us a couple of scares too! And just before submission, Laura and I discovered we have a third child on the way: no doubt he will have arrived by the time anyone reads this in print, bringing ever more joy to our lives. My parents, and Laura's parents Colin and Mary, deserve a special thank you too. I must also note the insights I have gained from conversations about pension investments with my dear friend Colin Wray. Colin is a contradiction in the best possible sense: an old-school socialist who has zestfully embraced the world of individualized pensions saving, and a man who never lets his appetite for hedonism, and a morbid sense of humour, outweigh his compassion for those in strife.

The book is dedicated, however, to my grandma, May Littlewood, who died while the book was in its early stages, in the year Sylvia was born. I was lucky enough to grow up with the love and attention of two wonderful grandmothers. Miriam shares her middle name with my paternal grandmother, Doreen, who died in 2009. Fortunately, the birth of my niece, the indefatigably lovely Lyla May Berry, just two months before Miriam, spared me from having to agonise over which of my grandmothers to honour in this way. So I sincerely hope that the gesture of this dedication goes some way to make up for my inadvertent snub! Of course, no gesture can ever possibly convey how blessed I feel that she was part of my life. I will always be grateful for all of her love and generosity. We were kids, so naturally we never let on, but Grandma's Thursday night visits were always one of the highlights of the week for me and my brothers. We drove her mad, especially when she was left holding the fort alone, but it was, truly, the time of our lives.

My grandmother worked harder than she should ever have had to, for her entire life—yet her contributions to our economy and society were not reflected in her paltry retirement income. Cases of women like May make the notion of a post-war 'golden age' in UK pensions provision seem like, frankly, a sick joke. I did not really choose the pensions path, but as soon as I embarked on it, I knew it was something I wanted to devote a large chunk of my life to, in the hope that the hardship my grandmother endured could be addressed before the same fate is inflicted upon another generation. Rubbish pensions are an affront to our essential humanity. Moreover, they are economically wasteful, making capitalism more ruinous than it needs to be.

But it is not enough to just will things to be different. To change things, we need to start by understanding why they are as they are now—and who is benefiting. That is why I returned to academic research (albeit with a heavy heart), and why I wrote this book. This is also not enough, but it is also, I hope, not nothing. There remain significant financial and cultural barriers to a successful academic career for people, like me, from working-class backgrounds (far more so than in the civil service, I might add). And it is deeply regrettable that generations of academics have sought to enrich themselves via institutionalized back-scratching and phoney 'impact' while their work becomes ever more irrelevant to the basic but essential task of using our cognitive skills and intellectual freedoms to make stuff better in the real world (or at least try). Too much of what now passes for political economy, in particular, focuses on describing economic problems without interrogating the power dynamics which enable these problems to exist—ruffling as few elite feathers as possible. The higher education policies of successive governments have of course moulded this model of the modern academic, so there is plenty of blame to spread around. But there is also hope—there is always hope. As a profession, we can do more for society. As a society, we can do better for each other. The book is written in this spirit. Save the whale.

Craig Berry
Manchester and Sheffield (and the land between)
September 2020

Contents

List of Figures and Tables

Figures

Tables

List of Abbreviations

ABI	Association of British Insurers
AFP	Administrators of Pension Funds (Chile)
AMC	annual management charge
AUM	assets under management
AVC	additional voluntary contribution
BIT	Behavioural Insights Team
BSP	Basic State Pension
CalPERS	California Public Employees' Retirement System
CBI	Confederation of British Industry
CDC	collective defined contribution
CMU	Capital Markets Union (EU)
CPI	Consumer Price Index
CWU	Communication Workers Union
DWP	Department for Work and Pensions
EET	exempt, exempt, taxed
ESG	environment, social, governance
EU	European Union
FAS	Financial Assistance Scheme
FCA	Financial Conduct Authority
FRR	Fonds de reserve pour les retraites (France)
GAR	guaranteed annuity rate
GDP	gross domestic product
GMP	Guaranteed Minimum Pension
GPIF	Government Pension Investment Fund (Japan)
GPP	group personal pension
IGC	independent governance committee
ILO	International Labour Organization
ISA	Individual Savings Account
LISA	Lifetime Individual Savings Account
M&A	merger and acquisition
MAEW	*Making Automatic Enrolment Work*
MIG	Minimum Income Guarantee
ML	Metropolitan Life (New York)
MPAA	money purchase annual allowance
NAPF	National Association of Pension Funds (now Pensions and Lifetime Savings Association)
NDC	notional defined contribution
NEST	National Employment Savings Trust

NICs	National Insurance contributions
NPA	Net Pay Arrangement
NPSS	National Pensions Savings Scheme
OADR	old age dependency ratio
OAP	Old Age Pension/old age pensioner
OECD	Organisation for Economic Co-operation and Development
ONS	Office for National Statistics
PADA	Personal Accounts Delivery Authority
PEPP	Pan-European Pension Product (EU)
PFM	pot follows member
PPF	Pension Protection Fund
PPI	Pensions Policy Institute
PTR	pensions tax relief
QE	quantitative easing
RAS	Relief at Source
RPI	Retail Price Index
S2P	State Second Pension
SERPS	State Earnings-Related Pension Scheme
SPA	State Pension Age
STSP	single-tier state pension
TEE	taxed, exempt, exempt
TPR	The Pensions Regulator
UCU	University and College Union
UK	United Kingdom
US	United States
USS	Universities Superannuation Scheme
WTW	Willis Towers Watson

1

Introduction: Pensions Imperilment and Political Economy

The United Kingdom (UK) pensions system is in danger. How did we get here? Moreover, what exactly is it that is endangering UK pensions? In short, the UK's dysfunctional political economy. This book contends that private pensions provision has become increasingly incompatible with the development of the UK's financialized economy—precisely because key aspects of provision have been transformed in the image of financialization, and the political-economic forces the process privileges. It shows policy-makers grappling, quintessentially, with a single dilemma: how to mitigate the impact and imperatives of financialization, in a system entirely entwined with the process. Amid a wider process of welfare retrenchment, the state is being dragged into private pensions provision in the UK, in ad hoc, unthinking, and occasionally perverse ways. In a sense, at the root of pensions imperilment is the failure of the present (that is, the early/mid-twenty-first century) to look remotely like the future imagined in the relatively recent past (that is, the mid-/late twentieth century). Specifically, today's workers—that is, today's pensions savers—are not only radically different to the future workforce imagined at the 'peak' of collectivist private provision in the 1960s and 1970s, arguably they are rather different from that foreseen even at the very end of the twentieth century, when the promotion of individualized pensions provision became an explicit goal of pensions policy and economic statecraft more generally. Futures fail. But has this ever not been so? Pensions provision is about transferring our income from the stage at life at which we can earn more, to the later stage when we probably cannot. However, it is also about our profoundly human *inability* to execute such a transfer, without the co-operation of future generations.

All economic activity in a capitalist economy is future-oriented. Pensions provision is sometimes understood in terms of its elongated time horizons; that is, its focus on the very, very long term. Yet this is a misrepresentation: pensions provision is actually about how we mitigate our own inevitable failure to accurately foresee the futures to which our economic activity is

Pensions Imperilled: The Political Economy of Private Pensions Provision in the UK. Craig Berry, Oxford University Press (2021).
© Craig Berry. DOI: 10.1093/oso/9780198782834.003.0001

oriented. And so, this, in short, is where we are: no longer able to tolerate our own temporality. The design and regulation of private pensions provision has become ever more fixated on the mitigation of future risks, but has become increasingly detached from the mechanisms by which uncertainty is addressed, and as such its own quintessential function. The state is (reluctantly) mopping up (some of) the spillage. Of course, pensions provision is not simply the victim of financialization. On the one hand, in long intersecting the dominant features of British capitalism, private pensions provision in the UK has also served to drive the process. On the other hand, as this book shows, pensions policy-makers have enjoyed a degree of autonomy in developing UK pensions provision amid financialization; for myriad reasons, they have used it unwisely.

Anybody who has taken an interest in the recent development of UK pensions policy, and/or pensions provision, will recognize that the notion that the UK is suffering a 'pensions crisis' has become incredibly prevalent. It is promulgated by tabloid editors eager for an eye-catching headline, and frequently invoked by politicians needing to justify their latest initiative—to the extent that it has almost become a cliché. Among the most popular explanations for how the UK pensions system finds itself in crisis are: population ageing (above all); government incompetence (or that of the previous government); government malevolence (ditto); a failure to save on the part of irresponsible individuals (particularly the young); an inability to save on the part of poorer groups (ditto); the self-interest of employers undermining their workers' hard-fought pension rights; the vested interests of trade unions making unaffordable demands; the self-interest of financial service providers leading to 'rip-off' pension products; over-regulation; under-regulation; the European Union; and the implications of the 2008 financial crisis. None of these explanations will suffice in accounting for the present state of UK private pensions (whether or not we accept the narrative of crisis), but each tells a part of a story which is invariably multi-layered, contradictory, and contested. Some are certainly more relevant factors than others in accounting for the imperilment of private pensions provision in the UK—yet even the mere *invocation* of each one tells us something about how we got to where we are, and where things might go next.

As indicated above, the explanation for the 'pensions crisis' which is invoked most often—certainly among elites, but also within popular discourse to some extent—is population ageing (referred to more colloquially as 'the ageing society'). Its extent and impact (and political implications) will be explored further in the next section. Population ageing is the apparent meta-trend which underpins many of the other explanations listed above;

sometimes explicitly, sometimes only implicitly. The fact that there are more older people alive today than ever before, in part because of increases in life expectancy, means that most of the traditional ways of funding retirement incomes privately have become unsustainable—or at least this is how the argument goes. The ageing/longevity argument obviously has some merit. But we must be careful not to accept at face value the notion that population ageing is inherently dangerous for pensions provision. If there is an ageing-induced crisis, its genesis lies in how the UK pensions system *interacts with* the apparent fact of demographic change, rather than any inevitable consequences of demographic change. The population has been ageing at a steep rate for a very long time—indeed, for much longer than the UK has had large-scale private pensions provision. Moreover, the book will suggest that it is precisely how policy-makers, providers, and employers have decided to *respond to*, and indeed *define*, population ageing that has placed the UK pensions system in greater peril. The inter-generational bargains at the heart of pensions provision are coming unstuck—but this is partly because we have started to neglect the importance of these bargains in the first place. To clarify, the book does not dispute the possibility that private pensions in the UK are, in many important senses, *in crisis*. The book is about this crisis, but it is also implicitly about the narratives of pensions crisis, most of which can be considered part of the problem they ostensibly seek to identify and resolve. The real crisis is not simply one of various exogenous processes impacting upon pensions provision; it is also of the way we understand what pensions are, and relatedly, of how pensions policy and practice relate to the UK economy as a whole.

In short, private pensions provision in the UK has been increasingly individualized, a process which has dismantled solidaristic pensions practice and, as importantly, served to obscure the inherently cross-generational nature of pensions provision. This process is intimately bound up with broader processes of neoliberalization, as individualized provision encompasses individuals being responsible for securing their own financial well-being via the market, and financialization, as individuals are required to engage ever more intimately with financial services providers. In a sense, pensions imperilment is a consequence of the *failure* of neoliberalization and financialization: as individuals have been largely unable to manage their own retirement risks, in part because capital market performance has proved an unreliable partner. However, individualization serves *by definition* to imperil pensions provision insofar as it conflicts with the temporality of pensions as a mechanism for managing future failures amid generational change. Can a sustainable pensions future be forged? We shall see.

The book contends that understanding these circumstances more satisfactorily—and therefore the possibility of transformative change—requires a political economy of private pensions provision in the UK. Crucially, this broad approach firmly locates pensions provision within the capitalist economy, but also, secondarily, acknowledges the role of pensions provision in the cross-generational management of capitalism. On this basis, while the book concentrates empirically on the UK, it places developments in the UK in a comparative context, and moves towards a new understanding of the relationship between pensions, temporality, and capitalism—in large part by documenting the marginalization of this (implicit) understanding within pensions policy. This introductory chapter will outline the book's key arguments in more detail. Section 1.1 considers what is meant by pensions provision, and the forms it has taken in the UK in recent years, and reflects briefly on the significance of population ageing in this regard. In order to explore the book's theoretical perspective in more depth, Section 1.2 focuses on the concept and relevance of financialization, and Section 1.3 considers the cross-generational nature of pensions provision. Section 1.4 elucidates the book's analytical approach and core argument, as well as its main contents (and recommendations).

1.1. Pensions and Pensions Policy in the UK

Defining what pensions are is not necessarily a straightforward endeavour. At the most basic level, a pension can be defined as a regular retirement income, ostensibly designed to replace earnings from employment. This is probably how most people would understand a pension. Increasingly, when we think about pensions (particularly private provision), we usually also think about the accumulation dimension too, that is, the means by which we put money aside (which can be understood as both *saving for* and *investing in* a pension) over the lifecourse so that we have funds to draw upon, or decumulate, when we reach retirement. Accumulation procedures actually receive far more attention than the decumulation phase in social science scholarship on pensions, particularly that which is focused on pensions as a form of welfare provision. This is probably because decumulation has traditionally been rather straightforward but, as explored in Chapter 6, this can no longer be taken for granted as individualized provision becomes more dominant.

A pension need not take the form of individuals putting money aside purely for their own retirement; in fact, pensions almost always do *not* take this form in any direct sense. The process of individualization means private pensions provision in the UK is coming to resemble this common-sense understanding (with deleterious consequences), although this would represent only a partial reading of recent developments. 'Collectivised' forms of private pensions provision, where risks are shared with fellow savers, employers, and providers (and occasionally the state, albeit usually only nominally) remain a definitive dimension of any pensions landscape. In the UK, private pensions provision has usually taken the form of collectivized 'defined benefit' schemes, although their coverage was never close to universal. The emergence of individualized 'defined contribution' schemes, replacing the defined benefit model, is the core focus of this book.

The fact that the saving process, whether individualized or collectivized, mainly involves sacrificing a proportion of our earnings during working age is important for understanding the form that private pensions usually take, since it means that ways must be found to maintain or enhance the value of that sacrifice over many years, and usually decades. In private provision in the UK, this generally means investment in capital markets by 'pension funds' which consist of the accumulated capital of scheme members (although the imaginary of a pension fund has been increasingly problematized in the UK by individualization). Crucially, it also means the underpinning of value across time by a 'temporal anchor' (that is, employers, in defined benefit provision), irrespective of capital market performance. This mechanism is central to the purpose of pensions provision regarding the management of failed futures, yet has been steadily eroded by policy reforms over recent decades. While this book's focus is pensions policy rather than pension outcomes, it should be acknowledged, beyond all doubt, that inequalities in pension outcomes reflect the inequalities experienced and disadvantages suffered by different groups within the labour market, specifically those with low earnings and incomplete employment histories (whether due to unemployment or caring responsibilities). Disadvantages arising from gender, class, ethnicity, and disability shape pension outcomes—as do the precarious labour market conditions increasingly experienced by young people. Individualization has arguably deepened this problem, yet has been pursued by policy-makers with little concern for the variable suitability of individualized provision across different groups (in fact, as explored in Chapter 5, the promotion of defined contribution provision is often justified by policy-makers in relation to its greater 'flexibility' for those with non-standard careers).

Although this book's focus is private pensions, it should be noted that the state pension remains a hugely important aspect of pensions provision in the

UK (as in most countries)—although an attempt by successive governments to tilt the balance from state to private helps to explain the book's focus on the latter. The various state pension benefits compensate for some of the inequalities in private provision (a mixture of basic or flat-rate and means-tested benefits), but far from adequately. As explored in Chapter 3, most pension systems are considered 'multi-pillar' insofar as they combine state provision with mandatory and voluntary private provision. (The UK does not have mandatory private provision but, until recently, had a 'second' state pension, on top of the 'basic' state pension, which performed a similar function.) State pension provision does not involve saving in any conventional sense, but rather the 'purchase', through taxation, of an entitlement to an income in later life (that is, after 'State Pension Age' (SPA)). In practice, this retirement income is funded by current taxation and borrowing, just as the taxes paid by today's pensioners during their working life paid for the state pensions of yesterday's pensioners. Accordingly, accumulated state pension funds are not invested in any direct sense. There is virtually no society in the world in which the main state pension benefit is financed directly via investment, by public authorities, in capital markets. The state is such a large component of the capitalist economy, with inimitable risk-spreading, revenue-raising, and money-printing capacities, it would unnecessarily jeopardize the solvency of provision to do so. Secondary state pensions are occasionally financed in this manner, but generally only when the resulting funds can be used strategically by the state as an (international) investment vehicle (admittedly, there are no straightforward examples of such arrangements). Similarly, even where a different form of tax is levied to fund state pension provision (as 'national insurance' in the UK is often understood), it again makes no economic sense for such revenue to reside in a hypothecated fund to pay only for pensions and related benefits—if it did, the money raised would lose value instantly and dramatically.

The non-investment of accumulated state pension contributions contrasts with most private pension vehicles, whereby the pension scheme itself is really a conduit for investing in a very large number of financial products, with the responsibility for investment decisions in this regard bestowed upon trustees—or scheme managers in the absence of trustees, who in turn usually outsource decisions to fund managers. Of course, while the state does not hypothecate the tax contributions made by tomorrow's pensioners in order to directly fund investment, the state itself can be understood to be making vast, collectivized investments in support of the economy, thereby helping to generate the economic value, and ultimately tax revenue, which funds the state pension (among other things). Problematically, however, this rather unremarkable situation has become quite contentious; this book contends that a failure to recognize the value of the state's role as a pensions provider—as the ultimate temporal anchor—is part of the story of how the UK pensions system has become imperilled.

Before outlining more specifically the arrangements that characterize UK pensions provision, it is worth at this point reiterating and reflecting upon the scope of the book. In short, the book is interested in the political and economic institutions and processes that provide for retirement incomes. Its specific, empirical focus is how public policy acts to produce and reproduce these institutions and processes. It is, in a sense, an account of how policy-makers have stewarded the development of the UK's 'pensions system'—albeit acknowledging the problematic nature of this term. We should *question whether*, rather than *assume that*, there is anything particularly *systematic* about the way different forms of pensions provision knit together. It is certainly not the case that every policy decision or initiative affecting pensions provision is devised with reference to how it interacts with other features of provision (even if greater alignment in this regard is occasionally lauded as a policy priority). Moreover, as suggested above, a person's retirement income (or financial security more generally) may come from sources that are not necessarily commonly defined as aspects of pensions provision. That said, however, there is a need to focus, firstly, on the most important dimensions of pensions provision, to ensure analysis relevant to how most people acquire most of their retirement income; and, secondly, on the issues that reveal most about how the UK tends to approach pensions provision, and indeed the apparent crisis in provision.

The book surveys, for the most part, a rather intense period in the development of UK pensions provision, focusing generally on the period in which promoting individualized provision became an important policy objective (we can date this to the 1980s, although the agenda intensified from the late 1990s onwards, under the New Labour government). It peers further back into UK pensions history where necessary, and specifically in Chapter 2. It was the Thatcher government which first signalled its support for defined contribution saving through the extension of 'contracting out' subsidies. In its first term, New Labour insisted that most employers offer defined contribution 'stakeholder pensions' for most employees, and later (based on the recommendation of the Pensions Commission, chaired by Adair Turner, which sat from 2003 to 2006) legislated for 'automatic enrolment' (or 'auto-enrolment') into a defined contribution scheme if no alternative existed. New Labour also sought to simplify dramatically the way that private pensions provision interacts with the tax system, through its 'A-Day' reforms in

2006—providing for pensions tax relief aligned to the emergence of defined contribution provision. New Labour was equally active in the state pension sphere, introducing the State Second Pension (S2P) in its first term and, following the Commission's advice, altering its design to facilitate over several decades the evolution of the main state pension into a largely flat-rate benefit. The other major reform triggered by the Pensions Commission was an increase in the age at which people become entitled to the state pension, from 65 to 68 by 2046. It is also worth mentioning the introduction of the means-tested pensioner benefit, Pension Credit, to mitigate the growth of 'pensioner poverty', as well as an array of other pensioner benefits, of which the Winter Fuel Payment is the most well known.

Recent years have been hardly less intense than the 2000s; the centrality of pensions policy to the Conservative–Liberal Democrat Coalition government of 2010–15, and the Conservative governments of 2015 onwards, has probably been underestimated. The Coalition took auto-enrolment forwards toward implementation (making several important modifications in doing so) and oversaw the operationalization of the National Employment Savings Trust as a key dimension of the auto-enrolment landscape. It also legislated for the introduction of fairly novel 'collective defined contribution' (CDC) schemes—albeit with limited impact to date—and, at the same time, and most notoriously, transformed defined contribution decumulation procedures by 'liberating' the annuities market (the so-called pension freedoms, discussed further in Chapter 6). An agenda on reforming pensions tax relief has been driven by the perceived need to reduce public expenditure (or, in this case, tax revenue foregone), although the most ambitious elements of this agenda have been abandoned. Investment decisions by pension funds have also become increasingly politicized, as policy-makers ostensibly sought to support economic 'rebalancing'—although, as discussed in Chapter 7, this agenda is largely illusory. In terms of the state pension, the Coalition legislated for a drastic reform of UK state pension provision by merging the Basic State Pension and S2P (or, arguably, abolishing S2P) into a 'single-tier state pension' (STSP), hastening New Labour's plans for a flat-rate state pension benefit. The state pension became far less generous as a result, thereby increasing the importance of private provision. The timetable for increasing SPA has also been accelerated significantly. It does seem, however, that the change of leadership from David Cameron to Theresa May, and subsequently to Boris Johnson—and, most importantly, the all-consuming Brexit process and impact of the COVID-19 pandemic—has brought about a period of relative quiet in the development of UK pensions policy. The departure of George Osborne as Chancellor of the Exchequer after the Brexit vote in 2016 has probably been decisive in this regard; Osborne made frequent incursions into the territory of pensions policy. If this book's contention is correct, the quiet will not last: policy-makers will frequently be drawn into addressing the implications of pensions imperilment in the UK—most obviously the flawed and hubristic decisions of their predecessors.

1.1.1   The Impact of Population Ageing

Recent pensions policy developments in the UK—as elsewhere, to some extent—have been driven ostensibly by concerns about population ageing (Berry, 2016a). What exactly has been the impact of population ageing on UK pensions provision? There are several ways to answer this question. Yet there are also several ways in which to ask it: too often, analysis of the pensions crisis assumes that this question is an unproblematic and largely neutral one. In fact, asking the question in this way serves to silence a number of contestable assumptions. As such, given that population ageing is part of the framing of most perspectives that claim the UK pensions system is in crisis, or severely imperilled, there is a need to reflect briefly here on the book's perspective on this issue, before its broader perspective on pensions imperilment is outlined.

The book does not intend to understate the difficulty of providing decent pensions in a rapidly ageing society. Population ageing is undoubtedly a real phenomenon. But this does not mean that how pensions policy-makers, employers, and the pensions industry have chosen to respond to this trend represents the only possible response, or indeed the most effective response—and certainly not the most progressive response. As John Macnicol (2015: 66) argues, '[p]opulation ageing today tends to be debated in a manner less than wholly rational, with long-known demographic trends being presented as entirely novel, historically unprecedented and apocalyptic'. We must be clear, for instance, that population ageing is very much a global phenomenon, and ageing in the UK is relatively unremarkable in the context of other countries' experiences (Philipson, 2013). In 2018, the proportion of the UK population aged 65 or over was 18 per cent.[1] This is higher than the proportion in the United States (US) and Canada (16 and 17 per cent, respectively) but lower than aggregate figures for the EU-28 (20 per cent), and France, Germany, and Japan (20, 22, and 28 per cent, respectively). Indeed, based on

---

[1] The population data in this section are taken from the OECD's elderly population dataset, which is available at https://data.oecd.org/pop/elderly-population.htm.

this measure, the UK population has aged significantly more slowly than the rest of the Organisation for Economic Co-operation and Development (OECD) in the post-war era, since in the 1950s only France and Austria had 65 or over populations comparable to the UK's (11 per cent in 1955)—and both of these now have higher proportions. The notion that population ageing is a uniquely British problem requiring unique British problems is therefore far too simplistic. Ultimately, how UK pensions provision responds must be—and will be—in tune to a significant degree with existing practices, as the impact of ageing will affect each country's dominant forms of pensions provision in relatively distinctive ways. But we must remain alert to the (very strong) possibility that the challenges arising from population ageing in the UK are the product of flaws and vulnerabilities in traditional UK pensions practice, rather than the experience of ageing per se.

The most contestable assumption in prevailing discourses around longevity in the UK is that population ageing is a novel phenomenon—with the implication that it is therefore inherently threatening insofar as it disrupts a hitherto well-functioning model of pensions provision. The actual evidence is rather complicated. In 2014–16, male life expectancy in England and Wales was 79.2 years, and female life expectancy was 82.9 years.[2] Just over a hundred years earlier, in 1910–12, the figures were, respectively, 51.5 and 55.4. The increase is stark, yet perhaps serves to underline the fact that increasing longevity has been a feature of the UK pensions landscape for a very long time. Life expectancy has been rising rapidly since the late nineteenth century, before most of what we now know as 'traditional' forms of pensions provision in the UK were established. Adjustments to provision were made throughout the previous century in order to mitigate increasing longevity, but we have also seen during this period—and even in recent decades—an enormous extension of some forms of provision in terms of both generosity and coverage, including a sizeable reduction in SPA in 1940, consistent efforts to improve women's state pension entitlements and outcomes, and the inclusion of a far greater proportion of employees within occupational schemes.

Arguably, of course, the more relevant measure for the impact of population ageing on pensions provision might be life expectancy at 65. The increase in this regard has been more recent; to simplify, earlier progress was

---

[2] The life expectancy data in this section are taken from the ONS's decennial life tables and national life tables. The latest information at the time of writing was published in, respectively, September 2015 and September 2017, and is available at http://www.ons.gov.uk/peoplepopulationandcommunity/births-deathsandmarriages/lifeexpectancies/bulletins/englishlifetablesno17/2015-09-01 and https://www.ons.gov.uk/peoplepopulationandcommunity/birthsdeathsandmarriages/lifeexpectancies/bulletins/nationallif etablesunitedkingdom/2014to2016#life-expectancy-at-older-ages.

due to success in largely eradicating childhood mortality, but progress since the 1950s has been due to advancements in the treatments of conditions affecting older people, such as heart disease, as well as lifestyle improvements more generally. As such, it is not simply the case that, on average, people are more likely to reach retirement, but also that, when they do, they are in receipt of pension income for longer. This is obviously an important consideration for forms of pensions provision whereby the 'sponsors'—whether the state or private employers—commit to funding pensions at a certain level (and with automatic or near-automatic indexation) for the rest of the recipient's life. In essence, these sponsors rather than individuals shoulder 'the longevity risk' in a direct sense. But are increases in life expectancy at 65 as significant as we tend to assume? In 1910–12, men reaching 65 in England and Wales lived on average for a further 11 years, and women for a further 12.4 years. In 2014–16, the figures were, respectively, 18.5 and 20.9. The question of whether this represents a substantial increase, enough on its own to seriously undermine, for instance, defined benefit pensions provision, can only be answered subjectively. There are clearly far too many variables regarding the particular demographics of pension schemes' membership, and other changes to how pensions are funded and regulated, to determine objectively what the impact of these increases has been on the actual risks shouldered by specific sponsors. We know, for instance, that life expectancy varies sharply by geography and social class, as a result of (worsening) health inequalities (Thomas et al., 2010).

We can also question the conventional wisdom that this increase has occurred unexpectedly. Female life expectancy at 65 has been rising steadily, at around a year per decade, since the 1930s. Of course, men are more likely to have been in work, and to have worked for employers with occupational pension schemes; male life expectancy rose more slowly from around the middle of the twentieth century, but then more quickly since the 1970s. However, even this trend throws doubt upon the conventional wisdom that longevity increases have occurred at an unexpectedly rapid rate, since the trend was already evident as pensions provision, generally speaking, was expanding. (It would of course have been unreasonable *not* to expect that male life expectancy would begin to catch up with that of women, perhaps even more swiftly than has actually been evident.) It is also worth noting that, while life expectancy from 65 onwards might be the more relevant measure for considering the direct impact of population ageing on pensions provision, simultaneous increases in longevity in general mean that, as noted above, greater numbers of people are reaching 65 in the first place. Other things being equal, this provides for a larger population of savers and taxpayers through which current pensions for those in retirement can be funded, mitigating the (very welcome) decline in morbidity.

None of this is to suggest that 'old age dependency ratio' (OADR; i.e. the proportion of people in retirement whose income is generally funded by working-age cohorts)—something which is relevant to individualized as well as collectivized pensions provision, as explained in Chapter 4—has not increased. In 2002, there were 298 people aged above SPA in the UK for every 1,000 aged between 16 and SPA.[3] This had risen to 311 people by 2012 (actually a lower ratio than had been forecast a few years earlier). According to the latest estimates, by 2022, as a result of increases in SPA (which are not necessarily automatically implemented in private pensions schemes), the OADR will have *fallen* significantly, with 295 people aged above SPA for every 1,000 aged between 16 and SPA. However, this will have risen again to 335 by 2032. It is worth pointing out that analysis of the OADR often overlooks the fact that the child dependency ratio is simultaneously falling. What matters in the real world of pensions provision is not necessarily the numbers dependent, but rather the actual implications of 'dependence'. If there are fewer children to care for as a proportion of the population then, other things being equal, there are more resources for older people (Macnicol, 2015: 81).

Yet the proportion of older people in relation to younger cohorts is not related solely to longevity. As a result of 'baby boom' periods, some cohorts are significantly bigger than others, and the recent and forecast increase in the retired population is partly a result of the major baby boom cohorts of the early post-war era reaching and approaching retirement, surviving in greater numbers than other cohorts irrespective of longevity improvements. There are other baby boom cohorts currently moving through the lifecourse, such as the large cohort of people in their mid-twenties born in the early 1990s, and the very large cohort of people born in the early 2010s. There was also a significant increase in the birth rate in the UK in the early 1970s—this cohort are now in their mid-forties, notionally approaching their peak earning potential, and much more likely than not to be saving for a pension in some form. Clearly, it is much more difficult to predict future birth rates than it is to predict future increases in longevity, because the former will depend on a range of cultural and economic factors—some of which are rather intangible—whereas the latter results for the most part from advances in

---

[3] The OADR data in this section are taken from the ONS's national population projections, specifically an ad hoc report published in July 2015, available at https://www.ons.gov.uk/peoplepopulationandcommunity/populationandmigration/populationprojections/adhocs/004889underlyingoldagedependencyratiodatafromthenationalpopulationprojectionsaccuracyreportreleasedjuly2015.

medical science. However, and furthermore, it may be that forecasts of further longevity increases prove to be overoptimistic. The possibility that there is an inherent limit to the amount of time that human beings can live, and that we may be approaching this limit, is not a variable that can be controlled for in longevity modelling in any satisfactory way. This is even more acutely so in relation to *moral* limits, which might dissuade future generations from continuing to invest in medical research that extends longevity to the same extent, perhaps due to concerns about declining quality of life beyond a certain point. At the time of writing, COVID-19 is disproportionately affecting older populations, especially in terms of morbidity. It remains to be seen the extent to which this is reflected in a lower OADR in the years ahead, but serves to tragically underline the volatility of any demographic trend.

Clearly, the OADR is also influenced by the level of immigration, which is in many ways an inherently political choice. The volume of immigration into the UK may fluctuate significantly, and unpredictably, based on a combination of push and pull factors, and the extent and effectiveness of immigration control. A high level of working-age immigration in the UK has actually tempered the impact of longevity increases on the OADR in recent years—and indeed has been permitted and encouraged, in part, for precisely this reason. At the same time, periods of high immigration tend to precede spikes in the birth rate. Brexit will in all likelihood transform this dynamic, albeit in ways that are not yet foreseeable (there might be a significant impact on, for instance, outward as well as inward migration). Essentially, lower immigration will increase the OADR in the short term, but may temper increases in the ratio over the longer term as there will be fewer second-generation immigrants reaching retirement. It is also worth noting here the similarly uncomfortable fact that, even when birth rates spike, chronic health inequalities (discussed further below) mean that many members of baby boom cohorts are unlikely to reach retirement, or to live in retirement for long before dying.

The OADR is also an oversimplification, obviously, insofar as it takes no account of the level of employment within the economy. In practical terms, only those in employment, and indeed only those paying tax and/or contributing to a private pension, are contributing directly to the retirement income of the supposedly dependent population. Yet the OADR captures virtually everyone. The OADR and, far too often, the discourses around longevity and the pensions crisis within which the OADR is frequently invoked, also takes little account of the fact that the output of capitalist economies (and therefore wealth of their participants) tends to grow steadily, due in large part to improvements in productivity. As such, countries like the UK should, other things being equal, be able to cope with an ever larger retirement population, so long as the economy continues to grow (in per capita terms). The choice of how to distribute the proceeds of output growth, especially but not exclusively tax revenues, are the subject of political struggle. Of course, it is entirely reasonable to argue that the UK can no longer rely on steady output and productivity growth; one of the book's core motifs in fact is that the pensions crisis is constitutive of and constituted by a wider economic crisis. However, this serves to underline the need to understand the line of causality between variables such as demographic change and pensions crisis in a more sophisticated way, chiefly by recognizing the political and economic context within which it operates. There is little, if any, evidence that policymakers have sought to untangle such dynamics before pressing the 'individualization' and 'retrenchment' buttons in the name of population ageing.

There is nothing inevitable about increasing longevity (see Dorling and Gietel-Basten, 2017b). Pensions reforms being enacted today are based on assumptions that today's young savers will be alive for significantly longer than previous cohorts; of course, this is probably still likely to be the case, but cannot be taken for granted. Life expectancy increases began to stall after 2010, associated with the impact of healthcare spending cuts on mortality, and then in fact slightly reversed (Dorling and Gietel-Basten, 2017a). Recent Office for National Statistics (ONS) population projections at first treated the mid-2010s as a blip, with the rate of increasing life expectancy accelerating immediately afterwards before returning to trend. The latest release, however, sees the trend rate (rather than an accelerated rate) resuming after the recent fall (as well as projecting slightly slower increases in the coming decades than had been projected three years earlier).[4] A 2018 ONS study confirmed that life expectancy increases from 2011 to 2016 had slowed drastically compared to the previous five years. Increases in life expectancy at birth slowed by 90 per cent for women, and 76 per cent for men, and increases in life expectancy at 65 slowed by 90 per cent for women and 71 per cent for men. Crucially, the study compared the UK experience to twenty similar OECD countries: across all categories, life expectancy had slowed more in the UK than any other country, with the single exception of male life

---

[4] Life expectancy data are available at https://www.ons.gov.uk/peoplepopulationandcommunity/birthsdeathsandmarriages/lifeexpectancies/bulletins/nationallifetablesunitedkingdom/2016to2018. See also https://ourworldindata.org/whats-happening-to-life-expectancy-in-britain?mc_cid=15bd79a411&mc_eid=c7b77ba6cf.

expectancy at birth (where the slowdown in the US was slightly larger than in the UK).[5]

Overall, we need to be careful not to assume that the impact of population ageing on pensions provision can be isolated. In practice, pensions provision evolves in relation to a wide range of demographic, political, economic, and technological changes at various scales. We must be careful too, as discussed above, not to assume that there is an identifiable pensions 'system' with normal modes of functioning, in relation to which population ageing can be assessed as an exogenous threat to pensions normality. This is not to understate a priori the significance of population ageing, but rather to suggest that its significance has to be understood in association with other developments that shape its significance, and indeed prevailing interpretations of the trend. One of the ironies of the present-day political economy of UK pensions provision—albeit not one this book has space to speculate on in detail—is that a stalling of life expectancy increases should of course alleviate, or at least mitigate, the pensions crisis, if indeed population ageing is its main source. Alas, such alleviation will not come to pass: the crisis in UK pensions is primarily one of political economy, not demography.

1.2. Financialization and the Political Economy of Pensions

Section 1.1 began, indirectly, to outline the book's analytical perspective. This section discusses it in greater depth via the concept of financialization, which is both analytically and empirically significant for the present purposes. A political economy understanding of UK pensions provision and pensions policy has been relatively absent from the pension crisis literature, and is required to more completely account for the recent development and endangerment of UK pensions provision. The literature on UK pensions policy is dominated by social policy scholars, with branches also in political science and public policy analysis more general. As such, pensions provision and pensions policy is generally studied via the analytical lens of welfare, with state pension arrangements privileged accordingly. As explored further in Chapter 3, private pensions provision is not ignored, but is viewed primarily as the 'other' in typologies based primarily on the notion that the market begins where the state ends. The key analytical issue therefore is

---

[5] See https://www.ons.gov.uk/peoplepopulationandcommunity/birthsdeathsandmarriages/lifeexpectancies/articles/changingtrendsinmortalityaninternationalcomparison/2000to2016.

determining where (and why) certain regimes place the boundary where they do, rather than interrogating how private provision operates (and indeed the state's intimate role in this). The unique nature of pensions provision as a form of welfare is therefore (inadvertently) obscured. This is not to suggest that political economists are currently succeeding in providing a critical appreciation of the relationship between pensions policy and real-world pensions provision as an aspect of the capitalist economy. Insofar as pensions are a subject of research, investment practice of private pensions funds are the primary focus. As explored in Chapter 7, given the immense role of pensions investment in global capital markets, this is understandable. But this scholarship has (again, inadvertently) distanced itself from analysis of how investment practices relate to developments in social policy and welfare provision; problematically, the analytical space around this relationship has been vacated in favour of the narrow approach of mainstream economics (as discussed further below).

It is possible to outline at this stage two principal connotations of any attempt to construct a political economy of UK pensions. Firstly, the study of any economic processes within a capitalist system should be located within a framework that recognizes capitalism as a social order with political, cultural, and economic dimensions, which is both reflected in and shaped by the distribution and exercise of power. Public policy ostensibly shapes capitalism, but also reflects its power dynamics. Secondly, and relatedly, such study must also acknowledge that the mechanics of capital accumulation are not given, but produced and reproduced in social and political institutions. The monetary system, credit relations, private property rights, and corporate governance forms are among the most pertinent of countless such mechanics that determine the nature of pensions provision.

Accordingly, financialization designates a key trend within the development of the capitalist social order in the UK which has impacted profoundly on pensions provision as a set of economic processes, and the role of public policy in shaping provision. The concept of financialization is one of those very rare beasts within social science: sufficiently pliable to enable application to a large range of socio-economic phenomena, yet with a relatively narrow meaning, allowing the implications of its application to be almost immediately clear. In short, it is about finance, but at the same time, the relationships between finance and wider social and economic practices. Financialization, according to Gerald Epstein's widely cited definition, represents 'the increasing role of financial motives, financial markets, financial actors and financial institutions in the operation of domestic and international markets' (Epstein, 2006: 3). Crudely, it means that debt is more prevalent across most dimensions of society, that capital markets and their constituent institutions have more influence over social, political, and economic life, and that short-term financial returns are pursued ahead of a more holistic range of objectives that might once have helped to shape capitalist economic practice (see Froud et al., 2006; Gospel et al., 2014; Leaver, 2018a, 2018b). Andrew Leyshon and Nigel Thrift add helpfully therefore that financialization has 'agency at a range of scales' (2009: 103), emphasizing individuals' experience of and participation in financialization, as well as changes within the economy at the macro and meso levels. Certainly, the micro-level household or individual dimension of financialization has become more important within the literature in recent years: Paul Langley (2004) spotted the shift at its earliest stage, charting the evolution of the concept away from its origins in Marxism and regime theory and towards cultural political economy, where the relationship between individual behaviour and embedded institutional and discursive practices is emphasized as a constitutive aspect of economic life (see also Langley, 2006; Froud et al., 2007; Montgomerie, 2008; Christophers, 2012; Lapavitsas, 2013; van der Zwan, 2014; Berry, 2015a). Of course, the cultural turn also has roots in Karl Marx's work (as opposed to perhaps Marx*ism* in its classical variety), as epitomized by Max Haiven's (2014) use of Marx's concept of 'fictitious capital' to survey both the saturation of popular culture with practices sympathetic to finance, as well as the creation of new financial products profoundly dependent on certain individual behaviours at the individual level.

Financialization, as an analytical concept, is useful for the present purposes in a number of ways. Above all, given that pensions provision is understood here as a dimension of capitalist organization, the concept—quite apart from the specific claims made about finance—is valuable insofar as it helps to locate analysis of economic trends with a framework that recognizes that the capitalist social order is founded in political and cultural as well as economic life. Pensions provision interacts with a vast range of economic practices and is shaped by a large number of areas of public policy, both domestic and international; it also depends profoundly upon how individuals engage with accumulation and decumulation processes. Specifically, the financialization concept invites us to consider some of the commonalities in developments across different aspects of pensions provision, such as the shouldering of greater financial risk directly by individuals, a more extensive role for financial institutions within provision (often resulting from their influence among policy-makers), and a greater focus on financial metrics by the firms that establish and sponsor pensions schemes. This third aspect is, in fact, central to the value of the financialization concept: insofar as the privileging of short-term financial returns constitutes a key condition of financialized economies, it helps to account for an apparent failure to maintain mechanisms by which pensions saving can be rematerialized over the very long term. Financialization, in short, is a shift in our experience of economic time—one which challenges the essential temporality (and therefore inter-generational co-operation) of pensions provision.

Yet a word of caution is required. Financialization has to be the opening question, not the final conclusion. Precisely because the concept refers to such a wide range of phenomena, to conclude simply that the UK pensions system has 'been financialized' would be rather unsatisfactory. Inquiry must focus therefore on *how* and *to what extent* financialization has affected pensions provision. There is already a growing body of work producing important insights in this regard, including Matthew Watson's (2013) analysis of how financialization in UK pensions provision constrained the Labour government's response to the 2008 financial crisis, Paul Langley's (2008) account of the downshifting of pensions investment risks to the individual or 'everyday' level in the UK and US, and the current author's earlier work on the fit between austerity, the individualization of private pensions saving, and the move away from social insurance principles within the state pension system in the UK (see Berry, 2016a). Deborah Mabbett (2020) refers to the role of financialization in instilling 'reckless prudence' with UK pension fund investments as risk management practices serve to shorten investment time horizons. An emerging literature on the state's role in producing certain forms of financialization is also worth noting here (see Trampusch, 2015; Davis and Walsh, 2016; Fastenrath et al., 2017; Grady, 2017), as is Adam Dixon and Ville-Pekka Sorsa's (2009) research on cross-country variations in the financialization of pensions provision arising from inherent variations in institutional practice (see also McCarthy et al., 2016; van der Zwan, 2017). This is a theme also taken up by Anke Hassel, Marek Naczyk, and Tobias Wiß (2019) and other contributors to a special issue of the *Journal of European Public Policy* on 'pensions financialization', although Hassel et al. tend to treat financialization in rather simplistic terms as the growing importance of funded pensions provision (particularly defined contribution) and/or pension funds' role as active shareholders. Neither feature could be considered novel in the UK case.

As such, and despite the advances achieved by this literature, the inherent limitations of the financialization concept for the study of UK pensions provision in particular have to be considered. Most obviously, given that the finance sector has traditionally played a very substantial role in UK pensions provision, analysis framed only by the financialization concept risks overstating the nature and extent of change in this sphere. Indeed, it would not be unreasonable to suggest that both the perceived imperative to save (more) for a pension as life expectancy rises, the finance sector growth enabled by pensions saving, and the role of pension funds as shareholders have been among the most important *drivers* of financialization, in the UK economy and indeed in similar developed countries, at the macro and micro levels (see Engelen, 2003). This financializing dynamic emanating from the world of pensions would have been evident even if UK pensions provision had remained unchanged over the last few decades, that is, if the pensions system had not itself embodied the financialization process to some extent. Related to this, we must be wary also of deploying financialization as a catch-all concept for other developments within UK pensions provision. Processes of, for instance, the liberalization of regulation, the individualization of risk, or the securitization of pensions capital are not simply derived from finan-cialization as a meta-process. They help to constitute what might be under-stood as financialization in broad-brush terms, but also have their own genealogies which should not be overlooked.

1.2.1 The Financial Crises

Any discussion of financialization demands attention to the impact of the 2008 financial crisis. The crisis is an important touchstone for the book in general, since it focuses empirically on the relatively underinvestigated post-2008 period in UK pensions policy development, while acknowledging that post-2008 practice is rooted to a large extent in the pre-crisis period. There has undoubtedly been substantial change since 2008. In part, therefore, the book contributes a case study on pensions policy to the large literature in political economy on the 2008 financial crisis—which shows that it was indeed a crisis, but also that its aftermath can be characterized by continuity rather than change in terms of economic governance (Crouch, 2011; Hay, 2013; Berry, 2016b; Lavery, 2019). As such, using the 2008 crisis as an analytical hinge is not equivalent to claiming that the crisis *triggered* a trans-formation in pensions practice or statecraft. The equally significant impact of the COVID-19 pandemic on financial assets and capital markers—which is still unfolding, at the time of writing—means any attempt to parcel reality neatly into pre- and post-crisis periods will always be challenged by the next crisis. The vulnerability of individualized pensions provision to recurrent financial crises has become increasingly apparent, yet has never been ser-iously contemplated by policy-makers in the UK.

The investment environment for private pension funds, particularly in defined benefit provision, was clearly affected by the 2008 crisis, or its constituent elements, and indeed the policy aftermath. Throughout 2008, the value of assets held by occupational pension funds among OECD countries declined by around US$3.3 trillion, a negative return of around 22 per cent in real terms. Losses in personal pensions plans were estimated at a further US$1.7 trillion. The UK's occupational funds declined in value by around US$0.3 trillion or 17 per cent in real terms (OECD, 2008). Beyond the immediate financial hit, pension funds in the UK, especially private sector-defined benefit funds, have led a process of de-equitization, that is, a significant shift away from investment in equities. The decline in equity values explains this trend only very partially. Interestingly, and as explored in Chapter 7, it is largely UK equities which have been dumped—investment in overseas equities has been much more stable. The average allocation of private sector-defined benefit pension funds to equities fell from 53 per cent to 37 per cent between 2006 and 2016, while average allocation to overseas equities was stable at around 20 per cent. In local authority funds, the average equity allocation fell from 71 per cent to 53 per cent, while average allocation to overseas equities was stable at around a third (Berry and Barber, 2017).

Yet the move away from equities has been problematized by the equally challenging environment for gilt investments. Loose monetary policy has kept interest rates and gilt yields low (effectively negative, in the UK, at some points). Of course, holding down gilt yields, and therefore the cost of government borrowing, has been one of the explicit aims of quantitative easing (QE). The safe haven of government debt has become rather expensive—just not quite prohibitively so, given the volatility of other traditional asset classes. The Bank of England concluded that the impact of QE on pension assets was rather mixed: it boosted equity values as funds de-equitized, and there is some evidence that funds moved bond allocations towards corporate bonds over gilts (Joyce et al., 2014). QE has returned in the wake of COVID-19, demonstrating that measures considered temporary after 2008 are fast becoming part of the new macro-economic normal. Some in the pensions industry lobbied for the introduction of 'smoothed' valuations so that one-off crises did not unduly affect assessments of their financial sustainability, but the attraction of this fix waned as it became clearer that the 2008 crisis was a little more serious than a statistical outlier. That its significance has now been eclipsed by the pandemic-related crisis underlines this point. We know relatively little about how the 2008 crisis affected defined contribution pensions in particular, not least because the volume of accumulated assets in defined contribution provision remains so much lower than defined benefit.

Since the victims of volatility are individuals rather than employers, the implications are largely invisible within public discourse—although the much younger age profile of defined contribution savers helps to sustain an assumption that funds will outgrow the impact of the financial downturn before scheme members retire. Of course, this is an assumption which relied on the 2008 crisis being a once-in-a-generation or even once-in-a-century event, rather than the start of a prolonged period of volatility.

In terms of pensions policy, the key post-2008 shift—the introduction of automatic enrolment—was set in motion well in advance of the financial crisis. So too were the increases in SPA, although the Coalition government accelerated the implementation timetable. The more novel changes introduced by the Coalition were the STSP and the end of compulsory annuitization. Even in these areas, however, the policies adopted were not unfamiliar to pre-crisis policy-makers. Both had been considered by the Labour government, and indeed some practices had been modified in the hope of achieving the same aims as these later initiatives, albeit more modestly. It is too soon to say what impact on policy the pandemic-related crisis will have, but the 2008 crisis has largely acted to reinforce the general drift in provision towards individualization which preceded the crisis. This underlines the importance of understanding the development of UK pensions provision in relation to financialization more generally, rather than simply the financial crisis. However, our understanding of financialization must recognize that financial crises are probably a recurring feature of the process. Financialization and crises of financialization are largely indistinguishable. If it is correct, as argued above, to understand the relationship between financialization and pensions provision in the UK as one of the latter's essential temporality being disrupted, then this applies not only to the process in 'normal' economic conditions, but also the role of financial crises in accelerating an undermining of the temporal anchor within pensions provision.

Arguably, the most significant implication of the 2008 crisis has been an ideological one, as the legitimacy of individualization has been reinforced. The austerity narrative has combined powerfully with an extant narrative on population ageing, discussed above, to valorise the notion that the limits of the welfare state have been breached, making the public finances too vulnerable to shocks, and requiring individuals to take greater responsibility for their own financial security (Berry, 2016a). Hassel et al. (2019) note a similar trend in other European countries, with crisis reinforcing the move towards financialized provision (as they understand it) despite crisis-related concerns about the efficacy of funded pensions provision (in part because the crisis led to more significant concerns about state solvency, impeding a rebalancing from private to public provision). In this sense, albeit with significant national variation (discussed further in Chapter 3), European pensions provision has become more Anglicized since the financial crisis (see also Wiß, 2019).

1.3. Generational Time and Pensions Provision

It is important to understand that pensions provision is, by definition, an inter-generational affair—something which has been strangely underacknowledged in the literature on pensions from across the social sciences (although see Barr and Diamond, 2008, 2009). However, this does not mean that we should adopt a generational lens on pensions policy or pensions provision, at least not without critical interrogation of the implications. Studying pensions from the perspective of the relationship between different age cohorts—although integral to how provision is organized—privileges the question of whether generations are in harmony or conflict. This implies, in turn, that a generation is a static unit of analysis (see Mannheim, 1952). This perversely obscures the biological fact of generational ageing which is, after all, the essential purpose of pensions provision: to allow people to manage their consumption across their lifecourse as their needs and capacities differ as they grow older. Nevertheless, it is essential that pensions provision is understood as something which spans several generations, and for pensions policy to be assessed for the impact it has on how this essential feature operates. The length of time which generally passes between the commencement of accumulation and the realization of decumulation means that we cannot simply understand pensions provision as an aspect of a given social order. All of human relations are of course organized and conducted *in time*, but pensions provision is probably a quite acute example of the temporal dimension of human relations in the political and economic spheres. Generations must not be seen as distinct entities interacting within a fixed social, political, and economic landscape. In practice, each generation transforms the landscape. This is both an existential threat to given forms of pensions provision, but also the defining characteristic of pensions provision in general, as a mechanism for coping with our failure to project the future accurately.

At a basic level, the nature and complexity of pensions provision as a set of socio-economic goods which, by definition, almost span individuals' entire lifecourses, means that its functioning requires the sustained participation and co-operation (whether willing, conscious, or otherwise) of countless individual agents in myriad and multiple roles. The life-stage of these individuals will have a profound influence on how they participate in the most common roles, that is, contributing financially to a pension scheme, or drawing upon pension capital or entitlements in retirement. Crucially, pensions provision generally relies upon people at a certain life-stage behaving in a way that is conducive to the maintenance of provision for people at different life-stages. Most obviously, the income of retirees would be jeopardized were younger cohorts to fail to participate in provision in various ways—this is applicable irrespective of whether schemes are 'pay-as-you-go', which signifies how funds are administered, but does not alter the quintessential need for providers of any form of pension scheme to have funds available from current savers to pay for current retirees. Equally, however, the future provision that younger cohorts will be expected to utilize will be significantly affected by how those decumulating pensions saving use their funds—a large-scale turn away from annuities by people reaching retirement, for instance, may mean that the pension products that future pensioners were expecting to rely upon in later life are significantly disrupted if annuity providers are forced to alter their business models.

It is only possible for accumulated funds to be available for decumulation if, in the cases of privately funded pensions provision, capital investment processes continue to function, or if, in the case of pensions funded via the state (whether 'unfunded' private pensions or state pensions), the public finances continue to be organized on broadly the same terms. Clearly, the actual money paid into a pension is of course not the same money that comes out of it. The dematerialization and rematerialization of pensions capital relies on innumerable individuals—alive, dead, and not yet born—maintaining the incalculable aspects of both the public and private sectors that enable money to be available to people upon and throughout retirement (irrespective of whether their actual pension income is at the level they were expecting). This would extend to any part of the world where investments are made, not simply to the country in which saving takes place, and indeed to the transnational political and economic processes within which any domestic economy is situated. Pensions provision therefore relies on people at different life-stages behaving or contributing in particular ways. Forms of provision develop, and are designed, on this basis. The problem, however, is that they may not behave or contribute as envisaged. To be more precise, they *will* not. Our inability to forecast the future with precision is endemic—even more so our pensions future, given its constitution in a dynamic and unstable capitalist system. Part of the rationale for this book is a recent effort by UK policymakers to allow for, and indeed deliberately establish, forms of pensions provision which offer far more freedom to age cohorts to act in their own, immediate interests. The consequences of diluting the expectations and regulations which generally underpin inter-generational co-operation may be profound, and imperilling of pensions provision as we currently experience it.

At the same time, it is recognized that, from the perspective of the cross-generational organization of pensions provision, individualization is ultimately impossible. Pensions are by definition organized generationally, even if inter-generational co-operation becomes less explicit as an organizing principle, and even if people are encouraged to behave selfishly *within* their age cohort. The ambition here therefore is to understand how and why policy-makers have sought to impose individualism on a sphere of capitalist organization which is inherently inhospitable to its values and imperatives. The processes of financialization and neoliberalization do not simply give rise to pensions provision which sets generations against each other, but to the unravelling of pensions provision altogether. This in itself forms a structural transformation of the landscape upon which future generations will interact. No cohort can expect capital markets or the public finances, for instance, to be organized in their retirement exactly as they anticipated when they began interacting with them as a pensions saver or taxpayer. We rely not on the fantastical notion that different generations will leave the world untouched, but rather on the reality that successor cohorts usually support the delivery of pensions to those in retirement which approximate to those expected or promised during accumulation. Yet each generation (most obviously, each generation of political and economic elites) will leave an imprint on the basic functioning of pensions provision—an imprint which affects those who have already finished accumulating a retirement income in various ways, and indeed those who have yet to begin. In short, each generation shapes the nature of inter-generational relations. Projected futures are fundamental to the organization of pensions provision across generations, but sustainable provision requires failed futures to be baked into its organizing institutions.

That pensions provision has emerged to help us to manage the problems which arise from generational change has been marginal, at best, within the growing body of think-tank (Cribb et al., 2013; Gardiner, 2016) and popular literature (Little, 2010; Malik and Howker, 2010; Willets, 2010) on inter-generational relations. There is an implicit, and often explicit, account of inter-generational 'injustice', with some authors arguing that today's young people (especially in the UK) have been *unfairly* disadvantaged (or even betrayed) by earlier cohorts. The depiction of pensions provision in such accounts, however, leaves a great deal to be desired. The state pension is frequently depicted, for instance, as a 'drain' on public finances which *directly* impedes greater spending on working-age benefits (see Toynbee, 2014), with little reference to the entitlements built up through paying tax, the millions who will be made worse off by the STSP, and indeed the vital role of the state pension in supporting the social care system (essentially 'saving' money for the public sector) (Berry, 2016d). Worse, defined benefit pension funds are depicted as *inherently* problematic from an inter-generational perspective. There are clearly severe problems in defined benefit provision in the UK—some real, some exaggerated—but the problem for the young is not the nature of defined benefit provision, but rather that schemes have closed to new entrants or accruals, as the role of a key component of provision—the employer as temporal anchor—is being undermined.

The non-academic literature is on safer ground in relation to housing, where some older people have clearly benefited from the unearned windfall of higher property prices, undermining the prospects for many younger people becoming home-owners. That said, even in relation to housing wealth, class-based inequalities are far more pronounced than age-based inequalities, and are indeed enabled by inter-generational transfers within families (Piachaud et al., 2009). In the academic literature, however, the focus of generational analysis has been on cultural and political rather than economic life (see for example Pilcher, 1995; Price, 1997; Edmund and Turner, 2005; Davidson, 2012; Berry, 2014b; Grasso, 2016; Milburn, 2019). There is a very substantial literature on the attitudes of different age cohorts in the workplace, but this largely overlooks the different structural conditions which different generations experience in the labour market (see for example Cennamo and Gardner, 2008; Deal et al., 2010; Kowske et al., 2010; Ng et al., 2010; Cogin, 2012). The most promising intellectual turn therefore is the emerging literature around young people's experience of precarious labour market conditions, and how this has been intensified by public policy (see; France, 2016; Prosser, 2016; Bessant et al., 2017; Green, 2017; Berry and McDaniel, 2018, 2020; Furlong et al., 2018). Yet pensions provision is largely absent even from such analyses (although see Berry, 2012; Foster, 2018).

It is important, however, to caution against a conservatism almost inherent in any invocation of the generational timescape. The depiction of the cross-generational nature of pensions provision offered above almost invokes the view of conservative philosopher, Edmund Burke (2012 [1790]), who described society in general as a partnership 'not only between those who are living, but between those who are living, those who are dead, and those who are not yet born'. The problem here is not the recognition of such cross-generational bonds—this book argues that they are integral, for instance, to the nature of pensions provision—but rather the valorisation of them as a bulwark against radical change. In fact, while generally advancing the notion that today's young people have been materially harmed by older cohorts, Ben Little and Alison Winch argue persuasively that the Burkean conception of generational harmony often works effectively to steer attention away from historical inequalities and struggles over class, gender, sexual orientation, etc. (see Little and Winch, 2017a, 2017b; also Little, 2014). Jonathan White (2017) makes a similar point regarding the deployment of a generational 'timescape' in relation to climate change. As in pensions provision, while concern for future generation informs action to address environmental damage, it simultaneously dilutes the insight that members of the same cohort may be impacted differently by climate change, and indeed that some members may be far more responsible for having brought it about.

Classical political economy, by problematizing the means by which socioeconomic structures are reproduced (implicitly, across several generations), contains the tools by which this dilemma can be resolved. Indeed, one of Karl Marx's most famous quotes, from *The Eighteenth Brumaire of Louis Bonaparte*, concerns generational change: 'Men make their own history, but they do not make it as they please; they do not make it under self-selected circumstances, but under circumstances existing already, given and transmitted from the past. The tradition of all dead generations weighs like a nightmare on the brains of the living' (Marx, 1852: 5). It is not unusual to see the second sentence reproduced in isolation from the first, but it is clear that, for Marx, structural and generational change are intimately related. The issue received slightly more attention in an earlier work, *The German Ideology*, in which Marx described history as:

> Nothing but the succession of the separate generations, each of which exploits the materials, the capital funds, the productive forces handed down to it by all preceding generations, and thus, on the one hand, continues the traditional activity in completely changed circumstances and, on the other, modifies the old circumstances with a completely changed activity.   (Marx, 1970 [1843]: 57)

This might seem rather obvious—and there is of course little theorization here of the political processes through which generationally bound actors might modify practices and structures. Yet it is useful to understand structural change as both enabled by the succession of new generations, while at the same time constrained by the new generation's dependence on their predecessors. Pensions provision embodies and is shaped by this dynamic. At the same time, it mitigates the impact of generational change insofar as it threatens to uproot the mechanisms of achieving financial security across the lifecourse. It loses its ability to mitigate in this regard when cross-generational co-operation is undermined.

1.4. Pensions Imperilled: In Brief

1.4.1 The Book's Analytical Approach

In the most basic sense, this is a book, as noted above, about *policy*. It is of course also about the problems policy is trying to solve, and its success in this endeavour. But it is mainly about the framing of policy problems, and how and why some policy problems are prioritized over others in policy-making institutions. It is about the consequences of policy decisions, but also the way in which certain outcomes are actively pursued at the expense of others by those making policy, not least due to the influence of those who benefit from these outcomes. Clearly therefore this book is also about the process of policy-making, and how this process serves to favour certain approaches, actors, and outcomes. It is worth noting, additionally, that the book takes a broad view of what policy consists of. Policy is not simply a final decision by a minister, or legislation passed by parliament, etc., but rather the real-world processes through which such things are actualized. These will include the (tacit) agreements on how policies will be delivered (especially if implementation involves non-state actors, as most policies do), the ways in which policies are communicated to prospective recipients, and where developments in a particular policy area fit within wider governing agendas. It is also worth noting that, even if presented and understood as a problem solved, any policy is generally only a staging post within an evolutionary cycle of policy-making in which certain policy approaches become more or less palatable over time (Hall, 1993).

This broader view of policy encourages us to introduce the concept of 'statecraft', which was employed, with little explanation, at the beginning of the chapter. Statecraft encompasses policy but also the wider political context in which policy is devised, and indeed the political entrepreneurship which allows politicians to produce the outcomes they want through their control of certain institutional functions, and indeed their ability to shape and redesign these functions. Andrew Gamble (2014; see also Hayton, 2014; Berry, 2016b) has written about how austerity proved to be a successful execution of statecraft by George Osborne after 2010, insofar as the austerity narrative framed the terms of political debate, and the pursuit of austerity within Whitehall both bolstered his position and inevitably reinforced his own policy agenda. The notion of statecraft has its origins in the study of diplomacy and foreign policy, in the sense that statecraft refers to the positions that a particular nation may uphold within international politics, and more precisely the effectiveness of particular statesmen in devising such positions.

The concept's assimilation into the study of politics was therefore partly about establishing the importance of leadership (Bulpitt, 1986; Buller and James, 2012). But arguably the underlying notion that statecraft is about how the state's power(s) is used to make certain outcomes more or less likely is the more useful dimension of the concept. Rather than simply referring to the use of existing state powers, state-making and state-shaping should be seen as key elements of statecraft. Hence the reference above to 'neoliberal' statecraft, which can be understood as both the policy agenda and institutional forms which are established to instil a neoliberal ideological perspective. In this rendering, there is no single neoliberal statesman, but the perspective's hegemony is reflected in statecraft by a broadly defined political elite. Similarly, we can see 'economic statecraft' as a specific form of statecraft. This term's conventional use echoes the origins of statecraft as a term related to diplomacy, and therefore refers to specific policy areas such as trade and aid, especially insofar as these are used alongside the more traditional tools of international relations. However, economic statecraft can be brought into political economy, in the same way that statecraft in general has been brought into political science, to assist the study of how the use and shaping of state power(s) affects the economy, specifically processes of capital accumulation. In the world of pensions, the institutionalization of interactions between policy-makers and the pensions industry is a key element of statecraft which both inhibits and enables various policy possibilities.

Pensions policy is rarely a central focus for political economy or political science. Generally speaking there are two rather distinct literatures on pensions provision in UK scholarship. Firstly, as discussed above, there are those scholars who assess pensions through the lens of welfare or social security. They tend to focus on state pension provision, although how this interacts with private provision is often a feature of analysis, and are typically from sociology or social policy backgrounds in disciplinary terms (with overlaps into political science and public policy) (see for example Meyer et al., 2007; Lain et al., 2013). The welfare lens is useful but ultimately unsatisfactory insofar that pensions provision, especially in the UK, cannot be reduced to its role within the welfare state. Rather it is embedded in many of the core structures and processes of the capitalist social order, including private productive and allocative activity, as well as several aspects of state architecture beyond social security mechanisms.

Secondly, there is a large economics literature (encompassing financial economics and extending to actuarial science) focused on testing the efficacy of different pensions system designs, and/or explaining how individuals have interacted or will interact with different options (see Blake, 2003; Barr and Diamond, 2008; Mackenzie, 2010; and the majority of the contributions to the *Journal of Pension Economics and Finance*). The latter focus has been supplemented, and gently critiqued, by a growing behavioural economics literature which softens assumptions around rational decision-making by individuals and considers the myriad biases that might encourage pensions-related behaviours, such as saving (see Thaler and Benartzi, 2004; Blake and Boardman, 2010; Thaler and Sunstein, 2008; for critical discussion, see Langley and Leaver, 2012). This literature focuses on private provision but, again, will also consider how state benefits might affect the operation of pensions systems, or the behaviour of savers.

These welfare and economics lenses are obviously very different, but both tend to see policy in a rather technocratic way. They might focus on explaining how different forms of pensions provision function, but at the same time imply that different policy choices would lead to different functioning. The notion that certain policies and forms of provision are, to some extent, products of a wider structural environment is, at best, a marginal dimension of scholarship. This is not necessarily a fatal flaw: it is inevitable that different forms of social science will operate at different 'levels of analysis'—although commensurability between different analyses is aided when the limitations of our approaches are acknowledged. It is of course not necessary to be considered, or to identify as, a *political* economist in order to bring structure and structural change into analysis of pensions provision. Viewed in more heterodox terms, the economics literature includes a wealth of analysis of different structural contexts, most obviously labour market and corporate governance structures among business or management theorists and economic sociologists (recent examples include Ebbinghaus, 2011; Hinrichs and Jessoula, 2012; Whiteside and Ebbinghaus, 2012), and the valuable work on the relationship between pension funds, capital markets, and investment management in economic geography (Clark, 2000, 2003; Dixon, 2008) and legal studies (Davis, 2008). The work of Gordon Clark, Kendra Strauss, and Janelle Know Hayes on retirement planning is also worth noting (Clark et al., 2009, 2012). Even in these broader literatures, however, the relationship between economic change and political power is rarely a central feature.

There is a clear need for pensions policy to be studied with reference to its (capitalist) structural context (for an outstanding account of how the structural environment of capitalism has shaped pensions policy in the US, which is discussed further in Chapter 3, see McCarthy, 2017). While both the welfare- and economics-related pensions literatures tend to overemphasize the prospect of change via the decisions of policy-makers, an institutionalist political economy offers the correct balance between contingency and determinism (Hall and Soskice, 1999; Crouch, 2005; Streeck and Thelen, 2005; Hay, 2006a). Institutionalist political economy must not simply focus narrowly on formal policy-making settings (an orientation which arguably characterizes historical institutionalism, the dominant paradigm in UK political science, as well as rational choice institutionalism). Instead the focus should be on the institutionalized practices—both inside and outside formal, political institutions—including those which govern the private economic sphere, insofar as it is shaped by interaction with the public realm. Policy may be designed ostensibly to disrupt established institutional practice (Dixon and Sorsa, 2009), but also to reinforce it (Hacker, 2005). Institutionalism must 'take capitalism seriously', understanding how economic processes and interests structure policy-making, while also understanding capitalism itself as a set of inter-related, institutionalized practices (Streeck, 2011). This perspective clearly bleeds into the institutionalism of heterodox economics, which challenges the notion of self-organizing markets (see Chang, 2002). But we must avoid the functionalist implication that institutions simply evolve as the materiality of capitalism adapts to technological change and resource availability. It is power-wielding, strategic agents, with ideological commitments, who act through institutions, whether to disrupt or reinforce their routines (Hay and Wincott, 1998).

1.4.2   The Argument, in a Nutshell

Population ageing is a real phenomenon which clearly affects dominant pensions practices in the UK. However, it is not an existential threat: UK pensions provision became more generous, and more universal, amid rapidly increasing life expectancy. Yet pensions policy-makers have in recent years behaved as if population ageing is such a threat. This is in part due to the dominance of neoliberal ideas about individual self-sufficiency, the privileging of private economic interests, and the limits to welfarism. In interacting with pensions provision underpinned by private employers, or financed on a pay-as-you-go basis by current taxpayers, the extension of morbidity, and therefore greater preponderance of non-workers in retirement, is seen as a drag upon profitability and growth.

Financialization is related to but distinct from the process of neoliberalization. On the one hand, pensions policy has been driven by the growing power of financial service providers, now dominant within UK pensions provision (although many new providers have emerged *In response to* public policy decisions). On the other hand, however, and more generally, financialization denotes the new temporality that has driven pensions policy and practice in the UK in recent decades. A fixation on short-term financial metrics—as a measure of both economic success and security—undermines the critical role of public and private institutions in anchoring pensions provision across time, maintaining the approximate value of entitlements, as generations change and forecasts of the future fail to materialize. The failure of the present to resemble the past's imagined future—of which population ageing is an example, alongside myriad social, economic, and technological shifts—is seen to undermine the very possibility of collectivized pensions provision, when in fact the future's inevitable failures are part of the fabric and rationale for pensions provision within all capitalist economies.

Policy-makers' perverse responses may have insulated the UK's 'pensions system' from failed futures, to some extent—but since pensions provision is part of the way capitalism in general manages generational churn, they have also served to intensify these failures. Imagined futures fuel financialization—and their imperfect realization unravels it. Individualizing pensions provision is the worst of all possible responses to pensions financialization. In subjecting greater numbers of people to investment risks, requiring a more direct, intimate form of engagement with financial services providers, and producing ever more complex accumulation and decumulation processes, means more people will be directly and materially affected by the failure of the future. The mechanism we use to insulate ourselves against future failure—pensions provision—will instead become the instrument of harm, ironically bringing to life the imagined inter-generational conflicts which the champions of individualization often claim they are seeking to alleviate.

However, we should avoid the simplistic assumption that the state is becoming increasingly absent from pensions provision. It remains the most important provider of defined benefit private pensions—and this will continue for generations to come. More generally, while policy-makers have resisted the rather statist set of solutions proposed by Adair Turner's Pensions Commission, the state is nevertheless acting to enforce and encourage individualized and financialized pensions provision in various ways. To some extent, pensions policy—still falling to some extent within the imaginary of the welfare state—is intent upon resolving a perceived crisis, in innovative ways. For the most part, the state's interventions are paradigm-reinforcing; alas, the paradigm *is* the crisis. Yet as the cracks in financialized pensions widen, the state is being called upon, and will continue to be called upon, to support private provision. The champions of welfare retrenchment imagine the boundaries of state intervention are becoming more rigidly demarcated, but this will prove to be just another failed future. The shape that pensions statecraft will take in the decades ahead is far from settled.

This is in part because the shape that the UK's economic model will take in the decades ahead is plagued by uncertainties—which are symptomatic of significant and ongoing shifts in the worldwide organization of capitalism, and the UK economy's place (and that of its constituent territories) within it. Pensions provision is a creature of capitalism, in that it arises in large part from industrial relations: the 'golden age' of collectivized pensions was not an aberration, but rather well suited to the UK's extant accumulation regime. What model of capitalist development will emerge from circumstances in which productivity gains are meagre, profits unstable, and business models depend on a highly flexible labour market? Or indeed from the wide-ranging implications of COVID-19? Pandemics notwithstanding, policy has in many ways been driven by these economic realities—yet it has not equipped UK pensions provision to be adequately resilient in this regard. The 2008 financial crisis served to intensify the individualization, and imperilment, of pensions provision. The economic crisis associated with COVID-19 may not.

It is essential that we understand the role of capital markets in the dematerialization of savings, and eventual rematerialization as a retirement income. This is why, as suggested above, the notion that UK pensions provision has 'been financialized' is somewhat misleading; UK pensions provision has been undergoing a degree of financialization for a very long time, and in many ways serves as a key progenitor of financialization within other capitalist institutions. Yet providers of pensions saving vehicles cannot choose how to dematerialize pensions saving as capital with complete autonomy—and they certainly cannot dictate the returns they will generate in support of rematerialization. The process of pensions individualization is characterized by a creeping, and occasionally sudden, shift in the balance of power from pensions providers to investment intermediaries. This may be problematic in itself, but also speaks to a wider trend of pensions provision increasingly being organized and operated in accordance with capital markets' pursuit of future returns, rather than pensions provision's management of future failures. To date, policy-makers have responded by 'liberating' individuals from some of the lingering features of 'institutional' investment: if control is illusory, individuals might as well fail on their own terms. There are signs that policy-makers have sought to reimagine a role for pensions capital in the construction of a new developmental path, yet they have not yet challenged the financialized impediments that constrain a progressive future in this regard

1.4.3   Outline of the Book (and Preview of Its Recommendations)

Chapter 2 offers a historical overview of UK pensions provision and pensions policy, describing in detail the experiment with 'liberal collectivism' and its unravelling during the 1980s neoliberal revolution. It also introduces key aspects of more recent developments, and helps to situate pensions developments in the UK in relation to wider economic trends such as deindustrialization and finance sector expansion. Chapter 3 provides a comparative perspective on pensions provision, surveying key dimensions of, and reforms to, pensions provision across 'the pensions multiverse'. It builds upon Chapter 2's distinction between collective and collectivism to situate pensions provision within the temporal management of capitalist relations. Importantly, it argues that the main ways of categorizing pensions systems within both academia and officialdom fail to adequately capture the nature of pensions provision (and therefore its relationship to capitalism) as a mechanism for managing failed futures.

Chapter 4 considers in more depth the demise of collectivist private pensions in the UK. As well as outlining the transition from the 'golden age' of defined benefit provision, and the essential differences between defined benefit and defined contribution provision (which are often significantly understated), the chapter accounts for the main approaches to pensions regulation, efforts to salvage collectivism amid the disappearance of defined benefit schemes, and the ever increasing demands upon the state to manage the defined benefit's demise. Chapters 5 and 6 move on to the emergence and entrenchment of individualized private provision, principally via the Pensions Commission and auto-enrolment. They focus on two key contradictions: firstly, between the expectation of greater individual engagement with workplace pensions provision, and the reliance of post-Turner policy on inertia; and, secondly, between the intent to revitalize pensions provision as a dimension of universal welfare provision, and the reliance in practice on delivery via financial services providers. Chapter 5 looks specifically at the individualist ontology underpinning defined contribution provision, and Chapter 6 considers the state's role in managing—or reinforcing—these contradictions (including the recent 'pension freedoms' reforms, and the role of tax relief in incentivizing pensions saving). Chapter 8 is distinguishable from earlier chapters insofar as, in focusing on the investment environment, it demonstrates the limitations of pensions policy in shaping how pensions provision functions in practice. That said, it also details several attempts in recent years to shape how private pension funds are invested. Moreover, it demonstrates the role of pensions provision in shaping capitalism, rather than simply responding to it—albeit a role increasingly abdicated in the context of defined contribution provision, as the time horizons of investment practice are inappropriately applied to unanchored pensions provision.

While much of the book veers towards fatalism in depicting (explicitly and implicitly) the development of UK pensions provision in recent decades as driven by a dysfunction capitalist regime and associated ideologies, in combination Chapters 2 and 7 show us that alternative futures are possible. The history of pensions provision is, after all, and at root, the history of expected futures that failed to materialize. Chapter 8, as well as summarizing the book's main arguments, therefore offers a series of proposals for policy and practice, some more modest than others. Although the state pension is largely outside of the scope of the book's analysis, it is clear that the state is uniquely placed to act as the temporal anchor of pensions provision, and that a significant uplift in the proportion of people's retirement income accounted for by the state is warranted. There is also a strong base for the nationalization of struggling defined benefit schemes, including the Pension Protection Fund (PPF) (and perhaps some defined contribution schemes). This is not necessarily because defined benefit provision is beyond salvaging, but because nationalization would represent an opportunity to capitalize and reconstitute an earnings-related state pension, at the boundaries of public and private provision. For continuing defined benefit schemes—especially if the above reforms are not enacted—there is a case for making it easier to adjust scheme retirement ages. However, this would only be permissible on the basis of clear, specific evidence that scheme demographics have radically changed, and should be introduced only on the basis of much tighter eligibility rules for the PPF. In practice, the likelihood of retirement age changes would be limited, but the *possibility* of change should the life expectancy of scheme members rise unexpectedly would assist the long-term planning of sponsoring employers.

Within defined contribution, three key, immediate reforms are required. Firstly, increase the scope of auto-enrolment, to ensure the scheme mitigates rather than reflects labour market inequalities based on gender, ethnicity, disability, class, etc. This would mean higher contributions from employers, and public credits for employees (and self-employees) unable to access employer contributions. Secondly, large-scale CDC provision must be substantively supported by government, with new expectations on employers to share investment risks with their employees—even where this contravenes current pensions law. Thirdly, introduce public annuities, either through a *de facto* nationalization of the annuities industry or, more modestly, by establishing a state-owned annuities provider to compete with private providers (in the way that the National Employment Savings Trust competes with the private sector for customers during the accumulation phase). This third reform would essentially build upon already forgotten recommendations of the Pensions Commission. A more radical solution to the problems of defined contribution would be for the state to establish a notional defined contribution scheme (increasingly popular across Europe) in place of private pensions saving, and establishing the state as a temporal anchor for the bulk of private pensions saving.

Across defined benefit and defined contribution provision, we must move towards abolishing pensions tax relief, the benefits of which skew heavily towards the highest earners. This would ideally be part of wider reforms to the taxation of income and wealth, which would increase greater fairness in how the already retired are taxed. Incidentally, the removal of pensions tax relief would help to justify the 'freedoms' now afforded to defined contribution savers to keep their savings invested rather than converting them into a retirement income. Abolishing tax relief should not be done to raise revenue (or reduce revenue foregone); instead, the benefits to the Exchequer should be recycled into new forms of fiscal support for collectivist pensions provision such as CDC. Insofar as pension funds remain reliant on generating returns in capital markets, much stronger action is required to strengthen their ability to protect members' interests in relation to investment intermediaries. Yet this agenda will be inherently constrained by the need to access particular asset classes to satisfy cashflow and regulatory requirements, and indeed paradigmatic thinking on what constitutes members' financial interests. We need to think more imaginatively therefore about new locally rooted and democratically organized investment vehicles which would route pension funds away from conventional investment practices. It is clear that these suggestions—even the least radical—are based on a much more expansive view of the state's role in ostensibly private pensions provision, which will be resisted by many. However, as the book explores, the state is already intimately and increasingly involved in private pensions provision, in compensating for the failures of financialization and neoliberalization. The question is whether this continues in a fairly ad hoc manner, with many perverse implications, or instead is rationalized as part of a more sustainable pensions settlement in the UK, better reflecting the unique and indispensable temporality of pensions provision.

2

The Liberal Collectivist Experiment: The Historical Development of UK Pensions Provision

All forms of pensions provision are collective in practice. It is possible for an individual to provide for their own retirement by storing money under their mattress, or more realistically, to save or directly invest their money and draw down any funds (plus interest or returns) in retirement. Similarly, people can, and often do, partly fund their retirement by releasing equity from their home. But such practices do not represent forms of pensions saving. In pensions provision, all of the money you save or invest is dematerialized, to be rematerialized at a much later point in time by mechanisms largely known in advance. This means that a reliance on other people's money, and their willingness to behave financially in a way complementary to your own behaviour, is a quintessential part of an individual's own pension. Of course, most economic processes in a capitalist system involve similar monetary practices; even in the mattress example, the saver would be reliant on others to recognize the value of their stash when it was retrieved. But the inherent temporality of pensions makes this reliance particularly acute, so much so that the process by which rematerialization will occur—albeit not necessarily the value that the rematerialized fund will possess—is generally written into the contract (including, in the case of state pensions, primary legislation) between saver and provider.

To clarify, however, 'collective' is not synonymous with '*collectivist*' in this context. The latter is a political-economic formation which amplifies the collective nature of monetary processes by making them an explicit part of the savings model from the individual saver's perspective. There are moral as well as economic arguments in favour of collectivism. UK pensions provision includes collectivist elements, or elements that conform to collectivist principles to varying degrees, most obviously the state pension, tax relief for pensions saving and certain investment forms, defined benefit pension schemes, and even defined contribution decumulation processes (to some

Pensions Imperilled: The Political Economy of Private Pensions Provision in the UK. Craig Berry, Oxford University Press (2021).
© Craig Berry. DOI: 10.1093/oso/9780198782834.003.0002

extent). (Alan Walker and Liam Foster refer to defined benefit schemes in the UK as 'quasi-collective' because members have no control over investment decision in practice (2006: 435).) Overall, however, UK pensions provision can be said to be less collectivist now than in the recent past. Arguably, collectivism was never really embraced in UK pensions, with arguments derived from liberal thought influential in presenting collectivism as a potential barrier to individual freedom, or an encumbrance upon market dynamics in the private economic sphere. The efficacy of such ideas in the development of pensions policy of course cannot be isolated from the financial practices in which UK pensions provision originated, as retirement savings products became both more necessary and more practicable. As explained in Chapter 1, UK pensions provision—as in all other countries—is not a self-contained 'system', but rather intertwined with the country's broader model of (capitalist) economic development.

This chapter provides on overview of the historical development of UK pensions provision, focusing on the main philosophical or ideological foundations of different elements of provision, how they fit together, how they have evolved, and the major policy initiatives that have both instituted and transformed UK pension provisions at different points in time. Its key interest is the post-war period, but Section 2.1 actually dates the birth of the UK pensions system to the late seventeenth century, before detailing developments throughout the nineteenth century and early/mid-twentieth century. Section 2.2 focuses on the period after the election of the Thatcher government in 1979, including the early years of New Labour, when many elements of the post-war system were unravelled. Section 2.3 focuses on the later years of New Labour, when the Pensions Commission led by Adair Turner was established to devise a new, sustainable blueprint for UK pensions, and the recent Coalition and Conservative governments, which have to some extent moved away from the post-Turner consensus. As such, the chapter introduces many of the policies and practices relevant to private pensions provision that will be explored in more depth in subsequent chapters. Section 2.5 seeks, among other things, to locate the development of UK pensions provision within broader economic practices, and Chapter 3 situates this development alongside those of comparable countries.

2.1. Collectivism, Constrained: From the 1670s to the 1970s

The 1670s were a relatively quiet decade in an otherwise tumultuous period in English history, occurring in the Restoration period between Oliver

Cromwell's rule, which ended in 1658, and the Glorious Revolution of 1688. It was, however, a momentous decade in the history of UK pensions provision, insofar as it witnessed the creation of the first 'organised' occupational pension scheme, for members of the Royal Navy. The geopolitics of the era perhaps played a significant part in the pensions milestone: the decade had begun with the Third Anglo Dutch War, a naval conflict focused on control of North America, part of the Netherlands' long-running conflict with France. England's King Charles II had formed an alliance with Louis XIV of France in 1670, and in tandem sought to mitigate the persecution of Catholics in England, yet despite the Royal Navy's military victory, the English throne was of course surrendered to the Dutch within twenty years (with the repression of Catholicism subsequently revived).

As tempting as it is for a pensions enthusiast to speculate that it might have been decent occupational pensions provision that enabled the Royal Navy to conquer the globe in the eighteenth century, rewarding military personnel with an income in retirement was becoming common among European nations during this period—and indeed represented a revival of practices evident under Roman rule for elite soldiers. In modern terms, the history of British occupational pensions provision begins in the mid-/late nineteenth century. Although there were already pension schemes for civil servants in the early nineteenth century (a profession which, unlike today, represented a miniscule proportion of the workforce), 'retirement' was not a significant feature of the early Victorian period. Bucking the dominant trend in favour of provision for men that would emerge, women were among the early beneficiaries of the development of provision, as many nurses became entitled to a retirement income in 1874. Teachers and the police received similar benefits from the 1890s onwards.

Private-sector provision began to develop too, with pensions schemes at, for instance, Reuters, WH Smith, and Colmans. The Bank of England, then situated in the private sector, established one of the earliest schemes (Walker and Foster, 2006; Hunter, 2015). While some early pioneers of occupational pensions provision (such as Quaker-owned firms) were motivated by paternalist sentiment, generally speaking in supporting the recruitment and retention of skilled workers (and smoothing the retirement of older workers) employers found defined benefit provision compatible with their interests within the wider growth model (Hannah, 1986: 22; Pendleton and Gospel, 2017: 14). Essentially, private pensions provision was introduced by large employers in industries that were, at the time, stable or growing industries—benefiting from the state investing more in public services, and expenditure on domestically produced consumer goods due to higher disposable income among low- and median-income households.

However, this parsimonious account overlooks a hugely significant actor within the development of occupational pensions provision in the UK private sector: the trade union movement. It is certainly the case that the increase in higher-skilled, blue-collar jobs during the late industrialization period enabled workers to demand better remuneration, and establishing pension funds was a convenient way of providing it, since employer contributions were mitigated by the expectation of strong investment performance as the economy expanded, and employers themselves could control the associated funds (as discussed below). However, this dynamic was most relevant in the *post*-war period, in conjunction with nationalization. In the earlier part of the century, defined benefit provision was largely an employer initiative (insofar as it helped employers to manage their workforce), to which unions were initially sceptical (Gospel, 1992). There were two main reasons for scepticism. Firstly, because of an apparent preference for up-front rather than deferred pay (at a time when manual workers would not necessarily have expected to live long enough to retire in any substantive sense).

Secondly, and crucially, because trade unions themselves were early providers of occupational pensions provision, alongside trade-based friendly societies (that is, mutual associations for financial risk-sharing). This provision often took the form of unemployment and illness payments, which members were more likely to be in receipt of as they aged. However, some groups had a highly developed pensions regime, most notably the Northumberland and Durham Miners Permanent Relief Society, which was actually the UK's largest occupational pension scheme by the end of the nineteenth century (with 140,000 members, including 4,000 retirees). The scheme had no formal retirement age, and many members worked until death without ever claiming a pension payment. There were similar schemes in other industries, notably the railway industry, where employers had already established pension schemes for management and clerical staff. Railway industry employers effectively took over the manual workers' pre-existing schemes. A similar pattern emerged in utilities industries, and eventually manufacturing industries. The remaining worker-led schemes were wound down as state pension provision expanded (as discussed below). But it is worth noting that, in many parts of the manufacturing sector, a bifurcation between schemes for blue-collar and white-collar workers persisted beyond the Second World War (see Hannah, 1986: 6–7, 11–13).

The precise form that employer-sponsored occupational provision took in the early twentieth century has had long-lasting implications for UK pensions provision. One of the early movers, mustard manufacturer Colmans (as noted above), realized they could use trust law to circumvent the need for a pensions contract between the firm and its workers. (This is hugely ironic given that, as later chapters of this book argue, trust-based pensions provision is now rightly seen as superior to contract-based provision, from the perspective of employee protection—although in the present, the contract in question is between saver and provider, not worker and employer.) Run as an independent, 'self-administered' trust, firm directors could control all capital accumulated by the pension scheme through their power to appoint the trustee board. The legality of workers' right to a retirement income from the scheme was actually rather uncertain, until statute specifically related to pensions trusts developed in the post-war period. One of the key implications was that employers could use access to the pension scheme to ensure employee loyalty—since departing employees often relinquished their right to an income from the scheme when they reached retirement (see Hannah, 1986: 18–19, 24–5). While employee protections were eventually strengthened—including a role for trade unions in appointing trustees—the fact that trust law was utilized in the early formation of occupational pensions provision underlines the voluntaristic foundations of UK private pensions.

Arguably, developments in the late *eighteenth* century are as important as those a hundred years later, especially from the vantage of the present moment. In 1762, the world's first mutual insurance company, the Society for Equitable Assurances on Lives and Survivorships, was established. The company began by selling life insurance, but, crucially, life insurance 'with profits' whereby customers received payments when the investments funded by their premiums delivered a return. These products were important sources of income in later life for the very wealthiest—and the state actually introduced tax relief to support their development during William Gladstone's first stint as Chancellor of the Exchequer in 1853 (Hannah, 1986: 5). Generally speaking, life insurance products are not equivalent to pensions, but the development of 'with profits' products was instrumental in the development of annuities in the UK, even though the vast majority of annuities no longer encompass 'bonus' payments based on returns. The annuities market began to develop in the nineteenth century, well ahead of the spread of occupational pension schemes, in conjunction with advances in actuarial science, and available only to the very wealthiest (see Kopf, 1927). However, the earliest annuities looked *less* like pensions than the earliest life insurance products, because they typically did not involve a structured savings process during the accumulation phase. It is essentially the co-evolution of these two products—a life insurance model for accumulation, and an annuities model for decumulation—that led to the defined contribution pensions saving products as we understand them today.

Moreover, it tends to be forgotten that insurance companies were a significant presence in the development of *occupational* pensions provision in the early twentieth century (in many ways, foretelling the major role the insurance industry now has in the auto-enrolment world, as provider of defined contribution savings vehicles in the accumulation phase). The practice of insurers offering off-the-shelf collective schemes to employers actually originated in the US—where trust-based defined benefit provision in the private sector was rare—and was exported to the UK by a subsidiary of Metropolitan Life of New York (ML). Domestic firms such as Legal and General and Prudential were soon able to compete with ML, and Legal and General actually acquired ML's UK business in the 1930s. Crucially, the schemes offered by insurers included the provision of guaranteed retirement income. Clearly, these schemes resembled the defined contribution schemes that now dominate auto-enrolment, but were effectively what would be known today (or until recently—see below) as 'hybrid' defined benefit/defined contribution schemes. It is worth noting that these schemes did not qualify for tax relief until the 1950s (as discussed below, it was available to the employer trusts from the 1920s), by which point they had already largely disappeared from the occupational pensions landscape in the UK.

Yet insurers remained active in the decumulation phase. This was primarily related to personal rather than occupational pensions, yet they would also become major providers of the 'additional voluntary contribution' products that supplemented occupational pensions for high earners. The development of these products would nevertheless come to have a profound impact in the subsequent development of workplace pensions in the UK.

Equitable Life (as the Society for Equitable Assurances on Lives and Survivorships came to be known) itself began selling 'with profits' life insurance products with a guaranteed annuity rate (GAR) in 1957, alongside Prudential and several other firms. Equitable Life's offer came unstuck, however, when the nature of the pensions 'promise' (that is, the 'guaranteed' bit of the GAR) it had made to its customers was tested. In essence, the company's nineteenth-century business model came into conflict with a late twentieth-century understanding of pensions, and pensions law; the infamous *Equitable Life Assurance Society* v *Hyman* ruling (in which the final verdict was delivered in 2001) prohibited Equitable Life from reducing the value of annuity guarantees, ultimately adding £1.5 billion in long-term liabilities to the company's balance sheet. The company essentially collapsed, and the UK government eventually committed to compensate many of its customers that had lost their savings as a result, after a high-profile campaign fronted by actress and former 'Bond girl' Honor Blackman (a victim of the collapse)

(Sullivan, 2003: 95–8; Jones, 2014). Such problems notwithstanding, the historical and significant role of the insurance industry in UK pensions provision demonstrates that the seeds of the ongoing transition away from traditional occupational pensions were sown *before* these practices even emerged.

Moreover, while the Equitable Life scandal did not have a significant impact on occupational schemes, the approach to pensions embodied in these insurer-provided hybrids persisted in parts of occupational provision, as exemplified by issues explored in another landmark legal case, *Houldsworth v Bridge Trustees Ltd*, regarding the legal status of occupational schemes which offered elements of both defined benefit and defined contribution arrangements. The UK Supreme Court ruled on this case in 2011. The judgment in *Bridge*, that arrangements which looked like defined contribution provision (or 'money purchase', in legal terminology) should be regulated as such, therefore undermining the value of the pensions promise made by employers unless engaged in conventional defined benefit provision, was surprising to most observers (although upheld through all appeals) (Woods, 2011). The drift in pensions law had generally been towards respecting the sanctity of the promise. Although the government later legislated to clarify the law in line with its own perspective—therefore mitigating the future implications of *Bridge*—the case perhaps reminds us that collectivized provision had never firmly taken root in the UK pensions system. It is worth pointing out, for completeness, that there is plenty of evidence that annuity-like products were quite widely available in the Roman era, and indeed in earlier civilizations to some extent—although they were generally provided by public institutions (the argument that the state, as the ultimate insurance company, should provide annuities is still frequently heard among critics of UK pensions policy). Religious conventions around usury may have prohibited the development of annuities in Europe from the Middle Ages onwards, but indeed may have also helped to lay the foundations for the largely risk-free form of annuitization that eventually became dominant in economies like the UK (see Kopf, 1927).

The emergence of defined benefit occupational pensions from the late nineteenth century onwards was supported by the introduction of pensions tax relief (PTR) in 1921. As discussed in Chapter 6, the basic model of PTR remains in place today: contributions are made from pre-tax income, and fund investment returns are exempt from tax, but pensions in payment are subject to income tax. Generally speaking, when HM Treasury decides not to tax something, it is because the state is really very keen to encourage the activity. The introduction of PTR at this time was also a direct response to the inflationary conditions which followed the First World War, leading to concerns that employers would be unable to provide retirement incomes to their former workers of the value promised (albeit informally) (Hannah, 1986: 19–20). Limits on the volume of earnings that could benefit from tax relief were introduced in 1947, suggesting that the Treasury might have been too obliging, failing to foresee the extent to which high earners would be able to use pension schemes to shelter their income from tax. The operation of these limits, which are frequently adjusted, remains hugely contentious (as discussed in Chapter 6). Yet the limits were also related to the fact that defined benefit provision became increasingly widespread after the Second World War, in large part due to the nationalization of key industries and the enormous growth in public-sector employment. The Labour government clearly wanted to focus PTR on lower earners. This is not an approach which has been uniformly upheld by subsequent governments (tax advantages available to higher earners have been curtailed in some ways, but for fiscal rather than redistributive reasons).

The spread of so-called 'gold-plated' final salary pensions is now widely considered an act of exuberance and complacency on the part of the 'Butskellist' political elite in the 'golden era' of 'welfare capitalism'. The overuse of inverted commas in the previous sentence signifies that this account is rather ahistorical, and indeed mythical (Pemberton, 2010). While Labour politicians, in particular, might have been pleased to see decent private provision spreading throughout parts of the industrial workforce, this was to some extent a by-product of the post-war nationalization of key industries, and provision was never compulsory in the private sector. Indeed, as discussed below, Labour unsuccessfully sought in the late 1950s to introduce a more robust and redistributive layer of private provision. Not all that glitters is necessarily gold: the spread of defined benefit pensions provision can therefore be seen as part of a conscious demonstration of weakness, rather than overconfidence, insofar as it was associated with a defensive form of nationalization by policy-makers, and indeed efforts to persuade workers with obsolete skills to retire by large employers. In short, the trend was as much about managing the UK's relative economic decline on the part of political and economic elites, as it was about constructing a generous form of welfare provision for 'ordinary' workers. It is for this reason that the spread was never particularly wide—at least not until public-sector employment grew sharply in the 1970s and 1980s—and defined benefit pensions provision remained confined to a privileged minority. The fact that the finance sector was also reasserting itself around this time as the UK economy's 'cuckoo in the nest' is also relevant, as nationalization created a very stable source of pension assets to manage for the City.

The most important development of the immediate post-war period, however, was the introduction of what came to be known as the basic state pension (BSP) in 1948. The state is not a bit-part player in UK pensions provision—one of the ironies of a system that valorises private and voluntaristic provision has been that state provision has assumed an incredibly important role, often compensating for the limitations of the former. There had of course already been limited state provision in place, focused on the poorest. In 1909 the means-tested 'old age pension' (OAP) was introduced (establishing the term 'OAPs' which remains in popular usage in the UK) (Walker and Foster, 2006). It was available from the age of 70—and therefore not extensively claimed, since this was below life expectancy for low earners at the time. In 1925, under Winston Churchill as Chancellor of the Exchequer, a contributory state pension for low-paid manual workers (and some other low-income workers) was introduced, available from age 65 onwards. Unlike the original OAP, the benefit was not means-tested, and was available even if individuals remained in employment after reaching 65. State pension expenditure rose from 0.3 per cent of gross domestic product (GDP) in 1910 to 1.5 per cent by 1930 (Hannah, 1986: 17). The new benefit essentially facilitated the co-existence of state and occupational provision, as workers no longer lost state pension income if they also received a private pension (as discussed below, the reintroduction of means-testing in the 1980s, and its expansion in the late 1990s, would later reinvent this problem).

It is worth reflecting briefly here on the class dynamics evident in the early development of UK pensions provision. By and large, the main beneficiaries of the early forms of occupational pensions were white-collar workers, and the functionaries of the state machinery. As noted above, many manual workers sought to help themselves, via trade unions and friendly societies. Interestingly, as state pension provision emerged, resources were focused overwhelmingly on the poorest workers—precisely because these groups were not adequately served by private pensions. Universalizing state pension coverage moderated this trend but, as discussed below, the dynamic soon re-emerged, resulting in further attempts to use the state to compensate for the inadequacy of private provision for the working class (and women)—notably the State Earnings-Related Pensions Scheme (SERPS).

The National Insurance Act of 1946, which legislated for the BSP, was largely based on the blueprint for welfare provision that William Beveridge had constructed in his 1942 report, *Social Insurance and Allied Services* (more commonly known as the 'Beveridge report'). It built upon the provision established in the 1920s but, in establishing near universal state pension provision (as well as improving outcomes for existing OAP beneficiaries), represented a hugely transformative moment for UK pensions provision. Yet the BSP that was implemented after the war differed in many ways from Beveridge's vision—these differences are usually overlooked, but are perhaps quite pertinent in light of recent reforms in UK pensions provision. Beveridge had never intended to institute a state pension system which afforded contributors an income related to earnings during their working life, but rather a flat-rate income which lifted pensioners out of poverty. Crucially, the scheme was also intended to be fully funded, with contributions derived on an actuarially fair basis from the expected retirement income.

The actual system introduced encompassed no requirement of funding, in large part because the Labour government wanted to extend eligibility to older cohorts that would not have been able to fund a full entitlement through their own contributions. The system was instead 'pay-as-you-go', and the level of taxation (that is, National Insurance rates) was set solely with reference to the revenue required to pay for pension benefits currently in payment. It was also not strictly 'contributory', as eligibility related to the number of years that National Insurance contributions had been made, rather than the level of contributions. In other words, the state pension that was introduced ended up being rather more progressive and redistributive than Beveridge had envisaged. The Institute for Fiscal Studies' account of the history of the state pension claims that its loose contribution arrangements meant that BSP was never a 'social insurance' pension (Bozio et al., 2010: 9), due to its understanding of social insurance in quite narrow terms as a conventional insurance product, albeit provided by the state. Yet it is not unreasonable to assume—precisely because of the fact that the state is the provider—that such an insurance scheme would seek to balance the infallibility it offers all beneficiaries with a redistributive agenda in favour of the worst-off beneficiaries. This would necessitate a pay-as-you-go model in practice, to ensure promised entitlements could be delivered in full, without invalidating the principle of social insurance.

As discussed in Chapter 3, the 'Bismarckian' pensions of continental Europe, despite embodying a social insurance model in a more conventional sense, also tend to include redistributive elements (which vary considerably between countries) and are generally financed on a pay-as-you-go basis too (albeit usually with more autonomy from the state's balance sheet). Definitional nitpicking aside, in providing the BSP, the state in the UK was doing a job the private sector *could not do*, not simply a job it had *failed to do*. State pension provision of any type represents a recognition that there are limits to the private sector's ability to successfully dematerialize and rematerialize pensions capital across the lifecourse of savers. That said, we should not assume that the relationship between state and private provision was necessarily *planned* in line with this objective, at least not in any meaningful sense, or that the principle of social insurance became a defining hallmark of UK pensions provision. It is clearly the case that access for low-paid workers to occupational private pensions provision had improved by the immediate post-war era. Leslie Hannah (1986) refers to the state and large employers as 'rival pioneers of collectivism' in this regard. Of course, the rivalry was never resolved: instead, both sets of collectivist arrangements soon started to unravel.

In terms of the state pension, while the spirit of the Beveridge blueprint remains pertinent to understanding UK pensions, in practice provision has proved both more and less liberal than Beveridge envisaged. The gold-plated nature of private defined benefit provision did not last very long (though the legacy of the post-war expansion of defined benefit provision will be with us for a long time yet) as firms took advantage of a lax regulatory environment. And the state has been far more extensively involved, albeit sometimes incoherently, in providing pensions to combat widespread poverty in later life. Yet the redistributive nature of the UK state pension system, and particularly its near universality, is almost certainly a large part of the explanation for its historically low entitlement rate. More exclusive schemes tend to be more generous.

The messy contradictions inherent in the UK's liberal collectivist approach to pensions reached their zenith with the introduction of SERPS in 1978 (SERPS actually expanded, albeit very significantly, the similar Graduated Retirement Benefit scheme that had been in place since the early 1960s). Although the focus of this book is private pensions provision, and SERPS was ostensibly part of the state pension system, its introduction foretold the ongoing role of state intervention in compensating for the failures of a highly financialized private pensions system. (Ironically, its eventual abolition served the same purpose, as SERPS itself proved an inadequate income-replacement mechanism for many groups ill-served by private provision.) SERPS is invariably associated with the Labour Member of Parliament Barbara Castle, Secretary of State for Health and Social Services when SERPS was legislated for in 1975 (but sacked by incoming Prime Minister James Callaghan before the scheme was introduced) and notorious for her previous stance on industrial relations. SERPS typified Castle's somewhat maverick approach to social policy, extending state provision to groups excluded from private provision (especially women and very low earners), to some extent, without seriously threatening—and arguably even reinforcing—the primacy of voluntaristic provision in the private sector. It is worth noting that Labour had proposed a much more ambitious version of SERPS in the form of 'national superannuation' while out of office in 1957. In light of the ongoing exclusion of the majority of workers from defined benefit provision, national superannuation would have seen the state organizing a single, funded defined benefit scheme, with an element of redistribution from high to low earners. The idea faced significant opposition from the City, but also trade unions, who worried about the impact that the new scheme would have on the existing schemes inhabited by their members (Pemberton, 2010).

Whereas national superannuation would have created a new, colossal private pension scheme backed by the state, SERPS was largely an attempt to turn the state into a direct provider of defined benefit pensions (Walker and Naegele, 1999). The scheme offered pensioners with a full National Insurance record a replacement income of 25 per cent of an eligible band of working-age earnings in an individual's best twenty years of earnings. SERPS was a universal benefit, yet not one those who were due to benefit from an occupational pension actually needed; as such, the scheme was accompanied by complex 'contracting-out' arrangements whereby many employees (and their employers) paid a lower rate of National Insurance in order to forgo entitlement to SERPS. SERPS and contracting out sound incredibly complicated because they were incredibly complicated (and, again, despite the abolition of SERPS and later abolition of contracting out, their complex legacy is still working its way through the pensions system). SERPS typified the contradictions of post-war pensions provision in the UK; while in public policy terms it ostensibly filled in the gap between state and private provision, arguably it disrupted the internal logic (of sorts) of both forms of provision—at a time when the UK's relative economic decline was creating fears about the fiscal sustainability of welfare provision. SERPS is best understood as an attempt to salvage widespread defined benefit coverage for those in work, amid the emergence of a services-led economy and steady dissolution of the (male) 'breadwinner' labour market model. Paradoxically, as demonstrated by the failure of national superannuation, the resistance of private pensions industry (and even the trade unions whose members benefited from it) to the reform of private provision, given the embeddedness of the voluntarist principle, meant that the state was required to take on an enhanced role *in place of* private provision. Yet the case for the state performing such a function was never convincingly made and, moreover, the same demographic trends that deterred new services sector employers from establishing occupational pension schemes also concerned those responsible for the fiscal balance sheet (Millar, 2002: 164).

2.2. Neoliberal Revolution? From 1979 to the Early 2000s

The neoliberal era in UK pensions policy took its cue from the high point of the collectivist period: the Thatcher government which took office in 1979 greatly disliked SERPS. Margaret Thatcher's statecraft was far more cautious than her own rhetoric might have suggested (Campbell, 2007) but the government eventually succeeded in reducing both the SERPS accrual rate (to 20 per cent) and, later, the rate at which previous earnings were revalued. As noted below, the government had proposed the abolition of SERPS, but had faced strong opposition. Like any new benefit, SERPS had immediately created a new cohort of welfare 'winners', but employers were also fearful— quite ironically, given subsequent reforms—that responsibility for occupational pensions would revert back to them were SERPS to end (Millar, 2002: 164). Changes to contracting out were arguably of greater significance, and actually involved fiscal expansion rather than retraction. From 1988 onwards, contracting out was applicable to defined contribution as well as defined benefit pensions. SERPS had been accused of overloading the state, but such fears were seemingly put to rest when there was an opportunity to use the fiscal balance sheet—and one of the key provisions of SERPS—to support the further individualization of UK pensions through defined contribution provision.

Thatcher disliked SERPS for the same reason she disliked defined benefit pensions provision in general: it made institutions—whether the state or employers—rather than savers themselves responsible for the individual's financial welfare. Individualization would breed personal responsibility (Walker and Foster, 2006: 433). Ironically, however, without SERPS, there would have been no contracting out, and therefore no opportunity to effectively publicly subsidize individualized, defined contribution pensions provision. Crucially, whereas contracting out related to defined benefit provision required that employers funded pensions above a statutory minimum level (in return for lower National Insurance costs), contracting out related to defined contribution schemes required only that the National Insurance savings were invested in employees' pension pots. This was a rather timid stipulation, especially given that employer sponsors of defined contribution schemes were not required to make any other contribution into their employees' saving pots. Whereas contracting out was designed to reward employers' voluntaristic provision of collectivist pensions, the Thatcher government—ostensibly critical of state intervention—was quite content to use the same mechanism to simply subsidize individualist pensions. It should be noted, however, that the second-term Thatcher government had hoped to go much further. The Fowler Inquiry into Provision for Retirement, established by Thatcher in 1983, and resulting in the 1985 green paper *Reform of Social Security*, had not only recommended the abolition of SERPS, but also the compulsory membership of a defined contribution pension (moreover, via a personal rather than workplace pension scheme) with individuals contributing 4 per cent of their earnings (Pemberton, 2017). The Prime Minister, it seemed, supported compulsion—but it was resisted by the Chancellor, Nigel Lawson, on the grounds that the resulting expenditure on PTR would be prohibitively expensive (and seen as a tax rise by the self-employed, who would not qualify for it) (Morris and Palmer, 2011: 56–7). In practice, SERPS was spared, which meant the contracting-out mechanism could be used to incentivize fiscally, rather than compel legally, the take-up of personal pensions. Of course, compulsory membership of defined contribution schemes was back on the UK pensions policy agenda within twenty years.

The Thatcher government also sought to undermine the BSP, with arguably much greater consequences for the value of state provision over the long term than their changes to SERPS. The government infamously broke the 'earnings link' in 1980, that is, the practice of indexing BSP awards in payment in line with the annual increase in average earnings. This reform appears to have become central to popular understandings of Thatcher statecraft, but it is important not to overstate the transformative nature of the change. Earnings indexation had not been part of the state pension in the immediate post-war years; it was first introduced in the 1960s, and not made statutory until much later. Nevertheless, the Social Security Act 1980 formalized a system of indexation by price inflation, and as such served to temper the possibility that the social insurance-based state pension would become a more dominant feature in the UK pensions system as the population began to age. Subsequently, the value of the BSP was significantly eroded, contributing to the increasing numbers of pensioners in poverty throughout the 1990s. It was also under the Thatcher government that the shift (back) towards means-tested benefits in state provision began. As noted above, the state pension had actually started life as a means-tested benefit focused on alleviating severe poverty. Furthermore, means-tested benefits had been an important feature of the post-war UK pensions system for those without sufficient National Insurance records. The Labour government introduced

National Assistance to this effect in 1948, offering awards that were to some extent discretionary, adjudicated by the National Assistance Board. Given that the Conservative governments of the 1950s often elected not to increase the level of the BSP each year, increasing numbers of pensioner households became dependent on National Assistance despite also being eligible for the BSP. In 1966, the replacement of National Assistance by the Supplementary Benefit increased the amount available to pensioners through means-tested benefits, and removed administrative discretion, although rises in the BSP minimized overlaps between the social insurance and means-tested systems.

Although they are often seen in opposition, the 1960s and 1970s were arguably therefore a time when *both* social insurance and means-tested state pension provision became more important to the UK pensions system, underlining its patchwork character. In the 1980s and 1990s, however, the pendulum swung firmly towards means-tested provision. Income support was introduced for all adults in 1988, with a premium for pensioners. Income support made means-tested benefit awards for pensioners more formulaic, although the minimum income level varied on the basis of housing costs. The Blair government's first term after the 1997 election saw this legacy being taken forward. The pensioner premium in income support was rebranded as a 'Minimum Income Guarantee' (MIG) in 1999, and increased substantially over the next few years. In Blair's second term—although the policy was very much associated with Chancellor of the Exchequer, Gordon Brown—Labour introduced Pension Credit. This benefit was primarily a replacement for the MIG, with its 'Guarantee Credit' element becoming substantially more generous over time due to earnings indexation. In contrast, the BSP remained tied to prices, in fear of the long-term fiscal consequences of restoring the earnings links (whereas means-tested benefits create less of a sense of 'entitlement'); the government did, however, introduce an array of other universal pensioner benefits in partial compensation.

Pension Credit also included a nod towards Labour's real ambitions on pensions policy, however, via its 'Savings Credit' element. Savings Credit was designed to soften the rate at which means-tested benefits were withdrawn from individuals with income above a particular threshold (generally tied to the value of the BSP, until 2008), and therefore mitigate the possibility of means-tested benefits disincentivizing people from saving for a pension privately. In practice, Savings Credit increased complexity within UK state pensions provision quite significantly, and actually brought many more pensioner households within the scope of means-tested benefits by extending further up the income ladder, therefore theoretically *introducing* a fiscal disincentive to save privately for some groups where none had existed previously.

It is reasonable to speculate that the Blair government was not as enamoured with means-tested provision as its early record suggests. Path dependency matters here. A rapid increase in the value of means-tested benefits was deemed to be required precisely because so many pensioners had fallen into relative poverty by the mid-1990s, although the higher poverty rate was a product of the neglect of social insurance-based provision from the 1980s onwards and, paradoxically, an unwillingness among many pensioners to claim means-tested benefits (Thurley, 2011). The *idea* of Savings Credit, even if it was bungled in practice, demonstrates that the government was aware of the downside of a reliance on means-tested benefits. Labour also demonstrated their objective to strengthen the contributory state pension system by introducing S2P in 2002 to replace SERPS. S2P enabled access to an additional state pension to those unable to contribute formally to the labour market through greater access to credits in lieu of earnings for people with disabilities or caring responsibilities. More fundamentally, S2P was more redistributive than SERPS (or what SERPS had become under Thatcher)—and therefore looked much less like a state-run defined benefit scheme—enabling higher awards to low and moderate earners. Of course, such effects were not due to materialize in retirement incomes for many years, thereby requiring swifter action for the poorest pensioners in the form of Pension Credit.

New Labour's main legacy for UK pensions provision is the further entrenchment of defined contribution pensions via public policy (not least because S2P has now been abolished). Gordon Brown's impact on private pensions provision will be forever associated, it seems, with his decision in 1997 to abolish tax relief on defined benefit funds' income from dividends (discussed further in Chapter 7). Two decades on, the decision continues to attract hyperbolic coverage in the financial press (which is overwhelmingly supportive of the private pensions industry), not least after the Office for Budget Responsibility published analysis in 2014 which suggested the change had netted the Exchequer around £10 billion per year in additional tax revenue. Former senior *Daily Mail* journalist and *Financial Times* financial advice columnist, Tony Hazell, reported that 'it is reasonable to conclude final salary schemes, which are today closed to new members, would otherwise have still been going had Mr Brown not dipped into their coffers... Mr Brown's tax raid will always stand out as one of the great injustices perpetrated on the diligent investing public—and rightly so' (Hazell, 2014; see also Hyde, 2014). In fiscal terms, this is a fairly significant sum—one of many examples of the Treasury fiddling with technical pensions regulations in order to enhance revenue for the Exchequer. But it represents a tiny percentage of the assets held by defined benefit funds. Had the tax change never been introduced, the positive, material impact on defined benefit fund deficits that grew steadily in the 1990s and 2000s would have been negligible. New Labour was not in any significant sense an enemy to the array of commercial enterprises involved in UK pensions provision, but the reaction to Brown's 'tax raid' exemplifies perfectly the ideological climate it was operating within. As discussed in Chapter 4, defined benefit provision was experiencing a steep decline, for a range of reasons far more consequential than the dividend tax change, but Brown's decision provided the means by which the government alone, rather than the development of the UK economy more generally, could be blamed for the trend.

In reality, the state was actively involved in this period in supporting private pensions provision. The worst that could possibly be said about the 1997 'tax raid' is that it demonstrated the Labour government's general indifference to defined benefit pensions provision. But New Labour was strongly supportive of the development of defined contribution provision. The introduction of stakeholder pensions in 2001 broke new ground in this regard. Through this policy, the government essentially designed a new defined contribution pension product for the mass market and, crucially, required most employers to offer it to their staff (although there was still no obligation for employers to contribute). The stakeholder pensions policy was short-lived, dramatically superseded by the development of 'automatic enrolment' (known as auto-enrolment) in Labour's third and final term in office. But it sketched the blueprint for the more significant rollout of defined contribution to come—a blueprint which ensured that what appeared to be a major shift in policy direction after 2005 was actually rooted in the neoliberal politics of the 1980s and 1990s. It is also worth noting Labour's activism in the regulatory space in relation to defined benefit provision (also discussed further in Chapter 4). The Pensions Regulator (TPR) was established in 2005 to institute a more risk-averse form of regulation in place of the relatively weak Occupational Pensions Regulatory Authority. The creation of TPR was a largely defensive move, designed to oversee the managed decline of defined benefit provision, rather than herald its resurrection, and should be seen alongside the creation of the Pension Protection Fund and Financial Assistance Scheme for members of insolvent defined benefit schemes. TPR has become more active in terms of defined contribution regulation in subsequent years—but it is fair to say that Labour largely accepted that the regulation of defined contribution pensions was largely unnecessary, since outcomes would be determined entirely by the market rather than any promise by sponsoring employers. The scope for intervention by TPR into defined contribution provision remains limited, as a result of this judgment.

From the 1970s onwards, the dominant forms of UK pensions provision clearly moved away from the collectivist moment of the early and mid-twentieth century. State provision was undermined in favour of private provision. Within state provision, means-tested provision was favoured over social insurance provision. And within private provision, defined benefit schemes gave way to individualized, defined contribution pensions saving. These changes exemplified the 'welfare retrenchment' associated with the rise of neoliberalism, which was based on a perception that 'globalisation' had dramatically altered the context in which the UK economy and constituent parts were operating. Heightened international competition, as new technologies created both opportunities for less developed countries to 'catch up' to the West and new imperatives for economies like the UK to 'upgrade' their industrial base, required companies that were agile, workers that were flexible, and a lower tax environment. Greater economic interdependence also required convergence within welfare systems (Taylor-Gooby, 1997; Hay, 1998, 2006b; Berry, 2011). The long-term nature of traditional pensions provision, especially insofar as it was intertwined with complex entitlements for recipients, was incompatible with this brave new world.

There were counter-trends to this general picture, but as suggested above, schemes such as SERPS were essentially an attempt to use the state to mitigate the decline of collectivism in the private sphere—in a way which proved unsustainable, at least politically. Similarly, its successor S2P sought to anaesthetize the teething pains of the new order, but proved to be even more short-lived. Of course, the new order was in many ways also the reassertion of elements of the old order, with private provision most accessible to the wealthiest groups and a means-tested safety net for the poorest, despite its association with the emergence of a novel neoliberal paradigm. However, there were new elements too, as will be explored throughout the book. Changes associated with financialization meant that the finance sector was not simply important to UK pensions due to its role in selling pension products directly to savers or managing pension investments; the imperative to engage with financial services was becoming an ideological hallmark of the individualization of UK pensions provision, bound up with elite fears about the emerging impact of demographic change (principally population ageing) on collective provision. Moreover, and crucially, the state was assuming a new role, not simply getting out of the way of whatever form private provision might take, but establishing new markets for individualized provision. Irrespective of the economic case for and against collective provision, it became clear by the 2000s that the *political* economy of collectivism, after a relatively brief heyday, was beginning to perish.

2.3. Consensus, Subverted: From 2005 Onwards

The most important thing to say about the first policy paradigm of the post-collectivist era, however, was that it failed, or at least was deemed to have failed by the main political parties, who agreed in 2002 to support the Pensions Commission in establishing a new long-term framework for UK pensions provision. In other words, even before Pension Credit, S2P, and stakeholder pensions had been fully rolled out, the Labour government signalled its intent to construct a new pensions blueprint for the UK, such was its concern about the spending pressures that state pension reform would create if the promotion of defined contribution pensions, and related initiatives, did not succeed in producing higher levels of private saving (DWP, 2002). The era of defined benefit was over, but the era of defined contribution remained in adolescence. It is worth noting, however, that the Pensions Commission appeared to extend its own remit without the full consent of the Labour government (Institute for Government, 2011)—the Commission upheld a more expansive interpretation of how state apparatus might be used to increase private saving. At the same time, as Paul Bridgen and Traute Meyer (2011) argue, policy elites from across the political spectrum had accepted long before the establishment of the Commission that voluntarism was 'exhausted', pointing towards both the increasing spread of regulation in private provision from the early 1990s onwards, and state pension reform after 1997.

As noted above, the Commission was chaired by Adair Turner, former Director of the Confederation of British Industry and future Chair of the Financial Services Authority, alongside trade unionist Jeannie Drake and academic John Hills. It published its analysis in 2004, and its recommendations in 2005 (see The Pensions Commission, 2004, 2005, 2006). The Commission's most important legacy was its recommendation for the automatic enrolment of most employees into a workplace pension scheme, if they were not already members of a scheme which met minimum quality standards. As discussed at length in Chapter 5, auto-enrolment is perhaps the most important example of the British state's embrace of the notion of 'nudge', based on behavioural economics, as individuals would be automatically enrolled in their employers' pension scheme, with the freedom to 'opt out'. One of the most significant aspects of the reform was the establishment in statute of a minimum employer contribution into employees' pensions of 3 per cent of eligible earnings. Employees were eligible for this contribution if they themselves contributed 5 per cent (the default minimum for those automatically enrolled). The package was briefly marketed as a 10 per cent pension contribution, including also a government contribution of 2 per cent, that is, an approximation of the role of basic rate PTR (because the 8 per cent came from pre-tax income). Crucially, while auto-enrolment into a defined benefit scheme was certainly permissible, the Commission accepted that the vast majority would be enrolled into defined contribution products, a judgment which was reflected in recommendations for both regulation and communications. Auto-enrolment normalized defined contribution provision.

The Commission labelled the pension products associated with auto-enrolment 'personal accounts' (deliberately avoiding use of the term 'pension', although this boycott has not really stuck). Interestingly, they focused their recommendations on contribution levels and minimum standards for savers, rather than on delivery mechanisms—even leaving open the possibility that the state would itself provide personal accounts, a quiet but significant echo of Labour's proposed 'national superannuation' scheme in the late 1950s. Personal accounts would of course be based on a defined contribution model rather than defined benefit, but—in a move that seems utterly remarkable now, only fifteen years on—the Commission even considered recommending a 'notional' defined contribution (NDC) model (see Barr and Diamond, 2010: 7–8), as exists in Sweden. In an NDC system, the state would take responsibility for providing individuals a retirement income, based on their lifetime contributions and an imputed rate of return, without any pensions savings actually being invested. Ultimately, the Commission favoured an individualized, 'pure' defined contribution model. But it was the Labour government which decided that the private sector would be the principal providers, and moreover, that schemes would not have to replicate the trust-based governance required in private-sector defined benefit provision. As discussed further in Chapter 6, the Personal Accounts Delivery Authority evolved into the National Employment Savings Trust (NEST), a multi-employer scheme managed by the state in a trust-like structure and focused on the small employer market. It was apparently hoped that private providers would voluntarily treat NEST as a benchmark in terms of scheme governance, investment principles, and member communications, but employers, who choose a scheme on behalf of their employees, tend to prioritize factors such as ease of use and cost to the employer (both of which also generally favour NEST) (Pension PlayPen, 2016; Tapper, 2016).

The government was also responsible for final decisions on the range of people to be covered by auto-enrolment, or more precisely, the band of earnings to which minimum employer contributions would apply. As well as phasing in the minimum employer contribution very gradually, the Pensions Act 2008 stipulated that the qualifying earnings band would be £5,035–£33,540, with the lower and upper limits uprated each year. The upper limit is designed to ensure that employer contributions are focused on low and moderate earners, less likely to already be saving for a pension, but the operation of the lower limit ensures that the lowest earners have a smaller proportion of their pay recognized when the statutory minimum employer contribution is calculated. The system also relies on qualifying earnings being received from a single employer, meaning people with multiple jobs (more likely to be women and low earners) are disadvantaged. Furthermore, after the formation of the Coalition government in 2010, the Pensions Act 2011 introduced an 'earnings trigger', meaning only those earning above a certain amount—significantly higher than the lower earnings band limit—would be automatically enrolled (although those earning between the lower limit and the trigger could 'opt in'). The earnings trigger was originally set at £7,045, but the Coalition subsequently sought to link the amount to the income tax personal allowance, even though the government was committed to substantially increasing the allowance. The link between the two, which had no statutory basis, has now seemingly been severed, with the trigger for 2017/18 frozen at £10,000, but not before many thousands of low earners had been effectively excluded from auto-enrolment. These changes, although relatively minor, represented a clear attempt by the Coalition to dilute regulatory burdens in light of the economic downturn, albeit without unravelling automatic enrolment in any significant way. It is also worth noting here the obvious fact that the self-employed—a population which has grown significantly in recent years—are not covered by automatic enrolment, although they can become individual members of NEST.

While the Commission hammered a further nail into the coffin of collectivism in the UK pensions system by accepting the pure defined contribution, its advocacy of auto-enrolment and minimum employer contributions was based on its view of a clear public interest in addressing inadequate retirement incomes, and therefore a revised role for the state in the UK pensions system. But in accepting much of the legacy of the neoliberal turn of the 1990s—with the partial exception of the expansion of means-tested benefits—it is apparent that the Commission failed to (re-)establish the solidaristic principles upon which its new framework might have required to become self-sustaining. In short, the Commission's approach—characterized by John Macnicol (2015: 54) as one of 'libertarian paternalism'—left the pensions policy door open to some of the key tenets of neoliberal statecraft, which had become firmly established across UK social and economic policy by the mid-2000s. As noted above, it was the Thatcher government who first suggested compulsory membership of defined contribution pension schemes—at the birth of the previous pensions revolution. The notion of personal responsibility became more, not less, central to New Labour's pensions agenda following the Commission, which helps to explain the policy choices it made around the implementation of auto-enrolment, and demonstrates the clear continuities between Labour's pre- and post-Turner pensions policy. Insofar as the financial crisis made any significant difference to the nature of UK pensions policy, after 2010 the Coalition government often invoked the crisis as justification for its own emphasis on personal responsibility as the principle underpinning its support for automatic enrolment. As such, there were clear pre- and post-crisis continuities too—although the Coalition government invariably presented its own agenda as a novel departure from the Labour years (Berry, 2016b).

The Coalition government did depart from New Labour, and the consensus around the Pensions Commission's proposals, in a much more substantive way by embarking on the 'liberation' of pensions. In 2014, George Osborne announced the near immediate end of compulsory annuitization in defined contribution pensions saving. Interestingly, the financial crisis played little part in the public justification of the change, although arguably it reinforced a sense of personal responsibility in pensions provision. Technically, compulsory annuitization had already been abolished by the Coalition in 2011, but punitive tax rates, linked to annuity values, on individuals seeking to draw down their pension pot had remained largely in place, thereby significantly disincentivizing most people from using pensions saving for anything other than buying an annuity. This disincentive was already in the process of being loosened, but it was decided that from April 2015 onwards funds drawn down would only be taxed at marginal tax rates, for individuals aged 55 and over. The full range of consequences of this change will be discussed further in Chapter 6. For now, it suffices to specify the impact that this change has upon the apparent cross-party consensus established by the Commission. The Commission had sought to usher in an age of compulsion (or near compulsion), with individuals strongly nudged towards saving, but receiving greater state and employer support in the process. It had been largely taken for granted that the annuitization process would remain static as automatic enrolment became embedded, and indeed that the annuities market would become more competitive as it adapted to demand from future generations of auto-enrolees. The so-called pension freedoms disrupt these expectations. Most auto-enrolees will in all likelihood lack the resources to utilize their new freedoms, but will instead be forced to engage with an annuities market very different from what might have been expected when automatic enrolment was implemented.

The end of annuities has seen a revival for 'with profits' pensions products, as accumulated funds now tend to remain invested, through accounts belonging to individuals, and drawn upon directly, and partially, to fund retirement. Products of this nature had of course never gone away, especially for individual savers less dependent on tax-advantaged saving; indeed, making profitable returns was of course a feature of defined benefit saving (albeit one that benefited the scheme sponsor rather than individual members). In the context of defined contribution saving, annuities were perhaps the last vestige of the UK pensions system's collectivist heritage, insofar as the process spread longevity risks across very large populations of savers, relying on the very long-term nature of insurance industry investments to rematerialize savings as a retirement income—agreed at the point of purchase—as required.

Much like the prospect of NDC, the Commission actually floated the possibility of the state itself providing annuities, although it refrained from making any recommendations in this regard (discussed further in Chapters 5 and 6). Essentially, the contradictions in the Commission's framework were too pronounced to withstand a policy agenda set on reviving the neoliberal revolution. A reliance on individualized forms of private saving, largely provided by the finance sector, meaning the (naïve) hope that a regime based on auto-enrolment would endure for generations to come, has been extinguished by the ideological resilience of neoliberalism, and indeed the quest for new commercial opportunities among some individual savers and providers. Crucially, the Labour opposition, although it had moved to the left under the leadership of Ed Miliband and sought to 'move on' from the New Labour project, largely acquiesced to the changes. Part of the Commission's *raison d'être* was that it represented a new cross-party consensus on pensions policy, yet by 2014 all three main parties supported the removal of one of its core elements (the pension freedoms were very much Conservative Chancellor of the Exchequer's George Osborne's initiative, but were taken forward by the Liberal Democrat pensions minister Steve Webb). The effective end of compulsory annuitization chimed with concerns Miliband had raised about the historically low annuity prices being offered to those nearing retirement with little choice but to annuitize. As such, the long-term development of auto-enrolment was given lower priority than immediate political calculations. Even self-consciously progressive politicians were caught in the ideological trap of substituting the individualistic mantra 'it's my money' for a genuine attack on restrictive City practices.

The Commission's most eye-catching recommendations were those related to increasing the SPA, as discussed further in Chapter 6. The UK's recent journey in this regard actually began in 1995, when the Major government legislated, in accordance with European law, to gradually equalize the male and female SPAs at 65 between 2010 and 2020. Following the Commission, the Labour government legislated to an increase for both to 66 by 2026, 67 by 2036, and 68 by 2046. By and large, however, the increases proved to be relatively uncontroversial, insofar as they were broadly in line with forecast increases in average life expectancy, and of course planned for far enough into the future that the impact was seemingly discounted (or unknown) by the cohorts that would be affected—the magic of behavioural economics at work once more. The Coalition government began to dismantle the carefully constructed SPA consensus as soon as it took office, under the auspices of austerity. The pace of SPA equalization was accelerated after 2016, so that parity would be attained by 2018. The increase to 66 for both men and women was brought forward to 2020, and finally the increase to 67 was brought forward to 2028. The Coalition also sought to introduce a more for-mulaic dimension to future increases (with individuals expected to spend around a third of their lives above SPA), albeit adjudicated by a regular review process. All of these changes have been contested forcefully by vari-ous civil society groups, although the Labour opposition has generally only raised complaints (and only since Jeremy Corbyn became leader in 2015) about the women whose SPA will increase much faster than expected in the near future. As such, Labour under Corbyn (replaced as leader by Keir Starmer in early 2020) demonstrated support for the high-profile Women Against State Pension Inequality campaign (see Corbyn, 2017; see also Holman et al., 2018 for further discussion of the concerns underpinning the campaign).

Another of the Coalition government's flagship pensions policy initiatives was designed to advance upon, rather than unpick, the Commission's agenda. Despite its very recent introduction, Turner et al. concluded that S2P—and moreover, the complex relationship between S2P and the BSP—was not fit for purpose. Forecasting enormous increases in eligibility for S2P, and means-tested benefits for those poorly served by social insurance-based state pensions, the Commission sought to effectively abolish S2P over time by turning it into a flat-rate top-up to the BSP by reducing and harmonizing accrual rates; the BSP would itself increase in value by once again rising in line with earnings growth. The idea of returning to a single state pension scheme, with everyone receiving a flat-rate amount irrespective of earnings throughout their career, had been floated around the fringes of Labour's pensions policy agenda since the 2000s. The Commission was keen on the idea that the state pension should be a simple, universal platform for private saving. It concluded, however, that the complexities involved in abolishing contracting out (a product solely of additional state pension benefit) and the anomalous losers that would be created by any rapid introduction of a flat-rate benefit justified a highly cautious transition (Berry, 2016a).

The Coalition government had other ideas. Pensions minister Steve Webb had long advocated a flat-rate state pension (see Webb, 2004), and Chancellor George Osborne was seemingly persuaded by the possibility of using the reform to make savings on a growing state pensions bill. The STSP was introduced via the Pensions Act 2014, with S2P and contracting out abolished as a result (Savings Credit was also abolished for future retirees)—the implementation had originally been planned for 2017, but was actually brought forward by Osborne in 2016. As the Commission had anticipated, a rapid transition to STSP meant that there were many losers, as well as some winners, as S2P accrual was replaced by less generous STSP accrual arrangements. Complex arrangements (that is, benefit reductions) also had to be put in place for people that had benefited from contracting out at some point in their careers. Furthermore, the rather low introductory level decided upon for STSP meant that many people in age cohorts close to retirement would become eligible for means-tested benefits, including the guarantee element of Pension Credit in many cases, and that younger cohorts would generally receive much worse outcomes from the state pension system than had the Commission's recommendations been retained (Berry, 2013a; Crawford et al., 2013; TUC, 2013). Ironically, because STSP was introduced at a time when male and female SPAs remain unequal, it means that many men had access to the new system while women born on the same day did not (because they were already in receipt of BSP), and were therefore excluded from the uplift in state pension payments received by some men with limited SERPS or S2P entitlements—a problem which afflicts women far more than men (Berry, 2013b).

It is worth noting briefly that while the Labour government, after Gordon Brown had become Prime Minister, did eventually relent on the restoration of earnings indexation—the 2010 election happened before the deadline for restoration had been reached—the Coalition government actually implemented a 'triple lock' of annual indexation by the higher of earnings growth, price inflation, or 2.5 per cent. This actually built upon another Brown initiative, since the 'double lock' of indexation by price inflation or 2.5 per cent had been introduced from 2002 onwards, to avoid a repeat of BSP rising by only 75p per week in 2000 (1.1 per cent), a highly controversial consequence of indexation by only prices at a time of low inflation (Thurley, 2020). The Coalition's triple lock spared the state pension from the immediate impact of public spending cuts amid austerity, but actually makes very little difference to the value of state pension accrual over the long term. Although state pension provision is not covered in depth in this book's subsequent chapters, it is worth keeping in mind that the retrenchment of state provision is part of the story of why private provision is now being asked to work harder than it possibly can. Indeed, the flattening of the state pension is explained by policy-makers' embrace of, or at least indifference towards, these circumstances.

2.4.   A Brief Note on Capitalist Development

This issue was discussed in Chapter 1, and will be discussed again in Chapter 3, but it is worth reflecting briefly here on the economic context in which UK pensions provision has developed. The most obvious link in a direct sense between pensions provision and wider economic activity is the role of the finance sector in provision. Financial service providers have consistently developed products and services that have become central to UK private pensions—albeit largely targeting affluent savers—in terms of both the direct provision of savings vehicles and the management of pension investments (issues around pension investment are discussed in more depth in Chapter 7). The latter became the most significant element in this regard as large defined benefit funds emerged in the post-war era. Such activity has often been strongly supported by state action, such as the funded nature of public-sector pensions in local government (providing a steady flow of capital to the asset management industry). In recent decades, the rise of defined contribution savings has introduced a new range of finance-sector providers, principally insurers. The extension of contracting out to defined contribution products (rewarding the new breed of insurers operating in the personal pensions space) means the state has been instrumental in this process too. Of course, the move into accumulation products is an extension of the insurance industry's traditional role in defined contribution decumulation products. The role of the asset management industry is no less important, although it is worth noting that both foreign-owned investment houses and insurance companies' own investment wings have become important in this regard.[1]

In general, it is difficult not to see the role and influence of the finance sector as instrumental in establishing the material and ideational context in which decisions about the nature of auto-enrolment were made, especially where the Labour government ignored or diluted the Pensions Commission's proposals. The finance sector has grown significantly in recent decades, in terms of size, proportion of UK GDP, and political influence (Hopkin and Alexander Shaw, 2016; Rhodes, 2019). However, it is too simplistic to suggest that UK pensions policy is driven by the interests of financial services providers. Different types of firms have different interests—and even within industries that have generally benefited from auto-enrolment, such as insurance, the range of business models means that some firms have prospered more than others. Many of those most important to the delivery of auto-enrolment are relatively new players rather than established interests—they are reacting to opportunities created by public policy rather than shaping it. Crucially, while some investment managers immediately recognized the opportunity for new products, most of the insurance industry expressed dismay about the 2014 pension freedoms, insofar as they disrupted their annuities business (KPMG, 2016). In turn, some of those that have benefited from pension freedoms have expressed dismay about the proposed tightening of tax rules on some affected saving pots (Fordham, 2016). There is no doubt that the finance sector's construction of accessible defined contribution products—and its thirst for new markets to sell them into—was a key part of the auto-enrolment story, just as the development of the asset management industry enabled the establishment of defined benefit pensions. But the ideological commitments of political actors, often acting in the perceived interests of the finance sector but *without* the direct support of the finance sector, has also been decisive in determining the shape of private pensions provision in the UK, and indeed finance industry liberalization more generally (Macnicol, 2015: 54; Hopkin and Alexander Shaw, 2016). Interestingly, in exploring the role of the finance industry in promoting defined contribution pensions in the 1980s, Stephen Nesbitt (1995) shows that, while direct and indirect lobbying by new providers was an important influence on policy, these actors were very much speaking a language the government wanted to hear.

---

[1] Data on post-war trends in GDP and GDP per capita growth among developed countries is available at https://stats.oecd.org/Index.aspx?DatasetCode=SNA_TABLE1.

Historically, UK pensions provision has also relied upon large employers' willingness to back the promises associated with defined benefit pensions—what is termed in this book the temporal anchor role. Employers' approach obviously cannot be divorced from their wider growth expectations, as provision will depend upon employers' faith in their own profitability and stability. The growth of defined benefit provision was paradoxically a product of deindustrialization, as manufacturing companies continued to expand their output on the basis of employing more skilled workers (living longer lives). As such, well-organized trade unions were able to demand high-quality pensions provision, although we should not understate employers' own willingness to provide pensions on a voluntaristic basis (Pendleton and Gospel, 2017). As indicated above, the growing number of people employed in retail, as disposable incomes rose in the post-war period, was a trend also associated with growing defined benefit membership (as was growing employment in the banking sector) (PLSA, 2017). The nationalization of the energy and infrastructure industries also boosted defined benefit provision—a trend sustained by the terms of later privatization, although transitional protections have been steadily eroded.

Many of these industries are no longer able to rely upon steady expansion—and those that have expanded have done so via (overseas) merger and acquisition activity, which has undermined firms' commitment to defined benefit (such as banking) or through the development of a radically different employment model (such as retail). In general, lower-value services employment (where workers are more interchangeable) now make up a much larger share of the UK economy—with even manufacturing industries coming to ape this employment as higher-value processes are offshored (Berry, 2016e). As argued above, the introduction of SERPS in the 1970s was in many ways driven by this unravelling; an attempt to nationalize a collectivist approach to private provision which, in the context of a liberal market economy, was already reaching its zenith. In general, while the UK growth rate (in terms of GDP, and GDP per capita) has not slowed down in the post-war period in any significant sense, it has failed to keep pace with many similar economies in Europe, North America, and East Asia, and has become significantly more volatile since the 1970s (arguably increasing the frequency and intensity of future forecast failures).[2] Pensions provision is obviously not to blame for this apparent endangerment of UK prosperity, but there is no doubt that

---

[2] Data on the historical performance of UK asset classes in Barclays' Equity Gilt Study series. See for example http://lwmconsultants.com/wp-content/uploads/2016/04/Barclays-Gilt-Study-2015.pdf.

right-wing political forces have succeeded in associating a liberation from pension-related obligations with economic renewal.

Issues around pension fund investment will be discussed in Chapter 7 (and, to a lesser extent, Chapter 4). However, it is worth noting here that investment performance has *not* been a fundamental factor in the story of collectivism's demise. From a long-term perspective, both UK equities (where defined benefit fund allocations have traditionally been allocated) *and* gilts have delivered stable returns in line with expectations for more than a century (gilts match inflation, and equities offer higher returns with greater volatility).[3] Capital markets are however part of the context in three main ways. Firstly, very poor equity performance in the early 1970s will have weakened pension funds just as membership was approaching its peak in the private sector. Secondly, however, following this trough, UK equities began to significantly overperform in the 1980s (as well as exhibiting slightly more price volatility)—yet the 'contribution holidays' offered by the Thatcher government to employers meant that many pension funds did not benefit in this regard, just as their cash payments to retired members began to increase sharply. Thirdly, and related to this, even though returns were fairly reliable, the ageing of scheme memberships (due to both increasing life expectancy and the inaccessibility of traditional funds to younger workers) meant funds came to demand ever higher returns on investment—to no avail.

2.5. Conclusion: End of the Experiment?

This chapter has sought to provide an overview of the historical development of UK pensions provision, focusing on the main philosophical or ideological foundations of different elements of provision, and the major policy initiatives that have shaped the evolution of pensions statecraft. Its development continues, but it is possible to conclude that the UK's 'experiment' with collectivism is effectively over (crucially, however, this does *not* mean that state intervention is going to disappear). 1979 heralded a decisive political shift away from collectivist principles, although it was only in the mid-2000s that support for defined contribution private pension schemes, and the notion of the state pension as a savings platform rather than a social insurance-based system (with a means-tested safety net) became firmly established in UK public policy. Collectivist forms of provision of course persist (albeit diluted

---

[3] The best source of information on the evolution of the UK (and global) asset management industry is *Investment and Pensions Europe*'s 'Top 400' series. See https://www.ipe.com/reports/special-reports/top-400-asset-managers.

in some ways) given that pensions promises are so difficult to unravel. As younger cohorts of savers will discover, it is far easier to simply not make the promise in the first place.

It is important to be clear that there was genuinely a collectivist moment in UK pensions provision—a historical reality easily overlooked by any characterization of UK welfare provision more generally as archetypally liberal (as discussed further in Chapter 3). However, it is equally clear that the UK's embrace of collectivism was held in check by an abiding liberal orientation in economic statecraft, favouring free markets and individual choice (Pemberton, 2018). This is one of the reasons that the UK pensions systems was, in general, only selectively collectivist. The state pension has traditionally been strongly tied to participation in the labour market, and has rarely been seen by policy-makers as alone providing a sufficient retirement income. Collectivist private pensions were generally only provided by large, stable employers, and therefore traditionally did not cover a majority of employees (although more than 50 per cent of employees were in defined benefit schemes for a brief period in the early 1980s (Maer and Thurley, 2009)). Walker and Foster (2006: 430) refer to 'two parallel systems of pensioning', as the worst off were covered by the state's means-tested benefit system, and a relatively small group of affluent employees (but occupying an exaggerated position in the historical imaginary), predominantly male, benefited from occupational provision. UK pensions provision looks quite different now, but arguably the two-nations dynamic is being recreated by other means. Many more people have access to a workplace pension, to top up outcomes from a state pension system which has returned to its origins in poverty relief, but relatively few will be able to save enough to provide an adequate retirement income.

In the twentieth century, as the workforce aged and expanded, and the economy deindustrialized (and parts of it were nationalized), occupational pensions in the UK became somewhat less exclusive. At the same time, however, the liberal collectivist compromise—especially its voluntaristic basis—was jeopardized. Paradoxically, the UK pensions system came to be seen in the late twentieth century as both insufficient to prevent impoverishment among older people, and so generous that it represented too great a burden on private enterprise. The evolution of liberal economic statecraft into neoliberal economic statecraft offered a solution to both sides of this dilemma. Since the 1980s, policy-makers and political elites have generally accepted a stronger emphasis on personal responsibility for long-term financial well-being, with a subsistence-level safety net for those unable to meet this expectation. This consensus manifests as a move towards defined contribution pensions saving—removing employer responsibility—and a larger role for means-tested benefits in the pensions system. Interestingly, Michael A. McCarthy (2014) characterizes the rise of workplace defined contribution pensions provision in the US as 'neoliberalism without neoliberals', since it constituted a response by employers to new defined benefit regulation that policy elites had not anticipated. This is not the case in the UK: policy-makers from the 1980s onwards pushed the replacement of (public and private) defined benefit provision with (mostly private) defined contribution schemes as a deliberate aspect of (neoliberal) pensions statecraft (Walker and Foster, 2006; Morris and Palmer, 2011; Pemberton, 2017).

Arguably, this orientation has evolved since the mid-2000s into something slightly more palatable for critics of neoliberalization, as the state pension is transformed into a benefit which generally offers a flat-rate cash amount (at or above the poverty level), and defined contribution saving is boosted by minimum employer contributions and the quality benchmarking role of NEST. Indeed, the Pensions Commission arguably sought to imbibe the next phase of development for the UK pensions system with a pseudo-collectivist sentiment, even as it further neglected to resist the drift away from collectivism in practice, by sketching a national mission to address undersaving. The state was tasked in this regard with ensuring that defined contribution provision worked efficiently, and that individuals were properly incentivized to save. While the state generally retains this orientation in a technocratic sense, it is fair to conclude that the intellectual legitimacy for an 'enabling' role for the state has failed to solidify, allowing some of the key elements of the Turner blueprint to unravel, first via key decisions on implementation, such as allowing schemes managed directly by insurance companies rather than trusts to be used for automatic enrolment, and more recently, via the abolition of compulsory annuitization. And as Chapter 5 explores in more depth, individualism has been retained as the (implicit) foundational principle of the post-Turner consensus, betraying its origins in the neoliberal revolution it ostensibly seeks to dislodge.

It is necessary to reiterate here the distinction between 'collective' and 'collectivism'. Pensions are collective by necessity. But where pensions provision is collective in practice, yet without being organized around collectivist principles, there are bigger opportunities for inter-generational exploitation, inadvertent or otherwise; as explored in Chapter 1, this is the pensions reality overlooked by the generational warriors that have (unwittingly, it seems) lent their radicalism to the opponents of collectivist state and occupational pensions provision. Pensions provision is increasingly becoming a sphere not of collectivism existing (partially) beyond the capitalist marketplace, but rather a sphere of individual disciplining and value extraction by powerful private enterprises. In combination UK pensions provision risks becoming rather exploitative. However, just as the Turner consensus has been fatally undermined by its roots in the neoliberal revolution, seemingly progressive responses have also absorbed elements of a neoliberal critique of collectivism in order to challenge financialized and individualized pensions provision, in the process undermining the rationale for pensions provision *sui generis*.

Yet as long as we recognize the essentially collective and generational nature of pensions provision, there are opportunities for rewiring collectivist principles and inter-generational co-operation via public policy. Pensions are not the victim of our failure to forecast to the future; they are part of how we manage this failure. Of course, we must be aware that naivety is often found on the flipside of hope. Even this chapter's cursory look at the over- view of UK pensions provision demonstrates its intertwine of the UK's wider capitalist growth model. The prospect of the UK political economy affording scope for a collectivist rebirth in the foreseeable future appears negligible. But this future is not nearly as certain as it seems. Moreover, this intertwine- ment means pensions provision—more so than any other form of welfare provision—is well placed to *shape* capitalist development in the uncertain years ahead. Most of this book is focused on exploring the *what* and *why* of how UK pensions policy has developed in more depth, before Chapter 8 sketches a potentially progressive future. Firstly, however, we need to pin down a more thorough understanding of how pensions provision functions (and how this is supported by pensions policy). Chapter 3 situates this dis- cussion in a comparative context, briefly discussing pensions provision across the developed world, and the ways in which it is (mis)understood.

3

The Pensions Multiverse: Capitalist Diversity and Pensions Transformation

That most ('advanced') human societies encompass pensions provision reflects the universal, ineradicable fact of biological ageing. Yet the form that pensions provision takes is far from uniform, even among the most affluent capitalist economies. This chapter surveys this diversity, but also the (flawed) ways in which pensions variation is usually understood or categorized. The intention, however, is not to replace one typology with another. While some of the most important differences across countries in terms of pensions provision are actually *understated*, there is also a tendency to *overstate* systemic differences based on a highly parsimonious account of varieties within (welfare) capitalism—with capitalist dynamics themselves left underinvestigated. There are of course common characteristics within pensions provision across countries, some of which are more prevalent in some countries rather than others. The overall aim here is to arrive at, or at least sketch, an understanding of the world—or 'multiverse'—of pensions in totality. And this means understanding how pensions provision connects to everything else. Cross-national typologies tend to partially bracket off the rest of social, political, and economic life when explaining what makes particular systems distinctive—yet this wider context is precisely *why* pensions provision varies.

Part of the problem with the urge to categorize pension systems is that provision, in every country, is constantly developing. As the social, political, and economic context in which pensions provision is determined is never completely fixed, the nature of provision is never completely fixed. More specifically, there is rarely a time when pensions provision, in all countries, is not in the midst of some reform programme. The costs of provision, and the number of people and organizations it affects at accumulation and decumulation stages, means that demands for change are constant, and constantly evolving. There are of course typologies for pensions reform agendas, as well as for the provision being reformed, but for the sake of parsimony these tend to depict the rationale for reform in singular and uncritical terms—most often as a response to population ageing.

Pensions Imperilled: The Political Economy of Private Pensions Provision in the UK. Craig Berry, Oxford University Press (2021).
© Craig Berry. DOI: 10.1093/oso/9780198782834.003.0003

As discussed further below, while typologies of pensions systems are often based implicitly or explicitly on a lifecourse understanding of pensions— that is, how different forms of accumulation result in different forms of decumulation—few capture the inter-generational co-operation that makes pensions provision possible. As discussed in Chapter 1, one of the definitional paradoxes of pensions provision is that it requires stability in inter-generational relations in order to function, yet this stability is unattainable. With the partial exception of categorizing recent changes in retirement (or entitlement) ages, pensions system typologies generally assume stability in inter-generational relations. Decumulation processes, for instance, are described with little reference to the messy circumstances which enable pension payments to be made—circumstances which might be quite different from those envisaged when today's pensioners were yesterday's savers. If we want to understand pensions not as ideal-types, but rather in the real world, we need to ensure their peculiar temporality is central to analysis. Pensions provision does not simply operate across a very long-term timescale; it also requires a vision of how this timeframe will be experienced, so that decumulation expectations are able to structure accumulation behaviour. Pensions policy seeks to institutionalize (and reinstitutionalize) these projected pensions futures, albeit based on the clear understanding that the real future cannot possibly imitate that which is (was) projected—pensions provision has as much to do with managing the failure of our forecasts as it does with producing the forecasts (or at least it *should*). Inter-generational relations cannot be stable, because each generation is, by definition, different from all others. Pensions provision therefore exists in a temporality which is at the same time acutely restrictive, and always imaginary. The moment we typologize, we risk taking pensions out of this temporal context, both real and imagined.

While focusing on pensions provision in countries other than the UK, one of this chapter's main aims is to further illuminate the nature and development of UK pensions provision, with reference to this comparative context. The chapter's core argument is that pensions provision cannot be divorced from wider capitalist organization—thereby supporting one of the book's core arguments, that is, that the imperilment of UK pensions provision is very much a story about British capitalism in general. When seen in the light of pensions provision elsewhere, the key plotlines in this British story start to become clearer. British capitalism is not amenable to the long-term timescale with which collectivist pensions provision must, as far as possible, be aligned. Yet this stems paradoxically from the UK's mastery of the other temporal dimension of pensions provision: the manipulation of projected futures. The imperilment of UK pensions is indelibly associated with its history as a pioneer of financialized pensions.

3.1. Categorizing Pension Systems

3.1.1   Pillar Talk: A Tautological Typology

Just as all human beings are mammals, all pension systems are 'multi-pillar'. So what? That all humans are mammals is not a question of observation, but rather definition, so the statement is tautological, and therefore logically redundant. Can we say the same about the statement that all pension systems are multi-pillar? Virtually every country has multiple forms of provision for older people no longer able (or obliged) to work, whether conventionally understood as pensions provision or not. This provision may be funded by taxation, private savings (in pension schemes or otherwise), or informally within familial groups. In practice, virtually every country now has a mix of conventional state and private pensions provision. Clearly, this statement encompasses a great deal more complexities than the human/mammals statement—containing observational as well as definitional elements—but nevertheless we can question its value as an aid to understanding pensions in the real world. More importantly, if its value is in doubt, it leads to a critical, supplementary question: why then is the 'pillar' framing used so extensively in typologies of pensions provision?

The notion that systems of pensions provision can be categorized into pillars came to prominence after the publication of the World Bank's *Averting the Old Age Crisis* report in 1994. The first pillar consists of near universal, unfunded defined benefit provision. Pension outcomes are linked to earnings from employment but, being supported by the state, generally also include a redistributive element, even if only implicitly. Contributions are mandatory for those in work, and there may be scope to credit nominal contributions for those unable to work. The second pillar consists of funded provision which is also mandatory, but generally provided by the private rather than public sector. In most systems this pillar would be formed of defined contribution provision. A third pillar resembles the design of the second, but participation is voluntary (and provision is less likely to be organized via the workplace). While ostensibly this three-pillar framework is designed to capture the varied forms pensions provision can take, perhaps its most important aspect is the conceptualization of pensions saving which is both *compulsory* and *privately organized*. This apparent contradiction is at the heart of contemporary pensions provision—almost everywhere—in terms of provision that exists now, but also, more importantly, in terms of the future agendas of pensions policy-makers.

In 2005, the World Bank, in an influential report authored by Robert Holzmann and Richard Hintz (2005), *Old-Age Income Support in the Twenty-First Century*, updated its framework to include an additional two pillars. Firstly, a non-contributory 'zero' pillar of benefits designed to alleviate poverty (this is obviously still dependent upon contributions, essentially in the form of taxation—although such contributions do not determine eligibility for a zero-pillar pension). The addition of this pillar owed much to criticism of the World Bank's initial omission of poverty-alleviation mechanisms from its pensions schema, not least by other international bodies such as the International Labour Organization (ILO) (see Gillion et al., 2000). Secondly, a miscellaneous fourth pillar of informal, non-financial old age support, or access to services such as health and housing which are formally outside the realm of pensions provision. The five-pillar framework is obviously more inclusive, although at the expense of analytical purchase. Clearly, treating myriad fourth-pillar arrangements as a form of pensions provision is an oversimplification. Moreover, while the zero pillar clearly captures forms of state pension provision excluded from the first pillar, it is no exaggeration to say that the vast majority of countries maintain a state pension system which lies somewhere between the zero- and first-pillar ideal-types.

The UK experience would have to be considered particularly anomalous within this framework, since it encompasses a social insurance-style state pension unlike either the zero or first pillar, and a large dependence on voluntary private provision which most resembles the third pillar of ostensibly supplementary provision. However, the most curious thing about this framework is that it does not really capture well the experience of *any* particular country. At best, we can speak of countries such as France having systems based on a first pillar of mandatory, defined benefit provision, countries such as the Netherlands having a larger second pillar of near mandatory occupational pensions (on top of quite generous zero pillar provision), and pensions provision in countries such as the US resembling, for most workers, the third pillar. In general, however, most countries encompass all five pillars, and differences amount to slight variations in how important each pillar is in the composition of retirement income.

In practice, most of the things we really need to know to appreciate the scope of pensions variation are encased *within* the second pillar and, to some extent, in *the relationship between* the first and second pillars. The form taken by private provision—especially in terms of how risks are borne—is usually the defining characteristic of any single approach to or tradition of pensions provision. Even if the multi-pillar framework is a useful way of describing the relative weight of zero- or first-pillar public provision in relation to second- or third-pillar private provision, it does not tell us about how public and private provision interact. And even judged on its own terms, the multi-pillar framework is not a useful guide to the *overall* level of resources available for pensions provision—since different systems with a similar distribution of pillars may commit different amounts to each pillar—and therefore the replacement rates achieved by pensioners (which is of course the outcome that really matters to those in retirement). Furthermore, the structure and operation of the financial markets in which accumulated savings are rematerialized within private provision is largely bracketed off by this framework; the pillar-based typology puts the focus on scheme and benefit design, rather than what happens to the product of saving once it enters the pensions arena.

Nicholas Barr and Peter Diamond (2009: 13–17; see also 2008) have criticized pillar-based typologies, particularly that upheld by the World Bank. While generally accepting the empirical accuracy of the depiction of multi-pillar pensions provision, Barr and Diamond argue, for several reasons, that the approach is analytically inadequate. They argue that the framework suffers from 'tunnel vision' in the sense that only one design objective is recognized—usually consumption smoothing—whereas in practice choices may be based on multiple policy objectives. There is 'an improper use of first-best analysis': pensions provision is not designed in optimal circumstances, and there are invariably trade-offs in design choices which mean 'distortions' are unavoidable, including, where necessary, a distortion of competition between providers within private provision. Barr and Diamond are also critical of an apparent, implicit bias towards funded pensions (ahead of state-provided, unfunded pensions) in the World Bank account. Even if a funded model were superior, there is a need to consider how the move from unfunded to funded provision is to be financed, and what the distributional consequences will be in terms of different cohorts of savers and retirees. They argue that the comparison of pensions debt across funded and unfunded provision is 'incomplete', not least because the government's ability to levy taxes and alter the real value of debt is a fundamental characteristic of the latter. Barr and Diamond agree with the point above that the scope of variation *within* private provision—involving choices around saving rates, compulsion, adjustment mechanisms, investment strategies, etc.—are as intrinsically significant

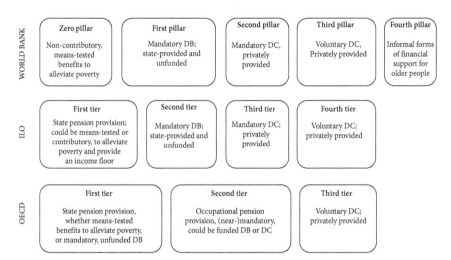

Figure 3.1 Comparison of World Bank, ILO, and OECD pension system typologies

as the distinction between private (funded) and public (unfunded) provision.

The OECD has refashioned the pillar-based typology of the World Bank, generally adopting an account of different 'tiers' of pensions provision (see Figure 3.1) (OECD, 2017, 2018). A first tier constitutes the most important poverty-alleviation mechanism, and may be state pension provision or publicly organized defined benefit provision (approximating, that is, the World Bank's zero and first pillars). A second tier constitutes mandatory (or only *quasi*-mandatory), occupational private pensions provision (which may be defined benefit or defined contribution). The third tier refers to provision organized by individuals, as in the World Bank's third pillar, albeit with a clearer distinction drawn between provision organized via the workplace and that which employers have no substantive role in. This framework has also been adopted by the European Commission (EU Directorate-General for Internal Policies, 2014). It is immediately obvious that the UK again does not quite fit in. Yet, as we will discuss below, the implicit depiction of the UK as a pensions pariah is somewhat misleading.

In fairness to the OECD, its pension system typology is, in contrast to how the World Bank framework is often employed, used as the *first* step in analysing pensions variation, rather than the *last*. The OECD's vast library of information on pensions provision among its member countries—published in its regular *Pensions Outlook* and *Pensions at a Glance* series—concentrates above all on detailing the myriad forms that provision may take across the three tiers. First-tier provision might range from non-contributory minimal benefits to social insurance-style provision, and even the regulation of guaranteed minimums within private provision. The defined contribution and defined benefit ideal-types are major fault lines within the second tier (and the OECD documents all the different forms of guarantees and risk sharing in-between the two ideal-types). It is recognized also that second-tier provision may be provided by the public sector (just as elements of first-tier provision may be privately organized). The OECD recognizes that different forms of provision have different foundational objectives (adequacy, redistribution, consumption-smoothing, financial security, etc.) which do not always map straightforwardly onto the different tiers, and that similar forms of provision may produce different outcomes in different countries, depending on coverage and contribution rates. It recognizes that changes in pensions provision produce behavioural change, and that some reforms are designed primarily for this purpose. It frequently details the variable impact of different forms of provision on different groups (low earners, women, the 'oldest old', etc.). And, crucially, the OECD recognizes that tiers interact: for instance, regulation for (and funding of) guaranteed pensions, or the provision of means-tested benefits to alleviate poverty, is first-tier provision which responds directly to outcomes in the second tier.

What should be noted, however, is that the OECD's framework is intended, above all, as a 'how-to guide' for pensions reform. The specific characteristics of pension provision among its members are described by way of demonstrating the array of options available to countries as they adapt their pensions systems. Means-tested benefits will ensure adequacy, at a cost; defined contribution pensions are sustainable, but with risks transferred to individuals; voluntaristic provision, of any type, might require a high degree of financial literacy; higher entitlement ages reduce costs, but with distributional consequences; and so on. As such, there is an other-worldly quality to the OECD's sometimes excruciatingly detailed analysis: pensions provision, and its multiple tiers, is described with almost no reference to the political (and ideological) or economic context in which it is situated. Pension system design is, in effect, a largely technocratic manner—with limited constraints on the model which technocrats may ultimately choose. The underpinning assumption is that policy-makers are currently *failing* to make the correct policy choices. But that policy-makers often 'fail' should not lead us analytically to a generalized account of 'policy failure'. It is more important to understand why certain policies are chosen over others: what looks like failure, from one perspective, might in fact be exactly what was intended, from another.

Obviously, typologies such as that advanced by the World Bank are not purely descriptive devices. The World Bank, with a specific remit to support economic development and poverty alleviation among low-income countries, was confronting an apparent trend of rapid population ageing in developing countries, before the private sector—and particularly financial markets—had developed sufficiently to enable private saving to alleviate the burden on the state. Pensions provision is a hallmark of economic development, but the World Bank considered the fiscal risks involved in pensions provided predominantly by the state could have impeded further development. This rather contestable judgement lies behind its identification of a realm of mandatory private saving, usually in defined contribution schemes—even though, as the OECD's work would attest, such provision still remains relatively rare, even among developed countries. This is prescription masquerading as description—or, at best, prescription entangled with description. Peijie Wang et al. argue perceptively that the three-pillar framework is based on the imaginary of modern portfolio theory, which advocates risk management via diversification (2014: 12–13). Three pillars are safer than one (and, of course, faith in modern portfolio theory underpins, to some extent, policy elites' faith in private pensions provision as a route to secure retirement incomes). Alas, it should not surprise us that such typologies serve an ideological as well as analytical purpose, or that the World Bank's framework has been adopted—and adapted—by those more focused on highly developed countries as a similar account of population ageing has taken root in elite thinking throughout the world. The ILO's alternative is equally guilty: it identifies a larger role for state pensions at least in part because its agenda is to protect workers against risks such as unemployment.

Similarly, the editorials prefacing the OECD's *Outlook* publications are highly prescriptive. In 2012, the OECD's Director for Financial and Enterprise Affairs, Carolyn Ervin, and Director for Employment, Labour, and Social Affairs, John Martin, wrote:

'Which country has the best pension system?' is a question the OECD is often asked. But it is one that is very difficult to answer despite the widespread appetite for rankings and league tables. The true response is that there is room for improvement in all countries' retirement-income provision. They all face at least some challenges: coverage of the pension system, adequacy of benefits, financial sustainability or the risks and uncertainties borne by individuals. The outlook for pensions in OECD countries is therefore one of continued—and necessary—change.

This passage does not stipulate a particular prescription, but nonetheless demonstrates the OECD's rather technocratic, problem-solving approach to pensions reform. Invariably, such an orientation overlaps with support for funded, individualized pensions, and accordingly the OECD's specific policy agenda has become clearer in recent years. In the 2016 version of the report, the editorial offered incredibly detailed advice to policy-makers on defined contribution decumulation strategies (see OECD, 2016a)—advocating an approach based on deferred life annuities in combination with flexible draw-down products—and was accompanied by a 'roadmap' briefing on 'the good design of defined contribution pension plans' (OECD, 2016b). In terms of mass provision, such advice is only relevant to a small proportion of the OECD's membership, or a small proportion of pensions savers in most OECD countries. Again, while the OECD recognizes that some finance sectors are more mature than others, the structure and operation of the financial markets that accumulated savings end up in is, at most, a marginal issue within the three-tier typology, which, like the World Bank's approach, focuses on how schemes are designed rather than how associated investments are governed.

3.1.2 Beveridge, Bismarck, and Beyond

Analytically, the 'worlds of welfare' approach to categorizing pensions provision across different countries is significantly more satisfying than the typologies discussed above. It has far greater purchase among most social science disciplines, including sociologists, political scientists, political economists, and institutionalist economists focused on how the endurance of certain policies and practices provides for diversity in capitalist organization. Nevertheless, for our purposes, it leaves a great deal to be desired. One of the earliest exponents of this approach—although it can perhaps be thought of as an epistemology which has long underpinned comparative analysis—was Gøsta Esping-Andersen (1990). Esping-Andersen posited three clusters of welfare state regimes: conservative-corporatist, liberal, and socialist or social democratic. It is worth stating initially that this approach is applicable primarily to Western and Central Europe—and attempts to broaden the empirical scope by subsequent scholarship have been constrained by this legacy.

The conservative-corporatist regime sees a significant role for the state in welfare provision. Yet it is not necessarily a *redistributive* state based on universal entitlements; welfare provision, including pensions provision, is instead strongly connected to individuals' industry and occupation, and often provided directly by employer-led groups even if mandated by the state. Many countries in this cluster traditionally, and perhaps paradoxically, maintain important roles for the family and church-based welfare support, to minimize demands from the poorest communities for public services. Esping-Andersen places a large number of European countries in this category, including Germany and Austria (which best embody the corporatist element), and Italy and Spain (which have a larger role for informal support for older people). The social democratic regime has a similarly significant role for the state, but with redistributive mechanisms grounded in a social insurance-based welfare state. Typically, Scandinavian countries such as Norway and Sweden offer generous state pension provision. In practice, the liberal regime, principally exemplified by the UK and Ireland, has elements of both the conservative-corporatist and social democratic regime, especially in pensions provision (regulated private pensions, basic state pensions, etc.) but generally focuses on providing a publicly funded safety net of means-tested assistance rather than seeking to transform market-based outcomes. Interestingly, many subsequent scholars were least convinced of the liberal regime category than any other (see Ragin, 1994; Shalev, 1996). Arguably, however, in pensions provision, the liberal cluster of countries, particularly the UK, has come to resemble Esping-Andersen's ideal-type far more *since* he published his major work than it did at the time, due to related trends of welfare retrenchment and financialization (although countries associated with other regimes have been 'liberalising' too!).

Esping-Andersen uses the concept of decommodification to distinguish regimes (that is, the extent to which different welfare regimes seek to replace, or simply mitigate, market-based distribution). Paul Pierson's (1994) seminal work on welfare *reform* employed the notion of *re*commodification to explain welfare retrenchment across all regimes and, as noted below, Mehmet Aysan and Roderic Beaujot demonstrate the value of this concept for understanding pensions reform in particular, as they demonstrate that pensions provision has undergone this process, especially in the liberal cluster. It is worth recalling, however, that Esping-Andersen had actually sought to quantify and 'score' the extent of decommodification across countries, as a key metric of the cluster to which they belonged. This has been unpicked by subsequent scholars, not least because of the limitations of some of Esping-Andersen's data sources (see for example Scruggs and Allan, 2006, 2008; Hay and Wincott, 2012; van der Veen and van der Brug, 2012). Colin Hay and Daniel Wincott (2012) generally update Esping-Andersen's typology, albeit arguing that welfare regimes cannot be classed in terms of models or 'types', by placing different countries on two axes: from liberal to conservative, and the extent of egalitarianism. Their typology depicts 'bundles of characteristics rather than ontological categories' (2012: 60). This provides for a relatively stable (but not unchanging) clustering of dominant forms of welfare provision across highly developed countries, with pensions provision in Italy, for instance, being classed as both conservative and inegalitarian (most countries in this cluster are shown to have become more liberal over time). In contrast: Sweden, for example, is egalitarian but relatively conservative; Denmark, for example, is both strongly egalitarian and relatively liberal; and the US, for example, is both liberal and inegalitarian.

Clearly, the larger the number of regimes that are identified, the more straightforward it is for any particular country to be classified. In terms of welfare provision in general, the UK fits into Hay and Wincott's typology less problematically than Esping-Andersen's, since it can be depicted as hovering close to the middle of both axes, but firmly within a cluster of liberal and moderately egalitarian countries. However, Hay and Wincott's framework arguably takes us slightly further away than being able to account specifically for pensions provision. The more specific the regimes, the less likely it is that the very messy world of pensions provision—which developed in many contexts quite separately from welfare provision more generally—will be aligned to the typology. It is perhaps for this reason that pensions regimes are often classified in terms of their relationship with a 'Bismarckian' or 'Beveridgean' ideal-type; again, however, this approach is overwhelmingly focused on Western and Central Europe. Confusingly, these ideal-types are relevant to welfare provision in general, not simply pensions provision, but whereas this typology has been supplanted in most parts of welfare provision, it retains some pertinence in relation to pensions.

The Bismarckian system (associated with Otto von Bismarck, the first Chancellor of the German Empire in the late nineteenth century) is based overwhelmingly on social insurance, essentially provided by the state. Bismarckian systems are associated with Esping-Andersen's conservative-corporatist regime since, although the earliest forms of welfare provision were designed to secure working-class support, outcomes are very much dependent on earnings from employment (and generally Bismarckian systems have limited provision for those unable to work). In terms of pensions, Beveridgean systems (associated with British academic and Liberal Party politician, William Beveridge, who led a landmark inquiry into the future of the welfare state in the UK in 1942) are based on basic state provision, which resembles social insurance but tends to offer flat-rate pension incomes, provided universally. Beveridgean systems may encompass both Esping-Andersen's liberal and social democratic regimes, with the former involving a larger role of occupational pensions provision (which would pre-date the state pension) and the latter offering more generous social insurance-style benefits. Both types of Beveridgean systems would be multi-pillar in practice.

This typology emphasizes the historical origins of pensions provision—its politico-institutional roots—at the expense of specific functions. It is obvious that pensions provision will have developed beyond its original blueprint, even in the countries of origin. The vast majority of pensions systems are influenced by both approaches; pensions provision in France, for instance, most closely resembles a Bismarckian system, but also traditionally includes an important role for a flat-rate state pension *and* private, occupational pensions provision. Indeed, the UK is often seen as an outlier of the Beveridgean approach, given that only the Nordic countries implemented the universal benefits in the manner envisaged by Beveridge (and with private pensions generally provided on an unfunded basis). The Netherlands sits somewhat awkwardly between the two systems, insofar as the main elements of pensions provision resemble that of the UK, but arise from corporatist or co-ordinated arrangements more typical of the 'pure' Bismarckian systems in Germany and Austria (see Figure 3.2 for a summary).

Clearly, the Bismarck versus Beveridge approach is not flawless, and risks distorting our understanding of what pensions provision actually looks like in practice. However, by emphasizing the historical roots of provision over the ideological connotations, it allows us to identify a truth which is often only implicit in comparative scholarship, that is, that *all* pensions provision is essentially socialistic. Although the state's role differs across regimes,

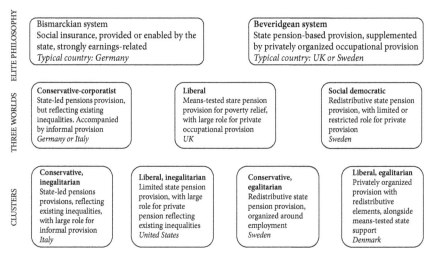

Figure 3.2 Comparison of elite philosophy, worlds of welfare, and cluster-based pension system typologies

pensions provision is very rarely something that happens without the substantive involvement of the state, either as provider or regulator, or both. And the long-term and cross-generational nature of provision means the principle of collectivism is almost always embedded in provision to some extent. That policy elites often introduced collectivist forms of provision as a way of defending social order against the rise of revolutionary socialist ideas perhaps only serves to underline the influence of socialism on the origin of pensions provision. The countries where socialism has traditionally had least influence do not simply have quite *different* forms of pensions provision from those that are evident in Europe—they also traditionally have *less substantive* provision overall.

Table 3.1 offers a more quantitative comparison of pensions provision among OECD countries, by detailing projected replacement rates arising from different forms of provision, and the expenditure committed to pension payments by the public and private sectors. It would be wrong to conclude that this information contradicts any of the typologies in this section—since there are cluster-like patterns—but there are some noteworthy cases. The inclusion of East Asian countries in the OECD data is useful, given that most typologies used in social science research are largely concerned with pensions provision in Europe. Korea's state pension system was introduced relatively recently, which explains the low levels of public expenditure. The replacement rates arising from this system will surpass those in Japan, but the development of voluntary, private provision in Japan means replacement rates are higher overall than in Korea. Based on these measures, Japan's system most closely resembles Germany's, in terms of the balance between mandatory, public schemes and voluntary, private schemes—this is not surprising given the corporatist traditions evident in both countries' overall development model. That said, Germany's system cannot (or can no longer) be seen as emblematic of a Bismarckian approach. The role of mandatory, public provision (and overall public spending) is far more significant in France and Austria, and formal provision in the countries of Southern Europe now enables much higher replacement rates (despite their greater reliance traditionally on informal support for older people).

It is not the case that the Scandinavian countries, steeped in the social democratic tradition, enable the highest replacement rates via public provision. Similarly, overall levels of spending are unremarkable. The US, arguably the archetypal liberal regime, has replacement rates and overall spending levels which are comparable to most European countries—indeed surpassing many, due to a combination of public provision providing an income floor, and very high levels of voluntary, private provision. (Of course, this

Table 3.1 Replacement rates and pensions expenditure by type of provision (selected OECD countries)

	Replacement rates (% average earner)				Expenditure on pension payments and related benefits (% GDP)		
	Mandatory public	Mandatory private	Voluntary	Total	Public	Private	Total
Austria	78.4	–	–	78.4	13.4	0.7	14.0
Belgium	46.7	–	14.2	60.8	10.2	1.1	11.3
Czech R	45.8	–	–	45.8	8.7	0.4	9.0
Denmark	14.8	71.6	–	86.4	8.0	1.0	8.9
Finland	56.6	–	–	56.6	11.1	0.2	11.3
France	60.5	–	–	60.5	13.8	0.2	14.1
Germany	38.2	–	12.7	50.9	10.1	0.8	10.9
Greece	53.7	–	–	53.7	17.4	0.4	17.8
Iceland	3.2	65.8	–	69.0	2.0	3.8	5.9
Ireland	34.1	–	38.0	72.1	4.9	0.8	5.7
Italy	83.1	–	–	83.1	16.3	0.8	16.7

Neth.	28.7	68.2	–	96.9	5.4	6.0	11.5
Norway	39.2	5.9	–	45.1	5.8	0.8	6.6
Poland	31.6	–	–	31.6	10.3	–	10.3
Portugal	74.0	–	–	74.0	14.0	0.6	14.5
Slovak R	39.6	24.8	–	64.3	7.2	0.4	7.5
Spain	72.3	–	–	72.3	11.4	–	11.4
Sweden	36.6	19.2	–	55.8	7.7	2.9	10.6
Switz.	24.2	17.9	–	42.1	6.4	4.9	11.2
UK	22.1	–	30.0	52.3	6.1	4.4	10.5
Australia	0.1	32.1	–	32.2	4.3	1.7	6.0
Canada	41.0	–	34.2	75.2	4.6	3.2	7.8
New Z.	40	–	18.8	58.8	5.1	–	5.1
US	38.3	–	33.0	71.3	7.0	5.0	12.0
Japan	34.6	–	23.1	57.7	10.2	3.4	12.9
Korea	39.3	–	–	39.3	2.6	0.0	2.6

Note: Replacement rates = Projected percentage of average earnings received in pension payments by full-time workers with a complete labour market history, based on policies in force in 2016. Expenditure data is from 2013

Source: OECD (2017, 2018, including embedded databases)

information does not offer insight to inequality among older people within these countries—while many Americans have substantial private pension income, many have little or none). Whereas Esping-Andersen and subsequent scholars treat liberal and social democratic regimes as distinct, their mutual heritage in a Beveridgean, multi-pillar approach is evident. It is also worth noting that, perhaps in defence of conventional typologies, the classificatory boundary between public and private provision is not always as clear-cut as the OECD data might suggest. Denmark and the Netherlands, for instance, stand out in terms of the low replacement rates arising from public provision. Yet the extensive role of mandatory, private provision in both countries means that they both achieve overall replacement rates which surpass all other countries. We could attribute this to the (anticipated) success of private provision—or we could recognize the variety of ways in which policy-makers might seek to achieve pensions policy objectives, outside of what might be strictly defined as public provision. The UK's embrace of auto-enrolment within private provision indicates a similar journey is under way (although the near exclusive use of pure defined contribution schemes to deliver this policy will hold back replacement rates).

3.2. Towards a New Understanding of Pensions Variety

Categorizing pensions provision across different countries should not be seen as an end in itself. The point, surely, especially from a critical perspective, is to better understand provision, its implications, and how it develops. We would of course not expect the World Bank, OECD, or other 'official' sources of comparative knowledge of pensions provision to offer a critical account in this regard. In their analyses, pensions provision is a policy problem to be addressed, and ideally solved. Of course, different organizations will have (slightly) different accounts of what the key problems—or gaps in provision—are, but the general analytical orientation is a shared one. Academic scholarship in the social sciences obviously gets us closer to a critical understanding of real-world pensions provision across different countries but, as argued above, the typologies generally drawn upon by social scientists are derived from comparative analysis of *welfare* provision in general. This creates a number of barriers to understanding.

Firstly, and perhaps ironically, the role of the state in pensions provision is underestimated. Section 3.1 argued that pillar-based typologies of pensions provision are flawed insofar as they suggest that the development of pensions provision is a technocratic matter, and that policy-makers can simply choose to add or grow particular pillars of provision. The various 'worlds of welfare' typologies are guilty, to some extent, of the opposite mistake. These typologies are steeped in an overarching account of the role of the welfare state in relation to the private economy—whether or not Esping-Andersen's concept of decommodification is explicitly endorsed or repurposed. This helps explain the literature's emphasis on state pension provision, at the expense of a more sustained focus on the specific characteristics of private provision (including pension-related investment practice). But the state's role is obviously not confined to state pensions. In the pensions multiverse, more acutely than other forms of welfare, every element of provision is beholden to state action, or at least the state's permission. As discussed below, the complex temporality of provision means this is unavoidable. Pensions provision across different countries invariably bears the hallmark of different, nationally constituted traditions in terms of state formation, industrial relations, corporate governance, etc. However, policy-makers are actively involved in reproducing—and occasionally contesting—such traditions. This trait may also help to explain why this literature has been slow to assess, for instance, the Europeanization of pensions regulation within the European Union (EU). As discussed in Section 3.3, Europeanization has not led to the decommodification or recommodification of pension provision in any direct, systematic way—but is nevertheless important as an emerging transformation of the policy environment in which pensions policy is made in EU countries.

Secondly, the emphasis on whether pensions are publicly or privately provided, and whether saving is mandatory or voluntary, tends to understate the distinction between collectivist and individualized provision. There is a general assumption that pensions provision is largely collectivist, where risks are shared with other citizens, either within schemes or via the state, or with employers. While this may once have been the norm in European pensions provision, it is increasingly less so. The difference between defined benefit and defined contribution saving is rather profound, and while it is traditionally most relevant to liberal regimes, it warrants greater attention in any comparative account of pensions provision, not least because defined contribution provision threatens to undermine the essence of pensions provision as a form of welfare. The embrace of 'notional' defined contribution (NDC) in countries such as Sweden suggests that individualized provision is becoming a feature even of state pension systems in ostensibly social democratic regimes, and there are several examples of defined benefit provision in Europe being semi-individualized through the establishment of 'collective' defined contribution schemes.

In concerning itself with the structure rather than operation of private pensions saving, the established literature also tends to bracket off from analysis the role (which is growing in importance, in many places) of the finance sector in pensions provision (Clark, 2003). A nationalist bias, methodologically speaking, in the comparative literature makes it difficult to incorporate the cross-border nature of financial markets into analysis of nationally constituted welfare provision. But how accumulated funds are managed and invested should not be seen as secondary to product design, but rather an integral part of provision. How financial markets interact with pensions provision is particularly important to the decumulation process, which receives very little attention outside specialist scholarly fields.

This is related to the third main oversight in the welfare-based literature: a failure to recognize the role of 'the pensions industry' (which might broadly include employers supporting provision, as well as product providers and investment managers) in shaping policy. The welfare lens encourages the identification of the relationship between individual well-being and public provision (for example, the extent to which the pursuit of well-being is decommodified) as the key dimension of pensions provision, and the key differential between provision across different countries. Analysis should be equally concerned with the extent to which state actors act in partnership (or otherwise) with private actors to support prevailing business models, and therefore profitability, in the pensions industry. The question of the state's responsibility for welfare may in fact be secondary for policy-makers to the question of what forms of welfare are permissible within a country's political-economic structure, including the distribution of power between employers and workers, and the structural power of financial services firms as delivery agents of private pensions provision.

Ironically, and fourthly, the welfare-based literature, despite largely originating in Esping-Andersen's analysis of 'welfare capitalism', struggles to account for the relationship between, or indeed dependence on, pensions provision and the wider capitalist system. This relationship is obviously not a feature of the technocratic analysis undertaken or supported by bodies such as the World Bank and the OECD. But welfare capitalism in the wider, academic literature is too often taken to mean little more than welfare provision which exists within capitalist countries. Esping-Andersen's concept of decommodification of course suggests that welfare provision in its purest, ideal form exists outside capitalist economic process—and this orientation has prevailed in the subsequent literature, perhaps more so than Esping-Andersen intended. At best, we are left with a largely implicit allusion to Keynesian theory, in which welfare payments to individuals are recognized as integral to aggregate demand. Hay and Wincott's (2012) *The Political Economy of European Welfare Capitalism*, discussed above, which is closer to the comparativist literature on 'varieties of capitalism' (Hall and Soskice, 1999; although cf. Hay, 2019) than most examples of welfare state analysis, is a partial exception. As such, Hay and Wincott are comfortable discussing the economic implications of different forms of welfare provision, and how this relates to nationally constituted models of capitalist growth. Again, however, while the 'profound interdependence of the economic, the social and the political' in the constitution of welfare capitalism is acknowledged (Hay and Wincott, 2012: 4–5), interrogating this interdependence empirically is not the book's primary purpose.

We should of course be careful not to reduce any form of welfare provision to the wider capitalist system—an oversimplification which tends to undermine the varieties of capitalism literature. For instance, this literature's tendency to distinguish financial systems across capitalist varieties as either bank-based or market-based has little relevance to the idiosyncrasies of pensions provision, in which macro-economic conditions (and policy) and financial markets (and their regulation) may produce very specific pensions practices which cannot be read automatically from wider practices of capitalist organization (Datz, 2016). That said, prevailing models of corporate governance, which are usually seen as central to the functions of particular capitalist varieties, help us to understand the specific issue of how employers approach their pension obligations across different countries (see Sikka, 2018). It seems, in general, that an overly parsimonious account of capitalist organization (see Hay, 2019) serves implicitly to frame accounts of pensions provision; in a way, paradoxically, that means the actual relations between capitalism and pensions is underinvestigated, meaning the essential features of pensions provision in *any* capitalist society are marginalized within typologies and related research.

Alongside the influence of capitalist organization on pensions provision, we should also consider the relationship between capitalism and pensions *policy*. This is the central thesis of Michael A. McCarthy's *Dismantling Solidarity* (2017)—a landmark account of the development of pensions provision in the US in the post-war era. McCarthy offers a broadly neo-Marxist account of pensions 'marketisation'—including the financialization of defined benefit funds, and the rise of individualized '401k' products—arguing that the state has been intimately involved in facilitating this process through (de)regulatory initiatives. Crucially, however, for McCarthy, policymakers' support for pensions marketization has not necessarily been deliberate. The development of pensions provision in the US has often been a secondary aspect of wider attempts to resolve (perceived) crises of capitalism, in terms of both capitalist production and its legitimation. For example, the passage of the Employee Retirement Income Security Act (ERISA) in 1974, which strengthened the regulation of defined benefit pension funds, is generally seen as a response to the collapse of firms which sponsored defined benefit provision, often leaving workers' pensions unprotected. McCarthy argues contrarily that ERISA was introduced largely to placate the older workers in heavy industries most likely to be negatively affected by President Richard Nixon's more significant agenda around trade liberalization (with these workers more likely to be in mature defined benefit schemes). Similarly, the fairly recent rollout of 401k pension plans in the American private sector was an almost inadvertent consequence of the introduction, in the late 1970s, of measures to extend tax relief to higher earners saving *outside* conventional pensions provision, which essentially responded to a perceived crisis of profitability.

McCarthy is guilty perhaps of overstating the generalizability of the American case. While it may be correct to argue that key pensions policy decisions in the US are driven by wider economic concerns, and not simply pensions-related policy ambitions, this is arguably less evident empirically in other domestic contexts. Precisely because most European countries, for instance, have a stronger welfarist tradition than the US, pensions policy, as with other welfare policies, appears to have a greater degree of autonomy from economic policy than found by McCarthy. This difference might, in turn, help us to understand some of the specific characteristics of UK pensions provision, since the UK can be seen to encompass a relatively developed welfarist tradition, albeit one in which welfare provision has traditionally been, and is increasingly, subservient to economic management. Exploring how this dynamic 'plays out' across different pensions policy domains is one of this book's key objectives.

Irrespective of how consistent pensions provision is with wider capitalist organization, and how well this is understood, critical analysis of pensions policy should also consider how pensions provision—principally, but not exclusively, accumulated funds in private pension schemes, and how they are invested—contribute to nationally constituted capitalist growth models. Gordon Clark's work on 'pension fund capitalism' offers an example of such analysis, albeit not one that has aged particularly well. Clark's thesis on the increasingly significant role of mature defined benefit funds in corporate governance—particularly in the UK and US—offered a snapshot of how certain forms of pensions provision seemed to be reshaping capitalist dynamics in some economies. However, the progressive potential of this shift, outlined by Clark, has not really materialized, as funds have begun to close at a rapid rate, or at least become more conservative in their investment strategies. Nevertheless, Clark was also able to show, more presciently, and contrary to his generally optimistic account, that elements of defined benefit provision were actually helping to facilitate some of the instruments of financialization which would later become prevalent within Anglo-American capital markets more generally. Giselle Datz (2014) draws upon examples from Latin America to distinguish alternative roles for pension funds in capitalist organization, including examples of pension fund capitalism, resembling Clark's account, in Chile and Mexico. She also describes 'pension fund developmentalism' in Brazil as pension funds invest in a collaborative manner alongside state enterprises, generally counter-cyclically, and 'pension fund statism' in Argentina, where pension funds have been nationalized and invested in a generally pro-cyclical manner to support Argentina's solvency on international credit markets.

Fifthly, and perhaps most importantly, the existing literature tends to focus either on the operation of pensions provision, or instead the political-institutional context which shapes provision. What pensions actually *is* as a form of welfare—its quintessential character as a means by which human beings may interact socially and economically—tends to be taken for granted. Chapter 1 discussed the inter-generational nature of pensions provision. Most analyses of pensions provision of course recognizes that it operates across the lifecourse, and indeed that specific forms of provision will involve and affect people at different life-stages in different ways. But the prevailing assumption is that different generations *co-operate* with each other in order to enable pensions provision (and are enabled to do so by the state)—this helps to explain the point, noted above, that the welfare-based literature is more comfortable discussing explicitly collectivist forms of pensions provision. In contrast, pensions provision should be seen in a subtly different way, that is, as a set of mechanisms of cross-generational co-operation so that generational *change* can be managed. To recognize that pensions provision is inter-generational is not to assume that it provides for inter-generational harmony, but rather to recognize that the experiences, interests, expectations, and behaviours of different generations will diverge quite radically over time. We are in danger of overlooking existential threats to pensions provision in the UK, for instance, if we assume that all forms of pensions provision are constituted by inter-generational co-operation. We need instead to interrogate the extent to which different forms of provision succeed in enabling very long-term processes of financial dematerialization and rematerialization to persist even as the worlds inhabited by different generations are transformed. The bracketing-off of finance-sector practices in most welfare-based scholarship is relevant here too—but the cross-generational rematerialization process also takes place via the state, and the economy in general.

Related to this, we must recognize also the peculiar temporality of pensions provision. We accumulate pensions saving, whether publicly or privately, collectively or individually, on the basis of a vision of the future in which our savings will later be decumulated. This future is always imaginary—the generational nature of human existence means it cannot possibly come to pass—but simultaneously real, insofar as it governs the temporal practices through which savings will be rematerialized as a pension income. There are some quite obvious elements of this temporality in conventional pensions provision, such as the discounting of future liabilities, whether *de jure* in funded schemes, or *de facto* in, for instance, state pensions. More generally, temporal imaginaries shape the terms on which employers agree to establish and contribute to pension schemes, and share risks, the terms on which savers defer their income, and the terms on which providers offer services, even if the projected future is not a specific aspect of product design.

Adam Leaver's (2018a) work on the temporalities of modern corporate governance are relevant here. He draws upon critical accounting to demonstrate that accounting practices do not report financial reality, but rather constitute financial reality, primarily via inscribing particular temporalities on both economic stocks and flows. Leaver explores the particular example of the collapse of construction firm Carillion to demonstrate the extent to which its business model relied upon the manipulation of future-oriented processes such as discounting and depreciation (the pensions policy implications of Carillion's collapse are discussed in Chapter 4). For Leaver, it is such practices, rather than, say, the prioritization of shareholder value in distributional struggles, which epitomize financialization—or, the two trends work in tandem. The most striking inference here is that such practices have always been a feature of pensions provision. Pensions are often likened to insurance (and indeed many insurers are in the pensions game too, especially in the UK), but whereas insurance services concern the probabilities attached to future events, pensions provision both builds in a probability that the future will resemble that projected at the point of interaction with the service, and the certainty that it will not. Yet mechanisms for managing future failures are being redesigned around inappropriate cross-generational institutions or behaviours, especially insofar as pensions reform overlaps with the financialization of corporate practices identified by Leaver (and many others). By not focusing on this characteristic of pensions provision, scholarship risks failing to identify when the approach to temporal management implicitly underpinning particular forms of provision becomes abnormally unsustainable; we are not seeing the pensions crisis for what it really is.

3.3. Pensions across the Multiverse

Pensions provision is messy. Arguably the main weakness in all attempts at cross-national categorization is the notion that we can capture the essential character of any nationally constituted 'pension system' by simply documenting the extent to which different forms of provision (usually deemed to arise from different political traditions) are present, relative to other forms. As a consequence, a great deal of expertise is mobilized in the service of simplifying the pensions experience. Parsimony is often useful, but in relation to pensions provision, its limits have been breached. This chapter, so far, has suggested that pensions provision can be understood in terms of:

- The role of the state in regulating and enabling pensions provision—this role usually includes providing pensions too, but the state's significance to pensions provision should not be reduced as such.
- The extent to which, and the ways in which, the risks involved in pensions saving are collectivized or individualized.
- The nature and objectives of the pensions industry, which will narrowly encompass the providers of pension products and services, but also more broadly encompass the financial markets in which private pensions saving is invested, and employers directly involved in supporting pension funds.
- The relationship between pensions provision and the wider capitalist system, including how efforts to manage capitalism are reflected in pensions policy and practice. Pensions provision varies because capitalist accumulation models differ, but it also has essential, cross-national features precisely because it exists within capitalism.
- The projected futures which are essential to enabling pensions accumulation in the present, and the mechanisms by which sponsors and providers manage failed futures as generational change unfolds.

While these five points certainly cannot be understood as a set of axes along which a country's dominant forms of pensions provision can be situated, the rest of the book endeavours to examine the recent history of UK pensions policy in accordance with this understanding, building upon the overview offered in Chapter 2. The remainder of this chapter briefly explores the recent history of pensions provision in other countries, both to contextualize the UK experience, and embellish the discussion in this chapter of pension system typologies.

3.3.1 Pensions Reform in Europe

The highly developed welfare states of Europe, particularly Western Europe, have been affected by policy-makers' efforts to balance welfare-related objectives with the perceived threat of increased longevity, and the perceived need to liberalize labour markets, for several decades. The 2008 financial crisis and subsequent fiscal tightening, especially in the Eurozone, has reinforced this agenda—but at the same time problematized one of its planks in the pre-crisis period, that is, the shift from unfunded publicly organized pensions provision to funded provision (see Casey, 2012; Engelen, 2003; Dixon and Sorsa, 2009). Germany began to move decisively away from its Bismarckian heritage in the early 2000s. In various stages, privately organized defined benefit and defined contribution funded provision has been introduced as the benefits arising from mandatory, social insurance provision have been reduced. The former, styled as UK-like occupational pensions and typically organized via collective bargaining and social partnership between employers and employees in particular industries, has had the most significant impact, especially in the large manufacturing sector. Introduced, ironically, as the decline of occupational pensions in the UK began to gather pace, benefits are less generous than in UK defined benefit provision, but state protections are stronger than in the UK, incentivizing participation even though provision is voluntary. Of course, access to occupational pensions, and their specific design, is uneven. The German state heavily subsidizes defined contribution provision, and regulates for guaranteed outcomes—the so-called 'Reister' schemes—in part to fill the gaps. These are provided directly to individuals, although typically organized in the workplace, with additional public support for schemes designed for the self-employed. Of course, the role of investment guarantees (fought for by unions in the context of state pension cuts) means that investment strategies tend to be conservative—both tempering the performance of funds and inhibiting the role of new funds in supporting business investment (which had been part of policy-makers' rationale for their introduction) (Naczyk and Hassel, 2019).

The German finance sector has grown in response to these new pensions markets—both in terms of direct provision of schemes, but also asset management, whereby assets under management by German firms have increased substantially in recent decades. Losses related to the financial crisis were relatively limited due to private funds' limited exposure to equities (Keeley and Love, 2010). Post-crisis adjustment of pensions provision has focused mainly upon raising entitlement ages for publicly organized provision, an agenda which had before been pursued more tentatively (although opportunities for 'early' retirement were more restricted). But the dilution of the standard employment model in Germany, a trend which has arguably accelerated since the crisis, clearly problematizes a situation in which more people are more dependent on earnings from employment to secure an adequate retirement income. It seems likely that Germany will be Anglicizing its pensions provision even further as more people become reliant on means-tested supplements within public provision, especially lower earners with limited appetite for private saving, and those who have experienced precarious work and lengthy career breaks (Riedmüller and Willert, 2007; Hinrichs, 2012). In other words, the present is already rather different from the future projected in the 'Neue Mitte' period of the early 2000s—although not inconsistent with a 'hollowing out' long evident in the German labour market.

Voluntary, funded provision has been growing in importance in France too, albeit not as quickly as in Germany. It was not until the mid-2000s that the state began to encourage private pensions saving by individuals, principally via the workplace, and defined contribution schemes (although there has long been a developed annuities market in France, utilized by very affluent groups). The development of funded provision came alongside repeated efforts to contain costs within public provision, which remains overwhelmingly the dominant form of pensions provision in France. The vast majority of private-sector workers are part of the Régime Généralé (RG), albeit with additional unfunded provision organized by industry, with public-sector workers part of various similar schemes. In the post-war era the Régime Généralé became increasingly responsible for administering non-contributory and means-tested benefits for all French citizens, although in recent decades the state has taken direct responsibility for these forms of provision, essentially representing the development of a UK-style state pension focused on poverty alleviation. The social insurance pensions schemes have, unlike the French economy in general, become rather more corporatist in recent years as trade unions have become more involved in fund governance, albeit in return for a reduction in benefit levels, and increases in entitlement ages, for most workers (Bonoli and Palier, 2008). Such reforms have been fiercely contested, even after the 2008 financial crisis, when elite concerns about fiscal sustainability were heightened, so the pace of retrenchment has been slow (Natali, 2011). The pace appeared to quicken after Emmanuel Macron became President in 2017, with the pursuit of a plan to merge dozens of unfunded pension schemes (including those for public-sector workers not covered by the Régime Généralé) into a single scheme with elements of both NDC and Bismarckian public provision (outcomes are based on 'points' accumulated, with the value of points linked to one's salary). The reform would also have penalized early retirement, although this element was later relaxed. Macron persisted with this agenda despite two years of industrial action and civil unrest, yet in early 2020 paused the reform in response to the COVID-19 pandemic. It is also worth noting the development of the Fonds de reserve pour les retraites (FRR) in the early 2000s—something which has received relatively little attention in the comparative literature. The French state began to build up the FRR in order to *pre*-fund public provision, with reserves built up through various sources, including the privatization of public assets. The FRR operates much like any pension fund responsible for defined benefit provision—seeking returns within global capital markets (Dixon and Sorsa, 2009). At the end of 2017, its assets were worth around €36 billion.[1]

The reforms introduced in Italy have followed a similar trajectory, albeit via an even bumpier path. Italian policy-makers introduced reforms in the early 1990s—earlier than in France—to contain the fiscal risks associated with its Bismarckian public pensions provision, most significantly increases to retirement ages and moving younger workers into NDC rather than defined benefit schemes. Supplementary, pure defined contribution provision was also encouraged by the state from around this time (Jessoula, 2012). Ironically, Italy had only firmly established its public pensions provision in the 1960s, later than France. However, its partial retrenchment was undertaken with very long lead-in times before implementation; it was not until the Eurozone crisis and formation of Mario Monti's 'technocratic' government that implementation was brought forward, through legislation known as the 'Fornero Law' in honour of Elsa Fornero, the neoclassical economist appointed to oversee cost containment in pensions provision. Italy's current leaders—belonging to the populist Five Star and far-right League parties— have vowed to reverse the 2011 legislation, appealing to younger workers whose atypical careers will be punished by defined contribution provision, and older workers whose retirement ages have risen. Any such move is likely to threaten Italy's (precarious) creditworthiness in international bond markets.

As noted above, although legislated for first in Italy, NDC is associated most with Swedish pensions provision. Traditionally, Sweden's Beveridgean

---

[1] For 2017 financial information on the FRR (in English), see: http://www.fondsdereserve.fr/documents/FRR-RA2017-GB.pdf.

system has combined a guaranteed, means-tested benefit and publicly organized, contributory defined benefit system. In the late 1990s, the latter element was transformed into an NDC system in which the state continues to shoulder the key saving risks, but is more able to alter notional rates of return in order to contain costs. Although the government chose not to reduce rates in accordance with the prescribed formula after the financial crisis, over the longer term rates will be set more cautiously (Natali, 2011: 19–20). At the same time, a portion of workers' savings were invested into mandatory—and very tightly regulated, and indeed publicly managed—pure defined contribution schemes. Caps on contribution into both systems means that funded, industry-based occupational provision—which may be defined benefit or defined contribution—has grown in importance in recent years, especially for higher earners (Trampusch, 2013). This provision is also highly regulated. Denmark stems from a similar social democratic heritage as Sweden but, unlike its neighbour, began to implement large-scale support for pensioners long before Beveridge—around the same time the Bismarckian system was emerging in Denmark's other, larger neighbour. That said, a system of means-tested support did not evolve into a universal, flat-rate state pension system until the 1960s. As the generosity and inclusiveness of state pension provision increased, Danish policy-makers began to introduce support for supplementary, occupational provision—now largely under a pure defined contribution model, albeit in very large-scale, industry-based schemes. These schemes are highly regulated, and typically designed via collective agreements between employers and trade unions.

Pensions provision in the Netherlands resembles that of Denmark, although state pension provision is considerably less generous, meaning occupational pensions have been more significant for a much longer period of time. This created a legacy of large, privately organized defined benefit funds—although the Netherlands' 'co-ordinated regime' has been more successful than in the UK, for instance, at protecting this provision, or replacing it with large-scale pure, hybrid, or, in many cases, 'collective' defined contribution schemes through 'negotiated retrenchment' (Bridgen and Meyer, 2009; but see Wiß, 2019 for a brief account of recent attempts to liberalize industry-wide funds in the Netherlands). Nevertheless, the difficulty of expanding private provision as it simultaneously de-risks has made state pension reform much more contentious (Anderson, 2012). It is worth reiterating a point made implicitly above: in Sweden, Denmark, and the Netherlands, trade unions have been centrally involved in the establishment of funded pensions provision, including defined contribution schemes, in place of or in addition to state pension provision. Yet unions have also served to ensure high levels of employer involvement, including risk-sharing, even in ostensibly defined contribution provision (Anderson, 2019). As Chapter 2 shows, UK trade unions were similarly instrumental in supporting private pensions, including favouring occupational provision ahead of public provision—the relative absence of trade unions in the sectors where workers are now being automatically enrolled surely helps to explain the individualized and lightly regulated nature of workplace pensions in the UK.

The countries of Eastern Europe clearly differ from their Western European counterparts. Poland, however, already had a strong Bismarckian tradition before the formation of the Soviet Union, and this was largely maintained throughout the post-war period. In the late 1990s, Poland established itself as an exemplar pensions innovator by implementing a largely wholesale conversion of its unfunded, defined benefit provision to NDC, alongside a mandatory second tier consisting of pure defined contribution schemes. The financial crisis was particularly difficult for Polish pensions provision—with Donald Tusk's centre-right government responding by reducing the level of mandatory contributions into second-pillar provision, boosting public pension provision, and effectively nationalizing many fund assets by taking gilts held by funds into the public sector (private pensions nationalization occurred on a much larger scale in Hungary after 2010) (Naczyk, 2016). The system is also, and increasingly—in contrast, but not straightforwardly, with the socialist era—leaving younger Polish workers worse off than envisaged in the 1990s due to labour market changes uprooting typical careers (Guardiancich, 2012). Other countries, such as Romania, the Czech Republic, and Slovakia, have increasingly followed Poland's lead, first by establishing various forms of private pensions provision and then, more recently, by undermining it in favour of first-pillar provision (Naczyk and Domonkos, 2016).

It is worth noting, finally, that pensions policy has increasingly come into the remit of the EU, albeit not in any straightforward sense, since 'pensions policy' is in practice a multitude of overlapping policy processes. At the most basic level, the EU upholds an approach to social and welfare policy—the so-called 'social model'—which ostensibly challenges neoliberal policy prescriptions. However, evidence of convergence has been relatively limited, in part due to the limited fiscal powers at the EU level, and in part due to the continuing influence of neoliberalism (this perhaps explains the limited interest in 'Europeanisation' within the comparative, welfare-based literature). Welfare has been retrenched across the EU, but not in a singular fashion (Hay and Wincott, 2012). Of course, one of the paradoxes of retrenchment is that it has coincided with a widening of entitlements to previously excluded groups, not least in pensions provision—contributing to perceived fiscal risks—and the EU's steadfast commitment to the protection of human rights across the continent is an important part of this agenda.

Although there is insufficient space here to discuss this issue in depth, Europeanization is far more evident in the regulation of private pensions provision. Institutions for Occupational Retirement Provision regulations have been introduced, and steadily strengthened, as more countries have encouraged privately organized provision. The intent of EU policy-makers is to ensure the greater portability of pensions entitlements—supporting the free movement of labour—while also protecting savers as the consumers of complex financial products (see Haverland, 2007; Hennessy, 2014). EU-level insurance industry regulation is also relevant to pensions provision in many countries, not least the UK. In both cases, Europeanizing the market for financial products is an important objective too. More recent moves towards a Capital Markets Union (CMU) will shape how savings are invested—the agenda focuses on mitigating macro-economic risks as well as protecting consumers and enabling EU-wide competition (Quaglia et al., 2016). The European Commission's efforts to create a single market in personal pension products (the so-called Pan-European Pension Product (PEPP)) has so far proven unsuccessful—in part because it has been approached as an issue of integrating financial markets, neglecting the profound role of defined contribution provision as an instrument of social policy in countries such as the UK. Interestingly, the prospect of encouraging greater levels of personal pensions saving was directly linked by the Commission with efforts to increase long-term investment by institutional investors (a policy agenda which also became central to the CMU, despite the reservations of the UK—the CMU's original champion) (Schelkle, 2019). The PEPP has yet to be realized, but we can perhaps expect this agenda to resurface if defined contribution saving continues to grow in importance across the EU, and if, probably more importantly, financial market integration remains an EU ambition.

EU-level pensions and financial regulation has certainly enhanced the transnational nature of pensions provision in important ways, but arguably also made private provision more challenging (and expensive for providers). Nevertheless, the key point here is that several aspects of pensions policy are now firmly part of the European policy-making arena; this is likely to intensify if the legacy of both the 2008 financial crisis and the economic impact of COVID-19 includes greater fiscal and financial regulatory alignment across the Eurozone. We will fail to understand how pensions provision is likely to develop in the EU—with or without the UK—if this process remains marginal to analysis.

3.3.2   Pensions Reform Elsewhere in the Anglosphere

It is always difficult to discern a single country's pensions 'system'—and nowhere more so than in the US. The different components of US pensions provision are not necessarily designed to fit together, and pensions policy is not determined by a singular or even coherent policy-making process. This fragmentation perhaps complements, or results from, a deep-rooted commitment to economic liberalism, which limits the extent of state intervention in the organization of pensions provision (although provision nevertheless remains rather extensive, compared to most other spheres of economic life). As such, while there is no system, there is certainly a dominant *approach* in the US, albeit one with very uneven outcomes for individuals. Old-age benefits are the lynchpin element of the American social security system. Individuals receive a state pension, from the federal government, based on their tax records. The amount received increases based on earnings, but nevertheless the system is progressive, with the lowest earners receiving proportionately higher pension payments, by way of alleviating poverty—the system's chief objective when first established in the 1930s. Arguably the social security system is the site of the most important reform in US pension provision in recent years, albeit a modest one, as the main entitlement age will gradually increase from 65 to 67 (individuals can also access their benefits early, in return for actuarially reduced payments).

Pensions reform has been relatively limited in the US precisely because coverage is so uneven. Defined benefit schemes in the private sector have followed a similar path of decline—and regulatory reform—as in the UK (see McCarthy, 2017). Yet most funded defined benefit provision is actually within the public sector (whereas most public-sector schemes in the UK are unfunded). Pensions provision in the private sector has become increasingly dominated by defined contribution saving, albeit with huge variation in the type of schemes, saving rates, and extent of coverage, and with associated financial services only lightly regulated compared to European countries. The majority of American workers are not saving for a private pension. The Obama administration sought to rectify this issue in various ways, but new initiatives to make pensions provision easier for employers, and pensions saving less risky for employees, have seen very limited take-up, and plans to automatically enrol workers without a private pension into a workplace scheme have stalled at the federal level. However, several individual states are proceeding with auto-enrolment legislation (Munnell, 2018). It is worth noting finally that the state pension in the US is technically a funded pension—as is nominally the case in the UK—and that the trust fund which finances pension payments (and other benefits), funded by general taxation, will be insolvent by the 2030s based on current tax and benefit rates (Borak, 2017). The state could of course underwrite the fund.

In other Anglosphere countries, policy-makers have embarked on reform agendas similar to that seen in the UK, and which remain at the embryonic stage in the US. Australia has a relatively generous, non-contributory state pension system, albeit with entitlements subject to means-testing, so that the wealthiest retirees receive lower, or no, pension payments. There has traditionally been little private pensions provision in Australia, although in the early 1990s, the government introduced compulsory, defined contribution saving into so-called 'superannuation' funds, with minimum employer contributions. The provision of defined contribution schemes resembles the market now emerging in the UK to some extent, with private trusts—often organized on an industry-wide basis—managing schemes on behalf of employers, within parameters policed by regulation. Many of these funds have become sizeable investors in international capital markets (Murdoch and Duran, 2019). However, Australia has an extremely limited market in decumulation products—with insurance companies, unlike the UK, not involved in pension provision. This problem is becoming more acute as the largest cohorts of early enrolees near retirement (Cooper, 2016). It is evident also in New Zealand, with similar provision to Australia, and where automatic enrolment into 'KiwiSaver' defined contribution schemes was introduced in the mid-2000s (Nolan, 2018). In Ireland, the state pension system resembles that of the UK, albeit with the earnings-related top-up (which has of course now been abolished in the UK). Private pensions coverage has traditionally been limited, with defined benefit schemes available to workers, and provision in the private sector—whether defined benefit or, increasingly, defined contribution—being patchy and under-regulated (OECD, 2014b). The Irish government did, however, embark on a programme of pensions reform in 2018, which included strengthening private pension scheme governance, and the extension of automatic enrolment in workplace pensions (previously only applicable to younger workers with relatively high earnings).

One of the most interesting developments in pensions provision among English-speaking countries in recent years is a reform that has *not* happened: Canada has opted not to significantly increase entitlement ages in its state pensions provision. This is despite offering *both* a UK-style universal basic state pension and a US-style earnings-related state pension to most citizens. Canadian provision is actually similar to that evident in Australia, insofar as private pensions accordingly play a rather limited role for most people. That said, funded defined benefit provision is available in many parts of the public sector and traditional industries (along the lines of American provision), although schemes are generally being 'downgraded' to defined contribution, either pure or CDC schemes. Defined benefit funds in Canada, especially public-sector schemes and the more universal state-run fund, have traditionally been significant players in international capital markets—similar size to equivalent schemes in the US, but far more likely than American funds to invest internationally than domestically (Duarte, 2019; *The Economist*, 2019).

The story of recent pensions reform in the Anglosphere is, in large part, one of individualization, albeit to variable degrees: state provision being scaled back, private provision being scaled up, and defined contribution replacing defined benefit (or limited private provision) as the dominant form of provision. However, it is a story also of increasing compulsion; that is, of governments making private saving compulsory, or near compulsory. As we will see in the UK case, the rationale offered by policy-makers will be grounded, rather shallowly, in behavioural economics, which preaches that individuals do not know best how to make decisions in their own interests. But there is a plotline here about the transformation of what Colin Hay (2013) calls 'Anglo-liberal capitalism'. Private- (and, in many cases, public-) sector organizations seek to abdicate long-term commitments to their workers, necessitating a transferral of investment risks in pensions provision to individuals. Yet the same drivers see workers less able to rely upon long-term employment contracts and regular wage increases, therefore undermining their ability and willingness to save in practice. The provision of financial services related to private pensions is also strained, as the financial crisis problematizes the development of new products for the mass pensions saving market. The 2008 crisis was not in itself hugely problematic for pensions provision in most English-speaking countries, since financial risks had in most cases already been shifted to the youngest workers, furthest from retirement. Yet the financial crisis typified and exacerbated a wider crisis of the Anglo-liberal growth model, which is reflected both in the unravelling of traditional provision and the ways in which policy-makers have chosen to respond. We can perhaps think of the COVID-19 pandemic as the first crisis of the era of defined contribution dominance, although the long-term consequences remain uncertain.

3.3.3 Pensions Reform in Latin America

While pensions provision across Europe and the Anglosphere is most directly comparable to that in the UK, it is worth noting that pensions provision in part of Latin America has undergone significant change in recent years (and duly received attention from scholars). Indeed, pensions reform in Chile is generally seen as a laboratory for changes that would later be rolled out across the Anglosphere and, perhaps more importantly, an exemplar of the kind of provision the World Bank has traditionally advocated in the developing world as populations age. In the early 1980s, under military dictatorship, Chile abolished its public provision and introduced a single-pillar, defined contribution system of private pensions saving. Workers are compelled to contribute 10 per cent of their income, whereby employer contributions were not mandatory. Individuals are able to choose (and switch) how their savings are managed, by choosing between different state-regulated Administrators of Pension Funds (AFP) schemes. A 'zero-pillar' means-tested benefit was retained for those whose AFP pension did not provide an adequate retirement income.

The resulting funds related to AFP schemes have become very large, and have helped to drive economic growth in Chile in recent decades. But the system has proved to be rather problematic, insofar as investment returns have rarely lived up to expectations, high AFP fees have been controversial, and coverage has been patchy due to Chile's large informal labour market. As in Australasia, a failure of markets for decumulation products to keep pace with private accumulation has been evident. All of the same problems have been evident in Mexico, which in the late 1990s introduced mandatory defined contribution alongside its Bismarckian public provision (Datz, 2014; Sinha, 2018). Chile has in recent years seen the state return to pensions provision through the establishment of a tax-financed 'solidarity' pillar for those outside the AFP system, better protections for those with limited employment records, and indeed a solidarity supplement within the AFP system for low-income workers (Barr and Diamond, 2010, 2016; Borzutsky and Hyde, 2016; Mander, 2016). State pensions, whether contributory or means-tested, have grown in importance throughout Latin America (OECD, 2014a). In Chile, AFP fees are now more strictly regulated, although proposals to allow state banks to administer pension funds—something more common in other parts of the continent—have yet to come to pass.

As noted above, in relation to private pensions provision, Datz (2014) contrasts 'pension fund developmentalism' in Brazil and 'pension fund statism' in Argentina, South America's largest economies. The key element of pensions provision in both countries remains public provision, although it has become increasingly strained. The end of military rule in Brazil in 1988 saw state pension entitlements enshrined in the country's constitution, giving rise to a generous and redistributive social security system, with a tax-financed, pay-as-you-go public pension for private-sector workers (similar but separate arrangements for public-sector workers were retained). Private pension provision has been encouraged by Brazilian governments since the

1990s, in the face of demographic pressures on public provision, and accumulated assets in Brazilian pension funds have grown enormously in the last 20 years to around 20 per cent of the country's GDP. As Datz explains, the Lula and Rousseff governments have ensured through strict regulations that these funds have been used to support Brazil's economic development, whether through investment in domestic gilts, property development, small and medium-sized enterprises, or, more recently, infrastructure. Limits on public equity holdings have recently loosened, but only if funds are invested in the Novo Mercado, a section of the Sao Paolo stock exchange with strict corporate governance rules. Of course, it would be naïve to expect private pensions provision in Brazil to continue without significant concerns—for instance, the direction of investment by policy-makers has invariably been linked to recent corruption scandals—especially if public provision is, as expected, retrenched further in the years ahead.

The links between capitalist development and pensions provision are also evident in Argentina. The retrenchment of public provision began earlier, and proceeded more quickly, in Argentina than in Brazil (following a similar path to Chile, Mexico, etc.). In the early 1990s, the Bismarckian public pension was itself part-privatized. We can see such moves as symptomatic of Argentina's embrace of the 'Washington consensus' and its pursuit of development through the internationalization of its economy (including financial markets). It is precisely the volatility seemingly inherent in this model which has led to the (re-)emergence of pension fund statism, as funds have been increasingly compelled to invest in domestic bonds to service Argentina's public debt, and workers incentivized to abandon private funds in favour of rejoining the public scheme. In the aftermath of the 2008 financial crisis, private funds (most workers had opted to remain in private provision, not least because benefits had been underpinned by government guarantees) were effectively nationalized, moving around 10 per cent of GDP—largely held in gilts—into the public sector (Datz, 2014).

3.3.4 Pensions Reform in East Asia

The concept of pension fund statism would probably be a familiar one in the East Asian context, although recent years have seen moves in the opposite direction, especially in Japan. Japan's Government Pension Investment Fund (GPIF)—with well over £1 trillion in assets under management—is regularly described as the world's largest pension fund. The Japanese state provides both a Beveridgean basic state pension and a Bismarckian earnings-related public pension, both funded by contributions into the GPIF. It operates ostensibly at arm's length from government, but has traditionally invested heavily in Japanese gilts and corporate bonds, as part of Japan's state-led, coordinated model of capitalist development (Fastenrath et al., 2017: 280). Pension funds are therefore central to economic stability in Japan, but more recently the GPIF has diversified its asset allocations significantly, with the help of deregulation. Domestic economic stimulation was clearly one of the goals of such reform, but it has also meant the GPIF has moved into international markets too (Flood, 2019). We should note also that there is some funded, occupational provision in Japan, occasionally in place of the earnings-related scheme (providing certain conditions are met), but often in addition to public provision. Voluntary provision is typically defined benefit, but increasingly defined contribution.

In a sense, pensions provision in Japan and Korea are converging on a three-pillar model. As noted above, pensions provision in Korea developed only very recently, alongside the rapid, 'catch-up' development of the country's economy. Means-tested assistance remains hugely important, but will decline in importance as its Bismarckian public pension system, introduced only in the late 1980s, matures. Means-tested assistance is becoming *more* important in Japan. Similarly, voluntary, occupational pensions provision—both defined benefit and defined contribution—was introduced as a central dimension of provision in South Korea, yet has developed relatively slowly in Japan. Understandably, much more attention has been placed on the development of pensions provision in China than Korea in recent years, although China has arguably been slower than Korea in growing, or regularizing, pensions provision. There remains a strong emphasis on China on informal, family-based support—and indeed new pension entitlements for older cohorts have (controversially, to some extent) been linked to the contributions of younger relatives. Recent pensions reform in China, amid rapid population change (primarily, increasing life expectancy and urbanization), has focused on expanding and centralizing public provision. As a legacy of piecemeal schemes for different categories of workers, rules on accessibility remain complex; coverage has spread significantly, but also led to the entrenchment of outcome inequalities (Zhu and Walker, 2018). Some provinces also provide mandatory, NDC benefits—replicating practice seen elsewhere in East Asia, such as Malaysia (Tolos et al., 2014). In general, private pensions provision in China is very underdeveloped, but this is expected to change dramatically in the decades ahead as financial services become more sophisticated. It seems that issues around scheme design and investment profile remain undetermined, but the direction of travel is not.

3.4. Conclusion: The British Mongrel?

In his final research paper, the late Stephen Hawking revised his conception of the multiverse. The 'Big Bang' may have created multiple universes, rather than simply the one everybody reading this book inhabits, but he concluded ultimately that these alternative universes were quite likely to resemble our own. The fundamental building blocks of matter, and therefore life, were likely to be common across the multiverse, even if each universe had taken a very different evolutionary path. There is of course more to life than pensions—but not as much as we might assume. The flaw in this analogy is that, while distinct universes *do not* interact (to the best of our knowledge), nationally constituted traditions of pensions provision *do*, at least to some extent. There is obviously a degree of learning across borders, and the economic processes underpinning pensions provision clearly have an international element (that is, labour markets, financial services provision, investment practice, etc.—and, in the Eurozone following the COVID-19 pandemic, even the issuance of gilts). The (partial) Europeanization of pensions regulation is a significant development in this regard, albeit one which the UK is now less likely to be affected by.

However, while it is correct that there are common traits across the pensions multiverse—a pension is, by and large, a pension—it is too often assumed that there exists a relatively limited range of types of provision or pension 'systems'. Even more misleading is the assumption in the technocratic literature, replicated in much (financial) economics scholarship, that countries can simply 'choose' an off-the-shelf system to implement, or transition towards. Pensions practice is deeply rooted in a country's political economy, or its social, political, and economic development, and as such any attempt to abstract and idealize system types is inherently flawed, even if useful for some purposes. Indeed, there is a danger that we actually downplay the importance of pensions provision's essential characteristics, as manifest in national practice, as we focus on the differences (and similarities) between nations. The possibility that existential threats to pensions provision are being marginalized as a result must be taken seriously.

Paul Bridgen and Traute Meyer (2011) argue that the UK's pensions system has become a 'hybrid'. This judgement is based on the fact that the expansion of the public-sector workforce means more people are covered by unfunded defined benefit provision, and that increasing regulation and state underpinning of defined benefit funds in the private sector leaves the UK system looking a little more Bismarckian for many. All the while, many in the private sector are left to rely only on the Beveridgean state pension. Very recent developments problematize this account, not least the decline in the public-sector workforce resulting from austerity (especially in local government, although local government pension schemes are funded) and an acceleration of the decline of defined benefit provision in the private sector. The more significant weakness is perhaps the notion that any particular country can be characterized as representing a hybrid of any two ideal-type systems. Indeed, the Netherlands, Bridgen and Meyer's point of comparison in their 2009 paper, is itself often seen as a hybrid of the Beveridgean and Bismarckian systems due to its highly developed multi-pillar model (Rhodes and Natali, 2003). With France being characterized as both conservative and egalitarian, and Germany moving away from its Bismarckian roots, both noted above, there are clearly only a limited number of hybrids permissible before it becomes necessary to question prevailing approaches to categorization.

It might be plausible from some perspectives to treat the UK as a hybrid regime, especially if comparative analysis encompasses only (Western) Europe and the Anglosphere. As Table 3.1 shows, pensions expenditure and typical replacement rates in the UK are on the less generous side compared to most countries of Western Europe—but also compare unfavourably with North America, where pensions provision is in some ways more European than in the UK, at least for some citizens. At the same time, the development of pensions provision in the UK clearly belongs in the European welfarist tradition—not unproblematically, but this could probably be said of most European countries—as demonstrated by its extensive system of tax-financed pension benefits and the state's longstanding role in shaping, supporting, or protecting private provision. Chapter 2 described the development of UK pensions provision as a distinctive experiment in 'liberal collectivism', insofar as the prevalence of collectivist provision in the private sector, and indeed the genesis of pensions provision as a form of insurance, depended very much on voluntarism, rather than compulsion, among employers and employees. The UK's large finance sector both enabled this voluntarism and grew larger on the back of it. Liberal collectivism has been unstable for some time, with the state stepping in to soften its contradictions—although generally in ways consistent with the essence of traditional practice—by first seeking to directly provide earnings-related defined benefit pension supplements, underpinning residual defined benefit provision in the private sector, and more recently by compelling and regulating the defined contribution alternative. It is tempting to conclude, pre-emptively, that the UK therefore constitutes a *failed* experiment. Yet all pensions provision is, to an extent, experimental, designed in the present on the basis of projected futures. All pensions provision therefore also fails, as the futures which underpin pensions provision and policy in the present invariably do not come to pass, and practice evolves as policy-makers and providers respond to generational change. It is especially important to acknowledge this characteristic of pensions provision in the case of the UK, given that the country's large and highly developed finance sector has created innumerable opportunities for designing provision around projected futures—in a way that has become a severe shortcoming as it interacts with the financialization of the UK economy and a dilution of temporal anchor function.

Clearly, the fact that pensions practice is deeply rooted in political economy does not mean that it is unchanging. Political contestation is also marginalized, unhelpfully, within the comparative literature. Although the welfare-based literature seeks to establish the political-philosophical foundations of pensions provision, it is too quick to assume that policy-makers merely embody such traditions, and that pensions reform is simply a product of traditional practice interacting with exogenous changes. This book will show that pensions reform is not apolitical; for instance, the way that new issues are interpreted as problems for pensions provision is an inherently political process, and there are political contingencies involved in how reform options are pursued and enacted. Pensions reform is often part of wider political agendas, or at the intersection of different agendas which overlap, occasionally in contradictory ways. The most significant reforms generally become possible when moments of political conjuncture are arrived at, even if such moments are produced by political and economic developments within which pensions provision is only tangential. The work of scholars such as Giselle Datz and Michael McCarthy, discussed above, offers an example of this understanding, albeit at the risk of reducing pensions practice to wider capitalist development. This is analytically dubious, but also empirically inaccurate in relation to the UK (perhaps in contrast to Latin America and the US), where pensions policy is established as a relatively distinct, but highly complex, policy arena. The question now is whether the choices made in this arena in recent years have imperilled, rather than simply transformed, UK pension provision. The story continues in Chapter 4.

4

A Good Innings? The Demise of Collectivism in (Mostly) Private Pensions Provision

In UK pensions provision, collectivism has not quite gone, but it is in danger of being forgotten. Chapter 2 of this book characterized collectivism in UK pensions provision as peculiarly liberal in nature—but this is an experiment that appears to have failed. Paul Bridgen and Traute Meyer (2011) write similarly of the UK's 'exhausted voluntarism', with defined benefit provision which relies on private-sector employers' willingness to shoulder investment risks approaching its final demise. Of course, we should avoid any insinuation that the providers and sponsors of defined benefit schemes have simply been unable to keep pace with economic and demographic change; such contexts are highly relevant, but the demise of collectivism is also a choice that has been made, and made again, by employers and policy-makers.

This chapter focuses mainly upon defined benefit occupational pensions in the private sector—perhaps the defining feature of pensions provision in the UK traditionally—albeit in the context of wider collectivist commitments in dominant forms of provision, and indeed acknowledging that the state plays a crucial role as regulator, guarantor, and provider of private, occupational pensions. The chapter begins by reflecting on the experience of defined benefit demise, and the false promise of its replacement by individualized defined contribution provision. Despite recent efforts to promote 'defined ambition' hybrid schemes, there is a vast gulf between defined benefit and defined contribution—with differences often obscured by an esoteric, technical discourse. Building upon the understanding of pensions provision developed in Chapter 3, this chapter argues that the key difference is the absence of a temporal anchor in defined contribution provision—a role performed in large part by employers in defined benefit provision. Yet the failsafe has failed. Section 4.1 actually notes also that the demise of defined benefit was identified even *before* its peak—with the state seeking, ultimately unsuccessfully, to provide alternative collectivist provision. Section 4.2 draws

Pensions Imperilled: The Political Economy of Private Pensions Provision in the UK. Craig Berry, Oxford University Press (2021).
© Craig Berry. DOI: 10.1093/oso/9780198782834.003.0004

upon critical scholarship to question the dominant explanations for the demise of defined benefit provision, including regulation, increasing longevity, and unfavourable economic trends. It suggests instead that defined benefit demise has more to do with the perceived incompatibility of traditional provision with new forms of capital accumulation and corporate governance (although, ironically, parts of the UK finance sector have found innovative ways to industrialize the demise of collectivism).

Section 4.3 briefly discusses attempts by the Coalition and May governments to mitigate the perceived shortcomings of residual defined benefit provision. Section 4.4 discusses the seemingly anomalous survival—and indeed expansion—of defined benefit in parts of the UK pensions landscape, that is, in 'lifeboat' provision and the public sector. The growth of the former sphere is a direct consequence of the demise of occupational pensions in general. The latter sphere has been subject to many of the same challenges as private-sector provision, and yet its survival demonstrates that there is nothing particularly inevitable about the demise of collectivist pensions in the UK. It is worth noting finally that, unlike many accounts, this chapter does not attempt to tell the demise story chronologically in any strict sense. The demise of collectivist pensions is not a singular story: it emerges from lots of overlapping trends, some of which contradict each other. Instead the chapter attempts to outline the various threads which have come loose, at various times and in various ways, wounding collectivism as a result—fatally, it seems, in the case of defined benefit provision in the private sector.

4.1. Definitionally, Maybe

The language of 'defined benefit' and 'defined contribution' pensions is conveniently technocratic, obscuring the vast differences between the two main forms of occupational pensions provision in the UK. In defined benefit provision, outcomes in terms of retirement incomes are guaranteed: every contribution made will confer a property right to a given pension payment—with these payments invariably revaluated to broadly keep pace with inflation. In defined contribution provision, contributions confer no rights: they are invested on savers' behalf, and the resulting retirement income depends entirely on investment returns.

How in defined benefit provision are these outcomes possible? How, in theory, is the imagined future made real? Simply, employers bear the risk that the scheme they 'sponsor' might not be able to deliver the pension promised from its own operations. The employer may of course be the state (and it is worth pointing out that the state imposes minimum expectations on private-sector employers regarding the formula for turning contributions into a retirement income, to ensure equivalence with its own experiments in occupational pensions provision for private-sector workers). Actual outcomes in defined benefit depend very much on actual scheme design. Traditionally the guarantee in defined benefit schemes has related to a member's 'final salary', providing for an additional layer of pensions futurology, as employers will not actually know the nature of the promise they are agreeing to keep until their workers reach retirement. A widespread move to promises based on 'career average' salaries offered a little future-proofing, although in practice both final salary and career average schemes can be more or less generous, depending on the accrual rate, that is, the proportion of the salary referent promised as a pension for each year (or part thereof) of contributions. The means by which pensions in payment are indexed (that is, protected against inflation) is also relevant here.

In generational terms, defined benefit provision obviously depends acutely on new and younger members making cash contributions and pooling their investments with older cohorts. But this is made possible by their employer (or employers in multi-employer schemes, which are relatively rare in the UK) acting as a temporal anchor which enables implicit cross-generational co-operation. Individual members pool investments, but generally share risks only with their employer—with ostensible control of the scheme's fund being one of the benefits to sponsoring employers. Pension funds associated with defined benefit provision are an enormously important part of the pensions landscape, traditionally—and still, for now—forming the key, direct interface between pensions provision and the wider capitalist economic model in the UK. Such practices constitute the real-world context within which defined benefit provision, and the employer's anchor role, actually exists—a context often neglected if we focus on the technical differences between different forms of provision. Because futures fail, there are clearly pressures on the state to intervene when employers are unable or unwilling to keep their promises, whether due to fund underperformance or otherwise. But the state has done so with great reluctance, and generally opted to tighten regulation on the nature of the promise, and how it is insured, in order to mitigate political and moral demands to reinforce or even replace the employer's role.

There is no equivalent anchor in defined contribution, other than individual members themselves, committing to saving throughout their lifecourse towards the goal of accumulating enough capital to produce a retirement income (as explored in Chapter 5). Obviously, as discussed in Chapter 1, an array of cross-generational practices is required in order for savings to be dematerialized and later rematerialized as a pension. But none have an underpinning role in ensuring that the future resembles at least to some extent that which is envisaged during the accumulation phase. As Peter Morris and Alasdair Palmer (2011: 25) argue—cutting through the technical language—'[t]he first and most obvious problem with a defined contribution pension is that it isn't actually a pension'. This is partly because in defined contribution saving 'you're on your own', and therefore unable to share risks (like uncertainty about how long you might live). Obviously, annuities allow this risk to be mitigated but, as Morris and Palmer also argue, defined contribution schemes do not actually provide decumulation products, rendering them fundamentally different to defined benefit schemes insofar as individuals accumulate capital without any guarantee that it can be converted to an actual income in retirement (and certainly no guarantee of what level of income it will provide for). It is highly unlikely that the state would act as an insurer or risk-hedger within defined contribution provision, to any significant degree, as in its 'lifeboat' provision for defined benefit schemes, since it would undermine the definitional responsibility on individuals within defined contribution provision to save. Welfare retrenchment in this regard is an additional nail in the coffin of collectivism. The closest thing to an *institutional* anchor in defined contribution is arguably the financial services provider, or the finance sector as a whole. While providers will not guarantee outcomes, the notion of a finance sector which is willing and able to deliver retirement-related products is integral to the imaginary of defined contribution providers. Financial products and providers themselves may over time reconfigure, but financialization, in this implicit account, is perennial.

4.1.1 A Lack of Ambition

It must be noted that it is possible to design 'hybrid' schemes which either collectivize defined contribution provision or individualize defined benefit provision, to some extent (as Chapter 3 noted), they are increasing in number in countries such as Germany and the Netherlands. The Coalition government's (or, more precisely, then pensions minister Steve Webb's) 'defined ambition' agenda launched in 2012 was designed to promote such hybrids, in the hope that 'final salary schemes are replaced by a model which offers greater flexibility to firms without loading all of the uncertainty on employees'. Webb added, without empirical verification, that he was 'hearing increasingly that firms would be interested in doing more risk-sharing if they had greater encouragement to take on risk'—implying defined ambition would 'level up' from defined contribution rather than 'level down' from defined benefit (Webb, 2012). Ironically, in 2011 the UK Supreme Court's verdict in the infamous *Bridge Trustees Ltd* v *Houldsworth and another* case led to many already existing hybrid schemes being reclassified as defined benefit schemes, insofar as they offered investment guarantees or, less commonly, forms of self-annuitization (a practice discussed below). These outlawed hybrid schemes are not to be confused with the practice of continuing defined benefit schemes which offer 'additional voluntary contributions' (AVCs) in the form of defined contribution; such practices entail two *separate* sets of pension entitlements from within a single fund, even if they are not explicitly communicated as such to members. AVCs are generally accessed by higher earners whose pay exceeds the 'pensionable earnings' definition against which their defined benefit outcomes are calculated. (However, *Bridge* ruled that where defined contribution savings built up via AVCs are annuitized via the main defined benefit fund, they are considered legally as defined benefit entitlements.)

The defined ambition agenda had an early, and probably unexpected, success when the supermarket chain Morrisons (with around 130,000 employees) decided to set up a 'cash balance' scheme to fulfil its auto-enrolment obligations. Cash balance is a form of defined benefit provision, whereby guaranteed incomes are linked explicitly to the employee's contributions (irrespective of fund performance), rather than earnings. However, this followed a decision to close the company's existing defined benefit schemes, first to new members, and eventually to new accruals—all employees were eventually moved to the cash balance scheme. Cash balance is far more common in the US, although the model has proved highly controversial (most notably in the case of IBM) insofar as employers have sought to replace final salary schemes with a less expensive alternative (Langley, 2004: 549). As indicated above, accrual rates are often as decisive as benefit design—and cash balance accrual rates are invariably lower, since they are linked to actual contributions rather than (future) salary. (This is a typical case of 'levelling down', albeit *within* defined benefit provision, rather than from defined benefit to conventional defined contribution.) Accordingly, the contributions that employers make into their employees' pension scheme obviously matters in cash balance provision (in salary-related schemes, employer contributions are effectively irrelevant to outcomes, and merely represent a way to manage the firm's pension-related obligations in a tax-efficient manner). Again, employer contribution rates tend to be much lower in cash balance schemes—only 2 per cent in the case of Morrisons. Indeed, by designating a defined benefit scheme as its vehicle for auto-enrolment, Morrisons were able to delay the application of statutory minimum contributions to their workforce (Frenkels Forensics, 2012). NDC schemes provided by the state are also a form of individualized defined benefit, strongly resembling a cash balance design; this model was briefly considered by UK policy-makers as auto-enrolment was being developed. It has been used in other European countries, as discussed in Chapter 3, but largely as a form of additional state pension provision rather than as a means for delivering occupational pensions provision.

The central imaginary of the defined ambition agenda was of course CDC provision. CDC has become increasingly common in the Netherlands, and has been promoted in the UK primarily by centrist think-tank the RSA[1] and David Pitt-Watson (an academic at a private university, better known for his previous careers as a management consultant and later Director of the fund manager Hermes) (see Pitt-Watson and Mann, 2012). In CDC, individual scheme members share investment risks with each other, but not their employer. They would then, ideally, 'self-annuitise', by drawing a regular income from the fund after retirement (as in defined benefit provision). This enables capital to remain allocated to return-generating investments, rather than disinvested at the point of an individual's retirement to fund an annuity purchase (and indeed invested more conservatively as retirement approaches). Under longstanding pensions law, self-annuitization would render CDC a form of defined benefit, since annuitization would rely on a formula, known in advance, for determining nominal annuity rates—a legal position reinforced by *Bridge*. The Department for Work and Pensions maintained the prohibition on self-annuitization until very recently. Indeed, the New Labour government had already considered the prospect of CDC before 2010, and indeed defined benefit/defined contribution hybrids more generally (new ideas are a rarity in pensions policy!). The *Bridge* decision seemingly took Steve Webb by surprise, but his Labour predecessors had already concluded that existing pensions legislation prohibited self-annuitization, and that it would not be possible to deregulate in this regard without creating 'loopholes' that employer sponsors of traditional defined benefit schemes could exploit (see DWP, 2008, 2009).

However, this position has now been modified. In early 2015, the Coalition government's Pension Schemes Act gave power to ministers to establish a new regulatory framework for risk-sharing through secondary legislation.

---

[1] The RSA is the widely used moniker for the learned society known traditionally as the Royal Society for the encouragement of *Arts*, *Manufactures*, and *Commerce*.

The initiative was abandoned as soon as the Conservative party was re-elected as a majority government, but resurrected after Theresa May became Prime Minister in 2016. The main trigger, it seems, was an agreement between the newly privatized Royal Mail and the Communication Workers Union (CWU) to establish a CDC scheme for Royal Mail's 160,000 employees, assuming the government could create the necessary regulatory framework (new primary legislation would be required in order to adjust the expected pension entitlements of workers transferred from the public to private sector). CWU seemingly saw the CDC model as an opportunity to establish a sustainable, collectivist pension scheme for all Royal Mail employees, while protecting accrued defined benefit entitlements. Crucially, however, the government has decided *not* to proceed in the planned 'third way' in pensions regulation, which had been explicitly promised in the government's 2014 response to the defined ambition consultation (see DWP, 2014). CDC will instead be regulated as a defined contribution scheme, 'so that employers have clarity about their liabilities to the scheme' (DWP, 2019a: 2). Royal Mail insisted on 'no possibility that the employer should later be found liable for the cost of any decline in the value of the fund' (see DWP, 2019a: 14). The possibility of self-annuitization means there is now a permissible grey area between defined benefit and defined contribution provision, but a relatively narrow one, categorically prohibiting the possibility of employer guarantees within CDC provision. Moreover, and crucially, in addition to 'target' benefits being modified (as in any defined contribution scheme), it will also be possible for the annuity payments to retirees to be reduced. This is the major downside of self-annuitization, leading to questions over whether CDC pensions—in not offering the kind of guarantees even available in pure defined contribution (albeit only at the point of retirement) are really even pensions at all. The Pensions Schemes Bill 2019–21 will, in all likelihood, make CDC under this framework generally permissible, but its passage through parliament was delayed by, firstly, the 2019 general election, and then secondly, the COVID-19 pandemic (see DWP, 2019a; Haves, 2020).

There are, however, two barriers to the success of CDC in the UK context. Firstly, private-sector schemes in the UK lack the scale of Dutch schemes, given the relative absence of industry-wide provision which is more common in more co-ordinated economies. It seems the only possibility of large-scale provision, which would enable investment inefficiencies and self-annuitization, arises from the levelling-down of defined benefit schemes to CDC (as in the Royal Mail case), which would be detrimental to present and future members. In other words, the 'loophole' reimagined as a legitimate corporate strategy for risk-management. Secondly, the Coalition government's (or, more precisely in this case, George Osborne's) pension freedoms agenda, discussed further in Chapter 6, which effectively ended compulsory annuitization. This means that CDC schemes could not rely on having the cash available to pay pensions to retirees, since members would be free to remove their savings at any point after the age of 55 without tax penalties. No such freedoms exist in the Netherlands.

Defined ambition was conceived—or at least presented—as a way to enhance pensions saving outcomes for the mass market of auto-enrolees, otherwise destined to end up in defined contribution schemes, by salvaging collectivist practices from the wreckage of defined benefit. Frank Field, Chair of the House of Commons Work and Pensions Committee, proclaimed in 2018, before the May government's decision, that CDC represented 'a new Beveridge' (cited in House of Commons Work and Pensions Committee, 2018b; see also 2018a). However, in practice its impact on the gulf between defined benefit and defined contribution will be extremely limited. CDC claims the mantle of collectivism, but lacks the temporal anchor upon which cross-generational collectivism in pensions provision depends, relying instead on the propensity of individuals to keep saving, and the permanence of the provider. Policy-makers are unwilling to utilize the state to provide an anchor, nor negotiate with employers to establish a genuinely new space between defined benefit and defined contribution. As explored in Section 4.1.2, there are powerful, historical trends acting upon collectivist pensions provision, related to capitalist development in the UK, which technocratic fixes such as defined ambition have failed to disrupt.

4.1.2 The Golden Age of Occupational Pensions

It is necessary to offer a basic account of the demise of defined benefit provision, in a historical context, before proceeding any further. Defined benefit provision, in terms of the number of active scheme members, peaked in the UK private sector in the late 1960s at around 8 million (at that time, active members outnumbered retired members by eight to one—the crossover came in the early 2000s). These members were predominantly male; women in full-time employment for firms with a defined benefit scheme were just as likely to be members as men in full-time roles, but women were far more likely to be employed on a part-time basis (Hannah, 1986: 66–7). Active membership dropped below 3 million before the 2008 financial crisis, and is now just over 1 million (there are now more than 11 million deferred or retired members). There are now only around 5,500 defined benefit schemes in the private sector—fewer than half of these are open to new accruals, and just over 10 per cent are open to new members. In terms of the size of funds, the peak came later, as the post-war baby boomers reached the peak of their career in terms of earnings in the late 1990s and 2000s—scheme assets were valued at around 90 per cent of UK GDP during this period, compared to below 20 per cent when active membership peaked in the 1960s.[2] Fund deficits have only been systematically tracked since the creation of the PPF. The aggregate funding level of private-sector defined benefit funds (on a full 'buy-out' basis) is now 72 per cent—alarmingly low, but significantly better than in recent years (it fell to 60 per cent in both 2009 and 2012) (PPF, 2018: 24–5). Of course, deficit figures from different years are not unproblematically comparable, since the schemes with the largest deficits are more likely to have closed, and are therefore no longer included in the data, in the intervening period. The overriding story in fund deficits is one of volatility.

It is not acknowledged sufficiently that defined contribution has not *replaced* defined benefit provision to any meaningful extent. Throughout the 2000s, while the defined benefit membership rate for employees fell from 43 to 32 per cent, the defined contribution membership rate only rose from 12 to 16 per cent (and within this, the proportion of people in *occupational* defined contribution schemes fell, in favour of 'group personal pensions' provided directly by insurance companies).[3] There are of course now around 8 million employees (around one in four) actively contributing to defined contribution schemes, as a result of auto-enrolment. Accordingly, the state is being called upon to serve as midwife for the rollout of defined contribution through soft compulsion but, having been required to fill the collectivist gap brought about by defined benefit's fairly rapid demise, is doing so on the basis that its responsibility for supporting collectivism in occupational provision is now strictly delineated, if not curtailed altogether.

Crucially, employer contributions are also significantly lower in defined contribution provision (and lower again in group personal pensions than occupational defined contribution schemes) (ONS, 2018a). The comparison is somewhat misleading, given that, as noted above, nominal employer

---

[2] Historical and current data on scheme membership, scheme status, scheme size, and contributions are available at https://www.ons.gov.uk/peoplepopulationandcommunity/personalandhouseholdfinances/pensionssavingsandinvestments/datasets/occupationalpensionschemessurvey, https://www.ons.gov.uk/employmentandlabourmarket/peopleinwork/workplacepensions/bulletins/annualsurveyofhoursandearningspensiontables/2018provisionaland2017revisedresults, https://www.ons.gov.uk/economy/investmentspensionsandtrusts/compendium/pensiontrends/2014-11-28/chapter9pensionschemefundingandinvestment2013edition#pension-scheme-funding-positions, and https://www.ons.gov.uk/economy/investmentspensionsandtrusts/compendium/pensiontrends/2014-11-28/chapter6privatepensions2013edition#participation-in-private-pensions. See also the PPF's *Purple Book* series at https://www.ppf.co.uk/purple-book.

[3] See note 2.

contributions in defined benefit provision are a function of anticipated liabilities, rather than the employer's benevolence—steady increases in contribution rates were therefore driven by higher liabilities (a risk not relevant to employers in defined contribution provision). Nevertheless, while employers are obviously not as committed institutionally to defined contribution as they were to defined benefit provision, they are undoubtedly now committing much less cash towards their employees' retirement (with no evidence that take-home pay has increased as a result). Furthermore, individuals are not contributing at equivalent levels either. Of course, the fact that minimum contributions in the new auto-enrolment system have been phased in gradually from a very low base makes such findings somewhat problematic; there are now many more employers sponsoring pension schemes than before 2008, and many more employees participating, but the new schemes tend to be clustered at very low contribution rates. The increase in legal minimums over time will partially alleviate this trend. Yet the default contributions of 3 per cent for employers and 5 per cent for employees (and these percentages only apply on a band of earnings, not necessarily full salaries) finally introduced in April 2019 are significantly below the rate of pensions saving typically evident in defined benefit provision (17.2 and 6.3 per cent (of entire salaries), respectively).[4]

Obviously, the demise of collectivism has not occurred in an economic vacuum. There are a series of principal characteristics of the typical defined benefit scheme sponsor which no longer pertain. Firstly, defined benefit provision was most likely to be found in one of three industries: manufacturing, retail, and financial services (PLSA, 2017). Deindustrialization and the decline of traditional 'high street' retailers means that many of the large employers sponsoring defined benefit schemes in the early post-war period are now much smaller, or defunct. One of the ironies of the financialization of occupational pensions in the UK is that many finance sector firms have retained defined benefit funds for at least some of their workforce—albeit generally not the largest employers. The utilities are relevant here too, although the picture is somewhat murkier. Defined benefit provision among utility providers became firmly established under public ownership, but survived privatization in the 1980s and 1990s—although protections have generally been eroded for more recent recruits.

Table 4.1 details the 2018 distribution of defined benefit scheme membership by industry. As we would expect, those industries dominated by public-sector employment are hugely over-represented among the defined benefit scheme members (education, for instance, employs 13 per cent of all UK employees,

---

[4] Ibid.

Table 4.1 Defined benefit (DB) pension scheme membership (thousands) in 2018 by industry

Industry	No. of jobs	No. in DB scheme	% of all workers	% of all in DB schemes
Agriculture, forestry, and fishing	147	8	0.5	0.1
Mining and quarrying	42	5	0.1	0.1
Manufacturing	2,663	293	9.5	3.8
Electricity, gas, steam, and air conditioning supply	188	75	0.7	1.0
Water supply; sewerage, waste management, and remediation activities	180	24	0.6	0.3
Construction	1,060	60	3.8	0.8
Wholesale and retail trade; repair of motor vehicles and motorcycles	4,295	230	15.3	2.9
Transportation and storage	1,126	282	3.9	3.6
Accommodation and food service activities	1,661	58	5.8	0.7
Information and communication	1,047	70	3.6	0.9
Financial and insurance activities	1,002	141	3.5	1.8
Real estate activities	387	65	1.3	0.8
Professional, scientific, and technical activities	1,980	142	6.8	1.8
Administrative and support service activities	1,677	88	5.8	1.1
Public administration and defence; compulsory social security	1,365	1,142	4.7	14.6
Education	3,844	2,834	13.3	36.3
Human health and social work activities	4,178	2,160	14.5	27.6
Arts, entertainment, and recreation	618	66	2.1	0.8

Note: ASHE is a survey of jobs based on information from employers. It therefore does not include the self-employed, nor account for individuals with more than one job. According to ASHE, the UK has 28,085,000 employee jobs, of which 7,801,000 encompass defined benefit scheme membership (to the nearest 1,000)

Source: Annual Survey of Hours and Earnings (ASHE) (2018) (including author calculations using ASHE data), available at: https://www.ons.gov.uk/employmentandlabourmarket/peopleinwork/workplacepensions/bulletins/ annualsurveyofhoursandearningspensiontables/2018provisionaland2017revisedresults

but encompasses 36 per cent of all in defined benefit schemes—this includes those employed by universities, discussed further in Section 4.5). The electricity and gas industry, with its legacy of public ownership, is slightly over-represented in this regard and, similarly, the transportation and storage industry is only slightly under-represented. The employees of most industries are very under-represented among the defined benefit membership, including retail, but manufacturing and finance—the other industries with a strong tradition of defined benefit provision—are somewhat better represented. Nevertheless, employees in these industries do now comprise a smaller proportion of the defined benefit membership than they do the employed workforce overall. Accommodation and food services employees are extremely under-represented, with almost 6 per cent of total employees, but less than 1 per cent of employees in defined benefit schemes.

Secondly, although the trend appears not to have been tracked in any systematic way, the growth of foreign ownership among the UK's largest firms—particularly evident in the manufacturing and retail industries—is also relevant. Pension scheme 'restructuring' is a common consequence of merger and acquisition (M&A) activity involving overseas firms, although in many cases the firms being taken over will have already actively sought to minimize their pension obligations. The more important trend is probably that new foreign-owned firms (and subsidiaries) in the UK are less likely to voluntarily establish defined benefit schemes. While in 2013 61 firms in the FTSE 100 list of the largest publicly listed UK companies had a defined benefit scheme open to new accruals, none had a defined benefit scheme open to new members. In contrast, twenty years earlier, *all* firms in the FTSE 100 had fully open defined benefit schemes (LCP, 2013). Foreign ownership of FTSE 100 shares increased hugely over this period (although the proportion of revenue arising from UK operations declined, making the FTSE 100 index a relatively unreliable indicator of the UK economy as a whole) (Brett, 2017). At the same time, restructuring seems to be just as likely in rare cases where 'British' firms transfer from foreign owners back to domestic ownership. Lufthansa's sale of low-cost airline bmi to British Airways is a case in point; in a highly unusual move, bmi's defined benefit pension scheme was 'dumped' into the PPF at the point of sale, despite both the selling and buying parents being solvent companies.

Just as the demise of defined benefit is symptomatic of wider structural changes in the UK economy, so too is the failure of defined contribution provision to replace defined benefit in terms of coverage. As the economy became increasingly dominated by the service industry, and indeed low-value, labour-intense service industries, the rationale for employers to voluntarily provide decent pension schemes was undermined. In the context of the weakening of employment protections from the 1980s onwards, and increasing conditionality in out-of-work benefits, employers had few incentives to invest in the remuneration and welfare of their workforce. Trade union density is much lower in service industries, particularly among young workers (BEIS, 2018), which largely removes the possibility of workers demanding (better) pensions coverage via industrial action. Indeed, recent years have seen a growth in self-employment—and specifically poorly paid self-employment (ONS, 2018c)—in such industries, and as such the absence of any access to a workplace pension scheme, or entitlement to employer contributions. Auto-enrolment is rendered irrelevant in the process. UK policy-makers are certainly aware of the possibility that the rise of the so-called 'gig' economy has seen the classification of many workers as self-employed when, in practice, they have contractual obligations to specific firms which resemble traditional employment relations. The May government asked Matthew Taylor to review such labour market practices. However, despite Taylor's role as Chief Executive of the RSA (champions of CDC), and indeed as a key Downing Street adviser at the time auto-enrolment was embraced by the Labour government, his report offers no specific recommendations on extending pension rights to this group of workers. Instead, it merely discusses ways in which pensions saving may be made easier for self-employed people (see Taylor, 2017).

Policy-makers have frequently insisted that the 'flexibilisation' of the UK workforce makes defined contribution a more appropriate form of pensions provision for contemporary labour market conditions. In the key 2006 green paper introducing auto-enrolment, the Labour government (during Tony Blair's truncated third term as Prime Minister) said the new pensions system must, among other things, 'fit in with modern life and the greater likelihood of people moving between jobs' (DWP, 2006b: 44). There were frequent references to the portability of defined contribution savings. For the avoidance of doubt, despite the white paper claiming to deliver the vision of the independent Pensions Commission—charged with reinventing pensions provision in the UK in the light of the perceived undersaving crisis—the Commission made no reference, across its many reports, to labour market flexibility in justifying defined contribution provision as the basis of auto-enrolment. Nevertheless, according to the government:

> [Defined benefit] schemes are those that offer a pension based on a certain formula (usually years worked and final salary). They are not necessarily better than [defined contribution] schemes, where the pension depends on the performance of underlying investments such as shares. For many people the greater flexibility of [defined contribution] provision better matches the greater mobility in the labour market and the increase in the number of jobs people may expect to do during their lives. (DWP, 2006b: 34)

It is an unsubstantiated argument which rests upon the slippery notion that defined benefit and defined contribution are broadly equivalent, and only technically distinct, forms of pensions provision—rather than fundamentally different approaches to risk-sharing, inter-generational co-operation, and consumption smoothing. Yet even the Pensions Policy Institute (PPI)—normally a reliable, independent source of research on pensions provision—fell victim to the logic around the time auto-enrolment was being determined:

> A [defined benefit] scheme may not be the most appropriate pensions saving vehicle for all employees. For example, for employees who frequently switch jobs a portable [defined contribution] scheme may be more suitable…Working patterns are changing. When [defined benefit] schemes were first established the workforce was mainly male and jobs tended to be for life. This is no longer the case. The employment rate for women has risen from around 56 [per cent] in 1971 to around 70 [per cent] in 2005 but women are still more likely to be working part-time than men. Also women are more likely to be economically inactive than men, taking career breaks to care for children or the disabled. So employers could see advantages in providing a flexible [defined contribution] scheme to cater for a more flexible workforce.　(Sanchez et al., 2007: 30)

There is no reason, at all, that defined contribution savings are more portable than defined benefit savings—the latter simply requires a 'transfer value' to be calculated in accordance with relevant regulation. In practice, as discussed in Chapter 6, the pots being accumulated as a result of auto-enrolment are proving to be incredibly difficult to switch from one workplace scheme to another when an employee changes jobs. Furthermore, the PPI's implicit argument that the increasing number of women in the workforce (that they are more likely to work part time or take career breaks is of no relevance to the funding model of a firm's pensions scheme) means that employers should be liberated from obligations to guarantee their employees' pension outcomes is rather outrageous. Obviously, the activation of female workers, especially in lower-skilled service industries, is part of the real-world context in which employers have become more reluctant to support collectivist pensions provision. However, we must resist attempts by academic researchers—let alone policy-makers—to obscure this political-economic process beneath highly technical and ultimately misleading arguments about the suitability of different benefit structures.

4.1.3　A Very Brief History of SERPS

UK policy-makers, particularly on the left, have long understood the importance of defined benefit provision, but also that access to collectivist pensions is highly uneven. As such, even in a largely Beveridgean system combining a limited state pension with voluntaristic provision in the private sector, we have witnessed an impulse for the state to provide a Bismarckian, earnings-related public pension—either as a floor for standards in the private sector, or to compensate for the absence of private provision. The temptation would be to see this impulse as a desire to mitigate or delay the historical demise of defined benefit, but in practice it largely coincided with the peak era of defined benefit provision.

This is not to suggest that policy-makers were particularly successful in such endeavours. The creation of SERPS in the late 1970s stands as this agenda's landmark achievement, but it followed the failure of earlier, more ambitious plans—and SERPS itself was undermined almost from inception. In 1957, the Labour opposition published proposals for a new system of 'national superannuation'. It was the *success* of collectivism in the private sector, and the failure of the state to provide an adequate state pension, that was its main rationale, as the party feared that access to defined benefit for a 'privileged minority' on the public and private sectors was creating 'two nations in retirement' (Labour Party, 1957; cited in Pemberton, 2010: 46). National superannuation would have provided retirement benefits broadly equivalent to typical occupational schemes, but with an element of redistribution from high to low earners (which is of course not particularly pronounced in many Bismarckian public pensions). The scheme was also designed on a funded basis, with the capital created used for investments that would modernize industry and raise living standards.

The idea was not taken up by the Conservative government in office at the time. The finance sector campaigned heavily against national superannuation, arguing that it represented the nationalization of private pensions. The characterization was not inaccurate: since the plan depended financially on new workers being compelled to enter the scheme, it would have led effectively to the closure of defined benefit pensions provision in the private sector. As such, most trade unions—upon whom Labour depended—joined the finance sector in opposing the plan. Unions were concerned about the potential impact on pension entitlements already accrued, but also the possibility that their members would be subsidizing the pensions of lower earners (Pemberton, 2010: 47–9; see also Bridgen and Meyer, 2011). By the time the Labour party returned to government in the mid-1960s, with Richard Crossman—national superannuation's main champion—serving as Secretary of State for Social Services, the proposals had been significantly scaled back. Crucially, the funded model had been replaced by an unfunded model; this would have meant the state using its fiscal powers to support occupational pensions to an even greater extent, albeit via a much less generous scheme.

But it also arguably challenged collectivist principles by denying the possibility of a state-run investment fund taking ownership of UK companies.

The revised plan never came to pass, but it is important to note that the Conservative government had already introduced Graduated Retirement Benefit in the early 1960s, providing a small, earnings-related top-up to the state pension. Limited in scope, the Graduated Retirement Benefit was nevertheless significant in widening the state's role in this regard. This role was enhanced by the introduction of SERPS in the late 1970s, under the stewardship of Barbara Castle. SERPS was more explicitly focused on providing benefits to those unable to access private provision, in recognition of the narrowing coverage of defined benefit provision in the private sector, even if membership levels remained high. This included entitlements for those with limited labour market records due to caring responsibilities. As noted in Chapter 2, the introduction of SERPS essentially echoed the dynamic fuelling the introduction of state pension provision more generally at the beginning of the century, that is, compensating for the inadequacies of occupational provision in the private sector. Yet SERPS also had distinctive elements which have profoundly shaped the recent development of UK pensions provision. Above all, the scheme encompassed the introduction of both the 'Guaranteed Minimum Pension' (GMP) and 'contracting out'. The former ensured minimal accrual rates in private provision, to ensure workers were no worse off by exercising the latter mechanism, which allowed lower National Insurance contributions for employees (and their employers) contributing to a private scheme. GMPs were revised to ensure indexation against inflation from 1988 onwards.

However, the Thatcher government had already begun to scale back SERPS by this point, principally by narrowing the band of earnings upon which SERPS entitlements were accrued (Macnicol, 2015: 56). As discussed in Chapter 2, New Labour replaced SERPS with S2P in 2002; this change was ostensibly progressive insofar as entitlements for lower earners and those with limited labour market records increased in generosity, but can also be seen as further undermining collectivism. New Labour then legislated to minimize the earnings-related element of S2P over time—a process which was accelerated by the creation of a STSP by the Coalition government. As such, we have witnessed in recent years the demise of the state's own attempts to provide collectivist, occupational pensions for citizens. These attempts had of course been rather limited due to concerns about the state crowding out private provision and taking on spending obligations deemed unaffordable, but the key point here is that the notion that the state was simply intervening (perhaps inadequately) in response to the demise of private-sector defined benefit provision is too simplistic. Approximately speaking, collectivism in state earnings-related pensions, and in the private sector, expanded in tandem—with each suffering from similar limitations and contradictions. The demise of private-sector provision has been attributed to a range of pressures acting upon employers' ability to sustain provision (as discussed further below). However, in the case of state provision, in which the potential scale of the scheme and ability to compel participation means such pressures can be minimized, an ideological and institutional aversion to fully embracing collectivism in UK pensions provision is much more apparent.

4.2. Bang, Storm, Crash

This section addresses in more detail the factors behind the demise of defined benefit provision in the private sector, or more precisely the political decisions and economic practices which have shaped the development of this dimension of pensions provision in the UK. It first addresses the issue of regulation, which is often seen as a decisive element in the decline story, before discussing how practices related to defined benefit provision have interacted with structural changes in the economy (and policy-makers' responses to these changes). It also briefly discusses how the finance sector has responded to, and benefited from, the evolution of defined benefit provision.

4.2.1 Regulation and Deregulation

The statutory rules on the form that defined benefit schemes and entitlements must take are often accused of raising the cost of provision for employers—and therefore causing, or at least accelerating, the demise of pensions collectivism in the private sector. Until around the 1980s, many elements of provision were determined on a discretionary basis by sponsoring employers, with limited protection for accrued rights in the event of employer insolvency. John Major's Conservative government of 1990–97 was responsible for some of the most significant changes (although building upon earlier practice). The introduction of indexation in line with price inflation (capped at 5 per cent per annum) for pensions in payment in 1995 has probably been the most significant (the cap was reduced to 2.5 per cent by New Labour in 2005).

The Major government had already introduced inflation protection for deferred pension rights (that is, for members who left a scheme before reaching retirement age) in the early 1990s. But this simply expanded protection for deferred members arising from the GMP system introduced alongside SERPS, which provided for annual indexation of GMP-related rights (with slightly different mechanisms for achieving this for rights accrued before and after 1988). It should be noted that it was not until the mid-1970s—or indeed when the relevant regulations were strengthened in the late 1980s—that deferred members (or 'early leavers') had any protection of their accrued rights within defined benefit schemes. Perhaps as surprisingly, it was not until the mid-1990s that regulation on how defined benefit pension scheme members are treated in the event of employer insolvency was regularized— up to this point, the loss of all members' accrued rights was not uncommon (for more detail, see Bridgen and Meyer, 2011: 270). Regulations were later strengthened to define the resulting unsecured debts in accordance with the buy-out costs (that is, the cost of achieving benefits equivalent to accrued rights via an insurance product), and TPR was given powers in 2005 to include connected employers within the scope of such regulations (to prevent M&A and restructuring activity liberating sponsoring employers from this debt).

A series of regulatory changes in the early 2000s affected how capital in defined benefit funds is invested, and how financial circumstances are reported. Most importantly, the introduction of the Financial Reporting Standard 17 in 2002 tightened accounting standards and increased transparency by mandating, among other things, that scheme funding levels had to be reported on the balance sheets of sponsoring employers. According to the PPI, '[t]his fundamentally changed the way that pension liabilities are viewed, making them more transparent to shareholders, as well as shortening the investment horizon for DB schemes in cases where trustees agree to invest in such a way that would help sponsors to meet their accounting objective' (PPI, 2016: 3). The mid-2000s also saw the introduction of the triennial valuation cycle, by which schemes must update TPR on the value of their assets and liabilities every three years (this includes the nominal financial value of the employer 'covenant'). This process was ostensibly introduced in order to determine appropriate levy payments into the PPF, with schemes at greater risk of failure paying higher levies. But it has also served to shorten investment horizons, insofar as investments that might produce higher returns, albeit over a timescale longer than three years, are disincentivized (Mabbett, 2020). (Research by the OECD has found, relatedly, that risk management strategies driven by regulatory or accounting standards tend to impede the ability of defined benefit pension funds to take advantage as investors of their long-time horizons (see Franzen, 2010).)

It would be disingenuous to deny that regulatory change (especially in the context of increasing life expectancy) has increased costs for sponsoring employers—even with the dilution of future rights seen in many defined benefit schemes, delivering the promised outcomes has become more expensive, and the promise itself more difficult to renege upon (see Turner and Hughes, 2008). The state, in essence, has become increasingly concerned with setting standards in defined benefit provision, in terms of both outcomes for members and the conduct of sponsoring employers. But we should not confuse this with the notion that the state is trying to protect or underpin pensions collectivism in general. The primary objective is to protect rights already accrued, rather than enable ongoing accruals. In this way, policy-makers can help to prevent members—who might have lost accrued rights, or seen their value eroded by inflation—falling back onto means-tested benefits, especially in later life. We can also speculate, with less certainty, that measures to strengthen employers' responsibility for employers, and the transparency of funding positions to investors, mean that accelerating the demise of defined benefit provision in the private sector has been an important objective for some policy-makers.

It is telling, therefore, that prevailing approaches to discounting the liabilities of defined benefit funds in valuation processes, linked to gilt yields, tend to overstate the future cost of pension obligations, at least from some perspectives. Con Keating (2010, 2011; see also Keating et al., 2013), the high-profile Head of Research at BrightonRock (an indemnity provider to pension funds) has devised the alternative 'internal growth rate' to defined benefit valuations, which generally eschews conventional discounting in favour of cash accounting. Similarly, the actuarial consultancy First Actuarial recommends a discount rate based on expected investment returns, which are generally much higher than gilt yields, and indeed produces an alternative index of defined benefit funding positions on this basis which invariably paints a rosier picture than official indexes.[5] Judged on their own terms, these alternative approaches to discounting and valuation are perfectly plausible. However, they also have an unfortunate, other-worldly quality, insofar as they implicitly build in assumptions about the shape of future labour and capital markets, and indeed the viability of certain employers irrespective of their pension obligations. The logic that discounting with reference to income from contributions or investments would actually encourage employers to maintain defined benefit provision by preventing the inflation of liabilities, therefore by definition making future income safer, is almost impeccable. But the notion that over the very long term pension funds can constantly outperform the wider capitalist economy is not a gamble that the funds'

---

[5] See https://www.firstactuarial.co.uk/resources/fab-index/.

guarantors—capitalist enterprises—are prepared to take. And the state will not ask them to take it. It is also worth pointing out here that inter-generational justice campaigners tend to be highly critical of even conventional, conservative approaches to discounting, for not inflating liability values enough, and therefore, so the argument goes, creating hidden debts for future generations (see Hanton, 2011).

It is difficult to make the leap from the acknowledgement that regulation has increased costs in defined benefit provision, to the argument that regulation has *caused* decline. However, it does seem that this logic was present in policy discourse by the mid-2000s. The Pensions Commission estimated that, as a result of the interaction of regulation and demographic change, the cost of a 'typical final salary pension promise' had risen from around 10–14 per cent of salary when schemes were initially established to around 22–26 per cent (Pensions Commission, 2005: 122–3). A study commissioned by the Labour government as part of a 'deregulatory review' around this time—after auto-enrolment had been legislated for—argued that 'the ever-increasing regulatory burden', alongside higher life expectancy, meant that employers were highly unlikely to use defined benefit schemes to meet their new statutory obligations (Lewin and Sweeney, 2007). The study was conducted by Unilever's former Head of Pensions alongside a leading trade unionist, Ed Sweeney of Amicus (later subsumed by Unite)—demonstrating again the peculiar role of British trade unions in resisting the state's role in managing defined benefit provision in the private sector. (The same dynamic was evident in the mid-2010s, when UK trade unions joined forces with the Confederation of British Industry and National Association of Pension Funds (NAPF) to oppose the European Commission's attempt, noted in Chapter 3, to introduce new solvency requirements on defined benefit pension schemes (see NAPF et al., 2014).) The government's response essentially endorsed this view, criticizing 'the weight of regulation' faced by employers while acknowledging that each individual instance of regulatory action had been well intentioned (DWP, 2007: 107). The PPI quite rightly pointed out that it was impossible to isolate the specific costs attributable to defined benefit regulation, nor indeed the impact on employer behaviour (Sanchez et al., 2007: 27). We must consider also the counterfactual: if regulation around, say, the protection of members' rights had not been strengthened, workers may have opted not to join schemes in greater numbers, arguably increasing the burden for employers in servicing older cohorts' guaranteed benefits.

We can say with more confidence that an accelerated decline has at least been an *inadvertent* consequence of regulatory activity. Responding to cost rises by instilling short-termist horizons upon employers and scheme managers fundamentally contradicts the tempo of inter-generational relations in defined benefits provision, effectively inhibiting the long-termist investment strategy traditionally upheld by older cohorts in return for the cash contributions of future cohorts. Defined benefit provision was being delivered in a context quite different to that which had been envisaged when the large cohorts approaching retirement had begun to save. Policy-makers responded to this failed future by seeking to insulate existing scheme members from the potential consequences, rather than seeking to make provision compatible with an emerging future. This is a pattern which has recurred in recent years, as discussed below.

The story of strengthened regulation would be incomplete without noting the part played by instances of *de*regulation in the demise of defined benefit provision. There are two key examples, both of which pre-date the regulatory strengthening that occurred in the 1990s. As discussed in Chapter 1, the 1986 Social Security Act made contracting out—but not GMPs—applicable in defined contribution schemes. This provided an enormous incentive to employers to establish defined contribution schemes to access lower National Insurance rates, without being required to ensure outcomes are above a certain level. There are 'protected rights' associated with defined contribution contracting-out arrangements, but these generally relate to the type of annuities that might be purchased at the point of retirement. (New Labour effectively abolished defined contribution contracting out in 2007—acknowledging that it was inconceivable that individuals would be better off saving in a defined contribution scheme rather than contributing to the S2P.) Another piece of legislation in 1986 (the Finance Act) encouraged employers to take 'holidays' from contributing to their defined benefit schemes. There was, on the one hand, a fear that employers were overfunding schemes in order to avoid corporation tax, and as such the maximum acceptable funding level was set at 105 per cent of present liabilities. However, given that this was before regulations on scheme valuations were tightened (and indeed before life expectancy improvements were sufficiently well understood) the change ultimately allowed for many schemes to become (chronically) underfunded (Sanchez et al., 2007: 24). It would be unfair to conclude that this was intentional on the part of the Thatcher government, but it is certainly consistent with elite-level indifference to the sustainability of collectivist provision in the private sector, and indeed wider ideological commitment to deregulating corporate governance. Interestingly, the Pensions Commission (2005: 122–3) suggested that contribution holidays were not designed to undermine defined benefit; instead, the policy was based on an 'irrational exuberance' underpinning the Thatcher government's belief that strong UK equity performance would endure indefinitely, ensuring consistent pension fund surpluses. Section 4.2.2 discusses the period in which this assumption was challenged.

4.2.2 From the Perfect Storm to the Great Crash

In the early 2000s, the notion of defined benefit pension provision being engulfed by a 'perfect storm' took root (see Clark and Monk, 2006). In this account, the storm had three main components. Firstly, a reduction in investment returns, especially in relation to equities, to which UK funds remained heavily exposed. There is no doubt that equities were performing less well in the late 1990s and early 2000s (even before the dot.com bust) than in the 1980s and early 1990s—as noted above, the earlier boom conditions had created the nominal surpluses which had permitted contribution holidays among employers. Secondly, low interest rates affected not only returns on investment in gilts, but, crucially, the rate at which future liabilities were discounted. In tandem, thirdly, with a growing appreciation of longevity gains and the impending retirement of the baby boomer cohorts, the value of scheme liabilities was revised upwards at precisely the moment when fund performance was becoming far less reliable.

This account, however, is too parsimonious. Most importantly, while many small schemes closed during this period, the rate of decline in active membership of defined benefit pension schemes did not actually increase during this period (Berry and Stanley, 2013: 13; ONS, 2014). Furthermore, a lengthy period of low inflation also helped to reduce the cost of pensions in payment, and a slowdown in earnings growth helped to mitigate the rising value of liabilities. (There appears to be an ideological blindness in this regard, whereby earnings are always forecast to grow steadily as a normal aspect of capitalist growth; on the other hand, scenarios in which defined benefit provision becomes less expensive are rendered unknowable.) The fact, moreover, that many schemes had *already* closed to new entrants deprived schemes of cash contributions—especially important when investment returns are disappointing.

In a sense, the notion of a 'perfect storm' merely validated a process that was already well under way. Did the 2008 financial crisis have a more profound impact? The rate of scheme closures seemed to accelerate around the time of the financial crisis, but has actually been slower since 2010 than the years immediately before the crisis (see PPF, 2010, 2018). The question was largely answered in Chapter 1. Although equity values fell sharply in 2008

(OECD, 2008), and have been volatile ever since, the process of de-equitization among pension funds in the UK has softened the blow. This trend has quickened in pace since 2008, but it was already evident before the financial crisis that funds were moving away from equity allocations in general, and specifically UK equities (Berry and Barber, 2017). There has been much concern over the impact of QE on pension provision in the UK—including from Ros Altmann (2017), a high-profile pensions consultant and campaigner who was briefly Pensions Minister after the 2015 general election—but no definitive conclusion. As funds moved into bonds instead of equities, the upward pressure on gilt prices—a deliberate objective of QE—will have affected returns, as well as compelling lower discount rates. However, funds had de-equitized by moving into corporate bonds rather than simply gilts (especially after 2008), and QE also injected cash into funds, as well as boosting the value of equities, bonds, and gilts that were already held (Joyce et al., 2014). While schemes were greatly concerned about QE, especially the impact on discount rates (NAPF, 2011), there is, again, little reason to conclude that the great crash, like the perfect storm, fundamentally altered the path of defined benefit's demise. Indeed, fund deficits have generally fallen in recent years, although we should of course be careful not to read a great amount into such results—schemes' funding levels have become rather volatile, and lower deficits may largely be a case of only the most viable schemes now being left standing. Clearly, the sudden and long-term economic impact of the COVID-19 pandemic will also affect defined benefit schemes. For instance, the Universities Superannuation Scheme (USS), the UK's largest private-sector scheme, saw its deficit triple virtually overnight in March 2020 (S. Smith, 2020). The pandemic is likely to accelerate the winding up of schemes already being wound up.

The particular investment portfolios of funds obviously shapes how they are affected by economic downturns—the issue of pension-related investments (in defined benefit and defined contribution) will be discussed further in Chapter 7. It is essential to point out here, however, that the financial conditions affecting the viability of defined benefit provision apply equally, if not more so, to defined contribution. Paul Langley (2004) made this case in relation to the early 2000s, before UK policy-makers boosted defined contribution through auto-enrolment. The OECD's (2008) analysis is clear that trust-based defined contribution schemes (where it is possible to track fund performance) were no less affected than defined benefit funds in 2008; the same will in all likelihood be found regarding the 2020 pandemic. The difference is that in defined benefit provision, the consequences are suffered primarily by the sponsoring employer. The consequences for individual savers in defined contribution schemes will be largely equivalent, and indeed particularly damaging for those reaching retirement, and therefore annuitizing, during a downturn. But downturns and even financial crises appear not to have dissuaded policy-makers from sustaining, and indeed enhancing, UK pensions provision's reliance on capital market performance.

The extent to which we can point to immediate financial circumstances in explaining the demise of defined benefit provision is limited. There is a bigger story here about the role of employers as the principal temporal anchor of collectivist occupational provision—a reliance on employers performing such a role voluntarily has made defined benefit pension schemes inherently vulnerable. At the same time, it is usually unfair to blame individual employers for abdicating this voluntary role in securing their workforce's financial well-being over the long term. In the majority of cases where defined benefit schemes have been closed, the employer in question has been in danger of collapse, or at least in the process of scaling back its business operations. (Some of the more controversial cases—essentially, where schemes enter the PPF—will be discussed below, but generally speaking these cases involve schemes which were already closed to new members.) However, at least part of the explanation lies in how these processes interact. Capital market volatility is not an exogenous threat to pension funds, but rather, as Minskyan theory suggests, a consequence of short-term, speculative investment activity, which funds themselves engaged in. Investment *in* defined benefit funds by employers became increasingly incompatible with prevailing accumulation strategies, even as investment *by* funds tended to reinforce the finance sector's amplification of speculative activity—precisely because they could no longer rely on cash contributions to mitigate their structural weaknesses (see Engelen, 2003). Regulators tend to support short-termism during periods of economic expansion—and it is no coincidence that New Labour strengthened the privileging of shareholders within UK corporate governance (legitimizing their pursuit of short-term, financial returns) during the 'perfect storm' period (Deakin, 2018). It would be easy, and not wholly unfair, to associate such dynamics with the wider process of financialization, especially in tandem with the state's support for individualized provision in response to the demise of collectivism in the private sector. However, defined benefit provision clearly already represented a highly financialized means of delivering pensions (see Pendleton and Gospel, 2017: 21–2)—albeit a form of financialization which proved unsustainable.

It is worth noting, finally, and relatedly, that the demise of defined benefit provision has led directly to the creation of new financial products, in the form of bulk annuities. Generally speaking, these could take the form of buy-outs, where pension funds pay a fee to an insurance company for the insurer to take over scheme liabilities (that is, the responsibility of paying members' pensions), or a buy-in, whereby liabilities technically remain the responsibility of the scheme, but a premium is paid to the insurer in return for pension payments being underwritten. The practice is common in the US and Canada—but the UK is the global 'pioneer' (Datz, 2017). By 2018, bulk annuity contracts valued at around £80 billion had been signed—equivalent to around 5 per cent of the total value of liabilities in remaining defined benefit schemes in the UK (Barnett Waddingham, 2018). The market is expected to grow significantly (Ralph, 2017), although it is worth noting that such products are, at the moment, prohibitively expensive for most funds. This is especially the case for smaller funds, in which deficits are typically larger (as such, although scheme deficits are routinely measured in relation to fund buy-out values, actual schemes in deficit usually cannot access the bulk annuities market that this value refers to). Since insurance companies generally require fees or premiums which *exceed* the value of liabilities, bulk annuities enable the transferral of risk, not a reduction of costs. However, as the market matures we may see insurers willing to accept lower premiums, if they are confident their products can remain profitable through economies of scale—there are also signs that the asset management industry (at a cost advantage due to the absence of solvency regulations) are developing new buy-in options to challenge insurers (Peters, 2018). These emerging practices demonstrate the intimate role of financial services in all aspects of UK pensions provision—financialization may have problematized collectivist pensions provision, but the development of collectivist provision would arguably have been impossible in the UK without the willing participation of the finance sector. We must be careful, however, not to accept the notion that buy-outs and similar practices represent 'de-risking': while this 'may make individual companies safer at the microprudential level…a series of transactions involving a limited number of longevity risk "buyers" (insurance and reinsurance companies) may produce more risk concentration…raising macroprudential concerns' (Datz, 2017). In other words, while population ageing may not represent the existential threat to pensions provision often assumed, finance practices ostensibly designed to combat longevity risks may indeed be amplifying them.

4.3. Regulating Defined Benefit amid Austerity

In recent years, UK policy-makers' approach to the regulation of defined benefit has followed a familiar pattern: concern about the ongoing financial burden for employers of sponsoring (closed) defined benefit pension schemes is expressed, consultations take place, and nothing changes very much. Commentators like to refer to 'zombie' schemes to characterize the UK's residual defined benefit provision: no longer alive, but—protected by law, and overseen by employers just about healthy enough to avoid insolvency—very difficult to kill. We can perhaps see contemporary efforts to reform defined benefit regulation through the same lens.

Again, it is important not to see economic shocks such as the 2008 financial crisis as the trigger for significant change in UK pensions policy. New Labour had looked extensively at how defined benefit pensions regulations could be relaxed, primarily through the Pensions Commission. The implementation of the Commission's main recommendations around auto-enrolment into defined contribution schemes provided the main impetus for seeking to reduce the burden on employers sponsoring defined benefit schemes. However, the 'deregulatory review' of defined benefit provision launched in 2007, cited above, was also justified on the basis of offering support to large employers during an economic downturn. Nevertheless, the review produced little of note. A series of radical changes supported by employers included making the indexation of pensions in payment conditional rather than mandatory, and even the widespread conversion of final salary defined benefit schemes to cash balance, hybrid, or CDC schemes (Maer and Thurley, 2009: 21–7). Yet none could be pursued without jeopardizing rights already accrued—which would have been legally difficult and politically risky (to say the least).

Having criticized the Labour government for its seemingly timid approach to 'the growing burden of regulation' on employers (see Conservative Party Economic Competitiveness Policy Group, 2007: 50–3), the Conservative party developed new proposals upon taking office (as part of the Coalition government). They allowed defined benefit schemes to index pensions in payment using the Consumer Price Index (CPI) rather than the Retail Price Index (RPI); the former usually shows a slower rate of price inflation. However, while CPI was adopted as a measure of inflation for public-sector pensions and the state pension by the Coalition, the legislation enabling the use of CPI in the private sector did not extend to new powers for employers to unilaterally change scheme rules where RPI was explicitly recorded as the scheme's inflation measure (that is, the vast majority of schemes). As such, the impact of this switch was negligible. The Coalition government also consulted, at the request of the NAPF, on the possibility of 'smoothing' valuations to mitigate the perceived negative impact of QE, but was unable to find a technical solution which would have actually benefited schemes financially (DWP, 2013c). One of the Coalition government's most consequential changes was a slight relaxation of rules around employer debt in so-called multi-employer defined benefit schemes (in practice, where subsidiaries of a corporate group participate in a single defined benefit scheme) when one or more subsidiaries is to cease employing any active member of the scheme. The triggering of debt (effectively, from one subsidiary to another) when groups restructured was said to 'inhibit corporate activity' (DWP, 2011: 6). The new regulations enabled a given subsidiary to transfer its liabilities within the group without triggering a claim upon its corporate assets.

Perhaps the most controversial measure proposed by the Coalition government was an attempt to consider the long-term growth prospects of employers alongside the protection of members' benefits when struggling schemes agreed a plan for 'deficit recovery contributions' with TPR (as part of the triennial valuation process). The initiative resulted in a new statutory objective for TPR ('in relation to DB [defined benefit] scheme funding, to minimise any adverse impact on the sustainable growth of an employer' (TPR, 2017a: 5)), alongside existing objectives around protecting member benefits, defending the PPF, and promoting good governance within pension schemes. The change was proposed as part of the same 'Pensions and Growth' consultation which also encompassed consultation on 'smoothing'; the government argued that it 'would provide employers with reassurance that in these difficult economic times their position will be taken into account' (DWP, 2013c: 5). The significance of the change is unclear, since ensuring the health of sponsoring employers is implicit within the existing objectives (as many trustees argued in response to the consultation). At most, it could mean deficit recovery contributions would end up being slightly lower, or more precisely, that deficits would be reduced over a slightly longer time-frame—thus reinforcing zombie dynamics. It is not apparent that this is actually in the interests of employers genuinely seeking to grow, since the presence of large pension scheme deficits on their balance sheets arguably impacts on their creditworthiness and attractiveness to investors more than expenditure related to deficit recovery. Nevertheless, the reform seemingly had a symbolic and ideological significance for the Coalition government. Defined benefit regulation was depicted without substantiation as 'a brake on investment and growth' in the 2012 Autumn Statement which launched the Pensions and Growth consultation (HM Treasury, 2012: 44).

Almost inevitably, the May government took up the cause of defined benefit regulation. Despite forecasting that enforcing a switch to CPI-based indexation could reduce defined benefit deficits by around £90 billion (close to half of total deficits), the government decided not to attempt any further change in this area. It is worth noting that ONS no longer classifies RPI as a 'national statistic', having lost faith in its accuracy as a measure of inflation. Remarkably, the role of RPI in pensions provision is the only reason that ONS is maintaining the index, somewhat reluctantly (see ONS, 2018b). This position obviously helps policy-makers' rationale for adopting CPI, but leaves private-sector defined benefit schemes where such a switch is essentially impossible in a very peculiar position—zombie schemes, overseen by zombie regulation, with a zombie measure of inflation. While relatively minor, the issue perfectly encapsulates the state's dilemma in relation to defined benefit pensions: the UK economy's capitalist development model—including even the ways in which key economic trends are measured—is increasingly incompatible with traditional defined benefit provision. Accordingly the state, lacking any purposeful strategy, is increasingly called upon to find patches in a defensive and ad hoc manner.

Interestingly, in a sprawling and rather cluttered report on defined benefit pensions in 2016, the House of Commons Work and Pensions Select Committee had actually recommended allowing trustees the power to make the indexation of pensions in payment conditional, with reversion to RPI uprating 'when good times return' (2016b: 3). The difference in perspective between the committee and government is clear: the former still considers that defined benefit provision has a sustainable future in the UK pensions landscape, and is prepared to contravene members' property rights through highly regressive means in order to secure this future. The latter, on the other hand, considers defined benefit a relic of an era that has passed, and so sees little point in adopting policies which may be legally unenforceable—thus resulting in a veneer of progressivism in support of members' accrued entitlements.

Alongside minor changes to TPR's guidance on scheme governance, the most significant change introduced by the May government was a set of new powers for TPR to fine company directors deemed to have recklessly endangered their (former) employees' accumulated savings. There will also be new criminal offences for those who have committed wilful or grossly reckless acts in this regard (see DWP, 2018c). These reforms reflect the specific political conditions in which the May government was operating—most notably, scrutiny of the sale by Philip Green of retail giant BHS to Dominic Chappell for just £1 in 2015, leaving the firm with a pension scheme deficit totalling £345 million (it subsequently rose to £571 million; the schemes had had a total surplus of £43 million when Green acquired the firm). TPR later found that the avoidance of pensions liabilities that would have fallen upon BHS's parent company had BHS become insolvent during Green's ownership was the 'main purpose' of the sale from Green's perspective (TPR, 2017b). Green, who served as the Coalition government's public finances 'tsar', agreed a £363 million 'settlement' with TPR. Green's main continuing business (The Arcadia Group, which owns several large fashion retailers) is also at the time of writing being investigated by TPR, as a restructuring plan appears to significantly reduce deficit recovery payments in the group's closed defined benefit schemes (see Butler and Wood, 2019). The select committee's 2016 report again offers a fascinating insight into the politics of defined benefit regulation, in describing the BHS case as 'an extraordinary tale characterised by behaviour very far removed from the usual standards of British business' (House of Commons Work and Pensions Committee, 2016b: 3). While perhaps an extreme case, most political economists would consider Philip Green and his handling of BHS as, in fact, depressingly representative of 'the usual standards of British business' (see Sikka, 2018). We must take great care not to confuse the voluntaristic nature of collectivist pensions provision in the 'golden era' with a sense of benevolence among UK employers: the select committee, especially under Frank Field as Chair, is guilty of a nostalgia which borders on naivety. The voluntaristic approach worked, because it worked for employers. It is undeniably exhausted now; alas, the state has no intention of—and perhaps even no *capacity to*, in any meaningful sense—introducing greater compulsion.

Finally, having also already introduced a slightly easier process by which separate funds can be 'consolidated' (requiring, for instance, a slight levelling down of GMP rights), the May government moved to permit the establishment of large-scale consolidator 'superfunds', which may allow employers with funds in deficit to be relieved of their pension obligations (DWP, 2018a). The move could represent a challenge to the provision of bulk annuities and similar products, noted above; accordingly, insurers have voiced their concern about it (Ralph and Cumbo, 2018), reminding us that the finance sector does not have uniform interests on pensions provision—although arguably superfunds represent this market's logical destination. However, serious question marks remain. Since superfunds would remove the employer covenant, new legislation will be necessary to allow them to operate—assuming this is financially viable—as defined benefit schemes without a guarantor, in the absence of a full insurance buy-out. Even before the necessary legislation has passed—which seems increasingly uncertain given the demise of the May government—TPR had issued rather cautious guidance to both employers and managers of prospective superfunds, warning that any transfer would automatically be considered 'materially detrimental' to members (TPR, 2018b, 2018c). The PPF would act as a guarantor if superfunds were eligible—but presumably the levy payments which would be demanded by the PPF (discussed further below) for such schemes would be substantial, perhaps prohibitively so, precisely because of the absence of a sponsoring employer. Interestingly, one of the earliest movers into the superfund market will be a fund managed by Alan Rubenstein, the PPF's former Chief Executive. Superfunds represent an eye-catching initiative, but whether they transform the path of defined benefit's decline remains to be seen.

4.4. The Collectivist Lifeboat: All Aboard?

The PPF came into being in 2005 to provide pensions for individuals whose defined benefit scheme had ceased to function as a result of the sponsoring employer's insolvency. As a general rule, individuals who end up in the PPF receive 100 per cent of the benefits their previous scheme would have provided if they were already in retirement (that is, receiving their pension), or payments equivalent to 90 per cent of the benefits they were expecting at retirement, when they reach retirement age. Compared to the possibility of losing their pension entirely, losing only 10 per cent of their expected retirement income is arguably, in colloquial terms, a pretty good deal. However, there is a catch, or indeed several catches. An annual payments cap (currently just under £40,000) overrides the 100/90 per cent rules. The PPF also only recognizes the main benefit offered by previous schemes, that is, the entitlement to a regular pension payment accrued by the point of retirement. It has its own arrangements for the subsequent indexation of pensions in payment, and related benefits such as payments to dependants in the event of a member dying—generally speaking, the PPF's offer is less generous than the benefits available in the insolvent schemes it has absorbed.

In its latest accounts, the PPF reported it had just over 236,000 members across both membership sections, with its assets under management valued at just under £30 billion (a large surplus). The size of the fund means the PPF would sit comfortably within the list of the UK's ten largest funded defined benefit schemes, if it were classified in these terms (which it probably should be) (see Blain, 2017; PPF, 2018). It has four main sources of income. Firstly, as noted above, a levy charged on pension schemes eligible to enter the PPF in the event of employer insolvency (that is, the overwhelming majority of private-sector defined benefit schemes). Levy income was £537 million in 2017/18. The levy is different for each scheme, calculated via a formula which takes into account the size of the scheme and the risk of insolvency. Levy calculations are always contentious, and the PPF consults widely on its approach each year (the formula for calculation has resultingly become far more complex since the PPF's inception). Secondly, the residual assets of the schemes whose members enter the PPF. Forty-six schemes entered the PPF in 2017/18, with assets valued at £507 million. Thirdly, the PPF also seeks to recover money and assets from insolvent employers. Fourthly, and usually most importantly, the PPF generates returns on its investments—making a net return of £907 million in 2017/18 (see PPF, 2018).

The PPF's funding model contributes to the sense that it is little more than a private insurance scheme, for private-sector employers. During the passage of the relevant legislation in 2003, then Pensions Minister Andrew Smith compared the prospective body with travel or car insurance, operating 'without recourse to public funds' (cited in Thurley, 2018a: 4). But participation— that is, the requirement to pay the levy—is mandatory (as Smith also acknowledged in the same breath, the PPF's power to set and vary the levy was absolute). The PPF is technically not a public body, rather a publicly owned corporation, but the need for the state to support the PPF is established in primary legislation, as are the PPF's main benefit arrangements. We should be in no doubt that the PPF could not exist or operate without the exercise of the state's sovereign power. The question, however, of whether the state has any responsibility for directly funding the PPF's liabilities, should the PPF develop an unmanageable deficit, remains unresolved. Of course, the first recourse would be for government to alter benefit levels to reduce the PPF's liabilities. But what if it were unable to do so, perhaps due to parliamentary opposition? It feels like a hypothetical question at the moment, but this may not always be the case—and the very fact that we cannot answer it definitively itself tells us something significant about policy-makers' indecisiveness regarding the state's ultimate responsibilities in this area. One, rather tragic consequence of this ambiguity is that many UK workers in private-sector defined benefit schemes are actually not eligible for the PPF, as a result of their pension scheme being registered offshore—as was the case with the airline Flybe, which collapsed in March 2020 (Sikka, 2020). The firm's (closed) defined benefit scheme has around 1,300 members, but was registered in the Isle of Man. If the PPF were more appropriately recognized as a public policy, not a private insurance scheme, then the moral right of Flybe's UK-based workforce to PPF protection would be beyond doubt.

The state is walking a tightrope regarding its responsibilities for the PPF. It has decided to establish a mechanism by which defined benefit scheme members have their benefits protected, for the most part, and as such replace the role of private employers, where necessary, in shouldering investment risks. But it is only doing so on the basis that the PPF's universe essentially consists of the dying embers of defined benefit provision. The state will bolster collectivism, in order to smooth the transition away from collectivism. The Work and Pensions Select Committee recommends taking this model to its logical conclusion, through the establishment by the state of an 'aggregator fund', administered by the PPF, by which small employers with legacy defined benefit schemes can shed their pensions obligations while solvent. The rationale for this is explicit: 'It would also increase the chances that small employers could continue to thrive, invest and employ' (House of Commons Work and Pensions Select Committee, 2016b: 19). As such, collectivist pensions are a problem for the private economy—and the solution is the state. Arguably, the May government's superfunds proposal delivers on some of this, but only by facilitating, rather than providing, the aggregators (and expecting multiple aggregators to compete for business).

It is worth noting that the PPF now also administers the Financial Assistant Scheme (FAS)—a much smaller compensation scheme for members of defined benefit schemes which collapsed from 1997 onwards, before the PPF began to operate. The Labour government introduced the PPF in response to significant political pressure invoking the experience of defined benefit scheme members who had been left with little or no private pension entitlements when their scheme's sponsoring employer became insolvent. FAS still offers benefits lower than the PPF, but it has become significantly more generous, with wider eligibility over criteria over time. Crucially, while FAS did absorb the residual assets of the funds which had ceased to function, the state is unambiguously responsible for ensuring that the agreed compensation is paid (Thurley, 2010a). That the state's commitment has increased significantly, and rapidly, since the establishment of FAS demonstrates well the logic of collectivist provision, with the state seen as the ultimate backstop to the employer's role as temporal anchor. The design of the PPF mitigates risks to the state, but perhaps not permanently. Crucially, that the state has sought to intervene to protect a narrow age cohort (or concentrate protection on a narrow age cohort) clearly undermines the legitimacy of this intervention in inter-generational terms. Paradoxically, the case for the state's *retreat* from pensions provision is reinforced by the terms on which it has *increased its interventions* in collectivist provision in the private sector.

We can perhaps expect the PPF to become a more controversial aspect of the UK pensions landscape in the years ahead, as it encounters more complex cases featuring the larger firms where defined benefit provision is increasingly concentrated. The case of BHS, noted above, is indicative of this trend. The case of Tata Steel is also highly illustrative. With Tata's UK business threated with collapse in the mid-2010s, the PPF faced the prospect of bringing in around 130,000 new members of Tata's defined benefit scheme, inherited from previous sponsors British Steel and Corus (an enormous 55 per cent increase in PPF membership, essentially overnight). The government was strongly opposed to the move. The pension scheme was eventually separated from the firm as a going concern, with a £550 million cash injection from the UK company's Indian-owned parent, to facilitate a merger with German steel-making giant ThyssenKrupp. It effectively now operates as a standalone scheme, with a 33 per cent stake in the continuing UK business. However, the PPF was required to underwrite this highly unusual move, and scheme members who chose to remain in the 'old' British Steel Pension Scheme— around 25,000—eventually entered the PPF instead (Tovey, 2016; *The Guardian*, 2017; Pooler, 2018). Clearly, very large companies such as Tata Steel UK, with valuable fixed assets, are unlikely to ever become insolvent by the conventional route provided for by PPF eligibility rules, but their ability and/ or willingness to sponsor collectivist pensions provision is nevertheless uncertain. Whether cases such as this become more representative of the PPF caseload remains to be seen.

The collapse of construction company Carillion saw around 28,000 individuals enter the PPF (around half already in retirement). Ostensibly a more conventional case of insolvency, the case is interesting insofar as, firstly, Carillion's significant pension scheme deficit was spread across several schemes—a result of the M&A activity which fuelled Carillion's growth. Secondly, regulators had defied their own guidance by allowing Carillion to make payments to shareholders at a significantly higher level than its deficit recovery contributions—seemingly a product of regulators' misplaced faith in the viability of Carillion's long-term revenue streams and creditworthiness (Leaver, 2018a; Reeve, 2018). The financialization of corporate practice, which is complicit in the undermining of collectivist provision, may also have been paradoxically helping to mask the scale of the crisis in defined benefit provision. Crucially, Carillion is by no means an isolated example. In 2016, FTSE 100 companies paid four times as much in dividends as they contributed to their defined benefit pension schemes—and forty-one of these firms could have cleared their schemes' deficit in its entirety with the value of just a single year's dividend payments (LCP, 2017). It is not clear that regulators have the powers—or the necessary information—to challenge such practices, as long as firms (and their auditors) self-report sound financial health (TPR acknowledged in 2016, for example, that it only learned of the sale of BHS by reading about it in the press (see Cumbo, 2018b)). It is worth being reminded here of Adam Leaver's (2018a, 2018b) work on the temporalities of modern corporate finance, first discussed in Chapter 3. According to Leaver, firms such as Carillion act as a time 'portal' by securitizing *future* income to produce *current* assets. This, for Leaver, is the essence of financialization. Of course, it closely resembles the defined benefit funding model, as workers are guaranteed that the value of pay they defer today will be available to them in the future, via capital markets.

As such, the business model typified by Carillion relies absolutely on the same processes of inter-generational co-operation which is the foundation of all pensions provision, albeit more implicitly and indirectly. The actual future must approximate to the one envisaged today. Perversely, Carillion was better able to obscure the failed future of defined benefit pensions provision as its ability to manipulate its future finances more generally increased—and the latter depended acutely on succeeding at the former, since it required the prioritization of short-term income for shareholders and creditors over other stakeholders. As such, the problem with defined benefit provision is not so much that it has been financialized—it has never not been—but rather that its temporal anchors have been financialized. Interestingly, an enormous defined benefit scheme deficit of £500 million is one of the reasons the airline and travel agent Thomas Cook collapsed in autumn 2019—and like Carillion, it had managed to temporarily sustain its business through a seemingly inflated 'goodwill' value (used by firms to value future cashflows arising from intangible assets such as branding and customer loyalty). This is the future which confronts the PPF, as its incoming cases become larger and more complex. It may be that the May government's superfunds plan, if taken forward by the Johnson government, means the next Carillion will have greater opportunities to dispose of their defined benefit liabilities before entering the PPF becomes necessary. However, it seems no less likely that superfunds will themselves end up requiring the PPF—and perhaps in worse circumstances than those which the PPF encounters at present, since superfunds will have been operating without employer covenants.

4.5. Public-Sector Pensions Provision

It is worth recalling that, while terminal decline of collectivist provision in the private sector continues, defined benefit pensions remain an integral part of the UK pensions landscape—in the public sector. Indeed, active membership of public-sector pension schemes has been rising since the mid-1990s, when it fell to around 4 million—it is now above 6 million, significantly higher than its earlier peak in the late 1970s (although it had dipped to close to 5 million in the years immediately following the financial crisis, before rising quite sharply). Eighty-five per cent of active contributors to defined benefit schemes are in the public sector (Thurley and McInnes, 2019: 5). Around a third of these are in the Local Government Pension Scheme, which is actually composed of dozens of *funded* defined benefit schemes—the largest, resulting from scheme mergers among several local authorities, are among the UK's largest pension funds. The majority, however, are in unfunded schemes, with the largest six being those for the military, the police, firefighters, teachers, National Health Service workers, and civil servants. Although benefits arise directly and exclusively from individuals' employment in different parts of the public sector, the schemes operate on a pay-as-you-go basis, with pensions in payment financed by the Exchequer via current taxation. This funding model—clearly the most efficient, given the unique characteristics of the state as an employer—has been increasingly politicized.

Inevitably, although the necessity of the Exchequer funding the 'shortfall' between employee contributions received (technically, held back from public-sector wages) and pensions paid out is equivalent in principle to the contributions any employer makes to their employees' pensions saving, in practice the scale of Exchequer contributions—and their forecasted increases—has invited scrutiny, especially as longevity has increased. Technically, most schemes already account for a nominal employer contribution (this is a fiscal irrelevance, but specified as departmental budgetary management); when these nominal contributions are added to employee contributions, it leaves an annual additional cost to the Exchequer of around £10 billion. Overall, expenditure on public-sector pensions, irrespective of contributions, is around 2 per cent of GDP.

Crucially, this cost is expected to fall dramatically in the years ahead. This is partly a result of recent wage freezes across the public sector, which have held back pension accrual even as the workforce has generally grown in size. (We should note that the expansion of the public-sector workforce is partly explained by a growth in part-time working, leading to a higher headcount.) (see ONS, 2019) But it is also, more importantly, the product of a series of attempts to scale back occupational pension entitlements. Concerted efforts in this regard began during New Labour's third term in office. Increases in employee contributions, reductions in accrual rates, and a later switch to using CPI rather than RPI for indexation, began to result in significant savings. Upon taking office in 2010, the Coalition government demanded further reform, appointing former Labour cabinet minister John Hutton to lead an independent review of public-sector pensions. Despite the then Deputy Prime Minister, Liberal Democrat Nick Clegg, claiming that 'unreformed gold plated' public-sector pensions were 'unfair and unaffordable' as part of a 2010 speech endorsing public spending cuts more generally (cited in BBC News, 2010), Hutton in fact acknowledged that the cost of public-sector pensions was already falling, and that for most recipients outcomes were 'far from gold plated' (cited in BBC News, 2011). Nevertheless, he recommended major changes, such as a switch from final salary to career average benefits (as such, a significant reduction in accrual rates), and increases in retirement ages for all schemes (see Independent Public Service Pensions Commission, 2011). As a result of these reforms, the cost of public-sector pensions is expected to fall below 1.5 per cent of GDP within thirty years (HM Treasury, 2017d)—and the additional, unfunded cost to the Exchequer has *already* fallen significantly.

What does the reform of public-sector pensions tell us about collectivist pensions in general? There are two main implications. Firstly, while defined benefit pensions in the public sector are likely to be secure for the foreseeable future, it is clear that the ideological basis of provision has been undermined by the politics of austerity. Technicalities have been politicized—even weaponized—to undermine the common-sense notion that public-sector pensions are merely part of public-sector workers' normal remuneration. A false dichotomy between public-sector workers and 'taxpayers' has been promulgated in recent years. For example, in establishing 'annual tax statements' in 2014, expenditure on public-sector pensions was (quite outrageously) classified by the Treasury as 'welfare' expenditure. Public-sector pension scheme design may be governed by statute, but this provision is essentially a private arrangement between employer and employee, not a citizenship-based entitlement. This decision was taken, it seems, simply to artificially inflate the figures for welfare spending, in service of the Coalition government's wider policy agenda around welfare retrenchment. Yet it clearly also reflects a reluctance to acknowledge the nature and purpose of defined benefit pensions provision in the public sector.

Secondly, if it was not already obvious enough, it seems clear now that the so-called 'pensions apartheid' between the public and private sectors will be addressed by levelling down the former, rather than levelling up the latter. It is worth a longer look at Clegg's, 2010 remarks at this point: 'Private sector workers have already seen final salary schemes close, while returns from defined contribution schemes fall. So can we really ask them to keep paying their taxes into unreformed gold-plated public sector pension pots?' (cited in BBC News, 2010). The whole point of unfunded pensions is that there are no 'pots'; pensions are a normal part of the employee remuneration essential for the delivery of public services. While most would agree public services should be funded by general taxation, the pension obligations arising from this model have been subtly lifted out of the narrative. It is of course instructive that Clegg cites the poor quality of defined contribution schemes as the justi-fication for this shift, conveniently ignoring the government's own inaction in this area (for a longer discussion of 'fairness' in relation to public-sector pensions, which interrogates the Coalition's narrative, see Cutler and Waine, 2013). It is also worth noting here that the public sector in the UK remains highly unionized, while union density has fallen dramatically in the private sector, particularly among young people, as the economy has deindustrialized. Public-sector pension reform has been accompanied by significant levels of industrial action, at almost every stage. With less union activity in the private sector in recent decades, the socio-political foundations of collectivism have been eroded to some extent—and indeed delegitimized as an image of public-sector workers behaving in a purely self-serving manner has taken hold. Invariably—and despite falling costs—insofar as the additional costs to the Exchequer are met through borrowing (albeit not in any direct sense, since the fiscal implications of the small amounts involved are impossible to track), public-sector pensions are often seen as an affront to 'future generations'. Such arguments have been made from both right-wing (see Moynihan, 2018; Johnson, 2019) and ostensibly left-wing perspectives (see Malik and Howker, 2010).

The UK's largest private pension scheme, USS (noted above), is effectively a funded public-sector scheme—it is usually described as 'quasi' public sector, given that the vast majority of universities rely largely on public funding, including the state's underwriting of the student loans system, despite technically being independent, charitable organizations. USS covers around 350 separate employers, with 400,000 members (around half are active), with around £60 billion in assets under management (USS, 2018) (note that employees of newer universities established since the 1992 education reforms generally belong to the teachers' pension scheme, that is, an unfunded public-sector scheme). As its funding deficit has grown, USS has undergone several stages of reform since 2010, including employee contribution and retirement age increases, a switch to career average for new accruals, and 'cap and share' arrangements which limit employers' exposure to rising costs. In 2018, with USS reporting its deficit at around £17 billion, the scheme's joint negotiating committee (representing employers and trade unions, although the unions opposed the proposals) recommended the near immediate cessation of defined benefit accruals, with all active members moved to the scheme's defined contribution section, hitherto used principally for AVCs. An extensive period of industrial action followed, leading to a withdrawal of the proposed reform, although at the time of writing the dispute remains unresolved—and USS has embarked on another valuation process. The estimated deficit fell significantly after 2017 but, as noted above, rose again sharply in early 2020.

At the centre of the dispute between USS unions and employer representatives are serious questions about the valuation process by which the deficit is calculated, including the method of discounting future liabilities. The argument made by the main union, University and College Union (UCU), that USS has overstated its deficit forecasts (see Grady, 2018; UCU, 2018) is a plausible one (although USS already uses a *higher* discount rate than most private-sector scheme sponsors, thereby deflating liabilities—this is justified on the basis of the scheme's reliable cash income (Ralfe, 2013)). However, it does leave unions in the strange—perhaps peculiarly British—position of arguing that capital market returns are more reliable than the array of finance industry professionals running and advising USS believe they are. The unique status of USS, caught between the public and private sectors, means generalizing from this case is difficult. However, it certainly seems to reveal some of the contradictory impulses produced by the UK's voluntaristic approach to collectivism, as beneficiaries make the case for the viability of the approach, while the state—even in an industry which is effectively nationalized—carefully polices its exposure.[6]

Generally speaking, only permanent members of the academic staff within universities are eligible for USS membership. With non-academic staff at least partially excluded, USS embodies the classist hierarchies which characterized the early development of occupational pensions provision in the UK (as discussed in Chapter 2). However, even academic staff at USS employers are no longer assured of access to the scheme. The fact that younger recruits are increasingly ineligible for USS—as a result of higher education's increasingly casualized workforce—means the growth in active membership has not kept pace with the growth of the retired membership, thereby undermining the scheme's long-term viability. The inter-generational underpinnings of collectivist provision are therefore lost, albeit as part of a wider process of labour market restructuring, rather than resulting directly from the preferences of those involved in pensions provision. The untold story of USS is therefore illustrative of the demise of collectivism in UK pensions provision more

---

[6] The text here cites Jo Grady, who at the time the cited pieces were published was both a leading UCU activist *and* an academic expert in pensions provision (among other things). Grady was subsequently elected as UCU's General-Secretary, due in part to activists' disappointment at the then UCU leadership's willingness to compromise during the initial 2017/18 dispute. The implications of this development for the wider politics of defined benefit provision in the public and private sectors remain to be seen. Although Grady was supportive publicly of Jeremy Corbyn's leadership of the Labour party, UCU remains an apolitical trade union (it has a political fund, but this is used only to support its own lobbying and campaign activity), with a limited record of working with other unions (generally representing lower-paid staff) within the higher education system. Nevertheless, in Grady, pensions collectivism now has an effective advocate with the platform and resources to amplify her positions on both policy and practice (see Grady, 2019).

generally. If the solution to apparent funding shortfalls is to make provision less accessible to younger workers, the risks to a scheme's sustainability will only be enhanced. The financial, political, and institutional basis of pensions provision depends on the management of inter-generational conflict.

4.6. Conclusion: A Good Innings?

While endangered in the private sector—and hardly thriving in the public sector—collectivist pensions arguably remain a major part of the UK pensions landscape, in the form of the state pension. It is not unreasonable to argue that a redistributive state pension (especially with the means-tested top-up), funded via general taxation, is a purer form of collectivist pensions provision. But where would such an argument get us? The UK's state pensions system is of course limited in ambition—and becoming more limited. It would be just as plausible to argue that the state's commitment to a Beveridgean state pension has actually impeded the development of a collectivist public pension in the Bismarckian tradition. SERPS is a case in point. While its unfunded model could be seen as embodying a purer form of collectivism, in practice it led to the scheme being designed in a fairly conservative manner, and ultimately morphing into another state pension top-up—more a social security benefit than a social insurance-based pension scheme.

Clearly, the meaning of collectivism is contestable. The focus of this chapter has been the voluntaristic organization of collectivist schemes, by which private individuals pool resources to insure against loss of earnings in later life. However, it will be clear by now that pensions collectivism requires more than the will (and capital, in the form of deferred earnings) of the collective. If this were not the case, defined contribution schemes would have some claim to collectivism, since saving pots are merged in practice. Certainly, CDC would be considered an unproblematic form of collectivism. In reality, collectivist pensions require an anchor, an entity which guarantees the promise individuals make to each other through time, because pensions provision is inherently cross-generational, and generational change is endemic. There must be mechanisms by which savings are guaranteed to rematerialize, once cash contributions have been allocated, and indeed mechanisms for ensuring inter-generational co-operation is renewed through the entry of younger cohorts. The demise of pensions collectivism is, in effect, the demise of the guarantee. We can point to economic trends such as deindustrialization and increasing foreign ownership, and demographic changes such as increasing life expectancy and increasing labour market activation, as well as more prescriptive or burdensome regulatory expectations, in explaining employers' apparent unwillingness to uphold this role voluntarily. It is also the case, however, that the UK's model of capitalist development has never been satisfactorily oriented towards supporting collectivist pensions provision on a large scale—defined benefit may briefly have been seen as compatible with employment practices in a small number of (large) industries, but the endangering of even short-term profitability has rarely been tolerated.

This is why the question of the state's underpinning role continues to surface as defined benefit provision interacts with generational change. The state is not simply a conduit through which promises can be delivered; its sovereign power makes its ability to act as a temporal anchor essentially inimitable. It is little surprise that the failure of *private* pensions saving mechanisms is invariably seen as a *public* problem—the state and collectivism are morally and ideologically entwined. Indeed, this is partly why regulation of the guarantee—a promise made between private actors—has been strengthened. More recently, demands for stronger mechanisms by which the state can underpin the private promise have increased, and been partially accepted in some contexts—but always somewhat reluctantly, and never unconditionally. Crucially, the state itself does not stand aloof from capitalism. When the Thatcher government diluted employers' pension obligations, it was in support of employers perceived to be operating in a more complex and competitive business environment. When policy-makers in the 1990s and 2000s strengthened reporting and valuation procedures around defined provision, it was in support of a shareholder-led investment model in which pension risks were seen to act as an investment disincentive. In an echo of Thatcher, the Coalition government offered to unpick some of the new regulatory burdens, but made few substantive changes: the slow logic of defined benefit decline is now well established, but cannot be accelerated without simply increasing demands upon the public safety net (and indeed challenging the interests of the UK's large asset management industry). The zombies are here to stay.

Should we be appreciative that collectivism has survived as long as it has in the UK, given the inhospitable environment? A good innings, on a sticky wicket? Perhaps. Yet, fatalism aside, this would also be to overlook the damage that the nature of the UK's liberal collectivist experiment has done to pensions collectivism more generally. As noted in Chapter 1, rather than the embodiment of inter-generational co-operation, defined benefit provision is now seen as emblematic of inter-generational injustice—with private-sector failures even infecting our understanding of public-sector pensions provision.

This unfortunate attitude will exist, it appears, for as long as defined benefit provision lingers. And as long as defined benefit persists, with the state's support, opportunities to demonize collectivist pensions provision will recur. That the problem is not pensions collectivism per se, but rather the voluntaristic and financialized nature of traditional, defined benefit pension provision in the UK, has been lost in the haze.

5

False Dawn: Individualization and the Perversion of Pensions Saving

Since pensions history repeats itself, genuinely revolutionary moments are rare. However, the introduction of auto-enrolment in the UK has to be seen as a transformative moment. While the earlier neoliberalization of wider economic governance processes encompassed important changes to pensions policy and provision, auto-enrolment encompasses an extensive set of reforms designed to alter how the vast majority of people engage with private pensions provision. The demise of defined benefit provision, in tandem with the expansion of the workforce and population ageing, had led to fears of a tendency to undersave for retirement (saving rates across defined benefit and defined contribution provision were discussed in Chapter 4). This would either intensify the trend of 'pensioner poverty', which policy-makers believed was politically (and perhaps morally) unpalatable, or instead create fiscal demands on the state which policy-makers did not believe it could possibly meet. The new system—legislated for by New Labour before the 2008 financial crisis—would (more or less) compel individuals to save for retirement, and (for the most part) force their employers to help them.

Has the apparent crisis of undersaving therefore been averted? In the sense that auto-enrolment and the new employer requirements will mean that many millions of people will be saving for retirement who would probably not otherwise have done so, the problem has at least been alleviated. However, it is far from certain that auto-enrolment will by itself produce decent retirement incomes for all participants. There are four principal reasons to be cautious. Firstly, and most acutely, as a system encouraging participation in workplace pensions, it reflects chronic (and arguably intensifying, from the perspective of today's young people) labour market inequalities, with lower earners, people out of work or only able to work part time due to caring responsibilities, and the self-employed by definition worse off. Only around half of working-age people in the UK are actually eligible for auto-enrolment (Silcock, 2015), and many others receive extremely low contributions from employers. Obviously, these problems intersect with

Pensions Imperilled: The Political Economy of Private Pensions Provision in the UK. Craig Berry, Oxford University Press (2021).
© Craig Berry. DOI: 10.1093/oso/9780198782834.003.0005

inequalities based on class, gender, ethnicity, and disability (Foster, 2010; Grady, 2015; Silcock et al., 2016).

Secondly, the auto-enrolment revolution actually masks a secondary transformation in UK pensions provision: the state's determination to promote and support individualized, defined contribution provision. The absence of a temporal anchor in defined contribution provision—other than the individual's own personal responsibility—is a major threat to future retirement incomes. Thirdly, the auto-enrolment revolution has been undermined by some of the operational decisions made by policy-makers in recent years around the delivery of the new system, especially where decisions have impacted directly upon financial service providers (the self-interest of which can be considered the real, if unreliable, anchor underpinning defined contribution provision). Fourthly, we have also witnessed counter-revolutionary policies in recent years which have undermined the consensual approach to pensions policy evident since the Pensions Commission (chaired by Adair Turner) in the mid-2000s. Of course, the counter-revolutionaries would argue that they are simply taking the system's individualized orientation to its logical conclusion—yet it is more plausible to argue that auto-enrolment's prospects depend on residual elements of collectivism (in, for example, annuities provision). As such, in the sense that auto-enrolment stretches the individualization of pensions provision to it apparent limits, the real crisis of UK pensions provision has barely even begun.

These issues will be explored across this chapter, and in Chapter 6. The focus here is on how individualism became embedded in UK pensions policy and practice. The chapter begins by exploring the rise of defined contribution provision, including the ascendant hegemony of an individualist ontology, and in particular the role of the Pensions Commission in institutionalizing defined contribution as the default form of private pensions provision in the UK. It also begins to explore the meaning and implication of decisions made by the Labour and Coalition governments in seeking to implement the Turner plan. Section 5.2 explores the behavioural assumptions of auto-enrolment—including the contradictions within these assumptions—and what experiences so far of the policy in operation tells us about its future. Section 5.3 considers recent efforts to support long-term saving away from pensions saving vehicles—locating such efforts in the origins of defined contribution provision.

5.1. Individualization and the Turner Consensus

Individualized pensions undermine immediately one of the key facets of pensions provision: inter-generational co-operation. As pensions offer opportunities to manage inherent differences between age cohorts based on different (expected) experiences of the economy across the lifecourse (which problematizes projections of the future including anticipated saving outcomes), provision which ostensibly assumes individuals will be responsible solely for their own retirement outcomes effectively rules out 'pay-as-you-go' funding models, irrespective of the financial rationale. This does not mean that implicit co-operation between generations is not inherent even in defined contribution provision. In a direct sense, for example, insurers will price annuities with reference to a wide range of considerations—including expectations of income from future retirees. Similarly, tax relief provided by the state to support pensions saving is funded by general taxation (and borrowing). And in an indirect sense, for example, large-scale, multi-employer scheme providers such as 'master trusts' obviously build capacity utilized by today's savers based on expectations that tomorrow's savers will be their customers too. (Annuities, tax relief, and master trusts will all be discussed further in Chapter 6.)

Yet this, precisely, is the problem: myriad forms of inter-generational co-operation are essential in order for pensions provision to function, but individualized pensions largely fail to incentivize and institutionalize such co-operation. Of course, pensions provision is organized not in a vacuum, but in the context of a capitalist economy in which volatility is endemic. In defined benefit schemes, employers generally take on the role of anchoring provision; this is interpreted as a cost by employers, but it would be better to see their role instead as conduits for inter-generational relations amid generational change, thereby mediating (and occasionally underwriting) inter-generational transfers. In the absence of a temporal anchor, inter-generational relations in defined contribution are framed only by the notion of individual responsibility: that individuals in one cohort will take responsibility for their own retirement income, rather than calling upon other cohorts, is the only constant. This section explores how this arrangement has manifest in UK pensions provision, as determined by pensions policy.

Auto-enrolment is now rightly seen as the flagship policy emerging from the Pensions Commission chaired by Adair Turner, alongside academic John Hills and trade unionist Jeannie Drake (as a former head of the Confederation of British Industry (CBI)—as well as future head of the Financial Services Authority—Turner was also the body's employer representative). To some extent, this outcome was baked implicitly into the Commission's remit from the beginning (as noted in Chapter 3, the introduction of auto-enrolment in New Zealand had influenced New Labour's thinking). The Commission concerned itself more with the question of *what* individuals would be enrolled into, automatically or otherwise. As such, 'personal accounts' were the major policy initiative arising from the Commission regarding private pensions saving—albeit one which looks rather different in implementation. The most important element of personal accounts is that they would be defined contribution pensions savings vehicles (although defined benefit schemes can be used for auto-enrolment, this possibility does not appear to have been envisaged by the Commission with any seriousness).

What was the rationale for the unequivocal adoption of defined contribution vehicles for the delivery of auto-enrolment? Incredibly, the Pensions Commission offered little explanation. In an academic paper summarizing the Commission's analysis and recommendations, John Hills (2006) mentions 'defined contribution' only twice: in noting the (overstated) trend that defined benefit schemes were being replaced by defined contribution schemes, and in accompanying, thirty-one-word footnote explaining the difference between the two. An analytical framework focused largely upon the impact of population ageing led to a series of 'unavoidable choices', chiefly the requirement for individuals to save more (Pensions Commission, 2004: 1; see Berry, 2016a). There is obviously an implicit affinity between personal saving and defined contributions pensions saving—with defined benefit pensions occupying a slightly different imaginary as a form of pensions accumulation—so, if more saving is required, defined contribution is the default assumption. There is also the implication that because it is *people* who are ageing, then people—not *firms*—are responsible for the consequences. The impossibility in UK law of defined benefit provision without a sponsoring employer (notwithstanding 'lifeboat' provision discussed in Chapter 4) again leaves defined contribution as the default. A *Financial Times* op-ed by Nicholas Timms, published alongside the Commission's interim report in 2004, takes us slightly closer to a justification:

> Why is there a pensions problem? Essentially because growing populations have allowed pensions to operate like pyramid, or Ponzi, selling schemes. Each generation has been able to promise itself more generous pensions in future because a bigger generation was coming up behind to pay for them. That has now ceased. The population is ageing as the baby boom generation nears retirement and is living longer. A man of 65 in 1950 could expect to live for a further 12 years; today the figure is 19 years. But just as important, the birth rate has fallen dramatically all around the developed world. Not only are there more older people living longer, but fewer younger people are coming along to pay their pensions.
>
> (Timms, 2004)

Timms actually had a significant role within the Commission's work: Mervyn Kohler of Age UK (a sage and seasoned observer of UK pensions policy) describes him as 'the fourth member of the Commission' (see Institute for Government, 2010). Without mentioning the terms 'defined benefit' or 'defined contribution' (at any point in the article), Timms outlines the apparent incompatibility of *any* pay-as-you-go provision with population ageing (despite the fact that the Commission eventually recommended expanded entitlements within the UK's pay-as-you-go state pension system) and suggests that individualized pensions provision is the only generationally fair, and sustainable, approach. (Timms' reference to the declining birth rate is particularly problematic—even if this simplistic account were accepted, there is no solid reason to assume that birth rates will continue to decline indefinitely.) Similarly, when reflecting on the Commission's work in 2010, Jeannie Drake remarked that their approach sought to distribute 'pain and benefits' around all stakeholders equally; yet the 'pain' for trade unions highlighted by Drake was solely the SPA increases, and therefore not the mass rollout of individualized pension schemes (see Institute for Government, 2010).

The Commission's reports also offer insight into the connection between welfare retrenchment and defined contribution provision in the context of population ageing. The Pensions Commission argued that 'the state plans to provide decreasing support for many people in order to control expenditure in the face of an ageing population (2004: x), and later that '[l]ooking forward the state is planning to play a reduced role in pensions provision' (2005: 2). Yet there was no such 'plan' or 'planning' on the part of the state in a substantive sense; in fact, the Commission's own (very thorough) analysis showed that pensions-related public expenditure was expected to increase significantly in the decades ahead. Indeed, their own proposals would have amplified this increase. The Commission presents as a fait accompli the expectation that state provision would retreat—and setting the state against the individual in dichotomous terms, ignoring the inimitable role of other stakeholders in pensions provision—therefore helping to lay the foundations for pensions individualization as a legitimate public policy goal. It is worth noting of course that this dichotomy was not imagined by the Commission independently, but established by New Labour (and political elites in general, given the cross-party support the initiative benefited from) within the Commission's terms of reference. The Commission's terms of reference, as 'Blair's project', focused narrowly on the adequacy of private saving by individuals, and asked the Commission to consider a move towards compulsory contribution (for employers and employees) (Brummer, 2010: 135).

As such, the Commission actually overstepped its remit somewhat, by settling on the notion of personal accounts. While accepting without objection the necessity of a defined contribution-based solution to undersaving, they argued that the state itself should become a *provider* of defined contribution pensions. A state-run entity—or entities—would collect contributions and make investment decisions on savers' behalf. Of course, governments might be expected to outsource the delivery of this system, in whole or in part, but from the savers' perspective, their individualized pension would be delivered by the state. The potential, operational implications of this approach are fascinating. For instance, would there have been a single, state-run mega-fund (or a small number of funds) for the investment of accumulated savings? And would the state also provide annuities? The Pensions Commission (2005: 383–5) actually floated this possibility, and the slightly less radical idea that the state would purchase annuities in bulk from the insurance industry on behalf of personal accounts members. Of course, such decisions were ultimately left to elected governments to adjudicate—and all of the most transformative possibilities have disappeared without trace.

However, it is important to note that the Commission itself baulked at the most radical implication of its approach: the establishment of an NDC scheme (also discussed in Chapter 3), in which individuals would receive a pension in line with nominal investment returns their contributions might have attracted—but in practice the outcomes are guaranteed (although amendable) by the state. The Commission justified its caution by arguing that the state's scarce resources should be focused on providing a basic income floor rather than matching the liabilities associated with NDC, and that pure defined contribution provision would create an individual pot with identifiable pension wealth that would be less amenable to future political tinkering. The Commission also claimed that individualization would provide people an opportunity to take on riskier investments should they wish to do so (2005: 172). None of these explanations are particularly compelling, and some are rather naïve, if not duplicitous. A pension scheme in which policy-makers may occasionally tinker with guaranteed rates of return (in accordance with identifiable criteria) is self-evidently better, from an individual saver's perspective, than a pension scheme without any guarantees at all (especially where guaranteed returns are linked, to some extent, to returns the saver *might* have expected to achieve by investing their savings). The notion that a large number of individuals might seek to gamble on achieving a higher rate of return than nominally offered by the state is probably (at best) overstated. Accordingly, it seems clear that NDC was simply politically impossible, insofar as it essentially represents a form of defined benefit provision.

The Commission's reports did not really pontificate on the concept of 'personal responsibility'—they spent more time emphasizing new *employer* responsibilities, even as the Commission's own support for defined contribution relieved employers wholesale of investment risks related to pensions accumulation. But it is a short jump from the Commission's analysis of the 'unavoidable choices' facing individuals and policy-makers to the establishment of personal responsibility as a foundational principle of auto-enrolment. In taking forward the Commission's plans for automatic enrolment, the Labour government emphasized the centrality of personal responsibility (the first of five 'tests of reform') to their agenda:

> We need to be clear that individuals must be responsible for their own plans for retirement. The reforms will ensure the provision of high-quality savings vehicles, and a solid state foundation to private savings. But the choice of how much to save, the level of risk to take with investments, and how long to work must be available to the individual. That provides the right balance of choice and support for individual responsibility.   (DWP, 2006b: 22)

The same rationale could perhaps have been applied to defined benefit provision (perhaps in conjunction with advocating higher employee contributions, or higher retirement ages, to minimize costs on employers). Yet the prospect appears not to have been entertained, to any extent. The only alternative to the state ever presented is the individual, acting to satisfy their own needs—the notion that individuals may co-operate for mutual benefit via collectivist mechanisms is entirely absent. As discussed in Chapter 4, the government also justified a defined contribution model with reference to changes in the labour market, chiefly the trend towards individuals changing jobs more frequently. This argument is, at best, inadequate; defined benefit savings are also portable and, as discussed in Chapter 6, the proliferation of small pots of defined contribution savings caused by individuals moving between jobs is a significant challenge for the operation of auto-enrolment. (It is worth reiterating that no such justification was offered by the Commission; reinforcing the argument here that defined contribution was the Labour government's choice, which the Commission was bound to follow.)

It should be noted that the government had, in its first term, already thrown its weight behind defined contribution provision, in the form of 'stakeholder' pensions, which were rolled out in 2001. These were essentially personal pension products, but most employers were mandated to arrange one for their employees if requested (and to make information available to all existing staff and new recruits). Employers were not, however, required to make financial contributions. Ultimately, as the government quickly acknowledged, stakeholder pensions failed, in that a voluntaristic approach led to low opt-in rates. Only around 5 per cent of private-sector workers were in a stakeholder scheme by 2008—on the eve of auto-enrolment's launch—as the steady rise of defined contribution membership more generally failed to keep pace with the rapid decline in defined benefit membership (ONS, 2013). Nevertheless, the salient point here is that New Labour had already demonstrated its accommodation of and support for defined contribution in place of defined benefit, thereby constraining Adair Turner et al.'s scope for action.

There were two elements of the stakeholder pension policy, however, which probably express the social democratic orientation of New Labour, especially during its first term in office, and which are largely absent from auto-enrolment. Firstly, the moniker 'stakeholder' (linked to the work of Will Hutton (1995)) is quite revealing, insofar as it suggests that defined contribution pensions saving in this regard was not conceived simply as a means for securing a retirement income, but also a way of connecting individual action to wider economic benefits by emphasizing the investment of accumulated savings (see Department of Social Security, 1998). Secondly, charges that could be taken out of individuals' savings by scheme providers were capped at 1.5 per cent per annum for active savers (falling to 1 per cent after ten years). This applied simply to scheme management charges, rather than the transaction fees hidden in the return on investment, but nevertheless represents an interventionist tendency which did not survive the shift to auto-enrolment—at least not while Labour was in office (the Coalition government's charge cap is discussed in Chapter 6).

As well as its opt-out rather than opt-in approach to member recruitment, the most novel element of auto-enrolment (or, in the Commission's vision, personal accounts) was the contribution model. Ostensibly, employers would be mandated to contribute 3 per cent of an employee's salary into their savings pot, assuming the employee contributed 5 per cent. These rates were only reached in April 2019, after a lengthy phase-in period lasting around a decade. It is of course disingenuous to refer to the employer contribution in terms that imply an act of charity—the employer contribution is part of an employee's remuneration, and indeed employers acknowledge that they tend to respond to higher pension costs by reducing wages (see DWP, 2018b). More importantly, the introduction of a qualifying earnings band and an earnings trigger means contributions are actually significantly below the headline rates for most people. In 2019/20, the qualifying earnings band is £6,136–£50,000 per annum—the 3 per cent minimum employer band only applies to earnings within this band.

The lowest paid workers, especially if they work part time, may not earn significantly more than the lower earnings threshold. For example, an employee working for twenty hours per week, paid at the minimum wage (even assuming the highest rate for people aged 25 or over), would have an actual employer contribution rate below 1 per cent. Moreover, they would not be automatically enrolled into the company's pension scheme in the first place—because the Labour government legislated for an earnings trigger set *above* the lower earnings threshold, and the Coalition government raised the trigger value significantly (it is now £10,000). People who earn less than £10,000 can opt *in* to schemes if they earn above the lower earnings threshold. The problem becomes even trickier when we consider that individuals may earn more than the lower earnings threshold, and indeed the earnings trigger—but not necessarily from a single employer (see Fernyhough, 2017). None of their employers will be required to enrol them in a workplace pensions scheme; or, they may be enrolled into one scheme, but still miss out on contributions from other employers. As such, there will be individuals prepared to behave exactly the way the Turner-based consensus demands of them: work, earn, and save. Yet they are denied employer contributions into their pension pot for purely administrative reasons; presumably, if the government had adopted the personal accounts model of state-managed schemes, this discrimination would have been eliminated. (There are of course also people unable to work/earn/save (to the same extent) for wholly justifiable reasons, such as informal carers.)

The earnings trigger was entirely a post-Turner invention. While the earnings *band* had to some extent been envisaged by the Pensions Commission, their rationale for the band was linked to the possible interaction of private pensions income with means-tested benefits. However, this complication is no longer as salient as it was when the Commission deliberated, given the introduction of an STSP which will lift most people out of means-tested benefits in retirement (see Berry and Stanley, 2013: 28). It is worth noting, for completeness, the obvious point (noted earlier) that self-employed people do not receive employer contributions. The number of people in self-employment has arguably grown more quickly in recent years than the Pensions Commission could have foreseen. As discussed in Chapter 4, the recent Taylor Review into 'gig' employment offered few, if any, substantive solutions for this emerging dilemma. (However, a footnote within DWP's auto-enrolment evaluation report, published in February 2020, noted that 'DWP is working with BEIS [Department for Business, Energy and Industrial Strategy] to ensure any changes [following the Taylor Review] are also considered in relation to who is eligible for automatic enrolment' (DWP, 2020: 96).)

Despite the embrace of defined contribution by the Pensions Commission, the government and the UK political elite more generally—effectively relieving employers of their risk-sharing role—the CBI opposed the establishment of minimum employer contributions, and indeed resisted auto-enrolment more generally (see Institute for Government, 2011). After the Commission's first report in 2004, the CBI's then Director-General John Cridland argued that 'compulsion is a complete blind alley' (cited in Brooksbank, 2004); in 2005, his successor Digby Jones described the 'soft' compulsion which the opt-out model represents as 'the sting in the tail' of the final report. Jones argued that mandatory contributions would cause wage cuts and job losses among small and medium-sized employers (cited in Newell, 2005; Jones was later appointed as a minister in the Brown government). While the pensions industry—represented at the time by the Association of British Insurers (ABI) and NAPF—were much more positive about the Commission's recommendations, employers were clearly lukewarm, at best, about their new obligations. Of course, ABI's view that employers belong 'at the heart of pensions provision' was no doubt shaped by insurers' own interest in encouraging higher saving rates (cited in Brooksbank, 2004).

5.2. Pensions Individualism and Responsible Behaviour

So, individuals are to be (largely) responsible for their own retirement income, via pensions saving. They must save, and accept the risk that their savings fail to rematerialize in future as the pension expected at the point of accumulation. However, while defined contribution requires that individuals are *responsible*, the auto-enrolment policy does not expect them to behave *responsibly*. The fallibility of individuals is built into auto-enrolment, even as UK pensions provision individualizes, precisely by ensuring eligible employees are enrolled without their consent into workplace pension schemes. Similarly, choices on contribution levels and investment strategies are made by default by employers and providers (within the scope of regulation).

The intellectual background to this understanding is the growth of behavioural science, specifically behavioural economics, and even more specifically the crude form of behaviouralism which has penetrated elite policy thinking, particularly in the UK and US. Individuals are sovereign, but not trusted to behave as the rational utility-maximizers of 'conventional' economics. As the 2006 white paper explained:

> Conventional economics suggests that people will try to smooth their spending over their lifetime...Behavioural economics is the combination of psychology and economics, and helps to explain people's decision making. It has identified a number of reasons why people do not save for retirement, even when it is their interest to do so. People may realise they should save for retirement but lack the

willpower to change their behaviour appropriately. Inertia often leads people to follow the path of least resistance in decision making, making the easiest rather than necessarily the best decision, and procrastination can lead to them not making any decision at all. In addition, people often live for today and struggle to see what their future needs might be. When presented with the option of having money now or more money in the future, people frequently choose to take the money now, even though they would be better off if they waited. This is reinforced by the fact that people often don't understand that inflation can erode the value of any money they have 'under the mattress'. (DWP, 2006b: 51–2)

The behavioural economist whom New Labour drew most upon in this regard is Richard H. Thaler, an American economist who would go on to win the Nobel Memorial Prize in Economics in 2017. Thaler's work on 'quasi-rational economics' pioneered the application of behavioural psychology to economic life, noting the many cognitive biases, attitudinal shortcomings, and informational blind spots which inhibited rational behaviour (Thaler, 1994). Thaler's work on pensions saving—advocating a 'save more tomorrow' model whereby individuals are not only enrolled into a private pension, but see contributions rise from a very low introductory rate over time—is cited in the white paper (see Thaler and Benartzi, 2004). Thaler came to prominence internationally and beyond academia in 2008 when he published *Nudge: Improving Decisions about Health, Wealth and Happiness* with Cass R. Sunstein, outlining the authors' 'libertarian paternalist' understanding of public policy interventions. 'Nudges' were depicted as interventions by the state to reshape the 'choice architecture' faced by individuals—not removing their responsibility for their own welfare, but ensuring, as far as possible, that they made the decisions deemed to be in their best (financial) interests.

The approach did not simply influence pensions policy, but instead became part of the Whitehall machinery when the Behavioural Insights Team (BIT; known colloquially as 'the nudge unit') was established by the Coalition government in 2010. (BIT was actually privatized in 2014—the first time civil servants responsible for policy *decisions* rather than *delivery* had been moved from public- to private-sector employment (Plimmer, 2014)—so that government departments drawing upon BIT's work now pay for the service.) However, as well as questioning whether behavioural economics provides for a sustainable solution to undersaving, we can question whether auto-enrolment actually represents the genuine integration of behavioural insights into pensions policy development. As Deborah Mabbett (2012: 121) argues, auto-enrolment 'is based on very partial lesson drawing from behavioural economics. It addresses the individual-level ghosts of inertia and reluctance to save for retirement, but it does not address the systemic ghosts that mean that retirement income security is not achieved by investing individual funds in financial instruments'. For Mabbett, one of the key insights of behavioural economics is that markets in general produce irrational outcomes—and yet, as this chapter and Chapter 6 testify, auto-enrolment has instituted a largely marketized approach to individualized pensions provision (see also Langley, 2006; and in particular Langley and Leaver, 2012).

5.2.1 The Rationality of Defined Contribution and Soft Compulsion

The influence of behavioural economics was also evident upon the Pensions Commission. The Commission (2004: 208–9) acknowledged a set of behavioural tendencies—principally, procrastination—as one of the main barriers to a voluntarist system, and accordingly a key justification of an opt-out ahead of opt-in approach. The other, main barriers discussed by the Commission were issues around complexity and lack of trust in the pensions industry (a key justification for the state-managed 'personal accounts' model which never came to pass), investment and management costs, the interaction of private pension income with means-tested benefits, and the variable tax incentives available to different groups of savers. There are, however, two major issues which may inhibit individuals' ability to save privately for a pension, irrespective of auto-enrolment—and which might actually render the decision *not* to save a rather rational decision.

Firstly, and most importantly, the question of whether individuals can afford to save. Incredibly, but quite deliberately, the 2006 white paper contains no analysis of whether groups at different points on the income distribution are more likely to opt out of workplace pension schemes, or even of whether income levels affect the likelihood they were already participating in a scheme or engaging in long-term saving more generally. The Pensions Commission was more obliging, with its initial analysis demonstrating that lower earners were far less likely to be saving for a pension—but at the same time far *more* likely to achieve a benchmark replacement rate when they reach retirement, as a result of accessing means-tested benefits (see Pensions Commission, 2004; DWP, 2006b). However, as suggested above, this is presented not in positive terms, but rather as a barrier to saving privately: in other words, the poor are not poor enough. Within the framing adopted by the Commission, the primary significance of undersaving is not whether it will leave individuals impoverished in retirement, but rather whether it will affect the state's fiscal position detrimentally, as more people become eligible for means-tested benefits (and for a longer proportion of their life) as private-sector defined benefit provision disappears. This perspective is implicitly replicated in the white paper which, despite positing fiscal sustainability as a key reform principle, largely focuses on the benefits of auto-enrolment and personal accounts to individuals in general. As such, while the Commission considered the mechanics of opting out very carefully, they did not assess in depth the likelihood it would occur on a significant scale among lower earners. The white paper contains only a brief mention of the likelihood of individuals opting out of their workplace scheme, having estimated that opt-out rates will be around a third, or ranged between a fifth and a half:

> Around 10 million employees will be eligible for automatic enrolment into a personal account. There are uncertainties about the number of people who might choose to opt out but we estimate that between 5 and 8 million employees will remain in personal accounts. Women, those working part-time, low and moderate earners are those less likely to have current pension provision and therefore will be well represented in our target group.   (DWP, 2006b: 45)

Clearly, if we assume lower-income groups are the most likely to opt out (because they can least afford to save, or means-tested benefits undermine the value of saving), then '[w]omen, those working part-time, [and] low and moderate earners' will accordingly be *under*-represented among auto-enrolees, and as a result will not be entitled to a statutory minimum contribution from their employer. Of course, as noted above, many in these groups are not eligible for auto-enrolment in the first place.

It is sometimes assumed that the introduction of the earnings trigger (and particularly the significant increase in its level that the Coalition government introduced) was to ensure that those most likely to opt out were not wastefully auto-enrolled. However, there was clearly no evidence upon which to base this assertion. As the Coalition's *Making Automatic Enrolment Work* (MAEW) review (which preceded many of the 'tweaks' to auto-enrolment undertaken by the Coalition) makes clear, the higher trigger was justified on the basis that the lowest earners are unlikely to benefit from accruing tiny pots of pensions saving—and so employers should be saved the administrative burden of enrolling them into a scheme and processing contributions (see Johnson et al., 2010). MAEW was undertaken by Paul Johnson of the Institute for Fiscal Studies, David Yeandle of the Engineering Employers'

Federation, and Adrian Boulding of Legal & General (there was no place at the table for any women, or workers' representatives, on this occasion). Interestingly, one of the most controversial elements of the new earnings trigger policy was that the level of the trigger was decided at the discretion of ministers—which MAEW had not recommended.

Remarkably, we *still* do not know whether the lowest earners (that is, those with earnings from a single employer just above the earnings trigger) are more likely to opt out, even with auto-enrolment fully implemented. DWP revised its opt-out assumption in 2013 from 20–50 per cent to 25 per cent (DWP, 2013b), but in practice the opt-out rate has actually been much lower: it was 9 per cent in 2017, generally in line with previous years (DWP, 2018b). Data on opt-outs comes solely from DWP's biennial Employers' Pensions Provision Survey—as such, it is employers who report how many of their employees eligible for auto-enrolment have opted out of workplace pensions saving. They are not asked to disaggregate their employees' decisions by earnings. (The survey also reports on how many employees stay enrolled for more than a year—that is, persistency—but, again, this is not disaggregated by earnings.)

Of course, while the opt-out rate has been lower than expected, this is almost certainly related to the fact that contribution levels have been phased in very gradually. Based on DWP's existing approach to data-gathering, it will be 2022 before we know the opt-out rate for the first full year (2020) in which the legal minimum contribution rate for employees (5 per cent) has been in operation. It is also worth noting that the earnings trigger has excluded from auto-enrolment many low-earning workers that the Pensions Commission had assumed would be automatically enrolled. Of course, while we do not know who is opting out, and why, we *do know* that, as a result of auto-enrolment, workplace pension scheme participation rates have increased very significantly among low earners, and young people. Table 5.1 presents data on scheme participation within the private sector by earnings and age since 2008. Interestingly, while lower earners generally saw participation rates fall between 2008 and 2012 (while rates for higher earners were stable), they have now 'caught up' to some extent. It is not clear whether the significant gap that remains results from a greater propensity to opt out among lower earners, or rather the fact that they are less likely to have (yet) been automatically enrolled. It should perhaps be acknowledged that, within all earnings groups, women have a slightly higher participation rate than men—although the gender gap among lower earners, where it had been most pronounced, has now largely closed (see DWP, 2019c) (and does not detract

Table 5.1 Employees' workplace pension scheme participation rate (%) in the private sector by gross annual earnings and age group, 2008–18

	2008	2010	2012	2014	2016	2018
£10,000–under £20,000	26	22	20	26	62	79
£20,000–under £30,000	40	37	35	39	70	85
£30,000–under £40,000	57	54	53	56	77	88
£40,000–under £50,000	66	62	65	68	82	91
£50,000–under £60,000	73	74	72	74	85	92
£60,000+	77	76	78	79	86	92
22–9	28	26	24	54	67	84
30–9	48	44	42	64	72	86
40–9	55	51	49	67	75	86
50–SPA	55	52	50	66	74	85

Source: DWP estimates using ASHE data, 2008–18, available at: https://assets.publishing.service.gov.uk/government/uploads/system/uploads/attachment_data/file/806507/workplace-pension-participation-and-saving-trends-2008-2018.ods

from the fact that women are less likely to be eligible for auto-enrolment, and receive lower contributions when they are enrolled).

Accordingly, we know that lower earners are now more likely to be enrolled in a workplace pensions scheme—yet we do not know if their earnings nevertheless mean they are more likely than higher earners to opt out. We therefore are unable to speculate on what the impact of raising minimum contribution rates—both to 5 per cent, and then potentially beyond—might be on participation rates. This is not because the answer is too difficult to ascertain, but rather because the question has not been asked by policy-makers. It seems that doing so would undermine the intellectual rationale of auto-enrolment, and in particular its delivery via defined contribution schemes. Ultimately, auto-enrolment is about disciplining individuals to prepare for, and cope with, welfare retrenchment amid financialization. Yet if we were to acknowledge that opting out of pensions saving has an economic rationale (that is, if it is deemed unaffordable), then this ideological project would be undermined. Undersaving is, so the story goes, a fundamentally irrational behavioural trait, to be countered by soft compulsion. But what if seemingly irresponsible financial behaviour were in fact the product of an entirely rational decision?

Secondly, while the Pensions Commission rightly acknowledged the *costs* of saving as a potential barrier to 'an effective pensions market', the question of whether individuals were prepared to accept the investment *risks* inherent in defined contribution provision was largely marginalized, both by the Commission and the Labour government (and subsequently MAEW and the Coalition government). Costs produce lower returns, but even a low-cost defined contribution vehicle cannot eliminate the risk that individuals will see their savings fail to rematerialize as a retirement income, or at least fail to rematerialize at the level expected. As discussed in Chapter 4, the difference between defined benefit and defined contribution provision is treated as a purely technical or operational issue—with the latter in fact seen as preferable due to its apparent flexibility and simplicity. Insofar as the relative interests of employers and individuals were considered in the choice between defined benefit and defined contribution, employers' unwillingness to shoulder investment risks is accepted a priori. As such, the question of whether individuals might be unwilling to save due to the risks inherent in defined contribution saving is never asked, because the necessity of such risks being individualized is inviolable. Again, we could argue that not taking such risks, by choosing not to invest in a defined contribution scheme, is a perfectly rational or responsible way to behave (see Casey and Dostal, 2013), especially if the Coalition government's changes to decumulation processes continue to undermine the value of accumulated savings.

Overall, auto-enrolment, and its delivery via defined contribution provision, asks individuals to accept personal responsibility, in place of state benevolence—while at the same time signalling individuals' lack of capacity to behave responsibly. Through pensions saving we atone for our inherent sinfulness. Pensions individualization has accordingly been accompanied by attempts to articulate a disciplinary narrative whereby policy-makers preach the importance of saving, even as the choice of whether to commence saving is (largely) removed from individuals. The contradiction is typified by pensions minister Guy Opperman's (pensions minister, at the time of writing, in the Johnson government) support for 'Pensions Awareness Day'. An op-ed Opperman wrote for *The Sunday Times* in September 2019 is worth citing at length:

> A private, auto-enrolled pension is one of the largest investments anyone will make in their life...But far too often they don't think about their pensions until it is too late to make a big difference. This is a bit like gardening: the hard work is in the planning, preparing and planting; the easy bit is sitting back and watching the flowers grow. You will reap the rewards when it comes to those autumn years and your pension is in full bloom. This is why Pensions Awareness Day, which is today, is so important, and why the government is launching a campaign to get the message out there...[The campaign] urges people to have their aspirations at

the forefront of their minds as they save for the future. If you help people to understand what they can do now to set themselves up for later life, they will do what is right for themselves and their families…Occupational pensions have been transformed since auto-enrolment began in 2012. More than 10m people have been enrolled into saving, many for the first time, through the scheme. We are not going to rest on this success. The next step is to get more people thinking about their pension.   (Opperman, 2019a)

Opperman (2019b) has also championed the 'pensions dashboard', so that 'retirement savers [can] keep tabs on all their pension pots at the touch of a smartphone screen'. The quote above demonstrates the ideological urge to valorise personal responsibility for pensions saving—imploring people to actively save, and think about saving, while simultaneously celebrating the removal of 'free will' which auto-enrolment embodies.

This agenda clearly echoes the financial literacy agenda which was pursued by New Labour, as part of the inculcation of asset-based welfare (Finlayson, 2009; Berry, 2015a). For the most part, New Labour upheld the notion that greater know-how regarding financial services would lead to, or enable, more responsible behaviour. We can associate this agenda with the provision of financial education, but also (short-lived) initiatives such as the Child Trust Fund (enabling people to build up a financial asset from birth), and indeed stakeholder pensions (signified by the branding). Fundamentally, auto-enrolment is a signal of the limitations of this agenda or, more cynically, that *too much* financial knowledge might encourage people to save less, if they are informed about, for instance, likely returns and the extent of investment risks being taken. This is not to suggest that low levels of financial literacy are not associated with low rates of pensions saving for some groups (particularly young people and women). However, the success of auto-enrolment depends more on auto-enrolees being convinced that it 'pays to save' (Foster, 2017: 77–8; see also Foster and Heneghan, 2017). Initiatives such as the pensions dashboard will not make it pay to save, but are based instead on the notion that greater access to information on our own pensions circumstances will breed trust in pensions saving. Yet given that we are already largely compelled to save in a workplace pension, why not simply nudge us into higher contribution rates too? This is the point at which the limits of the auto-enrolment system are confronted: policy-makers are unwilling to compel *employers* to contribute any more into their workers' pension pots, and so a mixture of literacy measures and moralizing discourses are mobilized to encourage individuals alone to save more.

Analysis of Labour and Conservative election manifestos from the early 2000s onwards demonstrates the UK political elite's determination to proselytize the importance of saving, albeit articulated in largely positive terms, that is, by promising to 'reward' individuals who behave responsibly (see Berry, 2017a). The interaction of this narrative with a pro-austerity narrative is worth noting. Labour's pro-saver and pro-saving narrative actually peaked in its 2010 manifesto, as saving was depicted as a responsible response to economic strife. The Conservatives' 2010 manifesto was less instructive, yet it is interesting that after five years in power, the party's 2015 manifesto adopted a very similar narrative around rewarding savers' responsible behaviour. An important argument from the 2010 manifesto, that savers were contributing to economic 'rebalancing' by supporting long-term investment, was entirely dropped in favour of a focus on rewards (and support) for individuals. However, it should also be noted that this discourse shifted at the 2017 election. The Conservatives' pro-saving agenda was undermined by then Prime Minister Theresa May's controversial proposals on social care finance, which were seen to punish savers by requiring higher contributions to the cost of their care by people with assets such as cash savings. And Labour offered virtually no reference to saving or pensions, other than a brief promise to challenge high management charges. Tellingly, however, despite this shift, neither party questioned either the principle or practice of auto-enrolment (or defined contribution more generally) in 2017, and nor is there evidence that such an agenda has been prioritized in the subsequent period (cf. Dromey, 2019).

5.3. Before, and Beyond, Defined Contribution

Although defined contribution may now be firmly entrenched in our imaginary of what a pension is, this does not mean that defined contribution pension provision is a settled part of the UK's financialized model of capitalism. Turner is far from the final word; even with auto-enrolment in its infancy, there are signs of the demise of defined contribution pensions provision. Indeed, the genesis of defined contribution (as discussed in Chapter 2) helps us to understand the relatively recent evolution of defined contribution as a product suitable for workplace pensions saving. Defined contribution provision is effectively the confluence of life insurance products as structured savings vehicles (particularly 'with profits' products in which customers benefited from returns on investments made using their premium payments) and annuities as a form of hedging longevity risks for those with sufficient capital. The co-existence of guaranteed outcomes (in both life insurance and annuity products) and the possibility of using savings to invest personal wealth served as the blueprint for personal pensions, and eventually the oxymoronic 'group personal pensions' (GPPs). GPPs emerged in the 1980s after the Thatcher government incentivized the establishment of defined contribution workplace pension schemes via the application of 'contracting out' tax incentives to defined contribution as well as defined benefit. Annuitization was the obligatory end point of accumulating savings in tax-advantaged pension products, even for individual savers. Crucially, however, despite annuities generally being purchased from the same insurance company providing the saving vehicle, the annuitization contract remains separate from that governing the accumulation phase.

Not all defined contribution schemes take the form of GPPs. There are also schemes governed by independent trusts—as in defined benefit provision—rather than by contractual relations between customer and provider, and which are classified legally as occupational schemes. We could therefore see trust-based defined contribution provision as a diluted form of traditional defined benefit practice. However, this would be a misreading: trust-based defined contributions schemes are individualized provision, only superficially resembling defined benefit. It would be equally plausible to suggest that trust-based schemes would not have emerged had defined contribution provision not first developed through contract-based provision (and, from the individual saver's perspective, the two models are—increasingly—indistinguishable). Developments in the pensions industry and its regulatory environment related to this distinction between contract-based and trust-based provision will be discussed further in Chapter 6. It is worth noting here though that occupational defined contribution provision—unlike defined benefit—is purely for accumulation purposes. As in GPPs, members of trust-based schemes are required to transfer their accumulated capital, principally to an insurer in the form of an annuity contract, to secure a retirement income. Smoothing this complex and risky transfer process for individuals, in both GPPs and trust-based schemes, has been a concern of policy-makers as a mass market for defined contribution provision has emerged—yet they have generally favoured industry self-regulation.

The trust-based model may at least offer opportunities for the development of CDC schemes, which would replicate some of the collectivist characteristics of defined benefit schemes. However, as discussed in Chapter 4, CDC is unlikely to significantly alter the UK pensions landscape—it is likely to be used to 'level down' defined benefit provision, rather than 'level up' defined contribution. We may instead be seeing long-term saving and financial management in the UK moving away from pensions products altogether, including defined contribution schemes. Crucially, such a shift has been encouraged by recent policy-makers, particularly George Osborne as Chancellor within the Coalition government. Osborne's decision to 'liberalise' pensions saving by abolishing compulsory annuitization will be discussed further in Chapter 6; we can note now, however, that this move does not so much abolish annuities as return them to their origins as an optional retirement product, clearly disconnected from the accumulation phase. Osborne also established the Lifetime Individual Savings Account (LISA) as an alternative to workplace pensions. Individuals aged 18–39 can open a LISA and save up to £4,000 per year, receiving a maximum bonus of £1,000 per year from the state, up to the age of 50 (in addition to interest on cash and/or returns on investment). Crucially, while LISA savings can be used to fund a retirement income after the age of 60, they are also designed to support home purchases. Savers can use LISA savings in entirety to fund property investments up to the age of 40. As such, the LISA replaces the Help-to-Buy Individual Savings Account, which operated in conjunction with the wider Help-to-Buy scheme to support housing purchases in the wake of the financial crisis, and was strongly criticized by the National Audit Office (2019) for largely helping savers who did not need helping. The LISA was launched in April 2017, and around 200,000 accounts were opened in the first two years, attracting total bonuses of around £170 million. Interestingly, almost a third of this amount (£50 million) had been paid to LISA customers of Hargreaves Lansdown—an investment services company catering predominantly for affluent clients, with a strong interest in non-workplace personal pensions saving (Cook, 2019). If the UK policy elite's commitment to defined contribution workplace pensions continues to wane, we may see long-term saving in the future come to resemble practices dominant in the era before employer-sponsored pensions provision emerged. This possibility has particularly vexed the House of Commons Work and Pensions Committee (2016a: 3). The committee argues that the LISA 'could jeopardise the success of [auto-enrolment]', and that 'the government should make clear that the LISA is not a pension'. Tellingly, the committee sided with DWP's view in this regard—and criticized the Treasury (and the then Chancellor) for promoting the LISA as an alternative form of pensions saving.

It is important not to overstate the short-term significance of these changes. But there is a paradoxical consistency between significant state support for the individualization of pensions provision and increasing opportunities and incentives for long-term saving outside formal pensions saving processes. With the latter linked profoundly to home-ownership, it speaks to the broader process of financialization at the micro level, with individuals compelled to build up financial assets by way of procuring their own long-term financial security. So, pensions saving is necessary, but so too are mechanisms more flexible than conventional pensions saving, as financialization cuts across multiple spheres of welfare—both/and, not either/or. Interestingly, in light of the state's willingness to cover only a small proportion of the cost of social care for older people, former Secretary of State for Health and Social Care, Jeremy Hunt, suggested during the 2019 Conservative party leadership contest (in which he finished runner-up) the introduction of a *second* system of auto-enrolment, to compel individuals to save separately for care costs. Boris Johnson, the new Prime Minister, has indicated his support for the idea (Clarke, 2019). Of course, the cost of care is itself intimately bound up with housing wealth; after several, failed attempts to include housing wealth more systemically in an insurance-based approach to social care finance—culminating in the May government's unpopular proposals at the 2017 general election, noted above—Hunt's plan was an attempt to circumvent this dilemma. Obviously, defined contribution pensions saving, as envisaged in the Turner consensus, is not about to disappear—by design, schemes will become increasingly populous—but the direction of travel is towards greater flexibility in, and beyond, the defined contribution model. This is not incidental: it is part of the same ideological settlement which compelled the Pensions Commission to accept an individualized saving model for auto-enrolment. In this regard, the compromise between individual responsibility, employer obligations, and state support has already failed—in part because the array of responsibilities is expanding, and in part because policy-makers since 2010 have prioritized supporting home-ownership in line with wider macro-economic objectives. Auto-enrolment will proceed in practice for the foreseeable future, but its foundational principles have been significantly weakened.

5.4. Conclusion: A False Dawn?

In many ways, the Pensions Commission was established to change course from the developmental direction UK pensions provision had taken since the Thatcher government. Its job was to both relieve fiscal pressure on the state resulting from undersaving and, relatedly, to mitigate the rising number of retired people below the poverty threshold (or, more likely, just above—given New Labour's introduction of new means-tested benefits). But the course correction was not only insufficient, arguably it further entrenched key elements of neoliberal statecraft. With individuals increasingly responsible for their own long-term welfare, and defined contribution now the default form of workplace pensions provision, the long-term, cross-generational co-operation that sustains pensions provision has been undermined. The post-Turner era in UK pensions policy is a false dawn. Moreover, as will be explored further in Chapter 6, the state is not simply 'getting out of the way' of financialization and a highly privatized approach to welfare provision—it is actively involved in advancing individualization. We are less able to rely on even the state to embody a collectivist approach to pensions provision— despite the faint allusions to collectivism that remained part of the Pensions Commission's initial framing.

Across the *longue durée*, we are of course only at the very start of the journey towards a largely individualized pensions landscape. Policy-makers may yet succeed in ensuring the majority of citizens are topping up, to a significant extent, their state pension entitlements through private provision. However, whether financialized capitalism delivers some approximation of the outcomes Turner et al. expected, we can be certain that it will not deliver them in the way that was expected. Pensions futures fails, because capitalism develops, and generations differ. The imperilment of UK pensions provision lies not simply in the likelihood that individualization is the wrong course, and that policy-makers will remain wedded to the neoliberal norms and financialized growth model that maintain it. Rather, it lies also in the fact that, by definition, individualization removes the mechanisms by which we manage future failures.

If employers are no longer willing or able to serve as the temporal anchor of pensions provision, and their substitution by the state is both messy and contradictory, then the only anchor available is individuals themselves. This reliance is baked into auto-enrolment; it is the assumption that individuals will always, and must always, act in accordance with their own self-interest to participate in, and therefore help to sustain, pensions provision that underpins the defined contribution model. This is an unreliable assumption, partly because individual self-interest is not timeless, but rather highly specific to its social, political, and economic context. Moreover, as the design of auto-enrolment itself shows, our understanding of what constitutes responsible or rational behaviour is far too crude. Individuals are deemed too irrational to behave responsibly, or too irresponsible to behave rationally. As Andrew Pendleton and Howard Gospel (2017: 26) argue, we can therefore see the shift to soft compulsion as both a recognition of the failure of neoliberalism and its advocacy of financialized pensions provision, and indeed the advancement of financialization. An approach to pensions provision that relies on individual engagement, but at the same time seeks to discipline individuals to ensure certain behaviours prevail, is, quite simply, asking for trouble—not least by, as we shall see in Chapter 6, inviting policy-makers to disrupt the fragile balance between choice and compulsion in service of their ideological commitments and/or immediate political interests.

6
Auto-Pilot: The State's Role in Delivering (and Endangering) Workplace Pensions

This chapters builds upon Chapter 5 by considering in more depth some of the key elements of the emerging landscape of individualized pensions provision in the UK, reflecting in particular on some of the state's emerging functions as facilitator, regulator, and provider of defined contribution pensions. At various times, and across various specific policy areas, we find policy-makers *diluting* the blueprint established by Adair Turner's Pensions Commission by curtailing the prospect of state intervention, embarking on new forms of intervention by way of *correcting* flawed aspects of the Turner plan, and indeed *undermining* the post-Turner consensus by intensifying the individualization of workplace pensions provision.

Section 6.1 considers the regulatory divide within defined contribution provision between trust-based and insurer-provided workplace pensions, and the role of NEST as a state-backed provider of defined contribution pensions. In both cases, policy (in)action has diverted UK pensions provision from the path established by Turner et al. Section 6.2 looks at the seemingly operational issues of, firstly, scheme charges and investment costs, and secondly, the proliferation of small pension pots as auto-enrolees move between jobs and providers. The Pensions Commission neglected to adjudicate on such issues—and policy-makers have made some rather contradictory decisions, while generally favouring financial services providers' interests. Section 6.3 looks at decumulation processes: annuities are an integral element of defined contribution pensions, but often marginalized in analysis focused on issues around accumulation. However, the introduction of 'pension freedoms' by the Coalition government has not only significantly affected the decumulation processes hitherto taken for granted, it has also further exposed the contradictions at the heart of auto-enrolment, and in the process jeopardized the inter-generational underpinning of UK pensions provision as a whole. Section 6.4 focuses on PTR—a controversial policy

Pensions Imperilled: The Political Economy of Private Pensions Provision in the UK. Craig Berry, Oxford University Press (2021).
© Craig Berry. DOI: 10.1093/oso/9780198782834.003.0006

instrument which complexifies the seemingly simple structure of defined contribution pensions provision. Here, we find the state unable to unravel its fiscal support for workplace pensions—in part because of the implications reform would have for zombie-like defined benefit provision and regulation. The chapter of course does not suggest that the imperilment of UK pensions provision is due solely to the distortion of the Turner plan by subsequent policy-makers: the Pensions Commission's approach was hugely flawed. Auto-enrolment—partly *de jure*, partly *de facto*—is itself part of the problem.

6.1. Regulatory State, Replacement State

The implementation of auto-enrolment has required a multitude of policy decisions by policy-makers—often exposing the contradictions of the policy in the process, as the Pensions Commission's broad-brush recommendations confront the institutionalized practices (and limitations) of extant defined contribution provision. This section considers in greater depth the messy divide between trust-based and contract-based defined contribution provision, and the emergence of NEST in place of Turner's 'personal accounts' model, and the apparent 'teething problems' of scheme charges and the proliferation of small pots. In practice, we find the state—as either provider or regulator—struggling to take on the role (vaguely, or only implicitly) outlined by the Commission, and instead adopting a subservient orientation towards private providers.

6.1.1 The Two Worlds of Workplace Pensions

The simplistic notion that defined benefit pensions provision has been 'converted' to defined contribution silently underpins much recent discourse on UK pensions provision. Of course, as explored in Chapter 4, closed defined benefit schemes were generally replaced by *nothing*, not defined contribution—although this is in part due to firm failure, with newer employers taking advantage of the lack of meaningful obligations to provide *any* form of pensions provision, in the context of industrial change and deunionization. As such, and as noted in Chapter 5, defined contribution's origins lie in the provision of personal pensions saving products, independently of the workplace, and generally to very affluent savers. Employer-sponsored schemes only emerged after contracting out was extended to defined contribution provision in the late 1980s. Yet pensions law requires *occupational*—a more specific, legal category than 'workplace'—pensions to be managed by

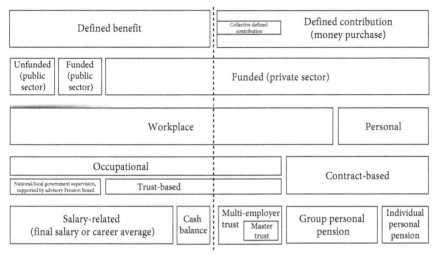

Figure 6.1 The overlapping (legal) categories of private pensions provision in the UK
Note: in defined contribution provision, only applies to accumulation phase

independent trustees (or at least trustees acting in an independent capacity, even if ostensibly representing employers) solely for the benefit of scheme members. This is, quite understandably, inconsistent with insurance companies' (the main source of personal pensions) objective of making financial gains from the customers they serve.

Figure 6.1 demonstrates the messy ways in which different legal, industrial, and financial categories of workplace pensions provision overlap, both within and across both defined benefit and defined contribution provision. While the governance of some defined contribution schemes is trust-based, as in private-sector defined benefit, the governance of some is based purely on a service contract between scheme provider (an insurance company) and the individual member. When contract-based schemes are used in workplace pensions provision, they are known rather oxymoronically as 'group personal pensions' (GPPs). In 2018, there were 8.5 million active members of trust-based defined contribution schemes, and 5.9 million in contract-based workplace schemes.[1] Given the manifold complexity of pensions saving, that many millions of individuals are now being automatically enrolled into schemes with no layer of oversight between themselves and the provider is highly problematic. (It should be noted that GPPs, as discussed in Chapter 7, are also now required to have governance committees, including

---

[1] Data on scheme membership by type is available at https://www.ons.gov.uk/peoplepopulationand-community/personalandhouseholdfinances/pensionssavingsandinvestments/datasets/occupationalpen-sionschemessurvey (ASHE) and https://www.thepensionsregulator.gov.uk/en/document-library/research-and-analysis/dc-trust-presentation-of-scheme-return-data-2018–2019 (TPR's scheme return data).

'independent' members, although these operate across a provider's GPP schemes, rather than at workplace level.)

The fact that a market-led approach to implementing auto-enrolment, with insurance companies at its heart, has important roots in much earlier occupational pensions practice in the UK has been almost entirely over-looked by scholars and commentators. Yet as Chapter 2 shows, insurance companies were major players in the rollout of occupational pensions in the inter-war period, offering schemes that would be understood now as defined benefit/defined contribution hybrids. The insurers lost the battle for supremacy with employer-sponsored defined benefit trusts—focusing instead on annuity provision and, in some cases, investment management. Yet they re-emerged as direct providers of personal pensions, beyond the workplace, in the 1980s, shorn of course of all features resembling defined benefit provision. In an important sense, auto-enrolment returns UK pensions provision to a firmly anti- or pre-collectivist imaginary that had been dormant for decades.

This outcome was not inevitable. While rejecting the Pensions Commission's plan for state-provided personal accounts, policy-makers could have insisted that all pension schemes used for auto-enrolment must be occupational or trust-based schemes—this would have been entirely consistent with traditional pensions practice in the UK. NAPF (representing trust-based providers) recommended such an approach to delivering personal accounts, when proposing the licensing of ten to twenty 'supertrusts'. The Labour government rejected this possibility, on the basis that 'a successful system must be designed around personal responsibility'. At the same time, the government also ostensibly rejected an ABI proposal for 'partnership pensions'; under this model, employers could choose whether to establish or join a trust- or contract-based scheme, but also facilitate their employees to divert contribution into an individual personal pension. Clearly, this proposal is rather close to where we have ended up, but the ability for individuals to reject their employer's choice of scheme was forgone on the basis that it created an administrative burden for employers, and exceeded an 'appropriate level of choice' for workers (a decision which embodies the contradictory individualism at the heart of auto-enrolment, as discussed in Chapter 5) (see DWP, 2006b: 47). (Fascinatingly, ABI also suggested a permanent Retirement Income Commission 'to oversee the system and ensure that it worked for individuals'; while TPR plays this role for trust-based schemes, no such equivalent for contract-based provision has ever come to pass.)

The main implication is that, counter-intuitively, around 2,000 workplace pension schemes (with an average of around 3,000 members)[2] are regulated

[2] See note 1.

not by TPR, but rather the Financial Conduct Authority (FCA; previously the Financial Services Authority). Insurance regulation focuses on the point of sale: ensuring that customers understand the product they are buying, or contract they are signing. (Annuities are regulated within this regime too.) Assuming such a regulatory approach is well executed, it is not necessarily unhelpful and has been strengthened since the financial crisis and the creation of the FCA in 2013. Yet the issue of how workplace pension schemes within the GPP space are managed post-sale (including the appropriateness of charges, even if savers agree to them) is largely overlooked by the FCA. Moreover, point-of-sale regulation is based on the assumption that customers are capable of understanding the terms they are agreeing to. Not only is pensions saving inherently complex, but the 'customer' is in practice usually the employer—who has no financial interest at all in the contract being signed between their employees and the provider. This ability to outsource scheme management to providers in entirety is a major incentive for employers to select a GPP for their auto-enrolment obligations (although, in practice, the largest, multi-employer trust-based schemes now offer similar arrangements).

There is obviously something inherently perverse about workplace pension schemes occupying quite different regulatory regimes, especially as individuals may build up savings in both regimes. This is not to suggest that TPR is unconcerned by savers in GPPs: it has worked recently with the FCA to strengthen guidance to providers on how pension schemes should be managed post-sale (FCA and TPR, 2018) (although similar initiatives have already been attempted (see FCA and TPR, 2014)). Yet it simply has no formal powers in this regard—and the FCA has few levers by which to intervene in GPPs beyond compliance with point-of-sale regulation. However, we must not assume that the TPR regime for trust-based schemes is unproblematic. TPR's main statutory powers relate, firstly, to defined benefit provision, and secondly, to employers' obligations regarding auto-enrolment. It has fairly limited powers to establish codes of practice for how trust-based workplace pension schemes are governed (although schemes are legally required to comply with codes, as well as trust law more generally). Indeed, in January 2020, TPR actually issued a £2,000 fine to the FCA, for a minor breach of disclosure rules regarding the latter's own pension plan (Espadinha, 2020).

The landscape of defined contribution regulation within the trust-based space was transformed recently by the Pensions Schemes Act 2017, and subsequent regulatory instruments, as 'master trusts' were recognized in law as a distinct form of trust-based defined contribution provision, with a new regulatory regime. (Arguably, this represents a diluted version of NAPF's super-trusts proposal, which was rejected more than a decade earlier. Ironically, however, whereas supertrusts were proposed in an attempt to hold off the full-scale nationalization of defined contribution saving implied by the Pensions Commission, master trust regulation is ostensibly an attempt by the state to strengthen regulation within the highly privatized approach that has actually ensued.) Master trusts are multi-employer pension schemes for unconnected employers, designed to cater for large numbers of members (in law, only two unconnected employers are now required for a scheme to qualify as a master trust). The development of master trusts can be seen as a market response to the establishment of NEST by the state—albeit, as discussed below, we should not therefore conclude that NEST's mission to provide a quality floor for large-scale, trust-based defined contribution provision has been achieved. In practice, most master trusts compete with NEST not on quality, but rather cost. Whereas NEST was established as a low-cost, 'no frills' default provider, master trusts now perform this function—with NEST instead focusing on quality provision, as well as smaller employers not well served by the private sector within either the trust-based or contract-based spaces. In effect, while master trusts occupy the trust-based regulatory regime, they resemble a typical GPP offer as much as they do the conventional image of a pensions-related trust, based on independent governance of the savings of a single employer's workforce. Indeed lighter-touch regulatory standards, in combination with scale, enables master trusts to compete also with formal GPP providers (Campion, 2013).

The problem with defined contribution regulation, therefore, is not simply that GPPs sit outside pensions regulation—which would in any case be too simplistic a reading—but also that, as suggested above, trust-based provision has been increasingly 'GPP-ised'. There are around 14 million members of master trusts in the UK (although not all of these master trusts have yet received authorization) (TPR, 2019a). As of 2018, NEST is the largest with around 6 million members, followed by People's Pension with around 4 million. NOW: Pensions has around 4 million (PLSA, 2018). Given that we know there are only 8.5 million active members of defined contributions trusts overall, a very large proportion of these memberships will be deferred and/or constitute individuals with multiple active and deferred pots. Some master trusts exited the market in the wake of the 2017 Act (which was designed in part to produce this outcome, that is, consolidation among the several dozen master trusts in operation).[3] Interestingly, L&G, the UK's largest

---

[3] The magazine *Professional Pensions* maintains an updated list of master trust providers; see https://www.professionalpensions.com/news/2352950/pension-master-trusts-list-providers. The withdrawal of some providers throughout 2018 was highlighted at this website at the time of writing (mid-2019), but information is regularly updated.

GPP provider, is now actively seeking to also become a dominant player within the master trust market by expanding its existing master trust offer. At the same time, GPP providers such as Royal London—where former Pensions Minister Steve Webb was until recently employed as Policy Director—have sought to emphasize the independence of the oversight of their pension schemes, by way of discrediting (or at least challenging) the notion that master trusts represent a step-change in the quality of defined contribution scheme governance (Royal London, 2019). The emphasis on cost ahead of quality has driven policy-makers' recent concerns with how master trusts are regulated. The 2017 Act therefore established 'authorisation criteria' by which master trusts can be licensed by TPR. The criteria focus on three key issues. Firstly, whether those involved in running the trust are 'fit and proper' (that is, whether they meet 'the standard of honesty, integrity and knowledge appropriate to their role'). Secondly, whether the trust has sufficient operational capacity to serve all members. Thirdly, whether the trust has a business model which means it is likely to endure—offering services to members—even in the event of adverse developments such as the withdrawal of certain employers (see TPR, 2018a).

Schemes meeting these criteria are then subjected to a different regulatory approach, whereby TPR has the authority to supervise the extent to which the business conforms to the criteria, as well as the key codes of practice—but in practice master trusts may face *less* regulatory scrutiny, as a result of clearing a higher entry barrier. It is obviously too early to say how effective master trust regulation will operate in practice. However, this book's primary focus is the rationale behind recent policy developments; it is clear that the new regime for master trusts helps to expose the inherent limitations of individualized pensions provision, even where defined contribution schemes are managed by independent trusts. The regulator's approach implicitly accepts that master trusts fail to accord to traditional expectations of trust-based pensions governance. In defined benefit trusts, trustees' most important task is policing the employer's role as guarantor or temporal anchor—a relationship which offers, at least in theory, a degree of leverage within investment processes by which workers' savings are rematerialized. In defined contribution trusts, the fact that outcomes are entirely dependent on capital market returns means an inherently weaker position vis-à-vis capital markets, since protecting scheme members' interests involves generating returns within these markets. Master trusts reflect this contradiction by muddying the distinction between those independently governing pension schemes and the finance sector with which schemes must engage. This was a highly predictable development, but one which the Turner Commission did not anticipate, and it remains to be seen whether TPR, however well intentioned, has the capacity or authority to effectively regulate these emergent pensions industry practices.

6.1.2 From PADA to NEST

As noted above, the Pensions Commission did not envisage the private sector would be directly responsible for auto-enrolment. Personal accounts would be a contract not between customer and supplier, but rather citizen and the state, collectively constituting the National Pensions Savings Scheme (NPSS) (although private firms would be commissioned to deliver scheme management in practice). As late as December 2006, the Labour government was maintaining its commitment to the NPSS, as seen in the white paper *Personal Accounts: A New Way to Save*, which announced the formation of the Personal Accounts Delivery Authority (PADA). Yet the paper also subtly implies that *alternative* employer-sponsored schemes could also be used for auto-employment (under the guise of allowing *existing* schemes to be authorized as appropriate vehicles, as had been accepted by Turner et al.). Furthermore, it also (very briefly) affirmed the government's commitment to allowing 'non-occupational' workplace pension schemes to be used for auto-enrolment (despite acknowledging that then European law prohibited automatic enrolment into a contract-based scheme) (DWP, 2006a: 119). The white paper contains only a single reference to 'qualifying' workplace schemes which could serve as an alternative to personal accounts/the NPSS. Yet by the time the government had published its response to the ensuing consultation, six months later, this concept had seemingly become central to the auto-enrolment delivery approach—with alternative schemes able to qualify based largely on applying the same minimum contribution levels envisaged for personal accounts (see DWP, 2007b: 68). Accordingly, by the time PADA was established in 2007, its remit had already changed, from delivering a defined contribution workplace pension scheme for all auto-enrolees, to providing a scheme for employers who would be underserved by private providers. The Pensions Act 2008 explicitly mandated PADA to facilitate the operation qualifying schemes beyond the NPSS (Thurley, 2010b: 35).

PADA became NEST in 2009, effectively becoming the first large-scale master trust. NEST operates at arm's length from government, albeit with public-service obligations, and is expected to operate at a profit (and 'pay back' to government its set-up costs). Technically, DWP owns the NEST

Corporation, which serves as sole trustee for the multi-employer, defined contribution pension scheme known as NEST (with trustee responsibilities shared by its board). As such, the notion that auto-enrolment into personal accounts would be delivered *by* the state via the NPSS has been entirely discarded. This is an outcome very much in line with the interests of the private pensions industry and financial services providers more generally—but in many ways represents a *more* privatized or marketized delivery model than they lobbied for in the wake of the Pensions Commission. It is likely that concerns that the state would be seen as responsible for retirement incomes accrued within the NPSS—morally and politically, if not legally—was also a factor (see Inman, 2006). The Coalition government was therefore able to later assert that NEST was designed to 'complement' private-sector provision (DWP, 2013d: 12). Crucially, the Labour government also placed restrictions on NEST's operations, notably an upper limit on contributions of £3,600 (in 2005 earnings terms). The Pensions Commission had suggested a similar limit for the NPSS. However, the impact of these limits would have differed significantly. The Pensions Commission envisaged that virtually all low to moderate earners would be in the NPSS, even if higher earners employed by the same company chose to save via other products—the limit allowed the NPSS to focus on providing for the auto-enrolment target group. In contrast, now that employers generally automatically enrol all of their eligible employees into a single scheme, the limit of NEST ensures that any company with employees earning around £40,000 or above—who are therefore likely to breach the limit—is incentivized to choose a private provider. The limit was abolished in 2017—but not before private providers had already gained a very sizeable share of the auto-enrolment target market.

Accordingly, while, as noted above, NEST is now the largest defined contribution pension scheme in the UK, the overwhelming majority of auto-enrolees are in schemes other than NEST. But if NEST is not delivering personal accounts, as originally envisaged, what is it for? It has a dual purpose. Firstly, representing best practice in master trust governance and scheme management. The issue however is not whether NEST itself represents best practice, but whether NEST has set a quality benchmark against which other private providers can be judged by prospective customers (that is, employers). There is no evidence for this. Secondly, offering auto-enrolment services to firms that insurance companies and other master trusts cannot profitably serve, principally small employers (see DWP, 2013d). In a sense, NEST was designed to correct a market failure that had *not yet occurred*, by offering very low-cost pension services to employers who would struggle to afford the costs typically associated with private provision. Ten per cent of NEST's members work in firms with fewer than five employees, almost 40 per cent work for firms with fewer than fifty employees, and more than 60 per cent work for firms with fewer than 250 employees (NEST, 2018). Clearly, the two purposes fit uncomfortably alongside each other. It is difficult to showcase best practice in scheme management with very low charges. The solution is 'contribution charges'. NEST costs employers who join the scheme *nothing* in either up-front or ongoing charges (the charging models employed, respectively, by the People's Pension and NOW), but members pay a charge of 1.8 per cent of each contribution they make (that is, before savings are invested), in addition to a 0.3 per cent AMC (that is, 0.3 per cent of the size of their pot, taking into account investment returns).

It is easy to dismiss NEST as a rather mundane aspect of UK pensions provision—it has accordingly received very little scholarly attention. In fact, it is an incredibly revealing development in terms of the state's role in the facilitation and maintenance of a highly individualized approach to pensions provision. As a form of state intervention in private pensions saving, NEST obviously represents a significantly scaled-back version of the Turner plan, serving only a segment of the market which private providers deem unprofitable, rather than effectively nationalizing a failing industry. Moreover, as a regulatory intervention, the notion of embodying 'best practice' in order to serve as a role model for private providers is a rather submissive approach. It is also worth noting here that most self-employed people are able to save for a pension in NEST. Yet pension scheme participation rates for the self-employed (now around 5 million workers) almost halved over the previous decade from 27 to 15 per cent (DWP, 2019c), as self-employment earnings have declined (ONS, 2018c). NEST does not therefore appear to be a suitable solution for undersaving among this group.

In sum, the state has elected not to provide a universal defined contribution pensions saving system, favouring delivery of auto-enrolment by the private sector directly. Yet the inability of the private sector to provide universal coverage has compelled the state to itself establish a provider which mimics private provision—while operating under the rather mythical assumption that the private sector will, in due course, come to mimic the practice showcased by the public sector. And because NEST is serving a segment of a market which the private sector cannot, or will not, the costs of this provision are largely passed onto savers who have little or no role in choosing to save within NEST. We should also keep in mind of course that the opportunity to profit from auto-enrolment only exists in the first place because of the state's willingness to (largely) compel individuals to participate in defined contribution pensions saving—and NEST is therefore only necessary because of the state's *un*willingness to simultaneously compel providers to ensure all individuals actually have opportunities to save privately.

6.2. Auto-Enrolment's 'Teething Problems'

The auto-enrolment delivery model instituted by New Labour placed key aspects of the policy's operation in the hands of private providers. This section considers two particular issues: charges and the 'small pots' problem. The first is probably the most significant, insofar as charges paid by savers directly affect the size of the pot they can accumulate to fund their retirement income—and, accordingly, impacts directly on the business models of providers. The second, however, is perhaps the most revealing, especially in terms of the state's emerging role in supporting defined contribution pensions saving.

6.2.1 At What Cost?

Unlike stakeholder pensions (discussed in Chapter 5), auto-enrolment was introduced without a charge cap on qualifying defined contribution schemes. There was a belief that the policy's implementation would itself achieve lower charges, with the Pensions Commission expecting average AMCs to fall to 0.3 per cent, as a result of improved persistency. Turner et al. demonstrated that high charges resulted from the fact that defined contribution saving in a single product rarely persisted beyond a few years, thereby requiring higher charges to recoup administrative costs involved in enrolment for providers. Closer to implementation, the Labour government said it expected charges to be 0.5 per cent, falling to 0.3 per cent over the long term. Crucially, however, it argued that lower charges are a result of regulation of providers rather than competition between providers: 'There is little evidence that competition for customers will provide significant downwards pressure on charges. Recent falls in charges have been a result of regulation, not competition. Similarly, international evidence from other countries shows that the lowest-cost systems are those with a limited choice of provider and/or investments' (DWP, 2006a: 26). Yet in practice, the government chose not to impose any regulatory standards on the level, or even disclosure, of charges on auto-enrolment qualifying schemes—and, at the same time, permitted a system whereby unlimited private providers compete (with a restricted NEST) for employer sponsors.

The impact of charges on final pot sizes can be considerable. DWP modelling in 2013 found that a 1 per cent AMC would result in between 12 and 28 per cent of a median earner's pot being 'lost', based on a range of typical career paths (including late commencement of saving, early retirement, and career breaks) (DWP, 2013a: 11). The loss is higher for people with higher earnings or full employment records—but such individuals also end up with much higher pots overall. Crucially, the DWP assumes here that annual investment growth will be 7 per cent, and that individual and employer contributions will grow by 4 per cent each year—both rather 'heroic' assumptions at a time of economic stagnation and sluggish earnings growth, especially given that costs and charges beyond the AMC are buried in the 7 per cent return. However, while criticism of defined contribution charges is not unreasonable, it is far from a straightforward issue. In a capitalist economy, there is no reason to expect private enterprises to provide their services for free—often public discourse on charges implies that they are wholly negative, indeed exploitative. A 2019 inquiry by the House of Commons Work and Pensions select committee is therefore correct to say that the problem is not charges per se, but rather whether charges represent 'value for money'. Yet, as the committee also rightly acknowledges, our understanding on this remains rather underdeveloped. Of course, it is also useful to consider why it is often assumed that pensions saving (especially under auto-enrolment) *should* be free, or very low cost. Surely this relates to a residual imaginary of pensions provision as an aspect of the welfare state. The Pensions Commission's state-led approach undoubtedly reinforced this sentiment, even if the delivery of provision was to be outsourced (as Mabbett, 2012 argues regarding auto-enrolment in general).

With pensions statecraft in this regard eschewing its welfarist origins, policy-makers have instead adopted a 'regulatory state' model. Accordingly, a cap on charges was eventually introduced in 2015, after a long and mildly controversial debate, and some experimentation with self-regulation (which is ongoing, to some extent). The cap was set at 0.75 per cent of an individual's fund (with rules on equivalence applied to alternative charging models, such as NEST's contribution charge), based largely on research by the FCA into different charging models in contract-based provision (see FCA, 2015). It applies only to default funds (the investment strategies people are automatically enrolled into), with individuals requesting more bespoke investment strategies likely to pay more. Recent interventions by policy-makers have been driven to a large extent by a damning 2013 report by the Office of Fair Trading (2013). The report concluded that auto-enrolment had not created, and would not create, a functioning consumer marketplace in pensions saving products (although as discussed in Chapter 5, the reliance on inertia shows this had never been policy-makers' intention). The report was also highly critical of industry self-regulation. By showing that auto-enrolees could not possibly make informed decisions about scheme charges, the Office of Fair Trading certainly provided the rationale for the charge cap subsequently introduced—the system required a failsafe. However, there is an important contradiction or silence underpinning such measures: while the case for a charge cap is essentially inarguable, it remains the case, hypothetically, that savers may ultimately benefit from paying higher charges, if charges support the provision of better services.

It is worth noting that DWP's latest analysis shows that average scheme charges are *below* the level of the cap, with average member-borne charges in trust-based defined contribution schemes of 0.38 per cent. Average charges for master trusts (before the new authorization regime) are 0.48 per cent, and in contract-based schemes it is 0.54 per cent (Wood et al., 2017: 2). As such, the cap is designed primarily to discourage the worst offenders, rather than bring charges down in general. That said, AMCs in most cases are not substantively higher than DWP's pre-implementation expectations. Does this mean a competition-based approach *is* actually working to bring charges down (the relationship between providers and savers may not, in the Office of Fair Trading's view, be a functioning consumer marketplace, but providers are certainly competing for business from employers)? It is difficult to say. If so, it will challenge the existing evidence base. In practice, however, it is also a consequence of what schemes are actually included in the AMC (and how they report this). The FCA now recommends disclosure of an 'ongoing charge figure', which adds the costs of services such as keeping a register of investors, calculating the price of fund units, and keeping fund assets safe, to the AMC (but still excludes transactions costs, and less predictable costs such as performance fees) (see FCA, 2016a, 2016b).

The pensions industry's attempts to self-regulate on charging refers of course to the *disclosure of* charges, rather than *limits on* charges. NAPF (now the Pensions and Lifetime Savings Association) worked with stakeholders including trade unions and consumer advocates to produce the Joint Industry Code of Conduct in 2012, producing a template for categorizing and presenting information on charges which it expected all providers to adhere to.[4] ABI and Investment Management Association (now known as the Investment Association) issued more unilateral protocols on disclosure

---

[4] The code is available at https://www.plsa.co.uk/portals/0/Documents/0273_Pensions_charges_made_clear_code_of_Conduct.pdf.

for their members, albeit to complement NAPF's initiative. Of course, there is no doubt that by pursuing self-regulation, providers hoped to avert the possibility of legislative interventions, in terms of both the level and disclosure of charges. At the same time, being seen to resist regulation by public authorities clearly invites further scrutiny of charging practice. An editorial in *The Guardian* in 2012, for instance, described charges as 'a conspiracy against the public'. There remains a degree of self-regulation—and, as such, providers can still choose what they disclose, and how—but the need to disclose information has since the Pensions Act 2014 (which gave ministers power to set the charge cap) been brought into statute. However, even Ros Altmann, who was briefly Pensions Minister in the Conservative majority government from 2015 to 2016, likens pensions saving, despite the 2014 Act, to 'shoppers going into a supermarket and seeing similar-looking products on the shelves, but the prices are hidden' (cited in Hayes, 2019). Following lengthy market study, and a 2019 consultation, the FCA brought in firmer rules on transaction cost disclosure in 2020 (see FCA, 2019, 2020).

Despite the clear shortcomings of the member-borne charge cap and new disclosure regime—in terms of the cap being set well above the market level, the crudeness of applying caps to ensure value for money in individualized pensions saving, and the incompleteness of the transparency requirements—Peter Tutyens of the London School of Economics describes the 2014 Act as 'a far-reaching legislative framework' (Tutyens, 2019: 562). This is a significant overstatement: Tutyens' account is insufficiently grounded in an appreciation of prevailing pensions industry practice, and indeed the Act's actual provisions. Nevertheless, there is some merit in Tutyens' *explanation* for why the state appeared to be taking a (slightly) more interventionist approach. He rightly demonstrates that issues around charges, governance, etc. had not become more salient among voters, and that financial services had become no less influential as a lobby group. Instead, the (limited) shift is due to policy-makers' own changed perceptions of how to continue to support individualized pensions provision, moving from disciplining individuals to engaging with the pensions marketplace, to ensuring that this marketplace is properly functioning. It is of course fascinating that New Labour, as noted above, identified regulation rather than competition as the key to lower charges, and yet opted for a lightly regulated system of auto-enrolment which encouraged competition among providers, whereas the Coalition government's zeal for *de*regulation eventually gave way, in pensions policy, to new regulatory interventions. However, viewed in its (recent) historical context, the Pensions Act 2014 represents an almost inevitable tilt towards a more regulatory approach. The Labour government did not introduce a charge cap because it was still, until very late in the implementation process, intent on enacting the Pensions Commission's proposal for state-managed provision, in which the government's procurement power would have made any cap unnecessary. Once the Coalition government committed to auto-enrolment—not without reservations—it was bound to be confronted with the messy consequences of a system in which the employer's choice of provider, on behalf of their consequences, had far greater impact on individuals than had ever been intended.

It is worth noting, again, the perverseness of the Department for Work and *Pensions* having to agree a cap with a Treasury agency, in order to regulate the pensions market which is conceived as singular—and indeed the fact that its own agency, the *Pensions* Regulator, does not have sufficient powers to regulate the pension schemes within the auto-enrolment programme it supervises. That said, TPR (alongside the Pensions and Lifetime Savings Association) actually expressed concern about the cap, rightly recognizing that the lowest cost schemes are not necessarily the best-run schemes. L&G, the largest GPP provider, argued for a *lower* cap (see Thurley, 2017; rather undermining Tutyens' 'far-reaching' claim). This issue seemingly lays bare the contradictions inherent in individualized defined contribution provision. What ultimately matters to savers—encouraged to be inert by auto-enrolment—is that they achieve the highest possible retirement income. It is impossible to say whether this will be more likely to be achieved by capping charges (and if so, a lower cap would indeed be preferable, other things being equal) or by having stronger governance standards (which involve higher costs for providers). There is little reason to believe that a 0.75 cap in itself strikes the correct balance in this regard—because any given level or model of charging, or any given governance processes, will in practice have a fairly limited impact on the returns individuals' saving might attract over the course of their career.

Of course, some charges are far less ambiguously negative for individual scheme members. With the FCA introducing restrictions on the commission that financial advisers may earn from providers for recommending their schemes to employers, the practice of member-borne consultancy charging saw employers pass on the cost of advice received when establishing a workplace scheme to their employees. In a series of steps, this practice has now been banned. So too have 'active member discounts', whereby previously deferred members of a scheme paid higher charges than those currently making contributions. As noted below, in the world of auto-enrolment, virtually all employees will simultaneously be active and deferred members of various workplace pension schemes. Restricting these practices is unquestionably correct. However, in a system dependent on financial services firms' ability to make profit from providing pensions saving products, it would be naïve to assume that equally problematic practices will not emerge in future—and indeed that the incentives for policy-makers to eradicate them can be relied upon. Indeed, the charge cap allows for flat charges, as well as charges consisting of a proportion of each contribution (the NEST model) and of the total pot. NOW, one of the largest trust-based providers, operated a flat monthly fee of £1.50. Such a model may work out cheaper than more common approaches for some active savers, but it clearly disadvantages those with small, deferred pots. At the time the government chose to permit flat fees, it insisted that it would soon introduce a new transfer and consolidation process to minimize the incidence of such pots (see DWP, 2013a: 5). As discussed below, it has not.

In addition to formal charges, much of the controversy around defined contribution charges relates to 'transaction costs' (specific member-borne charges, and costs which eat into investment returns, are frequently conflated and/or confused). Contesting this issue was Gina Miller's central contribution to UK public life (as head of the True and Fair Campaign), before she took up the cause of defending parliamentary sovereignty. Transaction costs may refer to fees paid to intermediaries and consultants as a routine—although not necessarily transparent or justified—part of allocating capital to specific investments, as well as the implicit cost of bid-offer spreads in securities trading. Chapter 7 will discuss the costs of investment and intermediation. In general, however, it is beyond the scope of this book to determine whether each instance of investment activity involving defined contribution pensions saving being subjected to transaction costs is fair or appropriate. It would be unwise to dismiss the accusation of endemic rent-seeking practices, in a market which is ostensibly competitive, yet too complex for savers to exercise genuine consumer choice (and, to reiterate, as discussed at length in Chapter 5, auto-enrolment is based on the assumption that they cannot and will not behave as rational agents). The Financial Services Consumer Panel (2014), for instance, reports that transaction costs are rarely fully measured, let alone declared—they are simply buried in returns, and fund managers are invariably unaware of all of the costs that may have affected the return value. At the same, the myriad services involved in dematerializing and rematerializing pensions saving over a lifecourse clearly must, in a capitalist economy, be paid for, one way or another—transaction costs *facilitate* as well as *moderate* investment returns. Some investment practices are labour-intensive, even if the labour in question is well remunerated. Even where some forms of investment practice are largely automated, this is not synonymous with being automatic. It is worth noting that transaction cost disclosure is part of the 2014 Act. The FCA has subsequently produced guidance on how to report transaction costs to fund managers, and this issue forms part of its latest consultation on charges in general, noted above.

It is instructive to consider, finally, how little defined benefit and defined contribution provision differ, in terms of exposure to transaction costs: there is essentially no difference regarding the type or extent of costs that might apply. The difference is simply that transaction costs can be tangentially linked to final outcomes for savers in defined contribution schemes, whereas in defined benefit they are essentially obscured by the employer's promise to pay the pension accrued. Transaction costs in funded local government pensions provision, where the employer's liabilities ultimately belong to taxpayers, have attracted some controversy (see Sier, 2012 for a comprehensive analysis). Obviously transaction costs cannot be capped in any meaningful sense—if they were capped, it would simply necessitate alternative investment strategies (avoiding costlier investments) which might overall reduce returns. Better oversight through scheme governance mechanisms is generally a good thing, and could mean the least justifiable transaction costs are swerved more often—but would increase scheme running costs, which would ultimately be passed on to members. Greater scale in defined contribution provision generally affords greater buying power, and therefore better deals from intermediaries—but the experience of the (mostly) very large local authority funds in defined benefit provision suggests that even scale is far from a panacea.

6.2.2   Does Size Matter?

While the issue of charges and transaction costs highlights some of the key features—and structural problems—of defined contribution pensions provision, the 'small pots' issue is arguably more revealing in terms of policy development, since it is an area where action (or, in this case, inaction) by policy-makers has much more scope to shape how provision functions. Policy-makers have known about the small pots problem for some time. The Pensions Commission's personal accounts model would have meant each individual accumulating pensions saving into a single pot throughout their career, irrespective of who their employer may be (although, admittedly, the practicalities of this approach were left rather vague by the Commission). Yet an approach which sees (mostly) private providers serving savers directly means individuals may end up with multiple pots of pensions saving throughout their careers, with many different providers (or even multiple pots in different schemes managed by the same provider) across both trust-based and contract-based provision.

We know relatively little about how frequently individuals change jobs, but various surveys suggest that people work on average for six different organizations during their career (Finnigan, 2015; Hope, 2017), and that today's younger people expect to switch employer even more frequently (Wilson, 2017) (this is notwithstanding the structural shift towards more insecure employment; ironically, if the 'gig' workers currently denied access to workplace pensions were to be brought into auto-enrolment, the small pots problem would multiply). The Coalition government's MAEW review, discussed in Chapter 5, reported results of DWP modelling (based on unidentified survey evidence) that people with a full employment record would change jobs an average of eleven times in their career (Johnson et al., 2010: 103). This was used in the small pots green and white papers in 2012 to argue that around 400,000 defined contribution saving pots valued below £2,000 would be created each year—leading to 50 million dormant pots being created by 2050, with 12 million of these below £2,000 (DWP, 2012a: 10, 2012b: 20). It is worth noting that a pot worth £2,000 or less is actually a miniscule pot, which would generate a negligible retirement income (in fact most annuity providers would not accept a pot of this size)—a figure of £10,000 would be far more reasonable, and on this basis we can expect many millions of small, dormant pots to be created each year. In collectivist, defined benefit provision, deferred membership is relatively unproblematic from the saver's perspective: final outcomes will be based on the terms of entitlement (and revaluation, so that deferred entitlements retain their value) agreed during the period of active membership. The pension due will be paid directly from the scheme (or an insurer if the buy-out has occurred), more or less automatically. In individualized, defined contribution provision, outcomes are not known until the point of retirement. The ultimate value of contributions made will remain uncertain, often for several decades.

Perversely, therefore, in a workplace pensions saving system defined around the behavioural assumption of inertia, savers are expected to actively decide to transfer savings accumulated with one employer to their new employer if they change jobs (and pay any transfer fees)—understanding the differences in charges, governance, and investment strategies this may entail. Most will not, and as such will leave their savings in schemes they are no longer actively participating in—making their management and investment performance more difficult to monitor (as noted above, the active member discounts which penalize deferred members have been outlawed—yet the flat fees applicable to all members, but disadvantage deferred members, remain permissible). Moreover, because the accumulation and decumulation phases in defined contribution provision are entirely distinct, if they do leave their savings in multiple schemes, savers are expected at retirement to independently arrange to combine their pots (usually incurring charges in the process) so they may convert their savings into a retirement income. It is worth noting here that it is technically not possible to be a deferred member of a GPP; leaving a GPP scheme means individuals become personal pension customers. Neither TPR nor the FCA tracks the number of people whose GPP savings are converted into a different product in this regard—and indeed nor does the ONS.

Two main solutions to the small pots problem were proposed by the Coalition government in 2012: 'pot follows member' (PFM) and 'aggregator'. While radically different, the Coalition government's position on both exposes some of the contradictions of its steadfast support for defined contribution provision. PFM would have seen an employee's pension saving automatically transferred to their new employer's scheme when they changed jobs (as is the case in Ireland). This was the government's preferred option, with automatic transfers of pots valued below £10,000 or £20,000 considered (which would have reduced the number of pots by 2050 by around half or three quarters, respectively). The white paper made reference to a customer survey by ABI which suggested individual savers preferred this model, yet it clearly has significant risks for consumer welfare, given that savings will be automatically transferred to schemes with different charging structures and governance standards. The government promised that 'effective safeguards' would be put in place (DWP, 2012a: 15).

The aggregator model would see many pots transfer to a scheme independent of both the individual's old and new employers—instead entering a state-managed consolidation fund, with only the scheme(s) they are actively contributing to remaining within the private sector. This approach was strongly supported by workers' representatives and consumer groups, on the basis that the aggregator would, like NEST, demonstrate best practice in scheme governance and charging—in fact, NEST itself could have provided the aggregator service. Interestingly, while ABI opposed *both* options, NAPF tentatively supported the aggregator model (while pointing out that a majority of its members wanted the system to be voluntary rather than compulsory) (see DWP, 2012a: 20, 23–4, 33). Of course, given the government's stated intention to outsource the aggregator service to the private sector, NAPF members running large trust-based schemes were rather likelier than

ABI's contract-based providers to win these lucrative contracts. In the event, the government thwarted the aggregator approach by insisting that only pots valued at less than £2,000 could enter an aggregator. To allow for larger pots—say, £10,000 or £20,000, the values modelled for PFM—to be aggregated would produce 'market distortion', that is, the vast majority of pots would eventually end up in the aggregator, supposedly reducing competition in the auto-enrolment market. In other words, Turner et al.'s personal accounts would have been reborn, via the back door. (The government also suggested that *multiple* aggregators could be established, with employers choosing a provider to transfer their departing employees' pots into—which obviously would simply produce *more*, not *fewer*, small pots.) Accordingly, it was deemed that an aggregator would have only a limited impact on the small pots problem.

In reality, the financial interests of providers were clearly prioritized over consumer welfare. While the pensions industry generally opposed either solution to the small pots problem (or at least either solution being compulsory), the white paper stated that '[t]he benefits to industry [of PFM] could also be substantial if the cost of transfers can be reduced to such a level that they are cheaper than administering dormant pension pots' (DWP, 2012a: 15). This is a rather interesting case of double-think by the government, given that providers had *not* complained about the cost of administering dormant pots, and ABI's opposition to PFM was *not* based on the cost of administering transfers. It is worth noting that the government's opposition to an aggregator approach was also due to this option's apparent failure to promote 'member engagement'—once again, highlighting the perversity of requiring individuals to be meaningfully engaged in a pensions saving system based fundamentally on inertia and a belief that individuals behave irrationally. Clearly, in allowing for the construction of a large, single pot of pensions saving, PFM is the only solution to the small pots problem that aligns with the post-Turner logic of auto-enrolment via privately managed defined contribution provision. Yet it is essentially unthinkable, insofar as it would involve both jeopardizing providers' customer base and over-riding the pretence of consumer protection within auto-enrolment regulations. An aggregator may in fact enhance consumer protection, but challenge providers' interests even more.

Faced with a choice between exacerbating the problems of under-regulation, or instead effectively nationalizing the provision of auto-enrolment—and with no compromise between the two approaches seemingly available—policy-makers have simply chosen neither PFM nor an aggregator. The eventual creation of a framework for enabling automatic transfers was one of

Steve Webb's final acts as Pensions Minister in the Coalition government (see DWP, 2015). Yet Guy Opperman, Pensions Minister in the May and Johnson governments, told parliament in 2018 that the government was focusing on continuing to deliver auto-enrolment in general, and it was 'therefore not the right time to implement automatic transfers' (Opperman, 2018). No further reasoning was communicated—which almost certainly means the growth of financial services providers' opposition explains the change of direction (see Cumbo, 2018a).

The number of 'dormant' pots is therefore steadily growing, in a way neither desired nor even imagined by the Pensions Commission, but as an inherent and entirely foreseeable feature of defined contribution provision in the UK labour market in the wake of government decisions on how to implement personal accounts and auto-enrolment. As noted in Chapter 5, progress has been made towards providing an online 'pensions dashboard' service so individuals can keep track of their own small pots, but these mechanisms will be unable to correct structural flaws in how auto-enrolment is delivered. As autonomy within work is increasingly undermined through new forms of work organization and surveillance (see Moore, 2017)—and arguably the compulsion to save for a pension is a tangential aspect of this shift in the UK—individuals are expected simultaneously to become masters of their own pensions destiny, using digital technology to correct one of the core, yet strangely unanticipated, flaws of the auto-enrolment programme and defined contribution pensions provision more generally.

Issues such as charges and small pots have been presented as auto-enrolment's 'teething problems' (a term frequently used regarding auto-enrolment, including by Steve Webb in relation to charges (see Webb, 2015)—he also used it in relation to the implementation of Universal Credit in 2014). Yet they are in fact endemic difficulties regarding individualized pensions provision, and especially an approach in which policy outcomes are acutely dependent on the delivery of services by the finance sector. Understandably, financial services companies are not going to provide services benevolently. If they are unable to charge savers for services, or forced to relinquish customers, their business models would falter. We can of course point to excessive profit margins in many cases, and righteously demand a 'fairer' pricing model—the long-term success of auto-enrolment may even depend on this outcome being achieved. Yet generally speaking finance sector profitability is not an aberration; it is tolerated, expected, and indeed encouraged by policy-makers, and integral to the UK's financialized growth model. In defined benefit provision, the temporal anchors—employers, for the most part—had incentives related to workforce growth and development in at least feigning benevolence as their balance sheets underpinned their employees' long-term financial security. This dynamic is entirely absent in the saver/provider relationship. Could the state compel providers to operate in ways that benefit savers to a greater extent? Probably. Could the state prevent providers exiting the auto-enrolment marketplace if their margins are threatened? Probably not. There is, it seems, a delicate balance which inhibits state intervention in, and/or regulation of, the private pensions industry: unsettling the balance will inevitably place demands upon the state which have barely been articulated, let alone accepted.

6.3. Annuitus Horribilis

One of the fallacies of the welfare lens on pensions provision is the implicit notion that the custodians of welfare states—part of the policy-making community, in the terms adopted in this book—have a significant degree of control over what individuals 'get' from social security systems and public services. The task for policy-makers, in this account, is how much people should get, and how they should get it (connected to questions around what they should first give, in order to then get). This is an assumption exposed by the reality of pensions provision, especially in defined contribution schemes. What people end up with is determined by processes which policy-makers have virtually no control over, that is, returns generated in capital market investment activity. (This was essentially also the case in defined benefit provision, albeit obscured by implicit and sometimes explicit bargains between the state and the employers responsible for pension outcomes). Of course, given the very long-term nature of pensions provision, policy-makers can usually design systems of accumulation around reasonable assumptions regarding investment returns—and adapt ahead of time to major shifts which might challenge expectations (albeit not necessarily successfully). Yet this is far less possible regarding decumulation in defined contribution provision, in which savers typically purchase an annuity to convert their savings into a regular, guaranteed income in retirement. Pensions policy-makers have very little control over the rates at which annuities will be offered— exacerbated by the fact that annuity rates tend to be volatile.

Furthermore, the purchase of an annuity is generally a one-off transaction. The switch between the accumulation and decumulation phases is inherently risky and largely unavoidable, and policies to alleviate these circumstances are characterized by futility (TUC, 2018). Auto-enrolment institutionalizes this process on a societal scale. It is worth noting that the Coalition government actually sought to introduce a 'secondary' annuities market in 2015. This policy is generally associated with George Osborne (and aligned with his pension freedoms agenda, discussed below), insofar as it was taken forward after the 2015 election. Yet Liberal Democrat Pensions Minister Steve Webb, and his future predecessor Ros Altmann, were its main champions (Thurley, 2015: 23–4). It was envisaged that people could sell the income streams arising from an annuity contract to institutional investors—including defined benefit pension funds (raising the remarkable prospect of defined contribution savers helping to support the risk-management strategies of defined benefit schemes) (see HM Treasury and DWP, 2015). They would be taxed on the lump sum received, thereby bringing forward revenue to the Exchequer, and indeed increasing revenue insofar as an annualized income would generally be below the personal tax allowance level (see HM Treasury, 2015a). The pensions industry generally opposed the plans—often with good reason, since individual annuity sellers would clearly have been at risk of striking a poor deal—and the policy was abandoned almost immediately after both Osborne and Altmann were sacked by Theresa May (Pickard and Cumbo, 2016).

Part of the reason for the Coalition government's enthusiasm for a secondary annuities market was the historically low annuity rates available recently. The story of annuity provision is one of endemic disappointment, from a consumer perspective—and the bad news has certainly intensified in recent years. As economist Joncqil Lowe explains:

> Over the last 25 years, annuity rates have fallen significantly meaning that individuals now have to build up a much greater pension pot if they are to retire at the same age as previously on the same nominal income. For example, taking as an indicator the standard level annuity for a single man aged 65, the rate has fallen from £1,537 per year for each £10,000 invested at the end of 1990 to £570 a year by end 2013...Put another way, an individual who wanted to start retirement with a nominal income of £10,000 would have needed a pension pot of [around] £65,000 in 1990 but over £175,000 by 2013.   (Lowe, 2014: 6)

Moneyfacts (a comparison website) reported in September 2019 that this figure had fallen, quite incredibly, to £410 (Clark, 2019). An individual wanting to secure an income of £10,000 (with no increases over time or protection against early death) would now need almost £245,000. To clarify, low earners are typically expected to accrue pots valued at around £100,000 through auto-enrolment: based on Moneyfacts' analysis of actual market rates, this would produce an income of around £70 per week—and

Table 6.1 Best available monthly annuity rates with variable pot size and protections, 2019 (£ per month)

Size of pensions savings pot	Lifetime annuity (without protection)	Lifetime annuity (starting rate—with inflation and survivor protection)
£50,000	208	108
£100,000	429	215
£250,000	1,095	511

Source: Quotes retrieved from www.moneyadviceservice.org.uk by the author on 1 October 2019

considerably less if, for instance, inflation protection is included. Table 6.1 details the best annuity deals available at the time of writing, according to the state-funded Money Advice Service. It shows the monthly income for a typical male[5] retiring on 1 January 2020 at the age of 66 in good health, showing deals for both fixed-income annuities with no inflation protection or post-death income for a spouse, and annuities which rise each year by RPI inflation, with a 50 per cent lifetime income for a surviving spouse.[6]

In practice, insurers will incorporate various factors to determine the annuity rates they offer, including the customer's health and lifestyle (O'Brien, 2013: 3–4). The main drivers, however, are of course expectations of longevity across the population, and long-term interest rates—structural factors largely beyond firms' control (although their own particular investment strategies, experience of increasing longevity among their customers, and profitability expectations will shape individual firm responses to this structural context) (Lowe, 2014: 13). So, with longevity increases stalling, it seems the primary reason that annuity rates have been particularly poor for savers in recent years relates to macro-economic conditions; this underlines the more intimate relationship between individuals' long-term financial well-being and immediate economic circumstances—a key hallmark of financialization. Moreover, it is the UK policy elite's policies and strategies for alleviating problems in the macro economy that form the key determinant of lower rates (as discussed further in Chapter 7). In short, annuity rates

---

[5] Insurance companies are no longer able to offer different annuity prices based on gender (other things being equal, women would obtain lower rates due to higher average life expectancy). However, comparison websites generally still require information on gender to produce quotes.

[6] Both sets of rates are based on a male reaching retirement on 1 January 2020, aged 66 exactly. His postcode is OX2 6DP (head office of this book's publisher), he has no health conditions, and average height, weight, and waist measurements. He does not smoke or exceed recommended alcohol consumption limits. In the first scenario, he is single. In the second scenario, he is married to a woman who has no health conditions, and average height, weight, and waist measurements. She does not smoke or exceed recommended alcohol consumption limits. The first scenario presents rates for lifetime annuities with no inflation protection or income protection for any survivors; in the second scenario, the annuity payments would increase according to RPI inflation each year, and the customer's wife would receive a lifetime income equal to 50 per cent of the annuity value if the customer dies first.

have been driven down by extraordinary monetary policy—very low interest rates and QE—since the 2008 financial crisis (Lowe, 2014: 13). This is an important caveat to the suggestion above that policy-makers ultimately have no control over defined contribution outcomes; they do, but they are exercising this control in support of wider economic policy objectives, largely irrespective of the implications for pensions savers (both now and over the long term).

Even with defined contribution pensions saving in its infancy, the annuities industry is sizeable. In advance of the reforms discussed below, ABI (2013: 1) estimated around 400,000 annuities were sold each year, worth more than £11 billion (with a total stock of around £210 billion—equivalent to around a tenth of UK GDP). We could probably have expected the annual value to be closer to £100 billion when auto-enrolees began to retire, even with the deliberate shift from servicing higher earners to lower earners. Chapters 2 and 5 noted the long history of annuity provision in the UK, and the Pensions Commission took for granted that it would remain in place—encompassing a reasonably competitive marketplace—when personal accounts holders came to retire (although it recommended a 'successor body' monitor in due course the markets' capacity to service millions of new annuitants). However, it is worth reiterating here that the Pensions Commission (2005: 383–5) actually pondered myriad ways in which the state could support annuity provision, including the state becoming an annuity provider for personal account savers, or at least buying annuities in bulk from the private sector on behalf of the NPSS. It also considered providing annuities for only savers with very small pots, and issuing longevity bonds to insurers so that the state effectively shoulders the risk of providing annuities to those who live unusually long lives (enabling lower prices for most people). None of these ideas were explicitly recommended, and so were ignored by the government. It would be wrong to suggest that the Pensions Commission envisaged a very active role for government in the annuities market—but they certainly imagined the possibility of such a role in future, partly because of their implicit assumption that annuities were the only game in town, for the mass market, in terms of defined contribution decumulation.

Without the state becoming a provider or underwriter, there is very little that policy-makers can do about annuity prices. The market is already competitive on the supply side, and there is very little scope for regulation, for instance, to produce better rates. There have been efforts, both by government and industry self-regulation, to improve transparency in pricing, and making it easier to 'shop around' (since most existing annuitants hold personal, contract-based pensions, and tend to stay with the same insurance company when they retire). There has also been some regulatory action around the provision (and cost) of advice and guidance regarding annuity transactions (Lindley, 2014; FCA, 2015; Thurley, 2015). Understandably, but nevertheless absurdly, the FCA's guidance on how people currently saving for a workplace pension are engaged by annuity providers applies only to those in GPP schemes—and their approach is generally focused on improving rates of switching from one provider to another at retirement. At the same time, NEST has sought to *reduce* the burden of choice for its members reaching retirement by acting as an annuity broker; crucially, however, private-sector trust-based providers have *not* followed suit. Instead they behave like typical GPP providers—albeit beyond the scope of the FCA's powers. The joint FCA/TPR workplace pension regulatory strategy of 2018, noted above, contains no substantive material on the annuities market.

6.3.1   The Pensions Emancipation Proclamation

And so, to 2014. The changes instituted by George Osborne, as Chancellor, to the annuities market will prove to be as significant a revolution *within* defined contribution decumulation as the changes to contracting out instituted by Margaret Thatcher were *across* defined benefit and defined contribution accumulation. The relative brevity of this sub-section is indication only of the rather obvious rationale for 'pension freedoms', and equally obvious implications, and not the insignificance of Osborne's policy to the story of pensions imperilment (although for a longer discussion see Berry, 2016c).

Osborne's emancipation of pensions consisted of the complete removal of the requirement to annuitize savings into a regular retirement income by the age of 75. He described it, only a little hyperbolically, as 'the biggest and most exciting reform to our pensions system in more than a century' (Osborne, 2015b). *Financial Times* later described it as 'Armageddon' (see Reichman, 2018). Compulsory annuitization had already been softened before 2014, essentially by allowing people to instead use 'drawdown' products (in which their savings remain invested rather than annuitize), albeit with limits on how much capital could be withdrawn from products. The pension freedoms reform therefore removed all legal restrictions and tax 'penalties' on capital withdrawal (Thurley, 2018b). Compulsory annuitization had been in place since the 1920s—long before occupational pensions, let alone the rise of workplace pensions—in recognition of the very significant tax advantages which pensions saving attracts, as Section 6.4 below testifies (the age 75 requirement was introduced in the 1970s). Pensions saving is incentivized insofar as it is actually used to generate a pension income.

The context for the reform can be inferred from the above discussion: the declining value of annuities. Existing defined contribution savers are of course a much wealthier cohort than future auto-enrolment retirees—often annuitizing small defined contribution pots accumulated via AVCs or a personal pension, on top of defined benefit pension entitlements. In short, they can live without annuitizing, especially if the price is not right. This will not apply to most auto-enrolees; accordingly, the Pensions Commission expected the annuities market to mature, rather than disappear, including the possibility of bulk purchasing (Adair Turner subsequently 'lambasted' the reforms (Cumbo, 2016)). Furthermore, policies such as promoting (discussed in Chapter 4) demonstrate an expectation of a much narrower range of decumulation options for defined contribution savers, in contrast to the Treasury's emancipatory zeal. Moreover, falling annuity rates are not synonymous with declining 'value for money' (Lowe, 2014).

Despite championing CDC, Steve Webb, as Pensions Minister, actually offered support to the policy. Webb infamously opined he would feel 'relaxed' if people used their pension pots to 'get a Lamborghini' instead of a retirement income (cited in BBC News, 2014). Writing in *The Telegraph*, Boris Johnson (2014b; then Mayor of London) proclaimed that Webb's bizarre comment 'made me stand on my chair and cheer'. (Other brands of Italian luxury sports cars are available, although for the sake of clarity, none were mentioned by Johnson or Webb.) Will Hutton (2014) decried the unravelling of risk-pooling which annuity provision offered, noting the traditional relationship between PTR and compulsory annuitization, yet Johnson responded that '[i]t isn't taxpayers' money, you Lefty bossyboots control freak: it's the money that the pensioners have saved up themselves—out of their *taxed income!*' (Johnson, 2014; emphasis added). As such, the UK's current Prime Minister not only ignored Hutton's point about tax relief, he brazenly asserted that no such relief exists. (Johnson has yet to repeat this falsehood since becoming Prime Minister in 2019.)

Hutton's comments allude to an element of defined contribution provision rarely articulated: annuity provision represents perhaps the final, or only, remnant of collectivism, with annuitants pooling their longevity risks. This is underpinned by insurance companies essentially acting in part as a temporal anchor, via investment in public debt. Pension freedoms undermine the 'liberal paternalism' of auto-enrolment, but amplify the broader agenda of pensions individualization—essentially as a response to the emerging failure of individualization. There is, arguably, a left-wing case for pension freedoms, articulated by *The Guardian*'s Patrick Collinson in a 2019 article. Collinson quite rightly pointed to insurers' relatively high levels of profitability, and in particular the apparent windfall they received when longevity increases slowed down—meaning they had in fact overpriced annuities in recent years. Accordingly, Aviva was able to fund additional dividend payments to its shareholders of £780 million, L&G paid out £433 million, and Prudential paid out £441 million (27 per cent of its operating profit). Again, there is no intention here to defend the profits of financial services providers, beyond the recognition that private pensions provision operates in a capitalist economy. Collinson is therefore not wrong to report the dividends, but we must also appreciate they result primarily from insurance companies shouldering longevity risks—and being surprised, at last, on the upside. (There is no reason to assume the profitability of drawdown products will be any different— yet as pots remain in investment, profits will arise from charges rather than returns.) As discussed in Chapter 2, collectivism in UK pensions provision has always operated under the constraint of an elite commitment to a (neo) liberal economic order. Arguably, the Pensions Commission sought to reinvent liberal collectivism (albeit in a much diluted form). Its flawed approach to doing so has already been undermined by the accumulation approach established by subsequent policy-makers—the same now applies to the decumulation process.

The 'business model' of auto-enrolment has therefore been severely jeopardized. In undermining one of the key mechanisms by which pensions-related savings are rematerialized, making this process more fraught for future retirees, the pension freedoms reform is a further blow to the implicit bargains across generations encapsulated by pensions provisions. Government policy and promotional documents demonstrate the lack of alignment with auto-enrolment. A 'fact sheet' explained the reform will benefit 'the 320,000 people who retire each year with defined contribution pensions'—a fraction of the number applicable once auto-enrolment is fully embedded (and today's retirees generally have much smaller pots) (HM Treasury, 2014c). Auto-enrolment only featured in the Treasury's consultation document as a *justification* for the reform:

In the past annuities only needed to support people for a short period in retirement. As people have started to live longer, annuity rates have reduced to the point that it is not clear they remain the correct product for everyone at the point of retirement, despite being the only realistic option for many. With the introduction of Automatic Enrolment, which will result in a large increase in the number of people with defined contribution pension savings, these are important issues that the government needs to address. There is a risk the lack of choice that people currently have at the point of retirement will undermine confidence in longer term saving. The introduction of the single tier pension will also significantly change the state support on offer to pensioners, providing greater certainty of their income and lifting a significant number above the level at which they are eligible for means-tested benefits. Thus, there is a strong case for the government to change its policy on how defined contribution pension savings are used in retirement and simplify the tax rules to increase the choice available to those with defined contribution pension savings. This will empower consumers to make their own choices and stimulate innovation and competition in the market.

(HM Treasury, 2014b: 15)

This explanation is disingenuous and nonsensical in equal parts. Firstly, increased longevity is used to justify individuals choosing not to pool the longevity risk. That the imperative is the precise opposite of what is claimed here is rather obvious. Secondly, the new 'certainty' (of lower payments) from the state pension (discussed in Chapter 2) is used to justify greater uncertainty in private pension payments. Yet this circumstance is a policy choice, not an inevitability. Thirdly, the reform hardly simplifies tax rules, since it was accompanied by the highly complex 'money purchase annual allowance' (MPAA) which restricts the amount people can put *back in* to a pension product—to attract further tax relief—having already exercised their new freedoms. In general, defined benefit decumulation freedoms are deemed necessary to create 'a new culture of saving' (HM Treasury, 2014a: 3)—whereas a curtailment of freedom in the accumulation phase remains the cornerstone of pensions policy. The government's response to the consultation contains only two inconsequential mentions of auto-enrolment (although it is also included in the glossary). (George Osborne's (2014) ministerial statement to parliament after the consultation does not even *allude to* auto-enrolment.) The response document summarizes 372 consultation responses (mainly from industry representatives) in barely three pages, and does not include a single reference to any trade union response regarding the complications for auto-enrolment.

Annuity sales have collapsed in the wake of the introduction of pension freedoms. Only around 80,000 are now being sold each year (FCA, 2018: 3; FCA and TPR, 2018: 6). There was an initial 'dash for cash', as savers withdrew their entire funds (incidentally, the UK is now the world's second largest market for new Lamborghinis, although sales have been increasing steadily since 2010. There is no data on sales of pre-owned Lamborghinis (see Lamborghini Media Center, 2019)). Yet the main implication has been a sharp increase in drawdown sales, with inflows of £22.4 billion in 2017/18 alone—a third higher than the previous year (FCA, 2018: 9). While the annuities market could, in theory, recover, the exit of several providers since 2014 suggests the industry may lack the capacity to service auto-enrolment retirees as Turner et al. envisaged. Prudential was the first large provider to withdraw from the market for new annuitants (citing strategic and regulatory factors in addition to the 'catalyst' of pension freedoms) (see Ralph and Cumbo, 2017). In recent years Reliance Mutual, Friends Life, Partnership Assurance, Standard Life, LV, and Retirement Advantage have also exited (although some as a result of M&As). As a result, only Canada Life, Aviva, L&G, Just, Scottish Widows, and Hodge Lifetime remain—and not all of these provide standard annuity products which most auto-enrolees will eventually require (Reichman, 2018). The Treasury's argument that pension freedoms will 'stimulate competition' therefore seems rather premature.

Interestingly, the House of Commons Work and Pensions Committee (2019) has called for caps on the charges that retirees may now incur on drawdown products. Thus the contradictions in the imaginary of individualized pensions provision are evident again: even those savers who have exercised the ultimate freedom—choosing not to generate a retirement income from their savings—still, according to the committee, require the protective shield of the regulatory state. In April 2020, the FCA published its 2020/1 business plan, and noted the 'significant risk' of harm confronting defined contribution savers as a result of pension freedoms (arising from making underinformed financial decisions). Individuals invariably express a desire for greater control over their savings, with a collectivist ethos declining in sync with collectivist institutions and practices, to the extent that risk-sharing is seen as inherently restrictive. Yet this desire is an antidote to a feeling of disconnection, rather than a thirst to become financialized pioneers (see research by 2CV reported in ABI, 2017: 40). A remarkable piece of research by the think-tank Demos (2018) suggests that drawdown customers tend to be more depressed than annuitants, partly as a consequence of the volatility of drawdown income (although we should note that the research was funded by annuity provider L&G!). The joint FCA/TPR (2018) regulatory strategy, discussed above, casually referred to both drawdown products and annuities as 'pensions'—this terminological imprecision should be questioned.

6.4.   The Exorbitant Irrelevance of Pensions Tax Relief

Section 6.3 noted some of the tax rules that shape *decumulation* processes in defined contribution provision. The main interface between private pensions provision and taxation is PTR—a major incentive designed to support the *accumulation* of pensions saving. PTR actually has its genesis in defined contribution provision, but developed as defined benefit provision became predominant. As noted in Chapter 2, its introduction for occupational pensions provision in the 1920s signified the state's willingness to assist (or even partially replace) employers in acting as the temporal anchor for the management of workers' accumulated savings. PTR is now of course being increasingly applied to defined contribution provision. The migration from defined benefit (back) to defined contribution has been a messy process. Above all, the most interesting thing about PTR is that, despite the significant amount of tax revenue foregone by the state to fund the incentive, its impact is rather limited, especially within defined contribution provision. It is perhaps the most significant pensions-related function of the state discussed in this chapter—and yet the state's objectives are, at best, unclear. George Osborne, as Chancellor, sought to reform PTR, seemingly in alignment with his own vision of highly individualized pensions provision, but—much like his attempted reforms to defined benefit regulation, discussed in Chapter 4—found pensions reality rather resistant to ideological parsimony.

PTR is, in theory, pleasingly straightforward—yet in practice, it is staggeringly complex. In essence, pensions saving is accumulated via pre-tax income, as part of an 'EET' system: both pension contributions and the investment returns they attract are exempt from tax ('E' and 'E', respectively), but pensions in payment are taxable (the final 'T'). If you are a basic-rate taxpayer, for instance, by definition you benefit from basic-rate PTR. (The middle E is actually rather more complicated, since the investment process is taxable in myriad ways, but generally speaking the returns that end up back in your pot are not taxed.) The New Labour government's 'A-Day' reforms in 2006 sought to regularize PTR and related mechanisms. The key changes were, firstly, a simplification of rules on 'lump sums'—the amount individuals can withdraw from their pension pot at retirement without having to pay tax (irrespective of PTR received during their working life). And secondly, and more significantly, the introduction of the lifetime allowance and annual allowance (not to be confused with the MPAA, discussed above), which restricted the volume of each individual's pensions saving which could benefit from PTR. The lifetime and annual allowances did not 'simplify' UK pensions provision. The A-Day reforms were essentially designed for defined contribution schemes—and were thus implemented around the time that New Labour accepted pensions individualization as a fait accompli. In defined benefit provision, where there is no 'pot', the allowances led to the necessity of complex regulations for the calculation of the real value of contributions.

Table 6.2 Annual expenditure on PTR 2013–18, selected years (£ million)

	2013/14	2015/16	2017/18
Income tax relief on:			
Occupational scheme contributions			
by employees	4,000	4,100	4,200
by employers	17,100	19,300	18,600
Personal and GPP scheme contributions			
by employees	1,900	2,000	1,600
by employers	4,200	5,600	5,600
Pension contributions by the self-employed	600	600	500
Investment income within pension schemes	5,900	6,800	6,700
Total PTR expenditure	*33,700*	*38,300*	*37,200*
Less income tax liable on pensions in payment	15,500	17,600	18,300
Total net PTR expenditure	*18,200*	*20,700*	*19,000*
NICs relief for employer pension contributions	13,600	15,900	16,500
PTR and NICs relief expenditure net of income tax liable on pensions in payment	*31,800*	*36,600*	*35,400*

Note: Figures rounded to nearest 100 million; HM Revenue and Customs assumes that income tax relief on investment income is applied at the basic rate

Source: Adapted by author from HM Revenue and Customs data available at: https://assets.publishing. service.gov.uk/government/uploads/system/uploads/attachment_data/file/833859/Table_6_Cost_of_ Pension_Tax_and_NICs_Relief__2012-13_to_2017-18_.pdf

Table 6.2 shows the recent cost of PTR. Clearly, there are various ways in which the costs could be calculated. While PTR cost £37.2 billion in 2017/18 (that is, HM Revenue and Customs estimates of tax foregone), we should recognize also that pensions in payment are taxed, suggesting a net expenditure of £19 billion. Obviously, however, the pension payments being taxed in any given year are unrelated to the pension contributions benefiting from PTR (in this sense, PTR is a mechanism of inter-generational co-operation). HM Revenue and Customs also publishes data on employer National Insurance contributions (NICs) foregone, as part of contracting out (that is, whereby employers pay lower NICs if their employees are enrolled in an eligible pension scheme in place of the S2P). It is worth noting here that contracting out now applies only to defined benefit provision: the Blair government reversed the Thatcher government's application of contracting out to defined contribution schemes when S2P was introduced in the early 2000s. The introduction of the STSP has led to the abolition of contracting out altogether.

The gross cost of PTR has roughly doubled since the early 2000s, for two main reasons. Firstly, as the 2015 green paper explicitly argued, defined benefit contributions have increased significantly in the last two decades in order to repair deficits—and therefore PTR has been nominally applied, without producing any increase in pension incomes for scheme members. Secondly, as the green paper implicitly recognized, there has been an increase in the proportion of individuals benefiting from higher-rate PTR during accumulation, yet paying income tax at only the basic rate in retirement (as discussed further below) (see HM Treasury, 2015b: 14). More recent cost increases have been held in check by the Coalition government's reduction in, and changes to, the lifetime and annual allowances, saving around £6 billion per year—including around £100 million in actual revenue in the first year as many high earners breached the new lifetime allowance (of just over £1 million) (Cumbo, 2017). Controlling contributions within defined benefit provision, in which PTR is an automatic function of contributing from pre-tax income, is far from straightforward. The new 'taper' applicable to the annual allowance, whereby people earning over £150,000 see the allowance of £40,000 reduced—falling to only £10,000 for those earning over £210,000—also proved controversial, particularly for highly paid surgeons in the National Health Service who, quite understandably, argued that the taper represented a complication (and perceived tax penalty) too far. (Very high earners were also affected by an alternative annual allowance, if they had already utilized the MPAA by exercising the new pension freedoms to access their defined contribution AVC savings.) The National Health Service has warned that surgeons were required to reduce their hours, or retire, as a consequence—with longer waiting lists for surgery the inevitable result. The rules for the National Health Service pension scheme were tweaked after Boris Johnson became Prime Minister—but sparing the surgeons led to demands for similar concessions from the highest earners in the private sector (see Brodbeck, 2019; Cumbo, 2019).

We should also note that auto-enrolment will lead to very significant increases in PTR expenditure, other things being equal. Given that minimum contributions only recently reached 8 per cent (even this figure is far below typical contributions into remaining defined benefit schemes, as discussed in Chapter 4), it is difficult to say with certainty how large the increase will ultimately be. However, PPI modelling in 2013 suggested that once auto-enrolment had been fully implemented, it would cost an additional £11 billion per year in PTR (in gross 2010/11 terms) (Echalier et al., 2013: 20–1). But to what end? There is no evidence that PTR provides for any meaningful savings incentive, largely because people do not realize it exists, or even if they are aware of PTR, do not understand how it operates (Echalier et al., 2013: 24–7; Blake, 2016: 577–80) (quite aside from the fact that auto-enrolment is based on inertia, not persuasion).

As well as failing to incentivize pensions saving, PTR is also highly regressive (see Sinfield, 2000). An EET approach assumes that tax on pensions in payment will be incurred at the same rate as tax on contributions is relieved. Invariably, it is not. The PPI reported in 2013 (see Echalier et al., 2013) that:

- Basic rate taxpayers make 50 per cent of total contributions to private pension schemes, but receive only 30 per cent of the value of PTR expenditure.
- Higher rate taxpayers make 40 per cent of total contributions to private pension schemes, but receive 50 per cent of the value of PTR expenditure.
- Additional rate taxpayers (that is, the highest rate) make 10 per cent of total contributions to private pension schemes, but receive 20 per cent of the value of PTR.

Clearly, any system which disproportionately benefits the highest earners will have uneven impacts by class, gender, ethnicity, and disability. It is also worth noting here two rather preposterous anomalies. Firstly, it is possible to bequeath any remaining defined contribution pot to one's heirs at death (that is, any capital which has not been annuitized or drawn down). Such bequests are exempt from inheritance tax; Paul Johnson, head of the Institute for Fiscal Studies, describes this policy as 'astonishing' (Johnson, 2018).

Secondly, whether very low earners (that is, people earning less than the income tax personal allowance, which generally means people working in part-time roles) actually receive their PTR entitlements depends entirely on factors outside their control. Under the 'Net Pay Arrangement' (NPA) system, contributions are deducted from a worker's salary before income tax is deducted—but if their taxable income is zero, PTR cannot be applied. Under the 'Relief at Source' (RAS) system, contributions are made by all workers from post-tax income, and the provider claims back the tax overpaid. Crucially, in RAS, non-taxpayers are awarded PTR as if they were basic-rate taxpayers—this mechanism is not available in NPA. Furthermore, and challenging the simplistic notion that trust-based pension scheme governance trumps a contract-based approach from the member's perspective, RAS is generally a feature of GPPs, whereas NPA is more prevalent in trust-based schemes (Royal London, 2019: 17–18). (However, the master trust People's Pension now advertises the fact that it applies RAS as its default arrangement, claiming that its rival NOW only offers NPA—while acknowledging that NOW does support members to claim back from HM Revenue and Customs the PTR they would have received had their employer operated the

RAS system.[7]) There is of course an important logic to NPA: the tax system cannot be used to induce behavioural change among non-taxpayers (and the lowest earners will probably be non-taxpayers in retirement too). But the notion that savers in the RAS system—which is effectively chosen by their employer—receive a fiscal boost to their pensions saving not available to all savers is very odd, and may indeed be illegal (see House of Commons Work and Pensions Committee, 2019: 34).[8]

As the government signalled its willingness to consider radical reform of the PTR system, a degree of momentum built around the proposal for 'flat-rate' relief of 30 per cent; basic-rate taxpayers would receive PTR at a rate higher than their income tax band, and higher-rate taxpayers would receive PTR at a lower rate. While this ostensibly constitutes a redistributive approach to PTR, in practice, according to the PPI, it would simply be a more 'equitable' approach whereby the benefits of PTR are aligned with the distribution of tax paid on pension incomes. It was also calculated to be fiscally neutral (Echalier et al., 2013). The RSA (champions of CDC, as discussed in Chapter 4) produced similar analysis with near identical results in 2018 (see Dellot and Wallace-Stephens, 2018). Adair Turner declared his support for a flat-rate system in 2016—although the Pensions Commission had not considered PTR design (see Cumbo, 2016). It would mean that all employers and providers would have to offer RAS; this would create significant administrative difficulties, but would mean PTR could be presented more simply as a (partial) 'matching contribution' rather than a tax relief.

It is believed that Osborne considered a move towards flat-rate PTR, before being dissuaded by a 'Save Our Pensions' campaign orchestrated by *The Daily Mail*, and supported by many backbench Conservative members of parliament (Cumbo and Pickard, 2018). (It is not clear whether flat-rate PTR for only defined contributions was considered, or indeed permissible—this would have neutralized much of the opposition). A *Financial Times* (2015) editorial voiced support for flat-rate PTR, but the newspaper's money editor Merryn Somerset Webb (2016) later described Osborne's approach to PTR as a set of 'stealth taxes', and criticized the plan's implications for those earning six-figure salaries (while also rightly describing the inheritance tax exemption as 'ridiculousness' and 'a sop to the right'). Somerset Webb is

---

[7] See https://thepeoplespension.co.uk/compare-auto-enrolment-workplace-pensions/.
[8] Note that at Budget 2020, the Johnson government promised to consult on alleviating the NPA/RAS anomaly (see HM Treasury, 2020: 89).

largely correct! Firstly, Osborne *did* seek to use PTR changes to raise tax revenue in less visible ways, and would undoubtedly have used the introduction of flat-rate PTR in such a way—he simply got caught. (One of his earliest decisions as Chancellor was to drastically reduce the annual allowance from £255,000 to £50,000.) Secondly, it *is* rather absurd to introduce a new category of income tax in order to ensure that PTR—*which does not incentivize pensions saving*—produces slightly more equitable outcomes, and in the process make pensions tax arrangements again *more* complicated, not less. Instead, it would be preferable to increase taxes on the wealth of very affluent older people, using the proceeds to provide targeted support for pensions accumulation for poorer and younger people, either within private provision or the state pension system.

It is not clear, in fact, that Osborne seriously considered flat-rate PTR. Instead, he appeared to favour moving towards a 'TEE' system (taxed, exempt, exempt). His radical reforms to the annual allowance can be read as revenue-raisers, but equally act to take large chunks of earnings out of the PTR system altogether. Under TEE, pension contributions would be made from post-tax income, but investment returns and pensions in payment would not be taxed, or at least would be taxed less than at present. Such an approach would deliberately bring pensions saving in line with the LISA model, and accordingly was christened 'the Pensions ISA [Individual Savings Account]' by commentators, although the LISA is probably best characterized as 'TST' (contributions from post-tax income ('T'), accumulated savings supplemented through fiscal subsidy ('S'), and subject to normal tax rules when withdrawn (the final 'T')). Osborne had already strongly signalled his support for this approach in his 2015 budget speech, before a consultation was launched:

> While we've taken important steps with our new single tier pension and generous new ISA, I am open to further radical change. Pensions could be taxed like ISAs. You pay in from taxed income—and it's tax free when you take it out. And in-between it receives a top-up from the government.   (Osborne, 2015a)

So, the Pensions ISA would also receive the subsidy element of the LISA (in other words, a 'TSE' model). Crucially, while Osborne said the consultation process 'takes care not to pre-judge the answer', the notion of a flat-rate PTR was *not* floated in the speech. Chris Giles (2015), *Financial Times*' Economics Editor, pre-emptively disagreed with his colleague Somerset Webb, and his employer's future editorial line, by applauding the plan—very few others did. It has not yet been taken forward, yet it was iced, rather than rejected, by the

Conservative majority government of 2015–16 (see HM Treasury, 2015c).
Watch this space.

6.5.   Conclusion: Hijinks or Hijack?

Adair Turner's Pensions Commission envisaged a new role for the state in
private pensions provision, as provider and procurer of financial services,
and at the very least facilitator of a more level playing field between individual savers and the pensions industry. The Commission focused on accumulation mechanisms, but also considered the state's functions in relation to
defined contribution decumulation. In both regards, this new role has not
come to pass. Instead, policy-makers have focused largely on regulating providers with a marketized approach to auto-enrolment. It has also replicated
market functions in some ways, albeit in seeking to provide pensions for
market segments which the private sector cannot service profitably—reacting pre-emptively to market failure. This highly submissive approach to state
intervention has led to various perverse circumstances, such as the build-up
of very small, dormant pots as workers change jobs, an apparent inability to
control the transaction costs which eat into investment returns, and, above
all, the absurdity of different workplace pension schemes being situated
across two very different (yet equally inadequate) regulatory regimes. On the
other hand, however, we cannot say with confidence that it would be in individuals' interest to be more protected by the regulatory state to any significant extent, since increasing the cost of provision within individualized
pensions ultimately affects the returns defined contribution savers rely upon.

The most important form of state intervention within private pensions
provision is PTR. Alas, it has no impact on saving incentives within defined
contribution provision, and, since PTR was redesigned at A-Day to suit
defined contribution, has complexified its application within defined benefit
provision. As is the case in other areas of pensions policy, we find the actual
policy rationale difficult to discern, with original objectives dissipated and
distorted over time. Yet PTR has proved impossible to unwind. The Coalition
and Conservative majority governments from 2014 onwards have responded
to such failures by seeking to refashion the nature of pensions provision in
the UK. This was enacted, firstly, by removing the compulsion to generate a
pension income from pensions saving through annuitization, despite savers
having benefited from PTR, and, secondly—and unsuccessfully, to date—by
abolishing PTR altogether in favour of a 'pensions ISA' model. The architect
of these measures, George Osborne, was of course seeking to score political

points and raise revenue for the Exchequer through such measures, appearing essentially to sacrifice long-term policy development in favour of his own short-term interests. Turner described them, ruefully, as 'rabbits out of hats' (cited in Cumbo, 2016). But is it correct to deduce therefore that Osborne was attempting to hijack the Turner legacy, and indeed even the diluted form of auto-enrolment that has characterized the post-Turner era? Perhaps, but only to a limited extent. The Pensions Commission's blueprint itself hijacked the (liberal) collectivist sentiment that had long been present within UK pensions policy. Employing the state to instil pensions individualization was a contradictory form of statecraft always likely to unravel at some point.

Essentially, pensions imperilment is a product of policy-makers seeking to compel the individual, rather than the state, to serve as the temporal anchor of cross-generational pensions provision. As discussed in Chapter 2, while the state pension still exists (forming a hugely important part of many people's retirement income), for future cohorts it has been reimagined as a flat-rate 'savings platform' which more or less guarantees relief from poverty, but not a decent standard of living. The state may still be acting as a temporal anchor in this regard, but does not want you to know it. Pensions futures always fail—this, paradoxically, is why we have pensions provision. But in an individualized system, the future fails harder, precisely because failures have become less tolerable. The pension freedoms reform is an exemplary case in point: it licenses individuals to abdicate inter-generational co-operation, despite being the beneficiaries of previous inter-generational bargaining, and remaining dependent on future cohorts to sustain the financial practices that enable opportunities for defined benefit decumulation. Furthermore, this approach has allowed political actors to exploit individualist sentiment as they seek, ironically, to secure their positions as custodians of the (potentially) collectivist state apparatus.

7

Many Happy Returns? Investment Governance and the Political Economy of Time in UK Pensions Provision

Investment activity by 'pension funds'—a term we must, increasingly, use rather loosely in this context—is supposed to be a means to an end. This is perhaps true of all investment activity, to some extent: we seek a return—that is, profit—on our investment not for its own sake, but because the returns enable a higher standard of living, both for ourselves and those with whom we share the proceeds. Usually, however, the investment mechanism is designed solely to produce the return; what we do with the return is a separate process. Traditionally, however, in pensions provision, investment returns are explicitly instrumental. We save or invest (or pay tax) in order to generate an income (deferred until retirement), which supports a given standard of living, and which is (more or less) known in advance. The notion that UK pensions provision has been financialized suggests, among other things, that the investment process, orchestrated by the finance sector, is not only the sole determinant of the incomes we may receive in retirement via private saving, but also that the mechanisms by which we accumulate and decumulate pensions capital are being reshaped around dominant capital market practices, irrespective of the utility of these practices for the ultimate beneficiaries.

In reality, there has always been a symbiosis between UK pensions provision and capitalist investment practice: the available means shaping the imaginable end. Even where certain outcomes are guaranteed, the ability of the state and, in particular, employers to deliver the pension promised depends on myriad processes by which pension contributions are dematerialized then rematerialized in order to sustain their value over time. The persistence of the employers and providers either guaranteeing or delivering retirement incomes itself depends on countless, cross-generational actions in this regard. In a paper published by Finance for the Future in 2010, economist and tax justice campaigner Richard Murphy (2010: 3) argued that there exists a 'fundamental pension contract':

Pensions Imperilled: The Political Economy of Private Pensions Provision in the UK. Craig Berry, Oxford University Press (2021).
© Craig Berry. DOI: 10.1093/oso/9780198782834.003.0007

This is that one generation, the older one, will through its own efforts create capital assets and infrastructure in both the state and private sectors which the following younger generation can use in the course of their work. In exchange for
their subsequent use of these assets for their own benefit that succeeding younger
generation[s] will, in effect, meet the income needs of the older generation when
they are in retirement. Unless this fundamental compact that underpins all pensions is honoured any pension system will fail...This compact is ignored in the
existing pension system that does not even recognise that it exists. Our state sub-
sidised saving for pensions makes no link between that activity and the necessary
investment in new capital goods, infrastructure, job creation and skills that we
need as a country. As a result state subsidy is being given with no return to the
state appearing to arise as a consequence, precisely because this is a subsidy for
saving which does not generate any new wealth. This is the fundamental economic problem and malaise in our current pension arrangement.

This gets us somewhat closer to understanding the symbiosis between pensions provision and the capitalist economy. For Murphy, crucially, the shift to
defined contribution provision and, relatedly, short-termist investment practice essentially breaks or jeopardizes the cross-generational pension contract.

However, while valuable, this account is unsatisfactory in two main ways.
Firstly, it suggests that there *ought to be* inter-generational co-operation in
sustaining the rematerialization of pensions saving. In practice, all pensions
provision, even if individualized, depends endemically on the ongoing contributions of people at different life-stages. We should think not simply about
generating inter-generational co-operation, but also about how pensions
provision governs the nature of existing inter-generational relations in this
regard. Secondly, it assumes that the relations between different generations
would ideally be rather static (while capitalist production gently expands).
Yet generational change is a perennial feature of human existence. Pensions
provision is not simply about fixing the parameters of inter-generational
relations, but also the creation and maintenance of the mechanism by which
we can cope with the inevitable failure of the future to resemble the present,
as a result of generational change. The notion that investment activity can
ever be merely a means to the end of decent retirement incomes is too simplistic; pensions provision will always be playing catch-up with capitalist
dynamics. At the same time, this does not mean that we should, or can,
accommodate the status quo.

It is clearly beyond the scope of this chapter to consider all aspects of the
pensions/capitalism interface in depth; it concentrates on introducing the
most relevant trends in the investment landscape, considering how they

interact with the rise of defined contribution, and drawing out the implications for the book's main arguments. Section 7.1 discusses the dominant investment practices across defined benefit and defined contribution provision, including the role of the asset management and insurance industries, and local government. Section 7.2 looks in more detail at the array of asset types pension funds engage with, the associated practices and strategies, and the prospect of reorienting funds (back) towards responsible and/or long-term investment. Section 7.3 discusses how investment is governed in defined contribution provision, including the attempted interventions of policy-makers in this regard. Section 7.4 reflects briefly on the implications for (our understanding of) financialization, inter-generational relations, and the inherent temporalities of pensions provision.

7.1. Asset Allocation, etc.

We know much less than we probably should about how large funds related to UK workplace pensions provision are invested, particularly in the defined contribution world. That said, calculating the value of assets held by each fund is obviously far from straightforward; the size of each individual's 'pot' in contract-based provision is essentially a reporting fiction rather than collectible data. And even in trust-based provision, methodological changes by TPR and ONS in 2017 significantly altered what we *thought* we knew. The OECD reports that UK pension funds were valued at 104.5 per cent of GDP in 2018—this refers only to funded, occupational provision, that is, defined benefit and trust-based defined contribution schemes.[1] Willis Towers Watson (WTW; leading investment consultancy) reports a similar 2018 figure, 101.7 per cent of GDP, with around 18 per cent of this related to defined contribution provision.[2]

The ONS produces comparable figures in the detailed National Accounts, and as such estimated total pension-related funds in the UK as 119 per cent of GDP in 2015. This was reported in April 2017, and as such incorporates the significant revising down of the size of trust-based funds in January 2017, which led to them being estimated as holding £38 billion (2 per cent of then GDP) rather than £355 billion (18.7 per cent of then GDP) in 2015.[3] The

---

[1] The latest OECD data are available at http://www.oecd.org/daf/fin/private-pensions/Pension-Markets-in-Focus-2019.pdf.

[2] The latest WTW data are available at https://www.thinkingaheadinstitute.org/en/Library/Public/Research-and-Ideas/2019/02/Global-Pension-Asset-Survey-2019.

[3] More information on the methodological change is available at https://www.ons.gov.uk/economy/nationalaccounts/uksectoraccounts/methodologies/theukenhancedfinancialaccountschangestodefined

total also includes pension-related reserves held by insurance companies, estimated as 40 per cent of GDP in 2015 (altogether, this means that the 2015 figure reported by the ONS for funds related to occupational pensions provision is very close to the 2018 figures reported by the OECD and WTW, even though the latter eschewed ONS data after the 2017 change). Crucially, the ONS National Accounts data for pension-related insurance reserves also, and rightly, include reserves related to annuities and drawdown products—which may, and increasingly will, derive from saving in trust-based rather than contract-based schemes. However, more than half of the pension-related reserves held by insurance companies arise from *personal* pensions (including decumulation products) rather than *workplace* pension schemes (the latter are technically personal pensions provided to a 'group' that is, GPPs).[4]

Tiptoeing through the statistical minefield, we can acknowledge nevertheless that UK pension funds are very large! Funded defined benefit provision is based upon funds worth close to the total value of the annual output of the UK economy; adding defined contribution, albeit with many caveats, takes us significantly above this value. How these funds operate, as capital, obviously depends on their liability structure and governance model—and as such the aggregate picture will change significantly as defined contribution takes over from defined benefit, and as the balance within defined contribution provision between trust-based and contract-based schemes becomes clearer. At the moment, while pensions *policy* is focused overwhelmingly on supporting defined contribution, the landscape of pensions investment *practice* remains dominated by defined benefit funds. (However, it would be premature to conclude that there are significant cleavages in investment practice between the two worlds of workplace pensions provision in the UK).

Tables 7.1 and 7.2 detail the aggregate asset allocation of private-sector defined benefit schemes in the UK, and how this has changed since 2006, as reported by PPF. Table 7.3 details the average asset allocation of the largest local authority pension funds in the UK from 2015 and 2016, based on

---

contributionpensionfundestimatesinthenationalaccountspart1themethods and https://www.ons.gov.uk/economy/nationalaccounts/uksectoraccounts/methodologies/theukenhancedfinancialaccountschangestodefinedcontributionpensionfundestimatesinthenationalaccountspart2thedata. Note also that TPR reported that, by 2018, the value of trust-based defined contribution funds (excluding schemes with less than twelve members) had risen to £60 billion. See https://www.thepensionsregulator.gov.uk/en/document-library/research-and-analysis/dc-trust-presentation-of-scheme-return-data-2018–2019.

[4] The latest National Accounts data related to pension funds and insurance companies are available at https://www.ons.gov.uk/economy/nationalaccounts/uksectoraccounts/articles/moneyinfundedpensionsandinsuranceintheuknationalaccounts/1957to2015. Note the Eurostat reporting rules now require national statistics authorities to report assets held for the purpose of annuity provision as defined *benefit* assets. It is not clear whether the ONS has implemented this change, or intends to do so if the UK leaves the EU.

Table 7.1   Aggregate asset allocation by UK defined benefit funds (summary), 2006–18 (%)

	2006	2010	2014	2018
Equities	61.1	42	35	27
Bonds	28.3	40.4	44.1	59
Other	10.6	17.6	20.9	14

Note: Annual figure refers to the date data were reported to the PPF (approximately 99 per cent of reports refer to asset allocation within the past two years)

Source: Adapted from PPF (2018), available at https://www.ppf.co.uk/sites/default/files/file-2018-12/the_purple_book_web_dec_18_2.pdf

Table 7.2   Aggregate asset allocation by UK defined benefit funds (detailed), 2010–18 (%)

	2010	2014	2018
Equities, comprised of:	42	35	27
UK-quoted	16.8	10.1	5
Overseas	23.2	21.8	18.7
Unquoted/private	1.8	3	3.2
Bonds, comprised of:	40.4	44.1	59
Government fixed interest	9.9	8.2	14.2
Corporate	17	17.8	17
Index-linked	13.4	18.1	27.8
Property	4.6	4.6	4.8
Cash and deposits	3.9	6.1	−2.5
Insurance policies	1.4	0.1	0.1
Hedge funds	2.2	5.8	7.0
Miscellaneous	5.4	4.3	4.6

Note: Annual figure refers to the date data were reported to the PPF (approximately 99 per cent of reports refer to asset allocation within the past two years). According to the PPF, negative 'cash and deposits' amounts are likely to be related to investments such as swaps and repurchase agreements by a number of large schemes

Source: Adapted from PPF (2018), available at https://www.ppf.co.uk/sites/default/files/file-2018-12/the_purple_book_web_dec_18_2.pdf

analysis of annual reports by the current author and Adam Barber (Berry and Barber, 2017). Local authority funds are valued at around £200 billion, and as such comprise a sizeable chunk of total defined benefit assets, although as public-sector funds they operate within different financial and regulatory parameters to private-sector funds. The focus here is on the largest funds, rather than all funds, in order to provide comparable data, since weighted average figures are not available (the majority of local authority pension fund capital is held by the largest twenty-five funds, given that these generally service merged schemes within high-population metropolitan areas). There is not the same degree of consistency (or detail) as in private-sector reporting: local authorities are required to publish financial reports, but not necessarily in a uniform, comprehensive manner given that they are

Table 7.3 Average asset allocation by largest UK local authority funds, 2005–16 (%)

	2005	2009	2013	2016
Equities, comprised of:	62	56	47	53
UK-quoted	35	28	16	18
Overseas	27	29	31	35
Unquoted/private	2	3	6	5
Bonds	13	16	19	16
Cash	5	5	3	3
Property	10	7	9	9
Infrastructure	1	1	4	4
Other (including hedge funds)	17	12	13	9

Source: Slightly adapted from Berry and Barber (2017), available at http://speri.dept.shef.ac.uk/
wp-content/uploads/2018/11/SPERI-Brief-29-Local-authority-pension-fund-investment-since-the-
financial-crisis.pdf

not part of the PPF. That said, the largest local authority funds, in contrast to the private sector, *do* distinguish infrastructure as an asset class (discussed further below). However, we cannot necessarily assume that all funds mean the same thing by 'infrastructure'; moreover, even where funds are investing significantly in infrastructure-related assets, this is likely to be captured within other asset classes, such as corporate bonds and private equity.

A number of recent trends are apparent; above all, the 'de-equitisation' of UK private-sector pension funds, as a 60/30 split between equities and bonds evident before the financial crisis has now virtually reversed at 30/60 (with 'other' investments still in the region of 10 per cent). This is actually a long-running trend—arguably intensified, but certainly not triggered, by the 2008 financial crisis (and we should not discount the impact of falling equity *values* on the equity/bond balance within funds) (Berry, 2014a). Local authority funds have also de-equitized, albeit to a much less extent, and generally not significantly increased investment in bonds. Private sector and local authority share a characteristic, however, in this regard: de-equitization is mainly a product of lower allocation to *UK-quoted* equities—with local authority funds actually increasing exposure to overseas equities in recent years. (The historical context of de-equitization will be discussed below.) Within private-sector bond allocations, the large increase is due mainly to investment in index-linked gilts. The PPF (2018: 46) also reports on asset allocation by fund size and funding status. Counter-intuitively, smaller funds with larger deficits tend to be more exposed to equities, and are more likely to invest in fixed-interest government or corporate bonds; larger, better-funded funds are more likely to have moved towards index-linked bonds. Such trends are undoubtedly linked to winding-up approaches, with smaller schemes more likely to be operating a short-termist investment strategy designed to address deficits before, or in order to secure, a buy-out. Larger schemes, even where closed to new members and/or accruals, generally expect to operate for much longer, and are therefore more conservative. Of course, from a member (or trustee) perspective, funding status matters far more than scheme size or how assets are allocated.

As discussed in Chapter 4, in general defined benefit pensions funds have liabilities that far outweigh their assets. The PPF reported in 2019 that the aggregate funding status of private-sector funds is around 77 per cent, with an aggregate deficit of almost £500 billion. Deficit levels are highly volatile, although broadly speaking the funding position of funds has improved in the last few years. This is partly a consequence of scheme closures (so new liabilities are not accrued), or insolvent schemes entering the PPF. Whereas it was the case until recently that the smallest schemes had the largest deficits, those that remain in existence tend to be the strongest, and the funding status of larger schemes has deteriorated (see PPF, 2019 for the latest analysis and further discussion). It is of course necessary to note that the immediate economic implications of the COVID-19 pandemic have affected pension funds, with investment consultants Hymans Robertson finding that around £100 billion had been added to defined benefit deficits in March 2020 (see *Actuarial Post*, 2020). As noted in Chapter 4, USS (the UK's largest private pension scheme) has seen its deficit triple. Falling market values are a key concern, but funds may ultimately be most affected by falling gilt yields, since these are used to discount future liabilities as well as being a source of cash (see Lamont, 2020). Deficit levels are not directly related to this chapter's focus, although worth noting insofar as a scheme's funding status will influence its investment strategy.

Unfortunately, we know far less about where defined contribution schemes invest. This is in part due to the fact that, by definition, they are not part of the PPF, and therefore do not operate under the same reporting requirements as defined benefit provision. As discussed in Chapters 4 and 6, since deficits are not possible in defined contribution schemes, the TPR valuation framework is not applicable. It is also due in part to the significant role of contract-based provision, in which the notion of a single scheme's asset allocation is incongruous. (Of course, that defined contribution workplace provision remains in its infancy means any direct comparison to defined benefit is inappropriate anyway; we can expect investment practice to evolve as auto-enrolment schemes grow and mature.) The ONS collects data on asset holdings by insurance companies and pension trusts, but does not distinguish pensions-related holdings within long-term insurance provision, nor between defined benefit and defined contribution within pension trust holdings. (The categories used to report asset types also differ from conventional asset allocation reporting.)[5]

However, PPI's survey of thirty-five defined contribution schemes (covering more than 20 million scheme members) offers some information, albeit with very broad categories of asset types. Usefully, PPI distinguishes between the asset allocation for members twenty years from retirement, and those at the point of retirement, and between master trusts and GPPs/stakeholder schemes. For master trusts, members twenty years from retirement have between 80 and 100 per cent of their pots invested in equities in 39 per cent of schemes. A further 23 per cent have between 60 and 79 per cent of their pot invested in equities. In contrast, in 54 per cent of schemes, members will have between 0 and 19 per cent of their pot invested in cash or bonds (with the remaining 46 per cent with an allocation between 20 and 39 per cent). This pattern is reversed for members at the point of retirement: in 38 per cent of schemes, these members will have between 80 and 100 per cent of their pot invested in cash or bonds, and in 46 per cent of schemes, these members will have between 0 and 19 per cent of their pots invested in equities. For GPPs/stakeholder schemes, members twenty years from retirement have between 80 and 100 per cent of their pots invested in equities in 44 per cent of schemes. A further 33 per cent have between 60 and 79 per cent of their pot invested in equities. In contrast, in 78 per cent of schemes, members will have between 0 and 19 per cent of their pot invested in cash or bonds (with the remaining 22 per cent with an allocation between 20 and 39 per cent). Again, this pattern is reversed for members at the point of retirement, but not quite as starkly as in master trust provision. In only 11 per cent of schemes, these members have between 80 and 100 per cent of their pot invested in cash or bonds, but in a further 44 per cent of schemes, these members have between 60 and 79 per cent of their pot invested in cash or bonds. In 78 per cent of schemes, GPP/stakeholder members have an equity allocation between 20 and 39 per cent (Pensions Policy Institute, 2019).

Reporting by ABI (2019) allows us to see that insurance companies strongly favour allocations to private-sector securities over UK or other governments' securities, and that bonds in general are strongly favoured over equities. However, ABI also reports that almost a quarter of its members' investments are in unit trusts, which typically include a wide range of asset

---

[5] The ONS's MQ5 series is available at https://www.ons.gov.uk/economy/investmentspensionsandtrusts/datasets/mq5investmentbyinsurancecompaniespensionfundsandtrusts (latest release March 2019). However, note that this series has actually now been discontinued pending a review of surveys covering the finance sector.

types, overlapping with the more specific categories. Such practices probably help to explain the imprecision in the PPI data. Although it has become common—including in pensions regulation—to refer to the 'default funds' that the vast majority of auto-enrolees are enrolled into (unless they actively choose an alternative investment strategy), default *arrangements* would be a more accurate term, since the various funds constituting the default will invariably be multi-asset funds in practice. Scheme managers (including trustees) may not have extensive information about such practices (and indeed are not required to collect it).

7.1.1 A Note on the Asset Management Industry

It is impossible to discuss pension fund asset allocation without noting the integral role of the asset management industry in shaping and/or determining investment practice. (This sub-section provides an overview of the industry, whereas its specific function as an investment intermediary is discussed in Section 7.2.) Few funds operate their own investment activity. With investment consultants, typically (a source of a conflict, according to some observers, given consultants' relationship with the asset management industry (Mooney, 2017; Jaiswal, 2018)), funds devise mandates for asset management firms to implement, either in whole or, far more often, in part (since the industry has become both more concentrated and specialized). Of course, the privileged access that asset management firms have to capital markets is part of what is being paid for, since this access would be difficult to replicate even for the largest funds. (This is arguably less problematic within defined contribution provision, insofar as 'funds' are managed by very large insurance companies, even if the associated workplace schemes are very small.) According to Investment Association (previously Investment Management Association) estimates, UK-based asset managers had more than £9 trillion in assets under management (AUM) in 2018, with around 60 per cent of total AUM accounted for by UK-based clients. Of the £7.7 trillion AUM by Investment Association members, £2.6 trillion belongs to UK pension funds, or £2.4 billion excluding in-house investment managers (who are able to join the Investment Association, but do not serve other clients)—nevertheless the overwhelming majority of pension AUM relates to 'third-party' asset management. Interestingly, the Investment Association reports that around half of this (£1.2 trillion) is now part of a liability-driven investment strategy, generally adopted by schemes expecting to wind up in the near future (Investment Association, 2019).

A much smaller—but still colossal—amount of total AUM belongs to insurance companies, that is, £0.4 trillion. Clearly, a large part of this will consist of assets built up through contract-based defined contribution pensions saving (just as a small part of the AUM for pension funds will relate to trust-based defined contribution schemes). In its most recent annual report, the key point made about defined contribution provision by the Investment Association (2019: 55–9) is the expectation that the asset management industry will increasingly become directly involved in decumulation as well as accumulation provision, partly, but not exclusively, as a result of 'pension freedoms', discussed in Chapter 6. This contrasts rather sharply with the tone of discussion in the organization's 2013 report, published as auto-enrolment commenced. This report focused on the challenge that the individualized nature of defined contribution will present to the asset management industry, and indeed the 'responsibilities' to savers the industry would take on in this regard (Investment Management Association, 2013).

One of the most important developments within UK asset management in recent years is the 'Americanisation' of the industry, with firms such as BlackRock, Vanguard, State Street, and Fidelity—the largest firms globally—now part-domiciled in London as well as New York. Many of the largest UK asset management firms are rooted in the insurance industry (and therefore defined contribution provision), most notably L&G Investment Management (with €1.1 trillion worldwide AUM in 2018; the UK's largest asset management firm, and the world's twelfth largest). As noted in Chapter 2, L&G has been a major provider of private pensions since the early twentieth century; as it began to lose market presence to defined benefit trusts administered by employers directly, the firm shifted to offering fund management services to the trusts in the 1950s. (Of course, as noted in Chapter 6, the rise of defined contribution provision means L&G is once again a major direct provider of workplace pension schemes.) M&G (recently 'demerged' from Prudential), Aviva, and Royal London are also in the UK top ten. The management of defined benefit pension funds remains concentrated, however, among 'traditional' UK firms, most notably Insight (with €620 billion pension fund AUM), Schroders (with €150 billion pension fund AUM), and Baillie Gifford (with €110 billion pension fund AUM). Each of these are among the world's largest 100 asset management firms, and for each firm UK pension fund assets constitute a very significant portion of total, worldwide AUM (in Insight's case, around 90 per cent), which underlines the significance of UK pension funds in global capital markets.[6]

---

[6] Information on the asset management industry in the UK, Europe, and globally is available at https://hub.ipe.com/top-400/uk-asset-manager-tables-2018/10007231.article.

As noted above, the UK asset management industry (as part of a global trend) has been consolidating as a result of M&A activity, reaching a peak in 2018 not reached since the immediate aftermath of the financial crisis (which led to unmanageable losses among some smaller firms). In fact, the *volume* of M&A transactions has been declining, while the *value* of transactions has been increasing—indicating the relatively new trend towards mergers among mid-ranking UK industry players in response to the arrival of larger, American rivals—the 2017 merger of Standard Life and Aberdeen Asset Management (to form Standard Life Aberdeen) is the most notable example (Walker, 2018). There are similar trends evident within the investment consultancy industry, especially as the largest firms (such as Mercer, WTW, and Aon) integrate asset management into their advice business through fiduciary management services. Regulators, in the form of the Competition and Markets Authority, have noted concerns around lack of competition, but so far have elected only to introduce stronger guidelines around transparency and tendering processes (Mooney, 2018). The asset management industry is regulated primarily by the FCA, further complexifying the perverse divide within pensions regulation: TPR is not only unable to regulate a large proportion of the auto-enrolment world, it has limited jurisdiction over investment intermediation arising from *any* aspect of UK pensions provision. It is worth noting, finally, that the Coalition and Conservative governments strongly signalled their support for the UK asset management industry through the development of *The UK Investment Management Strategy*, first published in 2013, and then renewed in 2017. The strategy promised a series of fairly limited tax and regulatory tweaks, as well as greater marketing support as the industry internationalized. It described the industry as 'critical to the financial future of millions of savers' (HM Treasury, 2013: 7), in order to justify government support for the asset management industry—of course, such a sentiment could also serve to justify intervention to reform the industry. The 2017 update (following the 'patient capital' review, discussed below) touched upon, with slightly less substance, the arrival of new asset types, such as cryptocurrency, as well as the need to standardize and scale up opportunities for profiting from responsible investment strategies (HM Treasury, 2017c).

7.2. Pension Fund Capitalism and Capitalist Pension Funds

An understanding of the allocation of pension funds between various asset types offers only a partial portrait of the relationship between pensions provision and capital market investment practice—this would be the case even if we had more complete information about asset allocation. This section considers (current and prospective) investment strategies in more detail, underpinned by an understanding of the intimate relationship between capital accrued via private pensions saving and dominant capital market practices. It considers policy-makers' efforts to reorient (and sometimes reinforce) investment practice, and the limitations that both neoliberal ideology and financialization place upon both action and ambition in this regard.

7.2.1 After De-equitization

An understanding of the allocation of pension funds between various asset types offers only a partial portrait of the relationship between pensions provision and capital market investment practice—this would be the case even if we had more complete information about asset allocation. This sub-section considers both the apparent process of de-equitization (in defined benefit provision), and the wider implications of pension funds' move towards ostensibly more conservative investment strategies. As noted above, de-equitization in UK pension fund investments is a very long-running trend. Before the Second World War, occupational pension funds tended to invest predominantly in fixed-income securities. Indeed, many of the largest funds invested predominantly in the bonds of their own sponsoring employers. This allocation shifted to public debt (a shift now being repeated, to some extent), and only in the 1960s and 1970s did listed equities become a major allocation, as the impact of high inflation demanded investment in riskier assets offering higher returns (Hannah, 1986: 73–4).

Allocations to particular asset classes clearly fluctuate in accordance with both scheme demographics and wider macro-economic conditions—and will continue to do so. Moreover, we should be careful not to assume that pension funds no longer invest in listed equities: they do, on a very large scale. De-equitization in the UK is not evident to the same extent as in other countries, including the US (McCarthy et al., 2016). Yet the balance in asset portfolios has certainly shifted away from equities in the UK—a situation which is likely to persist in the future. This is partly a story of supply: equity markets no longer consistently deliver the returns witnessed in the post-war era, and particularly the 1980s (part of the reason firms were encouraged to take 'contribution holidays' during this latter period). That non-UK equities have increased in importance recently underlines this trend. However, it is also a story of demand, as funds became less concerned about inflation risks in the 1990s. Perhaps more significantly, they also became wary of the apparent volatility of equity investments, a characteristic increasingly deemed incompatible with liability-driven investment strategies as schemes matured. As discussed in Chapter 4, the focus on managing risks and matching liabilities was reinforced by the regulatory environment, particularly the need for triennial valuations in the context of widening deficits in many schemes (which may lead to employers being mandated to make additional contributions to address shortfalls) (see Berry, 2014a). Deborah Mabbett (2020) accordingly refers to the 'reckless prudence' of defined benefit pension scheme governance, as funds adopt investment strategies which are more likely to hasten scheme closure. The harm to members and their employers of strategies with less risk (and therefore lower returns) is outweighed by a matrix of the risk aversion of policy-makers and regulators (seeking to avoid catastrophe rather than produce optimal outcomes) and the pseudo-academic portfolio management theories imported by investment consultants.

Another, possible demand-side explanation is the removal of the dividend tax credit by the Labour government in the late 1990s, meaning pension funds (and individual pensions savers in defined contribution provision) could no longer shield their dividend income—arising from equity holdings—from tax. As noted in Chapter 2, the policy is invariably depicted as Gordon Brown's 'tax grab' or 'tax raid', and is central to Alex Brummer's (2010) popular account in *The Great Pensions Robbery* (although the tax relief available had actually already been reduced by Conservative governments in the 1990s). A counter-factual analysis by the Office for Budget Responsibility suggested the change led to higher tax revenue of almost £10 billion per year by 2013/14, leading to hyperbolic commentary in the *Financial Times* by financial journalist Tony Hazell (2014) that 'it is reasonable to conclude final salary schemes, which are today closed to new members, would otherwise have still been going had Mr Brown not dipped into their coffers'. The analysis is rather flawed, due to an assumption that defined benefit funds would not have de-equitized to the extent they have, had the tax credit not been removed. Hazell's 'back-of-a-matchbox' calculation of a £230 billion loss also appears not to consider sustained periods of poor equity performance over the period in question. In other words, micro-economic analysis ignoring macro-economic context. Hazell concluded that 'Mr Brown's tax raid will always stand out as one of the great injustices perpetrated on the diligent investing public'. Of course, even if it were correct to argue that the policy has significantly affected pension funds, this would not make the policy unjust; as discussed in Chapter 6, taxation issues around pensions provision are extremely complex, with the temporal nature of tax treatment across the accumulation and decumulation phases invariably understated. Insofar as the dividend tax credit encouraged firms to prioritize shareholder income in profit allocation, it arguably supported the short-termist corporate governance practices which ultimately account for the demise of defined benefit. Nevertheless, Brummer's view that the change was undertaken primarily to raise revenue for the Exchequer—and arose from a rather complacent attitude regarding the wider vulnerabilities of private-sector defined benefit provision—is highly plausible.

In place of equities, UK pension funds now invest predominantly in bonds. As Table 7.1 shows, the average allocation by defined benefit funds rose from below 30 per cent in 2016 to almost 60 per cent in 2018. Table 7.2 shows that this increase is mainly due to a large increase in allocations to gilts, whether fixed interest (generally a short-term asset) or index-linked (for longer-term liability-matching). However, while allocations to corporate bonds have been stable at around 17 per cent since the financial crisis, there was a sizeable shift towards corporate debt holdings among defined benefit funds in advance of the crisis (PPF, 2010: 72). We can see this, on the one hand, from the pension fund perspective, as part of the long-running de-equitization process. On the other hand, it also speaks to pension funds' role in a wider shift within UK capitalism (in the context of the normalization of very low interest rates), as large firms have increasingly sought to issue debt rather than shares in order to raise capital (Booth, 2018). This effectively passes the risks of investment onto pensions savers (and fund guarantors) rather than existing shareholders.

There are two key implications of the move to debt-based assets for the development of UK pensions provision. Firstly, higher allocations to UK gilts have coincided in recent years with significant reductions in gilt yields—arguably, gilts effectively offer pension funds a mechanism for securing value, rather than an investment asset delivering an income. Pension funds have frequently expressed concern, especially as short-dated gilts began to trade in negative territory (Moore and Cumbo, 2016), yet there are few signs that alternative asset types will be attractive to funds on the same scale. In defined benefit provision, gilt yields are instrumental not simply on the asset side of the balance sheet—they also largely determine how liabilities are valued, via their benchmarking role in calculating discount rates (in accordance with international accounting standards). Pension funds have discretion in calculating the appropriate discount rate for their investment strategies (with funds invested in return-seeking assets generally adopting higher discount rates, driving down their liabilities to reflect expected future income), although they are accountable to TPR in this regard as part of the triennial valuation process (see TPR, 2018d; see also Meeks, 2017). The industrial dispute around the USS pension scheme (noted above and discussed at length in Chapter 4) essentially boils down to a dispute about discount rates, with scheme executives adopting a more conservative approach to calculating liabilities than would normally be expected in a very large scheme with a very strong employer covenant and an investment strategy generally seeking strong returns rather than liability-matching (see Casey, 2019).

As discussed in earlier chapters, QE—deliberately intended to reduce gilt yields, both to reduce the government's cost of borrowing and inflate the value of other asset types—has been problematic for defined benefit pension funds. While the Bank of England's assessment that—in terms of asset values—the impact of QE has been broadly neutral (Joyce et al., 2014) is generally accepted, the specific impact on gilt yields has affected the calculation of liabilities. This concern lay behind pension funds' advocacy of 'smoothing' for the calculation of liabilities, whereby valuations would be based on a multi-year trend in liability values rather than a single-year snapshot. The most recent round of QE, launched by the Bank of England after the 2016 Brexit vote, not only reinforced concerns about the impact on liability calculations, it also appeared to reach the limit of pension funds' willingness to actually sell their gilts. The Bank was compelled to pay above-market rates to purchase gilts from institutional investors, and indeed reduce its initial targets regarding how quickly the programme could be rolled out (Moore, 2016). As such, while possessing gilts has inflated pension fund liabilities, funds recognize also that there are few viable alternatives—and the benefits associated with new gilts may not match those of gilts already held. Moreover, even as the Bank seeks to purchase gilts from institutional investors, pension funds' role as a purchaser of public-sector debt is reinforced.

We know relatively little about the nature and extent of UK pension fund investments in complex and non-traditional assets. As investment in gilts has increased, as part of liability-driven investment, derivative products such as gilt swaps have been used to enable hedging of inflation and interest rate risks, and pension funds have engaged in 'repo' markets (that is, selling assets such as gilts on the basis of an agreement to repurchase the asset in the future) to boost their short-term cash holdings on the back of gilt allocations. However, both routes appear to have become less attractive in recent years. Swap yields now underperform gilt yields, and repo markets have shrunk as banks have partially withdrawn in response to regulatory change (since repo agreements are typically very short term, pension funds rely on 'rolling over' or refinancing agreements, but this becomes more uncertain with fewer market participants) (Gregory, undated; Moreolo, 2016; Pfeuti, 2016).

In terms of reporting on asset allocations, such activity is generally obscured in 'other' or 'miscellaneous' categories (if it is reported at all). However, it is possible to distinguish investment in hedge funds as a distinct asset class—and, as Table 7.2 shows, defined benefit pension funds' allocation to hedge funds has grown significantly in recent years. The attraction of hedge funds to pension funds is a paradoxical by-product of liability-driven investment and de-equitization: as mature pension funds are drawn to lower-risk assets, the inherent drawback of such strategies (lower yields), in combination with regulatory requirements, simultaneously encourage funds to pursue higher yields through less conventional investments (see Stewart, 2007). Hedge funds come in various forms, but it is highly likely that pension funds' engagement with hedge funds has increased exposure to debt-based derivatives such as collateralized debt obligations, thereby further increasing exposure to (riskier) corporate bonds, and indeed personal debt through products such as mortgage-backed securities. While UK funds' investment in such assets was, and is, probably limited, the role of US public-sector pension funds in fuelling demand for collateralized debt obligations and mortgage-backed securities in particular was seen by some at the time, including regulators, as a key cause of the financial crisis (see Ashcraft and Scheurmann, 2008). The California Public Employees' Retirement System (CalPERS), whose structurally significant role in pension-related investment practice is noted below, owned around $2.5 billion (around 1 per cent of its total fund) in securities backed by 'sub-prime loans' in 2007. A spokesperson explained: 'They are all AAA-rated, unlike other bonds that are subordinated and below our AAA holdings in the capital structure. We are well protected in this case and not at risk' (cited in Cometto, 2007). CalPERS ultimately rode the storm, despite the sudden confrontation of this set of assumptions with economic reality, but the more important story here is the role of large pension funds contributing to systemic, macro-economic risks.

Insofar as they drive demand for debt-based assets, and associated derivatives, pension funds are clearly implicated in one of the main features of the financialization process, that is, securitization. What is often underarticulated within such conclusions, however, is that this role derives directly from the peculiarities of defined benefit provision, especially where the fund sponsors—the temporal anchors—have signalled that they are no longer able or willing to guarantee outcomes. Safe assets become highly prized as a result—yet so do very *un*safe assets, to offset lower yields from conventional investment. This dynamic explains pension funds' role in securitization, but is also clearly evident in equity allocations. As noted above, within the broader process of de-equitization, funds have rebalanced listed equity portfolios towards higher-yield (and higher-risk) overseas equities (such as those listed in 'emerging markets' (Sharman, 2017)). However, as discussed further below, allocations to listed equities also now operate via passive, index-tracking funds—ostensibly smoothing volatility for individual funds, but arguably intensifying systemic risks. The absence of any institutional anchor in defined contribution provision means such dynamics are likely to be reinforced. High returns are necessary, but the associated risks are intolerable.

7.2.2 Pension Funds to the Rescue

The colossal size of pension funds—coupled, to some extent, with their foundation in the saving activity of 'ordinary' workers—gives rise to the expectation that they could (or should) serve a general public good, as well as the interests of their members. As discussed below, there was a moment in the late 1990s/early 2000s when some believed that pension funds had the scope to reorder the basic functions of capitalism, at least in the UK and US. This moment passed, but the notion that pension funds may serve a wider public good through shaping economic processes re-emerged after the financial crisis, in two main forms. Firstly, as long-term investors, pension funds could contribute to a sustainable economic recovery (and economic 'rebalancing') through increasing investment in asset classes such as infrastructure. Secondly, as shareholders in many large firms (de-equitization notwithstanding), pension funds could exercise an enlightened influence upon corporate governance practices.

Gordon Clark's (2000) *Pension Fund Capitalism* is perhaps the most significant book related to pension fund investment of recent decades. The notion of pension funds as stewards of the capitalist economy is central to its account, as Clark identified vast defined benefit pension funds in the UK and US—full of post-war baby boomers at the peak of their careers—as occupying influential or even dominant positions within Anglo-American capital markets. Clark's account was generally quite optimistic about the impact this would have on the capitalist economy, insofar as worker ownership of company shares via their pensions saving would incentivize firms to operate in line with wider public goods as well as seeking to maximize profits. While the 'pension fund capitalism' thesis is based on an account of power—with Clark essentially arguing that pension funds *could* reorient capital markets and corporate governance, due to their size and unique characteristics—it has also given rise to an ethical account of pension fund investment practice.

In short, the notion that pension funds *should* use their resources to generate disinvestment in various firms, sectors, and countries deemed incompatible with certain values. The first sentence of the mission statement of campaign group ShareAction (formerly known as FairPensions), for instance, is '[w]e exist to make investment a force for good'.[7] The United Nations' Principles of Responsible Investment for institutional investors, declared in 2006 adds weight to such campaigns. Its signatories agree to act in the long-term interests of their beneficiaries, while asserting that incorporating environmental, social, and governance (ESG) considerations into strategies can 'better align investors with broader interests of society'.[8]

Increasingly, this argument intermingles with the notion that a capital investment strategy oriented towards supporting public goods over the long term is also one best equipped to deliver healthy returns for the ultimate beneficiaries (that is, pension scheme members). This sentiment is reflected in ShareAction's agenda, alongside other groups such as the UK Sustainable Investment and Finance Association, which organizes, for instance, an annual 'Ownership Day' to encourage institutional investors such as pension funds to become 'active owners' of their investee firms. The occasion emphasizes links between delivering a broad ESG agenda and financial benefits to investors.[9] The agenda has been supported by 'centrist' politicians such as Chris Leslie and Chuka Umunna (2011), both of whom left the Labour party under Jeremy Corbyn's leadership to form ChangeUK (Umunna later joined the Liberal Democrats). It was boosted by a joint statement by sixteen large UK pension funds (including the BT Pension Scheme, BBC Pension Trust, and the Unilever Pension Fund) supporting a guide to ESG public equity investment *reporting* (and as such indicating a reorientation of their preferences) via NAPF in 2015 (note that NAPF/Pensions and Lifetime Savings Association has been publishing occasional guides to responsible investment *practice* in general since 2009). As discussed below, there are inherent

---

[7] See https://shareaction.org/about-us/.
[8] See https://www.unpri.org/. The key declaration is: 'As institutional investors, we have a duty to act in the best long-term interests of our beneficiaries. In this fiduciary role, we believe that environmental, social, and corporate governance issues can affect the performance of investment portfolios (to varying degrees across companies, sectors, regions, asset classes and through time). We also recognize that applying these Principles may better align investors with broader objectives of society. Therefore, where consistent with our fiduciary responsibilities, we commit to the following:

1) We will incorporate ESG issues into investment analysis and decision-making processes.
2) We will be active owners and incorporate ESG issues into our ownership policies and practices.
3) We will seek appropriate disclosure on ESG issues by the entities in which we invest.
4) We will promote acceptance and implementation of the Principles within the investment industry.
5) We will work together to enhance our effectiveness in implementing the Principles.
6) We will each report on our activities and progress towards implementing the Principles.'

[9] See http://ownershipday.co.uk/.

limitations in such campaigns and initiatives, not least a partial neglect of pension funds' mandates to deliver the strongest possible outcomes for *existing* scheme members—and the regulatory environment through which this is secured—even if defined benefit pension provision might arguably have survived to serve *future* cohorts had a longer-term and more discerning approach to investment been adopted.

This is a point made persuasively by Claire Parfitt's (2018) analysis of responsible investment practice (primarily in Australia). And pre-empting issues around intermediation discussed further below, Parfitt questions also the view of agency invoked by responsible investment discourse, given that in practice decisions around what qualifies as ESG is made by a small number of investment consultants and managers (see Parfitt, 2018). Moreover, as the *Financial Times* reported in early 2020: '[L]ook under the hood of some of the biggest ESG funds and it becomes apparent that they are heavily tilted towards tech stocks, including Microsoft and Alphabet [Google's parent company], plus a smattering of consumer-oriented companies, such as Johnson & Johnson and Procter & Gamble' (Wigglesworth, 2020). Why would this be the case? Effectively, because the 'G' (for governance) in ESG encourages investment in companies seemingly well run due to limited debt, and stable earnings growth. We might also point to a narrow understanding of the 'E' too, insofar as Silicon Valley firms do not themselves rely upon fossil fuels (although their energy suppliers, and many of their advertiser clients, most definitely do).

Nevertheless, it is clear that many institutional investors are now recognizing a responsibility to, and the opportunity of, divestment from firms and industries directly dependent on fossil fuel extraction, and adopting 'greener' investment strategies in particular, in the context of climate change (Croce et al., 2011) (of course the scale of this, effectively unmeasurable, should not be overstated). The environmental issue was given greater prominence by an 'intervention' by BlackRock—the world's largest asset management firm—in early 2020. An open letter authored by the company's chair and chief executive, Larry Fink (2020), outlined its intention to promote green investment strategies to its clients, precisely on the basis that 'climate risk is an investment risk'. NEST, the multi-employer defined contribution scheme owned by the UK government, came to a similar conclusion when it decided to 'tilt' its investments away from fossil fuels in 2017 (see Jones, 2017), and the Bank of England's then Governor Mark Carney opined in 2019 that unless climate risks were addressed, pension funds ran the risk of conventional assets becoming worthless (see Sardana, 2019). This intervention followed a joint statement by the Prudential Regulatory Authority, FCA, the Financial

Reporting Council, and TPR (2019) which had welcomed the UK government's wider 'green finance strategy' (which advocated an overwhelmingly voluntaristic approach) on the basis that '[f]inancial risks will be minimised by achieving an orderly transition'. The Fink letter is presented as a message to the firm's clients, but clearly BlackRock is—insofar as it signals a genuine shift—largely *responding to* the preferences being expressed by the clients themselves (such as NEST).

There are strong grounds for scepticism that 'pension fund capitalism' or campaigns for more ethical or responsible investment will substantively reorient investment practice, among pension funds and beyond. As discussed at length in Chapter 4, defined benefit provision in the UK private sector has declined sharply; given that the early 2000s was a key period in this trend, pension fund capitalism was probably over before it had even been theorized. There remains funded provision in the public sector among local authorities (and public-sector provision was always more significant in the American context, given the paucity of unfunded defined benefit provision in the US), but local funds do not constitute a commanding presence. As the NEST example shows, it is possible that defined contribution schemes will pack up the mantle—but most pure defined contribution schemes, even in the trust-based landscape, are not comparable to NEST, and fledgling CDC provision is unlikely to alter this picture in the foreseeable future. Even if defined benefit provision were sustainable in the UK economic and political context, the trend, noted above, towards de-equitization clearly undermines the notion that pension funds might have become responsible stewards of the corporate sector. The role of pension funds fuelling securitization through a growing preference for debt-based assets was an important, secondary strand to Clark's pension fund capitalism thesis.

Moreover, even if funds were opting to remain invested in UK equities, it is unlikely that responsible stewardship would be a priority concern. Firstly, as Clark also recognized, equity ownership by pension funds tended to reinforce 'shareholder value' and the short-termist investment practices often associated with the imperative to focus on delivering financial benefits to shareholders. He noted, for instance, 'the CalPERS effect', whereby the improvement in company performance that tended to be associated with receipt of investment around this time by CalPERS, the giant California public-sector fund, often led to herding into the same stock by other investors. As Gourevitch and Shinn (2007) note, pension fund investors typically press investee firms for stronger minority shareholder rights and a greater integration of shareholder value within the investee's business model (see also Gospel et al., 2014, and Pendleton and Gospel, 2017, for further discussion of the contradiction inherent in the notion of pension funds 'workers' capital'). Pension scheme and asset management trade bodies generally support the Financial Reporting Council's Stewardship Code, first established in 2010, which presses institutional investors to prioritize ESG considerations in their relationships with investee firms. Yet the fact that the code is non statutory—essentially unenforceable, and suitably vague—is probably not incidental to this support.

Secondly, and as discussed further below, equity investment by pension funds in the UK is often operationalized via passive, index-tracking funds— a symptom of pension funds prioritizing steady returns, therefore derisking *within* their equity portfolios, rather than active engagement with investee firms. Despite the allusion to a proactive green investment strategy, BlackRock's success in recent years is actually accounted for by the increasing popularity of passive funds in which asset choice (that is, between different listed equity stocks) is indiscriminate beyond immediate financial metrics (Dean, 2019; Henderson, 2020). This represents another side to the story of BlackRock's apparent fossil fuel divestment, since funds passively tracking indexes such as FTSE 100 or S&P 500, rather than being actively managed, cannot forgo investing in the firms which comprise major chunks of the index being tracked (Fichtner et al., 2020). As Billy Nauman (2020) explained following the Fink letter:

> It was a bold statement of intent. But a close look at the announcement shows the limitations of what BlackRock, with a huge chunk of its assets tied up in index funds, can actually do... [U]nless its customers choose to pick funds that exclude fossil fuels, the firm will retain its spot as a top-three owner in every major oil company for the foreseeable future, regardless of any environmental or fiduciary concerns about the investments. BlackRock committed to dropping about $500 m[illion] of coal stocks from its actively managed funds, but it has not promised a broader rush of divestments. For fossil fuel companies, the passive investment revolution clearly presents an opportunity. No matter how poorly they perform, they can count on investor money filling their coffers as long as they maintain their spot in the right indices.

While we can probably expect ESG-friendly passive funds to grow, to suggest that such a development would have a transformative impact would be to misunderstand why institutional investors are drawn towards passive investment, as discussed below. Furthermore, the type and scope of firms whose shares may qualify as ESG investments, noted above, indicates the potential for ESG concerns to be subverted by the passive revolution.

UK policy-makers have been far more interested in promoting investment in infrastructure, rather than ESG, by pension funds. However, the agenda is underpinned by a similar reasoning, with the evident size and apparent proclivity to invest over the long term of pension funds deemed to be aligned with a need to support productive activity in the 'real economy'. Pension fund investment practice was mobilized as such into the 'rebalancing' narrative within UK policy elite discourse following the financial crisis (Berry and Hay, 2016). The Coalition government established a National Infrastructure Plan in order to nudge private investors, chiefly institutional investors such as pension funds, towards particular 'shovel-ready' projects on the implicit understanding of government commitment. The Pension Infrastructure Platform was established by NAPF as part of this initiative, with asset management firm Dalmore Capital (infrastructure specialist) appointed to co-ordinate investment in infrastructure—largely via debt-financing—by a handful of local authority pension funds. Typically, the Coalition identified a lack of scale within UK pension funds as the main barrier to large-scale infrastructure investment: this was part of the rationale for the Pension Infrastructure Platform, and it was an agenda championed by Boris Johnson in his time as Mayor of London. Johnson's account, which focused on advocating a merger of public-sector pension funds to create a 'war chest' for 'the roads, railways, power stations and airports that this country is crying out for' was characteristically hyperbolic and duplicitous, insofar as he failed to acknowledge that 'funds' only exist for local government schemes, and identified only the 'vested interests' of those with 'non-jobs and sinecures' as the barrier to amalgamation (Johnson, 2014a). Yet it fed into the Coalition government's more modest efforts to allow for amalgamation among local authority funds, which achieved some success in terms of cost reduction—although the largest funds were of course already the product of mergers of several funds within city-regions.

Of course, scale is largely irrelevant regarding the ability of pure defined contribution schemes—increasingly dominant in the UK due to auto-enrolment—to invest in infrastructure. The individualized provision requires the possibility of rapid divestment irrespective of scheme size, not least due to the impact of the Coalition's 'pension freedoms' reforms, discussed in Chapter 6. (This barrier may be overcome, to some extent, by CDC provision, discussed in Chapter 4.) Section 7.3.2 also discusses a 2019 consultation by the Department for Work and Pensions (DWP) related to the regulatory barriers to infrastructure investment be defined contribution schemes (with some proposals to 'scale up' trust-based provision). Even within defined benefit provision, analysis by the OECD shows that while there is to some extent a correlation between fund size across different countries and a willingness to invest in infrastructure, the highly complex nature of infrastructure investment problematizes such straightforward inferences, and any attempt to devise policies which might increase investment. This work in fact suggests that viewing infrastructure as a single asset class is inadvisable, given the variety of ways in which pension funds may invest, from holding the shares or bonds of large, listed companies involved in infrastructure construction or maintenance, to the more irregular worlds of private equity and/or new debt-based instruments (with institutional investors often taking the place of bank or public-sector financing) (see Inderst, 2009; Croce, 2012; Inderst and Croce, 2013).

Peter O'Brien and Andy Pike's work on urban infrastructure investment demonstrates the financialized nature of investment by institutional investors in this regard. Pension funds are essentially capitalizing upon the decline of public *funding* of infrastructure projects in order to design bespoke *financing* arrangements to local authorities (in the UK and elsewhere), with capital ultimately repaid by taxpayers, or consumers via usage fees. The infrastructure 'providers' are themselves financialized entities, as they extract value from public sectors in order to service their investors' financial interests. Despite the rather moralistic discourse which surrounds infrastructure investment by pension funds, there is little doubt that maximizing returns is at the heart of infrastructure investment practice. This, in turn, influences the scope of projects available to public authorities, since financing requirements will be considered alongside public goods (see O'Brien and Pike, 2017; also O'Neill, 2013; O'Brien et al., 2019). The Greater Manchester Combined Authority's pension fund has been seen as a pioneer in investing in local housing, focusing on the private rented sector (including 'affordable' housing, but not social housing), in partnership with housing associations and private banks. It is not an act of charity: local housing comprises a tiny proportion of the fund's assets, and the expectation of a steady increase in rental income is required to ensure commercial viability (Wolf, 2019).

A slightly wider 'rebalancing' agenda is also visible regarding recent elite discourse on pension fund investments. In 2017, the Treasury conducted a review into 'patient capital', which focused on increasing opportunities for individual and institutional investors to invest in private equity (in order to increase the capital base for riskier, early-stage innovation). As discussed further below, the government reiterated that greater scale with longer-term investment practice, while in the same breath acknowledging that in practice the vast majority of defined contribution schemes are operating at sufficient scale (leading to the conclusion that it would be unwise for government to intervene, with the focus instead on an industry-led attitudinal shift) (HM Treasury, 2017a, 2017b). A related plan to relax PTR limits (discussed in Chapter 6) for pension contributions which were invested 'patiently' has not been taken forward (see Houlder, 2017). There have been some moves among local government leaders to articulate a more progressive version of the notion that local government pension funds could align their investment strategies with broader public goods, specifically within their home regions (Smith Institute et al., 2012). The Local Authority Pension Fund Forum— with around eighty Local Government Pension Scheme members—has led thinking among practitioners in this regard, and as such advises local government funds on responsible stewardship of investee companies, from conventional ESG issues to broader issues such as precarious employment and tax transparency.[10] John Clancy, then leader of Birmingham City Council, published *The Secret Wealth Garden* in 2014 to argue for a reorientation of local funds towards regional economies (partly enabled by a cap of asset management fees, discussed further below). It is worth noting that local government *workers* are not necessarily on board with such moves. When, in 2012, the Coalition government diluted restrictions on investment in 'partnerships'—encompassing private equity investments and the financing consortia through which local authority funds have sought to invest in infrastructure—in Local Government Pension Schemes, trade unions generally opposed the move due to concerns about the opacity of investment practice in this area. (Clancy's plan, however, involved investment by funds in bonds issued by local government and public banks.)

7.2.3 The Middle Men

The asset management industry, and its role in pension fund investment practice, was introduced in Section 7.1.1. This sub-section supplements the above discussion by briefly discussing the costs and connotations of investment intermediation. It is probably only a small overstatement to assert that this issue has consumed what little space exists for public debate on pension fund investments in the UK (in ways that have not necessarily been particularly informative). The issue of 'transaction costs' in pensions saving was first discussed in Chapter 6. It is impossible to say what impact the costs involved in these financial transactions (that is, investment activity) has on fund values and, ultimately, in a very direct sense for defined contributions savers,

---

[10] See http://www.lapfforum.org/.

retirement outcomes. This is, in part, because of a lack of transparency on investment-related costs incurred by pension schemes, inadvertently or otherwise. As argued in Chapter 6, it would be unwise to dismiss the possibility that some costs arise from rent-seeking practices over which scheme managers, and certainly individual savers, have little oversight. On the other hand, the myriad processes involved in dematerializing and rematerializing pensions saving over the lifecourse draw upon financial services which must be paid for. The scale of costs and fees for intermediation in local authority pension funds has been highlighted by campaigners and researchers, with Chris Sier (2012) arguing that funds which appear to incur higher levels of investment costs do not outperform funds with lower costs, thereby undermining the justification for many fees. Theoretically, information about charging practices in the management of local authority pension fund assets is more available than other market segments, due to local government being subject to the Freedom of Information Act. However, even where the extent of transaction costs is more widely known (or at least knowable), disquiet by members and taxpayers has been fairly minimal. If schemes are open, defined benefit pension benefits are paid, either way (and if private schemes become insolvent, the state steps in).

We might in future expect transaction costs to become politicized as large cohorts of defined contribution auto-enrolees reach retirement, assuming it can be demonstrated that costs have had a material impact on outcomes. The PPI (2019: 18) reports that total expense ratios (a measure of charges and costs, albeit one now seen as inadequate by some, including regulators) are higher in contract-based schemes, which lack genuinely independent investment governance, than trust-based schemes—although this is partly due to master trusts' propensity to invest passively (discussed further below). Accordingly, there has been a degree of regulatory interest in 'hidden' costs in defined contribution provision (it is also worth reiterating that the Pensions Act 2014, which allowed for member-borne charges to be capped, also required schemes to disclose transaction costs). As noted in Chapter 6, after many years of investigation into asset management practices more generally, the FCA implemented in 2020 firmer rules on cost disclosure (including modelling the impact of costs on returns) within contract-based defined contribution schemes (see FCA, 2020). The FCA's work appears to be ongoing, but there is little sign that the most radical proposals floated in the wake of the 2014 Act—such as the creation of independent governance boards *within* firms to protect clients' interests—will be taken forward.

Of course, the most effective way of reducing transaction costs is to reduce transactions—although this approach may displace costs from individual savers or schemes to the economy in general. The shift towards passive investment was noted earlier in the chapter. The speed and scale of this shift is rather astonishing, with passive funds globally now valued at more than $10 trillion, compared to $2 trillion in 2007 (with much of this increase mirrored in reduced allocation to actively managed funds) (Fichtner et al., 2020). Their leadership in passive investment helps to explain the growing presence of BlackRock, Vanguard, and State Street in the City of London. The Investment Association's detailed reports offer some specific insights on pensions provision, and suggest that the past decade has *not* seen a major reallocation of UK pensions capital from active to passive management. The proportion of AUM for 'corporate' pension funds (that is, largely defined benefit funds) passively managed has been relatively steady since 2009/10 (around 35–40 per cent), whereas for local authority pension funds the proportion has risen from 22 per cent to 33 per cent (Investment Association, 2019: 96–7; Investment Management Association, 2010: 100–1). This might suggest that the increasing popularity of passive investment strategies is due primarily to shifts within retail rather than institutional investment practice. Or, that retail investors are now replicating the strategies adopted earlier by pension funds as part of derisking from the early 2000s onwards (before comparable data were available). Nevertheless, pension fund managers themselves expect passive investments to grow significantly within their asset allocation in the decade ahead (Rajan, 2018). We can also expect passive investment to become a significant feature of defined contribution provision as auto-enrolment schemes mature.

Passive equity funds essentially track indexes such as the FTSE 100 or S&P 500 by buying shares in every company on the index to replicate its aggregate performance. As suggested above, passive investment turns a relatively volatile asset class into something far more predictable. It should therefore be seen as consistent with de-equitization, even if ironically this trend has recently held back increases in passive investment by UK private pension funds. As Jan Fichtner et al. (2018) explain, index-tracking is based on the logic of 'the efficient market hypothesis':

> because share prices incorporate all available market information, no single investor can ever outperform the market over the long term. Passive investment funds therefore do not trade individual stocks on the basis of their fundamentals, but rather assume that the market is 'right' and so only buy or sell a stock when the composition of an index like the S&P500 changes.

As such, the passive revolution, insofar as it has been instigated by pension funds, represents another way in which pension funds have driven neoliberalization, rather than pensions practice being seen as epiphenomenal. The fact that passive strategies involve lower fees—essentially because they involve less intense intermediation—helps to explain their attraction to pension funds (Rajan, 2018). But this does not mean passive investment is cost-free. The providers of the indices being tracked are private firms, with their profitability due in large part to royalties received from asset managers replicating their index. Some scholars have pointed also to the privileged role of these firms on global economic governance insofar as, by determining criteria for inclusion in the index, they are financial standard-setters (Petry et al., 2019; see also Büthe and Mattli, 2011). Fichtner et al. (2018) also identify the paradoxical implications for corporate stewardship. The passive revolution might make institutional investors the ultimate owners of a very large proportion of some of the world's largest companies. Yet the 'more voice, but less exit pressure' investment model creates 'passive-aggressive' exercise of voting rights by the asset managers, associated with maximizing dividend payments, reinforcing executive power at the expense of independent directors, and lower levels of capital investment.

Index-tracking funds are a form of investment 'platform', indeed arguably the archetypal and oldest form. Yet there are an array of platform-based investment practices worth noting. Increasingly popular exchange-traded funds are a subset of index funds, which restructure the fund management process as a two-sided market platform—shares in the fund are themselves (highly liquid) tradeable assets. In addition, Daniel Haberly et al. (2019: 171) report on the emergence of 'asset manager support platforms', which use data-driven analytics to provide portfolio risk management, trading optimization and execution, and regulatory compliance services to both passive and active funds.

Issues around intermediation were at the heart of the main attempt by (parts of) the UK policy elite in recent years to address pension fund investment practice. The Kay Review of UK Equity Markets and Long-Term Decision Making, overseen by economist John Kay (2012), asked whether both the ultimate asset owners (pension scheme members) and society in general were being poorly served by the asset management practices replete in equity investment (via active or passive). The review was commissioned by the then Department for Business, Innovation and Skills under the auspice of Secretary of State Vince Cable (who became Liberal Democrat party leader after the party left government). In a nutshell, Kay's conclusion was that asset management practices were based on a poor incentive structure which prioritized short-term, fee-attracting trading activity over a long-term commitment to effective corporate governance. Pension funds or pensions savers are harmed by excessive fees, and the economy in general is harmed by short-termism. Kay made suggestions around company voting rights to afford greater power to institutional investors, which were largely ignored by government. He also made specific recommendations around fiduciary duties in the asset management industry, arguing that asset managers should have a legal duty (as applies to pension fund trustees) to serve the interests of the pension scheme members whose capital they are managing. In line with the advocates of stewardship discussed above, Kay appears to assume that the interests of pensions savers and society are aligned over the long term. The government asked the Law Commission (an independent, statutory body which advises government on the operation of law) to review fiduciary duties in this regard, a process which resulted in 'clarification' of existing law rather than legislative reform (see Department for Business, Innovation and Skills, 2012; Law Commission, 2012). However, the Kay Review can certainly be said to have influenced the most robust approach to stewardship issues and cost disclosure taken by both regulators and industry self-regulation initiatives in recent years (discussed above).

The Coalition government's implicit conclusion on intermediation and fiduciary duties was that pension fund trustees already have sufficient powers to direct the activities of the asset management industry on both costs and stewardship, should they wish to do so. Interestingly, New Labour had in the early 2000s questioned this assumption through its institutional investment in the UK review, overseen by finance sector executive (and future government minister) Paul Myners. The review considered whether trustees had the capacity in practice to exercise power over investment intermediaries (including consultants). Myners concluded that they often did not, but his recommendations around strengthening the capabilities of trustees were, again, largely taken forward on a voluntaristic basis (see Myners, 2001; HM Treasury and Department for Work and Pensions, 2001). It is worth noting that, whereas the Kay Review focused on listed equities, the Labour government's motivation in commissioning the Myners Review was a sense that trustees' lack of capacity vis-à-vis intermediaries led to institutional investors eschewing opportunities to invest in *private* equity. As such, the review preempted, by a decade and a half, the May government's 'patient capital' review (discussed above), which also considered the ability of institutional investors to engage in venture capital investment. (Underlining that there is nothing new in pensions provision, Myners had also raised concerns about transaction costs. The Labour government responded immediately by encouraging trustees to develop their understanding of costs, and a 2004 follow-up review pointed to apparently encouraging developments in terms of asset management industry self-regulation in this regard (HM Treasury, 2004).)

7.3. Defined Contribution: Performance Anxiety

7.3.1 Investment Governance in Defined Contribution Provision

The preceding sections have addressed many issues relevant to defined contribution investment governance. However, it is worth discussing a number of specific issues related to defined contribution provision, not least because it has, in the context of implementing auto-enrolment, been the target of policy and regulatory action on this regard. Of course, such action should not be confused with *strategic* approach to intervention; an unsympathetic observer might conclude that UK policy elites sense that 'something needs to be done' on defined contribution investment governance, but they do not really know what. This section should be read in conjunction with Chapter 6's discussion of the regulatory divide between trust-based and contract-based provision (which was also briefly discussed above).

Ultimately, irrespective of the type of scheme, the key dilemma for policy-makers and regulators is whether intervention will improve investment performance, rather than simply adding to costs, since in defined contribution provision individuals' outcomes depend entirely on investment returns. In defined benefit provision, the temporal anchor role of employers—and increasingly the state—relieves individuals of this burden. As Chapter 6 also indicated, downward trends in the value of annuities (for decumulating accumulated capital) means individual saving must presently work even harder simply to deliver outcomes that might have been taken for granted a few years ago. Yet the same phenomenon driving falling annuity values—low gilt yields—is also affecting the performance of defined contribution funds in the accumulation phase, since defined contribution schemes are also heavily exposed to gilts, especially for members close to retirement. The double impact on defined benefit funds of low gilt yields following the COVID-19 pandemic—affecting both asset values and how liabilities are calculated—is visited upon individual scheme members in defined contribution provision: their investments produce lower returns during accumulation, and when they come to decumulate, annuity values are lower.

It is worth noting here that passive investment funds for bonds, rather than equities, actually represent the most significant growth area for passive investment. While equity trackers represent around 20 per cent of total AUM by UK asset managers (across all client types), having grown by around 30 per cent in the five years to 2018, AUM within fixed-income tracker funds quadrupled over the same period (Investment Association, 2019: 45).

These funds will include the private securities that are favoured by insurance companies during the defined contribution accumulation phase. We can speculate that the rise of defined contribution may further transform investment practice within UK capital markets in a way that, if passive ownership of corporate debt continues to grow in popularity, would further problematize the notion of pension funds as responsible corporate stewards.

The basic conundrum of defined contribution provision, explored throughout this book, should be restated here: pensions saving is individualized, but individuals have little or no capacity to manage the risks entailed, including the risks inherent in *not* saving—this is the cognitive foundation of the UK's auto-enrolment regime. Accordingly, the need for a 'default fund' (or, as suggested above, default arrangements) is established in relevant legislation, with default funds designed to minimize investment risks. NEST, for example, acknowledges that more than 90 per cent of its members have their capital in the default fund (its then Chief Executive said in 2013 that it was 99 per cent of members (Hughes, 2013)). Of course, since the risks cannot be fully mitigated—without forgoing returns—regulation generally requires that schemes simply demonstrate how they have properly appraised the risks inherent in the default strategy on behalf of members. (NEST has in fact been criticized for apparent conservatism in its default fund strategy, that is, avoiding losses rather than pursuing returns (see Brodbeck, 2017).) Naturally, with its regulatory powers focused on *schemes* rather than *providers*, TPR issues codes of practice[11] on investment governance within trust-based defined contribution schemes. TPR recently 'lifted the bonnet' (in its own terms) on default funds by surveying the nature and extent of default fund reviews (TPR, 2019b). Since it deals with insurers providing pension 'schemes' in name only, the FCA lacks similar powers for contract-based provision—yet default fund design features in the joint FCA-TPR (2018) regulatory strategy.

However, GPPs are now required by the FCA to have independent governance committees (IGCs), with a particular focus on the default arrangements for auto-enrolees in contract-based provision. These committees reside at the provider level, and as such oversee multiple 'schemes'. They are appointed by the provider but must include members independent of the company appointed through an open and transparent process. The IGC has no power to compel reform should it determine that services received by pensions savers do not represent 'value for money', but the provider must 'explain in writing why the provider has decided to depart in any material way from any

---

[11] Seehttps://www.thepensionsregulator.gov.uk/en/document-library/codes-of-practice/code-13-governance-and-administration-of-occupational-trust-based-schemes-providing-money-purchase.

advice or recommendations made by the IGC'.[12] Ultimately, IGCs lack the investment governance powers of trustees—yet as discussed in Chapter 6, the emergence of master trusts in trust-based defined contribution provision has diluted the supervisory role of trustees in practice. Moreover, the Coalition government's pension freedom reforms allows pensions savers not only to 'cash out' their savings, but also shift their investment in products into a largely ungoverned space (the FCA of course retains regulatory powers over the providers of these products, and has in fact suggested that the remit of IGCs should be extended to overseeing the investment pathway offers for customers exercising their pension freedoms (Espahinda, 2019)).

The inadequacy of governance in both trust-based and contract-based provision is one of the reasons policy-makers have applied a cap on management charges; the state compensating for the shortcomings of the privatized approach state actors have consistently championed. The specific issue of costs of investment practice is one in which contract-based provision may be superior. Whereas the FCA can compel asset managers to disclose costs to contract-based providers (and therefore their customers), trustees cannot. As the TPR code on defined contribution governance explains:

> The law requires the member borne costs and charges across all arrangements within a scheme to be disclosed in the annual chair's statement. This includes transaction costs, insofar as trustee boards have been able to obtain that information. Where trustee boards have not been able to obtain information about transaction costs, the law also requires the chair's statement to indicate the information they have been unable to obtain and explain what steps are being taken to obtain the information in future.[13]

As with the power of IGCs to insist on a particular (default) investment strategy, it amounts to little more than angry letter-writing (of course, we can probably expect the application of new disclosure rules by the FCA to filter through to trust-based provision). Michael McCarthy (2014) demonstrates that the higher the regulatory standards around investment governance, the lower the scope for trade unions to contribute to strategic decisions on members' behalf. This echoes the longstanding, and somewhat paradoxical, feature of private pensions provision in the UK, whereby trade unions favour funded over unfunded provision, even if the former places workers' capital in greater jeopardy, because the former is a platform for trade union

---

[12] See https://www.fca.org.uk/firms/independent-governance-committees.
[13] See note 11.

influence. Given that defined contribution provision, despite recent tweaks, remains a very lightly regulated domain, we might expect trade unions to be more present in investment governance processes. This is not the case, partly because, as noted above, policy-makers have allowed for the creation of far less intrusive governance forums than prevailed in private-sector defined benefit provision. Furthermore, the private-sector workforce in the UK has become largely deunionized: as unions have acknowledged, the typical auto-enrolee is unlikely to be a member of a trade union (Berry and Stanley, 2013). Even if trade unions were more intimately involved in defined contribution investment governance, it is not clear they would be able to unshackle the straightjacket of individualized provision in a financialized environment. What, at the ground level, would they ask providers to do differently? Unions rightly demand higher contributions from employers, but transforming what the finance sector does with these contributions without undermining returns is more problematic.

7.3.2 Mind the Macro

The prospect of stronger regulation to protect or support defined contribution savers as their contributions are dematerialized within capital markets would, it seems, raise an eyebrow on Threadneedle Street. Analysis by the Bank of England's Procyclicality Working Group of structural trends in asset allocation by pension funds and insurance companies concluded that regulatory protection for 'policyholders' (that is, workers saving for a pension) generally reinforces procyclical investment practice—since the intent is to maximize the value of the pot at any particular moment in time—and therefore may contribute to economic volatility:

> [I]n relation to the structure of long-term savings provision, policies primarily designed to deliver the appropriate degree of policyholder protection might have consequences at an aggregate level for long-term economic growth and financial stability. Policymakers are obliged to ensure the appropriate degree of policyholder protection is delivered, and may be compelled by statutory objectives, regulation and legislation to behave in a particular way. However, it is important that in addition policymakers are able to consider financial stability and the impact of the real economy as well. At times there may need to be a balance struck between these objectives…For both insurers and pension funds, consideration could be given to countercyclical regimes that ensure that resilience is built up in benign economic circumstances, in order that regulatory constraints can be relaxed safely in periods of stress.   (Haldane et al., 2014: 6)

It may well be correct that defined contribution investment practice is inherently procyclical. Defined contribution schemes are, for instance, major consumers of passive investment funds including exchange-traded funds and related investment platforms (HM Treasury, 2017a: 58). It would therefore follow that macro-economic policy-makers should be cautious about regulatory practices which reinforce this dynamic. If the solution, however, is to impose countercyclical strategies on schemes, it would essentially contradict the individualized nature of defined contribution provision. Asking savers to accept lower returns for the greater good undermines the notion of individual self-reliance at the heart of the UK pensions policy regime. TPR guidance on investment platforms to defined contribution scheme trustees is essentially focused on ensuring only that platform choice best serves members' financial interests.[14]

That defined contribution savers in general may over the long term be better off if the wider economy was developing in a more sustainable manner will be no comfort to those individuals asked to sacrifice their more immediate interests in maximizing their retirement income—and begs the question of who gets to decide what sustainability or long-termism looks like. The May government's deliberation on defined contribution pension provision's contribution to long-term investment is relevant in this regard. In 2019, DWP consulted on measures to increase the allocation of defined contribution scheme assets to illiquid assets, such as private equity (see DWP, 2019b)—an initiative which arose directly from the Treasury's patient capital review, discussed above. The government identified some minor regulatory barriers to illiquid investment, and argued that greater scale of schemes, and clarity around trustees' responsibilities, would also help. Its most important proposal, however, concerned the 0.75 per cent annual cap on management charges in default funds for auto-enrolees (which was discussed in Chapter 6). Given that investing in illiquid assets may require more time and specialist knowledge than investing in liquid assets, they are generally more expensive. (It is worth noting however that some private equity investments by institutional investors are now operationalized via digital platforms (Langley and Leyshon, 2017).) Crucially, they also tend to involve performance fees, meaning that costs are not known in advance. Most defined contribution schemes use the prospective rather than retrospective method of calculating member-borne charges, meaning that costs related to investment performance—even where arising from good performance,

---

[14] See https://www.thepensionsregulator.gov.uk/en/trustees/managing-dc-benefits/investment-guide-for-dc-pension-schemes.

which by definition benefits members—would conflict with prevailing approaches to regulatory compliance.

One of the problems is that what is included within the territory of the charge cap is already relatively unclear; transaction costs and the cost of owning 'real' assets such as property are, for instance, excluded, but fees owed directly to asset managers for facilitating particular investments would generally be included. Furthermore, given that some members will leave the scheme during a 'charging year' (by changing jobs, or exercising pension freedoms) modelling the potential impact of likely performance fees, paid only by remaining members, for funds which are pooled in practice is difficult; essentially, it cannot be ruled out that the remaining members' annual charge will breach the cap. Interestingly, the government did *not* propose that it was permissible for the cap to be breached in these circumstances. Instead it made proposals for an 'additional' assessment to supplement prospective calculations, to ensure that any performance fee likely to be levied was structured in a way that made a breach impossible (DWP, 2019b). As such, while the government reiterated its commitment to the charge cap, the episode clearly exposes the contradictions at the heart of defined contribution investment governance. Without an institutional guarantor or temporal anchor, the state is increasingly required to ensure that pensions savers' immediate financial interests are safeguarded. Such moves tacitly accept that the notion that pensions savers and the finance sector have a mutual interest in maximizing returns is flawed, if not fictional. At the same time, state actors are prepared to revise safeguards in service of an alternative imaginary of mutual interest, that is, between pensions savers and the long-term development of the economy in general—because the self-interest of asset managers is the grease on the wheels of this relationship. (At the time of writing—early 2020—the outcome of the consultation remains unannounced.)

7.4. Conclusion: The Political Economy of Time

Economic time is not monolithic. It is experienced very differently by, for example, the employed and self-employed, or by those paid to work a shift—a portion of time—and those expected to deliver certain results irrespective of the labour input. Similarly, capital does not have a singular timescape; its temporality depends on its form and purpose, or the mode of accumulation within which it is engaged. Some temporalities may be institutionalized, while some may be more malleable. The nature of economic time may be explicitly regulated by public authorities by, for example, making rules on employment protection, accounting standards, shareholders' rights to dividends, etc. Alternatively, time may be implicitly—even inadvertently—shaped by the type and availability of credit enabled by monetary policy, or by the forms of activity permissible amid a public health emergency.

Investment activity—including saving—is inherently future-oriented. But its relationship with time is frequently transmuted. The implications of an apparent increase in the scope for exploiting the multiple temporalities of capital has become an important area of study among heterodox and political economists in recent years. Martin Konings (2018) challenges a Polanyian understanding of 'disembedded' economic activity by showing how *embedded* a neoliberal understanding of time, typified by the notion of speculation, is within society (and supported by the maintenance of the monetary system by the state). Elena Esposito (2011) has explored the multiple, yet simplified, futures upon which products like derivatives depend, creating new risks under the guise, ironically, of risk management. Lisa Adkins (2016, 2018) has explored similar themes, emphasizing the ways in which securitization (including derivatives, but more specifically securitized debt) is essentially a process of *re*temporalization, developed to allow for accumulation even where capital's ability to generate returns is constrained. Research by critical accountants such as Adam Leaver (2018a, 2018b) has demonstrated that retemporalization has been adopted as corporate strategy in countries like the UK. As discussed in Chapter 4, firms such as Carillion orchestrate 'temporal balancing acts' in converting expected future cashflows into present assets, which can then be leveraged to cover operating costs (Carillion's 'inter-temporal gamble' eventually failed).

Pensions provision is implicated in much of these phenomena—as both victim and perpetrator. The collapse of firms such as Carillion leads to a loss of pension income for employees, yet Carillion's business model is in part driven by the inheritance of pension schemes in deficit from constituent firms. The risks inherent in securitization loom over pension funds, yet securitization is in part explained by funds' liability-driven investment strategies. However, pensions provision itself is future-oriented in quite a particular way. Private pension scheme capital—the product of workers selling their labour time—is invested in order to generate a return, and therefore relies on a forecasted future in which such returns might be realizable. Yet the aim is not simply profit maximization (however broadly conceived), but rather the maintenance of value over time, which may require returns either above or below the prevailing rate of profitability. This creates a highly unstable temporality at the heart of pensions investment practice, and pensions provision is therefore most appropriately understood also as a mechanism for maintaining value even where the future underpinning investment activity fails to materialize. The implicit purpose of pensions provision, in totality, is to eliminate or at least mitigate this uncertainty. This is precisely why the state pension system is *a form of* pensions saving, rather than *an alternative to* pensions saving. More importantly for this book's remit, it is also why the employer's traditional role as 'temporal anchor' in guaranteeing defined benefit pension outcome is integral to pensions provision, rather than a bonus feature relevant to only some (gold-plated) forms of provision.

It is ironic but inevitable that the centrality (and vulnerability) of this role only becomes clear as it falters. As explored in Chapter 4, defined benefit provision has been problematized by employers' efforts to, ultimately, exercise more control of their own temporality. The current chapter essentially explores the implications of capital markets becoming more temporally temperamental. Because the temporal anchor function has not been sufficiently institutionalized, pension funds' ability to impose their own temporality—a concern with mitigating failed futures—upon investment practice has been eroded. Policy is at least partly to blame, as UK pensions regulation generally demands defined benefit funds are valued around current asset prices. The tail is wagging the dog. This makes pension funds acutely vulnerable to capital market performance—a vulnerability underlined by COVID-19 (P. Smith, 2020). In defined contribution provision, where the temporal anchor consists of, at best, the individual's willingness to maintain contributions (as explored in Chapter 5), people reaching retirement during a downturn have no recourse. For example, in May 2020, while explaining that 'most NEST members are unlikely to experience a long-term impact from shorter-term market falls because they're young enough to ride it out', NEST conceded that members closer to retirement are likely to be much more significantly affected. However, '[i]f you're...in one of our main NEST Retirement Date Funds, we'll have taken steps to move your money out of the stock markets'. Even the young are only 'unlikely' to be affected—the caveat required because the impact of the COVID-19 pandemic on returns may be felt for many years to come—but the best that can be done for older investors is to try to prevent any further losses by abandoning equities in favour of (extremely low yield) gilts. And even this mitigation depends on the right investment strategy having been chosen by the member in advance of the pandemic which they, obviously, will have been unable to foresee. Vulnerability to capital market performances does not mean that pension funds or providers of defined contribution schemes have no agency as investors; as discussed above, many recent shifts in investment practice, such as the emergence of passive funds, appear to serve the interests of pension schemes. Yet these interests are essentially malformed, that is, arising from the removal from provision of temporal anchoring.

There are a number of complex and connected implications of the growing predominance of investment temporality within pensions provision, most of which have been discussed throughout this chapter. The first concerns the relationship between pension investments and wider economic benefits. Temporally anchored pensions provision appears to make pension funds 'better' investors, and as such serve an important function within capitalist economies, due to its role in generational reproduction. Today's worker-savers know they will be reliant on the productive capacity of tomorrow's worker-savers when they retire, and so are incentivized to invest accordingly. The UK government implicitly acknowledged this when it called upon funds to play their part in enabling economic recovery after the 2008 financial crisis, and it is a dynamic which underpins campaigns to reorient pensions capital towards (authentic) ESG investment. However, when this role is performed without guaranteed retirement outcomes, the unique nature of pensions capital is transformed from a strength to a weakness: since uncertainty in returns is intolerable, it forces pension funds to invest far more conservatively. UK policy elites have responded to this shift by, as discussed above, seeking to engender larger-scale pension funds, or seeking to augment trustee capacity to oversee the asset management industry, or even reshape the structure of assets such as infrastructure. Such measures focus on making pension funds more efficient as investors but, at the same time, reinforce a temporality which conflicts with the purpose of pensions provision. As work by Peter O'Brien and others shows, an expansion of financialization into ostensible goods such as local infrastructure is the outcome—so too the subversion of ESG. Pension funds serve societal welfare, and the wider economy, not by surveying the future for opportunities to profit, but by helping us to cope with our limited capacity to do precisely this.

Secondly, the growth in AUM—signalling what the Bank of England's chief economist, Andy Haldane (2014), refers to as 'the age of asset management'—has created new macro-economic risks, insofar as asset managers may now be 'too big to fail'. The Bank for International Settlements has warned of the destabilizing potential of passive bond funds in particular (see Burger, 2018). For regulators, the answer, essentially, is more regulation, specifically to encourage counter-cyclical investment practice when necessary. This agenda is reminiscent of the Bank of England's Procyclicality Working Group (chaired by Haldane), discussed above, which warned *against* regulation to protect pension savers in fear that this would further encourage procyclical investment by asset managers. In short, it is permissible for less efficient investment strategies to be imposed upon pension funds, because the means by which pensions capital is dematerialized threatens the wider accumulation model. Interestingly, we can draw similar conclusions regarding the possible impact of a 'financial transactions tax'—a measure supported by many left-wing political actors—upon capital market activity; that it increases costs for actually existing pension funds is secondary, at best, to the perceived interests of the economy in general (see Gray et al., 2012). The notion that pensions provision itself is uniquely important to the function of capitalism—rather than simply one source of investment among many—is absent from UK policy discourse around financial regulation.

Thirdly, and relatedly, acknowledging the absence of a temporal anchor brings into focus the defining characteristic of investment strategies in defined contribution provision: reducing costs. For all the cant about an adjustable matrix of choice, risk, and 'lifestyling', the abiding concern of policy-makers since the establishment of auto-enrolment has been to engineer a marketplace, and regulatory environment where necessary, which keeps management costs low. There is an element of circularity in the relationship between cost concerns and 'conventional' approaches to asset allocation. A predilection for off-the-shelf investment strategies is a near inevitable consequence of the need to reduce costs, while at the same time, scheme managers and trustees have little scope to produce above-trend returns for members, so prioritize instead reducing costs. Yet lower prices have a price: control. Defined contribution schemes are content to channel business to platform-based intermediaries and index-tracking asset managers to reduce costs. With traditional pensions temporalities excised from the saving vehicle, control serves little purpose. And as the volume of capital dematerialized within defined contribution schemes grows, it will become more difficult to envisage this imperilling dynamic being disrupted.

8
Conclusion: Summary and Policy Options

The future of private pensions provision in the UK is probably bleak. The drift, and occasional surge, towards individualized provision has been supported (implicitly and explicitly) across the political spectrum, with even the Labour party under a radical, left-wing leader failing to devise any substantive proposals for reversing the transition away from collectivist provision. Of course, it was under the last Labour government that pensions individualization in the UK made its most significant advance, through the introduction of auto-enrolment, albeit with new powers for the state to mandate employer contributions in workplace pensions providing a paternalist veneer for this agenda. Boris Johnson's Conservative government appears to have few ambitions for UK pensions policy. It has inherited from the May government pending legislation supporting *de jure* the rollout of hybrid CDC provision, although the *de facto* impact of this change remains uncertain (not least because implementation has been disrupted by the COVID-19 pandemic).

Johnson himself, before becoming Prime Minster, allied himself to two largely contradictory pensions policy agendas, that is, supporting freedom for pension scheme members to withdraw their savings to invest or spend as they wished, and supporting the merger of schemes to enable pension funds to invest members' pooled savings in large-scale infrastructure projects. Of course, these positions are not *wholly* contradictory, since the former applies in practice only to defined contribution provision, and the latter applies to defined benefit provision. Johnson's interventions typify the incoherent way UK policy elites have approached pensions issues in recent years: supporting *more* individualization as the answer to problems *caused by* individualization, and at the same time persistently intervening with little strategic intent into legacy collectivist provision in response to political and economic dilemmas arising from the slow demise of defined benefit pension funds.

On the other hand, however, as this book has argued throughout, futures fail. The gloomy forecast for UK pensions provision could be wrong. Crucially, it can be made wrong, as future generations—of both elites and

Pensions Imperilled: The Political Economy of Private Pensions Provision in the UK. Craig Berry, Oxford University Press (2021).
© Craig Berry. DOI: 10.1093/oso/9780198782834.003.0008

ordinary workers—come to influence not only pensions policy and pensions provision in a direct sense, but also the social, political, and economic landscape in which it is situated. This concluding chapter therefore offers a series of proposals, some more modest than others, for pensions policy and practice. First, however, it summarizes the key themes and arguments of the book, and the contributions it makes to the existing literature.

8.1. Summary of Key Themes and Arguments

Pensions provision is a set of mechanisms for dematerializing the contributions we make into various pensions saving schemes (including the state pension via taxation), and rematerializing the accumulated capital when required to finance a retirement income. Like all economic activity, pensions saving is future-oriented; moreover, pensions provision is designed around a particular vision of the future, so that a degree of certainty on the real value of the income we get in retirement can be generated (implicitly or explicitly) in advance. Rematerialization is an inherently cross-generational process, and the ultimate delivery of even an approximation of the future value of dematerialized pensions capital clearly requires innumerable forms of intergenerational co-operation.

The problem, in short, is that futures fail. The only certainty is that the forecasted future will not come to pass. The social, political, and economic landscape in which pensions provision is situated, and in which projections are determined, will change over time. Even in the last decade and a half, the 2008 financial crisis, the Brexit vote, and the COVID-19 pandemic have transformed the economic conditions of which private pensions provision is constitutive (and, in some cases, have challenged institutional practices intimately related to pensions provision). There are also a series of long-running (and overlapping) socio-economic trends which have disrupted private pensions practice in recent decades, including:

- Deindustrialization and the rise of low-paid services sector employment.
- A significant rise in employment levels for women, often alongside care responsibilities.
- The rise of insecure employment, including low-paid self-employment and individuals with multiple employers.
- A shortening of investment time horizons within corporate governance.
- The expansion and increasing complexification of financial services.

Clearly, these trends are not exogenous to public policy and the wider political sphere. They have been created or exacerbated by policy decisions and associated shifts, such as:

- A weakening of employment rights, and declining levels of unionization—coupled with a welfare system which compels recipients to seek and accept low-quality work.
- A political consensus around fiscal conservatism, culminating in severe public spending cuts after the 2008 financial crisis.
- The growing influence of the finance sector, either directly through lobbying or policy elites' own perceptions of the sector's economic significance.
- The privatization of publicly owned firms and industries, such as energy and telecommunications.
- The ascendance of neoliberal ideology and associated epistemologies.

As discussed in Chapter 1, population ageing is widely perceived as the most important socio-economic trend affecting traditional pensions practice in the UK. Even with later retirement ages for many schemes (and, for state pension provision, a higher entitlement age), increased longevity means that many people are in receipt of an income-for-life for longer than might have been envisaged during the time they were accumulating a right to this income through saving. Is it correct, however, to say that increasing longevity was not foreseen? Life expectancy has been rising rapidly since the late nineteenth century, before most of what we now know as 'traditional' forms of pensions provision in the UK were established. Adjustments to provision have been made throughout the previous century in order to mitigate increasing longevity, but we have also seen during this period—and even in recent decades—an enormous extension of some forms of provision in terms of both generosity and coverage, notably the inclusion of a far greater proportion of employees within occupational schemes in the post-war era.

Yet perceptions of the impact of population ageing have fuelled arguments that pension promises have become increasingly unaffordable for employers (and the state). Defined benefit pension schemes therefore make firms less competitive, at a time when 'globalisation' means they are facing ever more intense international competition (so the argument goes). The unaffordability argument is also fuelled by an increasing focus on short-term financial metrics, noted above, either deemed inherently legitimate as a tool of corporate governance, or deemed a pre-requisite of attracting investment from globally mobile capital investors. In other words, a gradual (and not necessarily permanent) process of demographic change is seen as more threatening than it is precisely because of the neoliberal lens it is viewed through—while at the same time it is used to justify the neoliberalization of pensions provision (Macnicol, 2015: 7–12).

Neoliberalization in response to population ageing is, in fact, unjustifiable; adherence to a neoliberal paradigm is not protecting UK pensions provision, but rather imperilling it. Social, political, and economic conditions are in constant flux: some practices disappear, some conditions abate; new practices emerge, or extant conditions are intensified. This churn invariably untangles the mechanisms of inter-generational co-operation which ostensibly underpin pensions provision. Yet this is precisely why pensions provision exists as a dimension of capitalist management. Pensions provision requires a vision of the future in order to shape behaviour in the present, but it is also based on the certainty that the future will not resemble the envisioned future—and thus uncertainty is hard-wired into institutional practices. In the UK, in the last century or so, employers have performed this temporal anchor function in private pensions provision, ensuring that pension outcomes conform approximately to those which were promised. The promise is critical: without it, capitalist labour relations would be more difficult, if not impossible.

As explored in Chapter 2, the UK has always managed the unique temporality of pensions provision in a voluntaristic manner. Because provision was not deeply rooted in collectivist values, employers have been able to abdicate the temporal anchor role rather unproblematically. The most important anchor mechanism is of course the state, but state pension provision in the UK has always been inadequate, and has now been refashioned as a 'savings platform' ostensibly to encourage individuals to pick up the responsibilities for pensions provision abdicated by most employers. The irony is that, without a temporal anchor to mitigate failed futures, private pensions provision now requires greater accuracy in its projections, to enable accumulated funds in defined contribution provision to be rematerialized as a retirement income—or, more precisely, to incentivize saving in the first place. This process is increasingly vulnerable to generational change, but has no failsafe. This is the real 'pensions crisis'—and it extends beyond pensions provision. There should be no presumption that the model of capital accumulation which prevails in the UK can persist once individualized pensions provision is fully embedded, especially if state provision remains meagre. An essential work incentive is being unwound, largely unthinkingly. Ironically, population ageing—the key driver of neoliberalization—is now arguably in reverse: tragically, as a result of the impact of austerity on health inequalities, and probably also as a result of the COVID-19 pandemic's disproportionate impact on older people. That there is no sign of a retreat from individualization is a clear indication that population ageing was never quite the immutable force it was claimed to be, but rather a convenient excuse.

The individual now serves as the core imaginary of UK pensions provision. Indeed, a (misguided) reliance on the individual's enduring capacity and willingness to take personal responsibility for their own retirement income now arguably functions as a form of temporal anchoring. This book's empirical focus has primarily been the way this conception has been advanced and sustained by public policy (and how UK policy-makers have sought to alleviate its contradictions). Yet the auto-enrolment agenda has been supported by only limited attempts by policy elites to justify why defined contribution provision is superior to defined benefit. As Chapter 5 explores, policy-makers have utilized a behaviouralist paradigm in focusing on how to encourage individuals to save more at the micro level (that is, soft compulsion) within a marketized private pension system, while ignoring the insight of behavioural economics that markets are inherently irrational at the macro level (Mabbett, 2012). The Pensions Commission of the mid-2000s (which established the framework for auto-enrolment) understood perfectly well the dangers of a market-led approach, but New Labour largely ignored (without explanation) its recommendation for universal, state-managed defined contribution provision. Recent governments have sought to counter the inadequacies of defined contribution provision by enabling CDC, that is, an opportunity for scheme members to share both accumulation and decumulation risks among themselves. But this initiative will only proceed voluntaristically, with employers in control—despite not bearing any risk. Furthermore, even this agenda is fundamentally undermined by the hyper-individualist 'pension freedoms' reforms which give savers the (illusory) opportunity to remove their accumulated funds from workplace pensions provision, despite benefiting from PTR.

As explored in Chapters 4 and 6, none of this means that the state is no longer involved in private pensions provision in the UK, whether in terms of attempting to clean up the very messy process of defined benefit demise, or attempting to correct the abundant flaws of defined contribution. The mandatory employer contributions encompassed by auto-enrolment are themselves the product of an interventionist state, and policy-makers have been compelled to both establish a state-owned, low-cost default defined contribution provider, and strengthen regulation on disclosure, charging, and governance, in order to mitigate some of the most alarming consequences of a market-led approach. Interventions are, however, ad hoc, and essentially designed to enable rather than disrupt private profitability. This explains the persistence of the perverse regulatory divide between TPR (for trust-based defined contribution and defined benefit provision) and FCA (for contract-based defined contribution provision), and the failure to address the chronic 'small pots' problem which arises when auto-enrolees change jobs. In legacy defined benefit provision, policy-makers have increasingly strengthened 'lifeboat' provision—essentially agreeing to (temporarily) assume the temporal anchor function, so that employers may (permanently) relinquish it. Chapter 3 argues that the main critical social science literature on pensions provision—arising from the study of pensions policy as a form of social policy, and pensions provision as an aspect of the welfare state—misunderstands the state's role in this regard. As well as inadequately distinguishing between collectivized and individualized provision within private provisions, this literature also tends to assume that any state intervention in private provision is inherently progressive (see for example Bridgen and Meyer, 2018). Challenging this assumption empirically is one of the book's core contributions.

More generally, the book also makes an important contribution to the varied literature on financialization, which is situated mainly across political economy and heterodox economics. Pensions provision is both cause and conduit of financialization, and some recent pension-related reforms are a consequence of wider processes of financialization within the UK economy (and their promotion by policy elites). One of the frustrations of the financialization concept is the flipside of its analytical value: the concept helps to emphasize links between transformations across disparate socio-economic domains, but loses explanatory force as it does so. To argue that UK pensions provision has 'been financialised' would be to say not very much. However, this book's subject matter has allowed for exploration more specifically of the relationship between financialization and time. By seeing financialization as, in part, a shortening of time horizons across multiple domains of economic organization (including the state's involvement in the economy), the distinctive temporality of pensions provision, outlined above, becomes more visible. The loss and undermining of temporal anchors has made pensions provision more dependent on generating financial returns, and exposed more people to risks arising from intimate engagement with financial services. In a sense, the temporal anchor function has been deemed incompatible with a financialized economy. However, we can also conclude that the transformation of pensions temporality has itself driven financialization, in creating demand from institutional investors for particular types of assets, and opening up new markets for the finance sector.

Financialization is particularly relevant to Chapter 7, which further explores the conflicted temporalities underpinning pensions provision. Clearly, in the UK, providers of pensions-saving vehicles cannot choose how to dematerialize pensions saving, as capital, with complete autonomy—and they certainly cannot dictate the returns they will generate in support of the rematerialization of savings as a retirement income. The process of pensions individualization leaves people more reliant on using their savings to generate a financial return in capital markets, and is also characterized by a shift in the balance of power from pensions providers to investment intermediaries. This may be problematic in itself, but also speaks to a wider trend of pensions provision increasingly being organized and operated in accordance with capital markets' pursuit of future returns, potentially undermining the very long-term investment horizons of pensions provision, and more importantly, displacing the underpinning temporality of pensions provision as a mechanism for managing failed futures. We can better understand hyper-individualist reforms such as pension freedoms in this light: with capital markets unable to deliver the returns and security required by pensions provision, individual savers are urged to take back control (to coin a phrase) from pensions institutions. But this control is an illusion, and serves to further subject individuals to the costs and risks of investment, while advancing the dissolution of pensions provision.

UK private pensions provision has always produced uneven outcomes, in part because outcomes reflect people's earnings during their working life, and in part because, even at its peak, defined benefit occupational pensions provision was only selectively inclusive. Where they are eligible for an occupational or workplace pension, the poorest groups obviously receive the worst outcomes—compounded by the inequity of PTR. Women are over-represented among low earners (alongside disabled people and ethnic minorities) but are also likely to be disadvantaged by the (cumulative) impact of career breaks and/or caring responsibilities on retirement incomes. Documenting these inequalities has not been a core aim of the book, given the empirical focus on the rationale for and implementation of pensions policies, rather than evaluating their outcomes. We can deduce, however, that it is not necessarily the case that pensions policy has deliberately discriminated against women, but rather that it has been gender-blind (Grady, 2015). Policy has also marginalized concerns around people in self-employment, and those with multiple jobs. In general, auto-enrolment widens access to workplace pensions (and employer contributions, for most workers), but it does so while shifting risks onto people least equipped to take them.

Furthermore, the impact of the pension freedoms reform on the annuities market will be felt most by those with the smallest pension pots at retirement. The Pensions Commission took for granted that auto-enrolees would be able to access annuities; if the most affluent savers are able to access alternatives to annuities, the entire business model of auto-enrolment will be undermined. Of course, the value of annuities has already fallen sharply in recent years, as a result of low yields on UK gilts (which helps to explain why the Coalition government introduced pension freedoms)—an important example of long-term pensions policy objectives being sacrificed in the service of sustaining accumulation strategies in the short term.

8.2. In the Face of Peril

This section briefly discusses ideas for reforming UK pensions provision. Some are more radical than others. Some are novel, while some draw upon the experiences and traditions of pensions provision in other countries, as explored in Chapter 3.

8.2.1 Improving the State Pension

Although state pensions provision has not been a core focus of this book, it is clear that the state is the ultimate temporal anchor (a role it is actually taking on within private provision, as policy-makers seek to manage the demise of defined benefit provision). From a pensions perspective, it is essential that state provision forms the bedrock, if not the bulk, of people's retirement incomes. It would not be realistic—or even necessarily progressive—to suggest that the UK could move swiftly from a Beveridgean to a Bismarckian system, but even within a Beveridgean system, the UK can and should offer a significantly more generous universal state pension. This should not be seen as burdensome: providing pensions is of benefit to the state's wider socioeconomic objectives too, insofar as it legitimates personal taxation, and therefore enables the revenues which fund all state activities. (It may also be worth considering alternative sources of funding for state pensions, such as social wealth funds with equity stakes in large firms (see Blackburn, 2006).) State pension provision is also an essential opportunity for redistribution, correcting inequalities entrenched in the labour market in a way that private pensions provision cannot. New Labour's introduction of the S2P briefly promised such an agenda, but the STSP (which merged the two state pension benefits) could be used for the same ends. The 'triple lock' on state pension indexation, discussed in Chapter 2, actually represents an important mechanism for increasing the value of the state pension over time, with benefits focused on today's young people (Berry, 2017b).

8.2.2 Legacy Defined Benefit and a New Public Pension

Defined benefit pensions provision in the private sector is, for the most part, in terminal decline. Policy-makers continue to search for solutions—generally speaking, to reduce costs for sponsoring employers, rather than to protect scheme members—while allowing the PPF to expand. The opportunity should be taken to nationalize all, or most, defined benefit schemes, including the PPF. Crucially, this would be the first step towards establishing a new Bismarckian public pension, in addition to the existing state pension. Legacy defined benefit scheme members and PPF recipients would be the first wave of beneficiaries, but the programme would eventually open to new members and new accruals. In providing an earnings-related supplement to the state pension (ideally, with a strong redistributive element) this would, in essence, reconstitute S2P and the earlier SERPS, although it could be operated on a voluntary rather than mandatory basis, with contributions made in a similar way to existing workplace pension contributions rather than via personal taxation. Some suggest that a scheme of this nature could be organized on a funded basis, with the accumulated capital invested to support public investment (with the state effectively borrowing from—and therefore paying interest to—the fund) (see Murphy, 2015).

Ultimately, it would be necessary to consider whether the new scheme would replace or complement existing private pensions provision. It is clear that a public scheme organized as a defined benefit pension represents a far superior proposition for individuals than the defined contribution schemes into which the vast majority of auto-enrolees are now contributing. The new scheme could be established on an NDC basis, with the state committing to provide retirement incomes on the basis of notional (and adjustable) investment returns which contributions, if invested, would generate, rather than accrued rights linked to individuals' earnings. The NDC model would be similar to that which the French government is seeking to introduce; whereas these proposals have provoked fierce resistance in France, this policy would represent a significant upgrade in the generosity and security of UK pensions provision. Even if operating alongside private provision, the state would be (re-)established as a temporal anchor for pension provision, and a bulwark against the retemporalization of pensions associated with financialization.

Increases to SPA have, understandably, been among the most controversial aspects of policy-makers' attempt to adapt UK pensions provision to the perceived challenge of population ageing. In theory, decisions are now subject to independent review—although this system has yet to be seriously tested. Raising retirement ages in private defined benefit provision has been more difficult. In the absence of the reforms suggested above, there is a case for making it easier to adjust the point at which members can access their pension in continuing defined benefit schemes. However, this would only be permissible on the basis of clear, specific evidence that scheme demographics have radically changed. Moreover, it should only be introduced in conjunction with much tighter eligibility rules for the PPF, as part of a comprehensive agenda to prevent scheme closure. In practice, the likelihood of retirement age changes would be limited, but the *possibility* of change, should the life expectancy of scheme members rise unexpectedly, would assist the long-term planning of sponsoring employers. It would of course also be possible for retirement ages to be revised down.

8.2.3 Collectivizing Defined Contribution

Many of the problems of existing defined contribution schemes are detailed throughout the book, particularly in Chapters 5 and 6. For some of these problems, relatively quick fixes are available (see Blake, 2016). For example, administrative barriers are no excuse for an auto-enrolment system which excludes the self-employed, and discriminates against people with very low earnings and/or people who work part time or for multiple employers. Similarly, employers can and must be compelled to make higher contributions into their workers' pension pots. Crucially, the state should contribute directly to the pension pots of those workers unable to access employer contributions, or those who receive lower employer contributions as a result of caring responsibilities. Radically improving the governance and transparency of defined contribution schemes would also be straightforward (although the impact on outcomes for members would probably be negligible). Bringing all defined contribution schemes into a single regulatory regime would be trickier, but should be seen as urgent. This objective could be achieved by effectively prohibiting the use of contract-based defined contribution schemes for auto-enrolment (see McClymont and Tarrant, 2013);

however, we should also acknowledge that the regulation of trust-based schemes (particularly master trusts) is far from ideal.

More substantive reforms to defined contribution provision are possible. Firstly, moves towards enabling CDC should be accelerated—with the model used to 'level up' defined contribution provision, rather than 'level down' defined benefit. Ultimately, employers should be compelled to automatically enrol their workforce into CDC rather than pure defined contribution schemes (as part of this, NEST would be converted into a CDC scheme (Berry, 2015b)). It should also be possible for employers to agree to share risks with their employees, by guaranteeing minimum outcomes, ensuring that CDC represents a genuine hybridization of defined benefit and defined contribution provision, rather than simply a largely superficial tweak to the latter. As noted in Chapter 2, trade unions and similar bodies actually performed the temporal anchor function in some of the earliest forms of pensions provision in the private sector (see Hannah, 1986): CDC therefore heralds a return to mechanisms of self-help organized among workers themselves. There is no plausible reason that their employers—particularly in multi-employer schemes—cannot share part of this responsibility.

Secondly, the provision of annuities should be nationalized, in full or in part—revisiting a reform seriously considered by the Pensions Commission. This could take the form of policy-makers establishing a default provider for defined contribution decumulation, in the same way that NEST is a default provider for the accumulation phase (of course, providing annuities is a much larger undertaking, in fiscal terms, than providing a savings vehicle). It could be that, rather than providing annuities directly to people in retirement, the state could instead offer bulk annuities to be purchased by private schemes. This approach would actually help to underpin the rollout of CDC (since schemes could purchase bulk annuities in order to partially guarantee outcomes to some extent, while continuing to generate investment returns to provide additional benefits to retirees). However, the direct provision of annuities would offer more scope for a redistributive system.

8.2.4 Abolishing Pensions Tax Relief

As Chapter 6 demonstrated, the benefits of PTR skew heavily towards the highest earners. Assuming private pensions provision continues in a similar form to the present, we should move towards the abolition of tax relief on pensions saving. (This policy would ideally be part of wider reforms to the taxation of income and wealth, which would increase greater fairness in how the already retired are taxed.) Abolishing PTR—essentially, requiring individuals to make pension contributions from post-tax income—would lead to materially lower contributions. However, in place of PTR, the state should subsidize the pension contributions of the lowest earners (incentivizing higher contributions in the process). As noted in Chapters 2 and 6, PTR represents an attempt by the state to assist, and even partially replace, employers in acting as temporal anchor for their workers' accumulated savings. If the state is going to take on this responsibility, it should do so directly. In general, the fiscal benefits of abolishing PTR should be recycled into state pension provision. Short of abolition, policy-makers could also introduce flat-rate tax relief of, say, 30 per cent (so that the lowest earners receive relief at a higher rate than their marginal tax rate, and higher earners receive it at a lower rate).

8.2.5   Reorienting Pensions Investment

In recent years, as discussed in Chapter 7, policy-makers have consistently sought to enable or encourage pension funds (primarily, defined benefit funds) to adopt longer-term investment strategies, and allocate more capital to assets such as infrastructure. The key proposals have focused on increasing the size of funds through scheme mergers (generally only taken forward via funded provision in the public sector, to a limited extent). Often, however, policy-makers have resorted to simply *imploring* funds to change the way they invest—without daring to revise the regulatory norms which necessitate short-termist investment practice, or seriously considering ways to strengthen the capacity of pension funds to steer the activities of investment intermediaries. Similarly, campaigns which encourage pension funds, as investors in listed equities, to become responsible stewards of corporate governance tend to focus on how pensions investment practice could help the wider economy, rather than on how to improve the sustainability of pensions provision or outcomes from pensions saving.

The inconvenient truth is that, without wide-ranging reforms to the finance sector and capital markets, any demand that pension funds modify their investment practice for the benefit of the economy in general is likely to increase the cost of investment—leading to a material reduction in retirement incomes for defined contribution savers. There is no straightforward solution to this dilemma. As well as considering whether pension fund investment practice should be constrained in some ways, we need to consider the supply of investable propositions available to institutional investors. Part of this agenda will involve thinking more imaginatively about locally rooted and democratically organized investment vehicles which route pension fund capital away from conventional investment practices. The state would be intimately involved in the establishment of these mechanisms.

8.3. And Finally...

> Lord, we know what we are, but not what we may be.
> Ophelia (in William Shakespeare, Hamlet, c. 1600)

There are few reasons to assume that the policy agenda sketched above is likely to be enacted in the foreseeable future. To some extent, the UK lacks the necessary political and economic conditions to render the most radical ideas realizable. A more collectivist approach would probably depend, for instance, on wider change to corporate governance and industrial organization. Similarly, a more long-term investment orientation probably requires different forms of finance sector regulation, with greater state intervention, and indeed an alternative development model for the UK economy, embedded in macro-economic management and industrial policy. Greater union density will probably be required, to press for reform from the front line. Ultimately, if private pensions provision is to be rescued, and refurbished, the UK will need to (re)discover an economic development model in which firms seek to nurture long-term, mutually beneficial relationships with their workers. This will not happen automatically; ultimately, it will require the state to drive change through its own investment and regulatory activity.

Radical reform to pensions policy is probably unlikely while pensions provision remains a low-salience political issue; by the time today's auto-enrolees begin to experience the consequences of policy choices made decades ago, it will be too late (for them). We must hope that the UK policy elite embraces collectivist values in a way that previous generations of elites never really have—but neoliberalism survived the 2008 financial crisis, and may yet survive the COVID-19 pandemic (Berry et al., 2020; Berry, 2016b). It will be a tall order but, if this book's diagnosis of the imperilment of UK pensions provision is correct, it is a task we must take on. The best place to start is seeing the pensions crisis for what it is: a neglect of the unique, temporal function of pensions provision in capitalist societies, that is, the management of failed futures. It is now up to us to ensure this book's pessimistic prophecy fails.

References

Actuarial Post (2020) Coronavirus adds £100 billion to DB pension deficits in a week. March. Available at: http://www.actuarialpost.co.uk/article/coronavirus-adds-gbp100bn-to-db-pension-deficits-in-a-week-17916.htm (accessed 1 April 2020).

Adkins, L. (2016) Speculative futures in the time of debt. *The Sociological Review*, 65(3), 448–62.

Adkins, L. (2018) *The time of money*. Stanford, CA: Stanford University Press.

Altmann, R. (2017) There is a magic money tree—it's called QE. *Financial Times*, 6 June. Available at: https://www.ft.com/content/3f9dd17e-47a2-11e7-8d27-59b4dd6296b8 (accessed 8 October 2018).

Anderson, K.M. (2012) The Netherlands: Reconciling labour market flexicurity with security in old age. In: *Labour market flexibility and pension reforms flexible today, secure tomorrow?* eds K. Hinrichs and M. Jessoula. Basingstoke: Palgrave, 203–30.

Anderson, K.M. (2019) Financialisation meets collectivisation: Occupational pensions in Denmark, the Netherlands and Sweden. *Journal of European Public Policy*, 26(4), 617–36.

Ashcraft, A.B. and Scheurmann, T. (2008) Understanding the securitization of subprime mortgage credit. *Federal Reserve Bank of New York Staff Report No. 318*. Available at: https://www.newyorkfed.org/medialibrary/media/research/staff_reports/sr318.pdf (accessed 1 December 2019).

Association of British Insurers (ABI) (2013) *The UK annuity market: Facts and figures*. Available at: https://www.abi.org.uk/globalassets/sitecore/files/documents/publications/public/2014/pensions/the-uk-annuity-market-facts-and-figures.pdf (accessed 1 September 2019).

Association of British Insurers (ABI) (2017) *The pensions dashboard project: Reconnecting people with their pensions*. Available at: https://www.abi.org.uk/globalassets/files/subject/public/lts/reconnecting-people-with-their-pensions-final-10-october-2017.pdf (accessed 1 September 2019).

Association of British Insurers (ABI) (2019) *UK insurance and long-term saving: The state of the market 2019*. Available at: https://www.abi.org.uk/globalassets/files/publications/public/data/abi_bro6778_state_of_market_2019_web.pdf (accessed 1 December 2019).

Barnett Waddingham (2018) Buy-outs and buy-ins. Available at: https://www.barnett-waddingham.co.uk/finance-directors-guide/liability-management-risk-reduction/buy-outs-and-buy-ins/ (accessed 10 March 2019).

Barr, N. and Diamond, P. (2008) *Reforming pensions: Principles and policy choices*. Oxford: Oxford University Press.

Barr, N. and Diamond, P. (2009) Reforming pensions: Principles, analytical errors and policy directions. *International Social Security Review*, 62(2), 5–29.

Barr, N. and Diamond, P. (2010) Reforming pensions: Lessons from economic theory and some policy directions. *Economia*, 11(1), 1–15.

Barr, N. and Diamond, P. (2016) Reforming pensions in Chile. *Polityka Społeczna*, 1(1), 4–9.

BBC News (2010) Public sector pension costs 'to double in five years'. 15 June. Available at: https://www.bbc.co.uk/news/10305817 (accessed 1 April 2019).

BBC News (2011) Public sector pensions report explained. 10 March. Available at: https://www.bbc.co.uk/news/business-11466273 (accessed 1 April 2019).

BBC News (2014) Minister fuels pension debate with Lamborghini comment. 21 March. Available at: https://www.bbc.co.uk/news/uk-politics-26649162 (accessed 19 July 2020).

BEIS (2018) *Trade union membership 2017: Statistical bulletin.* Available at: https://assets.publishing.service.gov.uk/government/uploads/system/uploads/attachment_data/file/712543/TU_membership_bulletin.pdf (accessed 3 April 2019).

Berry, C. (2011) *Globalisation and ideology in Britain: Neoliberalism, free trade and the global economy.* Manchester: Manchester University Press.

Berry, C. (2012) A contract between generations: pensions and saving. In: *Re:generation*, eds C. Coatman, G. Shrubsole, B. Little, and S. Malik. London: Lawrence and Wishart, 139–46.

Berry, C. (2013a) £144 is not enough to realise the benefits of a simple state pension. *Touchstone*, 17 June. Available at: https://touchstoneblog.org.uk/2013/06/144-is-not-enough-to-realise-the-benefits-of-a-simple-state-pension/ (accessed 1 February 2020).

Berry, C. (2013b) Gender inequality in single tier pension plans. *Touchstone*, 26 June. Availableat:https://touchstoneblog.org.uk/2013/06/gender-inequality-in-single-tier-pension-plans/ (accessed 1 February 2020).

Berry, C. (2014a) Pension funds and the City in the UK's contradictory growth spurts. Paper presented at CITYPERC/SPERI workshop *Capital Divided? The City of London and the Future of the British Economy*, November. Available at: https://www.academia.edu/9094932/Pension_funds_and_the_City_in_the_UKs_contradictory_growth_spurts (accessed 1 December 2019).

Berry, C. (2014b) Young people and the ageing electorate: Breaking the unwritten rule of representative democracy. *Parliamentary Affairs*, 67(3), 708–25.

Berry, C. (2015a) Citizenship in a financialised society: Financial inclusion and the state before and after the crash. *Policy and Politics*, 43(4), 509–25.

Berry, C. (2015b) *Take the long road: Pension fund investments and economic stagnation.* International Longevity Centre-UK. Available at: https://www.academia.edu/20835522/Take_the_long_road_Pension_fund_investments_and_economic_stagnation (accessed 25 May 2020).

Berry, C. (2016a) Austerity, ageing and the financialisation of pensions policy in the UK. *British Politics*, 11, 2–25.

Berry, C. (2016b) *Austerity politics and UK economic policy.* Basingstoke, Palgrave.

Berry, C. (2016c) The fallacies of freedom: George Osborne's pensions liberation agenda. Paper presented at Sheffield Political Economy Research Institute Conference, July. Available at: https://www.academia.edu/26680802/The_fallacies_of_freedom_George_Osbornes_pensions_liberation_agenda_draft_paper_ (accessed 20 September 2019).

Berry, C. (2016d) The government is right on pensioner protection—but for the wrong reasons. *SPERI Comment*, 14 January. Available at: http://speri.dept.shef.ac.uk/2016/01/14/the-government-is-right-on-pensioner-protection-but-for-the-wrong-reasons/ (accessed 9 March 2017).

Berry, C. (2016e) UK manufacturing decline since the crisis in historical perspective. *SPERI British Political Economy Brief No.25.* Available at: http://speri.dept.shef.ac.uk/wp-content/uploads/2018/11/Brief-25-UK-manufacturing-decline-since-the-crisis.pdf (accessed 10 August 2018).

Berry, C. (2017a) The declining salience of 'saving' in British politics. *SPERI British Political Economy Brief No.28.* Available at: http://speri.dept.shef.ac.uk/wp-content/uploads/2018/11/Brief-28-The-declining-salience-of-saving-in-British-Politics.pdf (accessed 1 August 2019).

Berry, C. (2017b) The long-term impact of the state pension 'triple lock'. *SPERI British Political Economy Brief No.29.* Available at: http://speri.dept.shef.ac.uk/wp-content/uploads/2018/11/Brief-27-The-long-term-impact-of-the-state-pension-triple-lock.pdf (accessed 1 August 2019).

Berry, C. and Barber, A. (2017) Local authority pension fund investment decisions since the financial crisis. *SPERI British Political Economy Brief No.20*. Available at: http://speri.dept.shef.ac.uk/wp-content/uploads/2018/11/SPERI-Brief-29-Local-authority-pension-fund-investment-since-the-financial-crisis.pdf (accessed 1 April 2019).

Berry, C. and Hay, C. (2016) The Great British 'rebalancing' act: The construction and implementation of an economic imperative for exceptional times. *British Journal of Politics and International Relations*, 18(1), 3–25.

Berry, C. and McDaniel, S. (2018) *Young workers and trade unionism in the hourglass economy.* London: Unions 21. Available at: http://unions21.org.uk/files1/YOUNG-PROFS-ECONOMY.pdf (accessed 4 September 2019).

Berry, C. and McDaniel, S. (2020) Post-crisis precarity: Understanding attitudes to work and industrial relations among young people in the UK. *Economic and Industrial Democracy.* Available at: https://journals.sagepub.com/doi/full/10.1177/0143831X19894380 (accessed 1 February 2020).

Berry, C. and Stanley, N. (2013) *Third time lucky: Building a progressive pensions consensus.* Trades Union Congress. Available at: https://www.tuc.org.uk/sites/default/files/third_time_lucky.pdf (accessed 1 February 2020).

Berry, C., O'Donovan, N., Bailey, D., Barber, A., Beel, D., Jones, K., McDaniel, S., and Weicht, R. (2020) The covidist manifesto: Assessing the UK state's emergency enlargement. *Future Economies Research and Policy Paper No. 9.* Available at: https://www.mmu.ac.uk/media/mmuacuk/content/documents/business-school/future-economies/covidist-manifesto-FINAL-PDF.pdf (accessed 25 May 2020).

Bessant, J., Farthing, R., and Watts, R. (2017) *The precarious generation: A political economy of young people.* London: Routledge.

Beveridge, W.H.B. (1942) *Social Insurance and Allied Services.* London: HM Stationery Office.

Blackburn, R. (2006) The global pension crisis: From gray capitalism to responsible accumulation. *Politics and Society*, 34(2), 135–86.

Blain, N. (2017) The top 100 pension schemes 2017. *Professional Pensions*, 14 December. Available at: https://www.professionalpensions.com/professional-pensions/analysis/3060952/the-top-100-pension-schemes-2017 (accessed 1 April 2019).

Blake, D. (2003) *Pension schemes and pension funds in the UK.* Oxford: Oxford University Press.

Blake, D. (2016) *We need a national narrative: Building a consensus around retirement income.* London: Independent Review of Retirement Income. Available at: http://www.pensions-institute.org/IRRIReport.pdf (accessed 1 September 2019).

Blake, D. and Boardman, T. (2010) Spend more today: Using behavioural economics to improve retirement expenditure decisions. *Pensions Institute Discussion Paper PI-1014.* Available at: https://mpra.ub.uni-muenchen.de/34234/1/MPRA_paper_34234.pdf (accessed 9 March 2017).

Bonoli, G. and Palier, B. (2008) When past reforms open new opportunities: Comparing old-age insurance reforms in Bismarckian welfare systems. In: *Reforming the Bismarckian welfare systems*, eds B. Palier and C. Martin. London: Wiley, 21–39.

Booth, J. (2018) UK corporate debt soars to all-time high after years of low interest rates. *City AM*, 2 July. Available at: https://www.cityam.com/uk-corporate-debt-soars-all-time-high-after-years-low/ (accessed 1 December 2019).

Borak, D. (2017) Social Security trust fund projected to tap out in 17 years. *CNN*, 13 July. Available at: https://money.cnn.com/2017/07/13/news/economy/social-security-trust-fund-projection/index.html (accessed 6 August 2019).

Borzutsky, S. and Hyde, M. (2016) Chile's private pension system at 35: Impact and lessons. *Journal of International and Comparative Social Policy*, 32(1), 57–73.

Bozio, A., Crawford, R., and Tetlow, G. (2010) The history of state pensions in the UK: 1948 to 2010. *Institute for Fiscal Studies Briefing Note 105*. Available at: http://www.ifs.org.uk/bns/bn105.pdf (accessed 9 March 2017).

Brett, D. (2017) How the FTSE 100 has changed over 33 years. *Schroders*, 30 June. Available at: https://www.schroders.com/en/uk/private-investor/insights/markets/how-the-ftse-100-has-changed-over-33-years/ (accessed 1 April 2019).

Bridgen, P. and Meyer, T. (2009) The politics of occupational pension reform in Britain and the Netherlands: The power of market discipline in liberal and corporatist regimes. *West European Politics*, 32(3), 586–610.

Bridgen, P. and Meyer, T. (2011) Britain: Exhausted voluntarism—the evolution of a hybrid pension regime. In: *The Varieties of Pension Governance: Pension Privatization in Europe*, ed. B. Ebbinghaus. Oxford: Oxford University Press, 265–91.

Bridgen, P. and Meyer, T. (2018) Individualisation reversed: the cross-class politics of social regulation in the UK's public/private pensions mix. *Transfer: European Review of Labour and Research*, 24(1), 25–41.

Brodbeck, S. (2017) Youngsters lose out in state-backed pension scheme as 50-somethings net 73pc gain in five years. *The Telegraph*, 6 July. Available at: https://www.telegraph.co.uk/pensions-retirement/news/youngsters-lose-state-backed-pension-scheme-50-somethings-net/ (accessed 1 February 2020).

Brodbeck, S. (2019) Boris's NHS pension fix must be available to us saps in the private sector, too. *The Telegraph*, 7 August. Available at: https://www.telegraph.co.uk/pensions-retirement/news/boriss-nhs-pension-fix-must-available-us-saps-private-sector/?WT.mc_id=tmg_share_em (accessed 1 September 2019).

Brooksbank, D. (2004) Pension Commission reaction. *Investment and Pensions Europe*, November. Available at: https://www.ipe.com/pension-commission-reaction/17252.article (accessed 1 August 2019).

Brummer, A. (2010) *The great pensions robbery: How New Labour betrayed retirement*. London: Random House.

Buller, J. and James, T.S. (2012) Statecraft and the assessment of national political leaders: The case of New Labour and Tony Blair. *British Journal of Politics and International Relations*, 14, 534–55.

Bulpitt, J. (1986) The discipline of the new democracy: Mrs Thatcher's domestic statecraft. *Political Studies*, 34(1), 19–39.

Burger, D. (2018) Passive bond funds rewarding debt danger stability, says BIS. *Bloomberg*, 11 March. Available at: https://www.bloomberg.com/news/articles/2018-03-11/passive-bond-funds-imperil-stability-by-rewarding-debt-says-bis (accessed 1 April 2020).

Burke, E. (2012 [1790]) *Reflections on the revolution in France*. Plano, TX: SMK Books.

Büthe, T. and Mattli, W. (2011) *The new global rulers: The privatization of regulation in the world economy*. Princeton, NJ: Princeton University Press.

Butler, S. and Wood, Z. (2019) Philip Green's retail rescue plan at risk over pension scheme. *The Guardian*, 23 May. Available at: https://www.theguardian.com/business/2019/may/23/philip-greens-retail-rescue-plan-torpedoed-by-pension-watchdog?CMP=share_btn_link (accessed 23 May 2019).

Campbell, J. (2007) *Margaret Thatcher: The iron lady*. London: Random House.

Campion, B. (2013) The winner is…*Pension Age*, January. Available at: https://www.pensionsage.com/pa/The-winner-is.php (accessed 25 August 2019).

Casey, B.H. (2012) The implications of the economic crisis for pensions and pension policy in Europe. *Global Social Policy*, 12(3), 246–65.

Casey, B.H. (2019) I am glad I am not the one carving up the USS turkey. *Times Higher Education*, 17 December. Available at: https://www.timeshighereducation.com/opinion/i-am-glad-i-am-not-one-carving-uss-turkey (accessed 18 December 2019).

Casey, B.H. and Dostal, J.M. (2013) Voluntary pension saving for old age: Are the objectives of self-responsibility and security compatible? *Social Policy and Administration*, 47(3), 287–309.

Cennamo, L. and Gardner, D. (2008) Generational differences in work values, outcomes and person-organisation values fit. *Journal of Managerial Psychology*, 23(8), 891–906.

Chang, H.-J. (2002) Breaking the mould: An institutional political economy alternative to the neo-liberal of the market and the state. *Cambridge Journal of Economics*, 26(5), 539–59.

Christophers, B. (2012) Anaemic geographies of financialisation. *New Political Economy*, 17(3), 271–91.

Clark, D. (2019) Annuity incomes fall to historic low. *Moneyfacts*, 10 September. Available at: https://moneyfacts.co.uk/news/retirement/annuity-incomes-fall-to-historic-low/ (accessed 1 October 2019).

Clark, G. (2000) *Pension fund capitalism*. Oxford: Oxford University Press.

Clark, G. (2003) *European pensions and global finance*. Oxford: Oxford University Press.

Clark, G. and Monk, A.H.B. (2006) The 'crisis' in defined benefit corporate pension liabilities—Part I: scope of the problem. *Pensions*, 12(1), 43–54.

Clark, G., Knox-Hayes, J., and Strauss, K. (2009) Financial sophistication, salience, and the scale of deliberation in UK retirement planning. *Environment and Planning A: Economy and Space*, 41(10), 2496–515.

Clark, G., Strauss, K., and Knox-Hayes, J. (2012) *Saving for retirement*. Oxford: Oxford University Press.

Clarke, S. (2019) What are Boris Johnson's plans for adult social care? *Home Care Insight*, 24 July. Available at: https://www.homecareinsight.co.uk/what-are-boris-johnsons-plans-for-adult-social-care/ (accessed 20 September 2019).

Cogin, J. (2012) Are generational differences in work values fact or fiction? Multi-country evidence and implications. *The International Journal of Human Resource Management*, 23, 2268–94.

Collinson, P. (2019) Annuities: A £4bn pension heist, or a great opportunity to buy? *The Guardian*, 16 March. Available at: https://www.theguardian.com/money/2019/mar/16/annuities-a-4bn-pension-heist-or-a-great-opportunity-to-buy (accessed 1 September 2019).

Cometto, M.T. (2007) 'Toxic waste' in pension funds. *Investment and Pensions Europe*, September. Available at: https://www.ipe.com/toxic-waste-in-pension-funds/25155.article (accessed 1 December 2019).

Conservative Party Economic Competitiveness Policy Group (2007) *Freeing Britain to compete: Equipping the UK for globalisation*. The Conservative Party. Available at: https://www.webarchive.org.uk/wayback/archive/20080411012057/http:/www.conservatives.com/pdf/FreeingBritaintoCompete.pdf (accessed 1 April 2019).

Cook, L. (2019) Is Lifetime ISA the right tool for pension savers and homebuyers? *Financial Times*, 7 March. Available at: https://www.ft.com/content/5979aaf4-3c52-11e9-9988-28303f70fcff.

Cooper, J. (2016) Australia. In: *Towards a new pensions settlement: The international experience*, eds G. McClymont and A. Tarrant. London: Policy Network, 19–28.

Corbyn, J. (2017) It's time to right a wrong: Message to WASPI lobby. Press release by the Labour Party, 8 March. Available at: http://press.labour.org.uk/post/158146497189/its-time-to-right-a-wrong-message-to-waspi (accessed 9 March 2017).

Crawford, R., Keynes, S., and Tetlow, G. (2013) A single-tier pension: What does it really mean? *IFS Report R82*, Institute for Fiscal Studies. Available at: https://www.ifs.org.uk/comms/r82.pdf (accessed 1 February 2020).

Cribb, J., Hood, A., and Joyce, R. (2013) The economic circumstances of different generations: The latest picture. *Institute for Fiscal Studies Briefing Note 187*. Available at: https://www.ifs.org.uk/uploads/publications/bns/bn187.pdf (accessed 9 March 2017).

Croce, R.D. (2012) Trends in large pension fund investment in infrastructure. *OECD Working Papers on Finance, Insurance and Private Pensions No.29*. Available at: http://www.oecd.org/

daf/fin/private-pensions/TrendsInLargePensionFundInvestmentInInfrastructure.pdf (accessed 1 September 2019).

Croce, R.D., Kaminker, C., and Stewart, F. (2011) The role of pension funds in financing green growth initiatives. *OECD Working Papers on Finance, Insurance and Private Pensions No.10.* Available at: http://www.oecd.org/finance/private-pensions/49016671.pdf (accessed 1 September 2019).

Crouch, C. (2005) *Capitalist diversity and change: Recombinant governance and institutional entrepreneurs.* Oxford: Oxford University Press.

Crouch, C. (2011) *The strange non-death of neo-liberalism.* Cambridge: Polity.

Cumbo, J. (2016) Lord Turner lambasts Osborne pension reforms. *Financial Times,* 13 March. Available at: https://www.ft.com/content/a7aa7420-e763-11e5-bc31-138df2ae9ee6 (accessed 1 September 2019).

Cumbo, J. (2017) Lifetime allowance curbs snare pension savers. *Financial Times,* 21 July. Available at: https://www.ft.com/content/db7cd4a2-6d34-11e7-bfeb-33fe0c5b7eaa (accessed 1 September 2019).

Cumbo, J. (2018a) Minister shelves automatic pension transfers plan. *Financial Times,* 20 April. Available at: https://www.ft.com/content/e0c62018-4483-11e8-93cf-67ac3a6482fd (accessed 1 September 2019).

Cumbo, J. (2018b) UK pensions regulator chief to step down after criticism from MPs. *Financial Times,* 31 May. Available at: https://www.ft.com/content/93964f5e-64b1-11e8-90c2-9563a0613e56 (accessed 3 April 2019).

Cumbo, J. (2019) Boris Johnson: I'll fix NHS pensions allowance crisis. *Financial Times,* 12 July. Available at: https://www.ft.com/content/5398331a-a491-11e9-974c-ad1c6ab5efd1 (accessed 1 September 2019).

Cumbo, J. and Pickard, J. (2018) Call for UK pensions tax relief at 30%. *Financial Times,* 18 April. Available at: https://www.ft.com/content/3044b990-423d-11e8-803a-295c97e6fd0b (accessed 1 September 2019).

Cutler, T. and Waine, B. (2013) But is it 'fair'? The UK coalition government, 'fairness' and the 'reform' of public sector pensions. *Social Policy and Administration,* 47(3), 327–45.

Datz, G. (2014) Varieties of power in Latin American pension finance: Pension fund capitalism, developmentalism and statism. *Government and Opposition,* 49(5), 485–510.

Datz, G. (2016) Unconventional monetary policy, debt management and pensions: Co-dependent dynamics in the UK. Paper presented at Public Debt Management in the EU and Beyond, workshop held at UNC-Duke, 11 November. Available at: http://www.academia.edu/30976549/Unconventional_Monetary_Policy_Debt_Management_and_Pensions_Co-Dependent_Dynamics_in_the_UK_1 (accessed 20 December 2018).

Datz, G. (2017) Longevity as transferable 'risk': The new financial dynamics of ageing. *SPERI Comment,* 9 May. Available at: http://speri.dept.shef.ac.uk/2017/05/09/longevity-as-transferable-risk-the-new-financial-dynamics-of-ageing/ (accessed 3 April 2019).

Davidson, S. (2012) *Going grey: The mediation of politics in an ageing society.* London: Ashgate.

Davis, A. and Walsh, C. (2016) The role of the state in the financialisation of the UK economy. *Political Studies,* 64(3), 666–82.

Davis, R.B. (2008) *Democratizing pension funds: Corporate governance and accountability.* Vancouver: University of British Columbia Press.

Deakin, S. (2018) Reversing financialization: Shareholder value and the legal reform of corporate governance. In: *Corporate governance in contention,* eds C. Driver and G. Thompson. Oxford: Oxford University Press, 25–41.

Deal, J.J., Altman, D.G., and Rogelberg, S.G. (2010) Millennials at work: What we know and what we need to do (if anything). *Journal of Business and Psychology,* 25, 191–9.

Dean, J. (2019) BlackRock investors go for passive funds. *The Times*, 16 October. Available at: https://www.thetimes.co.uk/article/blackrock-investors-go-for-passive-funds-3shk069ps (accessed 17 February 2020).

Dellot, B. and Wallace-Stephens, F. (2018) *Venturing to retire: Boosting the long-term savings and retirement security of the self-employed*. London: RSA. Available at: https://www.thersa. org/globalassets/pdfs/venturing-to-retire-report-2.pdf (accessed 1 September 2019).

Demos (2018) *The retirement income riddle*. Available at: https://www.legalandgeneralgroup. com/media/2796/demos-report-2018.pdf (accessed 1 September 2019).

Department for Business, Innovation and Skills (2012) *Ensuring equity markets support long-term growth: The government response to the Kay review*. Available at: https://assets.publishing.service. gov.uk/government/uploads/system/uploads/attachment_data/file/253457/bis-12-1188-equity-markets-support-growth-response-to-kay-review.pdf (accessed 1 September 2019).

Department for Social Security (1998) *A new contract for welfare: Partnership in pensions*. London: The Stationery Office.

Department for Work and Pensions (DWP) (2002) *Simplicity, security and choice: Working and saving for retirement*. Available at: http://collections.europarchive.org/tna/20031220221853/ http:/www.dwp.gov.uk/consultations/consult/2002/pensions/actionplanfull.pdf (accessed 7 March 2017).

Department for Work and Pensions (DWP) (2006a) *Personal accounts: A new way to save*. Available at: https://assets.publishing.service.gov.uk/government/uploads/system/uploads/ attachment_data/file/272383/6975.pdf (accessed 25 August 2019).

Department for Work and Pensions (DWP) (2006b) *Security in retirement: Towards a new pensions system*. Available at: https://assets.publishing.service.gov.uk/government/uploads/ system/uploads/attachment_data/file/272299/6841.pdf (accessed 7 March 2017).

Department for Work and Pensions (DWP) (2007) *Personal accounts: A new way to save— summary of responses to the consultation*. Available at: https://assets.publishing.service.gov. uk/government/uploads/system/uploads/attachment_data/file/243270/7121.pdf (accessed 25 August 2019).

Department for Work and Pensions (DWP) (2008) *Deregulatory review of private pensions: Risk sharing consultation*. Available at: https://assets.publishing.service.gov.uk/government/ uploads/system/uploads/attachment_data/file/220327/pensionrisksharing-consultation-June2008.pdf (accessed 7 March 2017).

Department for Work and Pensions (DWP) (2009) *Deregulatory review of private pensions: Collective defined contribution schemes*. Available at: https://webarchive.nationalarchives. gov.uk/20130125094449/http://dwp.gov.uk/docs/collective-defined-contribution-schemes-dec09.pdf (accessed 7 March 2017).

Department for Work and Pensions (DWP) (2011) *Employer debt (section 75 of the Pensions Act 1995): Consultation on draft regulations*. Available at: https://assets.publishing.service. gov.uk/government/uploads/system/uploads/attachment_data/file/220380/employer-debt-consultation.pdf (accessed 1 April 2019).

Department for Work and Pensions (DWP) (2012a) *Improving transfers and dealing with small pension pots*. Available at: https://assets.publishing.service.gov.uk/government/uploads/ system/uploads/attachment_data/file/184963/gov-response-small-pots-automatic-transfers-consultation.pdf (accessed 1 September 2019).

Department for Work and Pensions (DWP) (2012b) *Meeting future workplace pension challenges*. Available at: https://assets.publishing.service.gov.uk/government/uploads/ system/uploads/attachment_data/file/220405/small-pension-pots-consultation.pdf (accessed 1 September 2019).

Department for Work and Pensions (DWP) (2013a) *Better workplace pensions: A consultation on charging*. Available at: https://assets.publishing.service.gov.uk/government/uploads/

system/uploads/attachment_data/file/254332/cm8737-pension-charges.pdf (accessed 25 August 2019).

Department for Work and Pensions (DWP) (2013b) *Framework for the analysis of future pension incomes*. Available at: https://assets.publishing.service.gov.uk/government/uploads/system/uploads/attachment_data/file/254321/framework-analysis-future-pensio-incomes.pdf (accessed 1 August 2019).

Department for Work and Pensions (DWP) (2013c) *Pensions and growth: Government's response to the call for evidence*. Available at: https://assets.publishing.service.gov.uk/government/uploads/system/uploads/attachment_data/file/194217/pensions-and-growth-government-response.pdf (accessed 1 April 2019).

Department for Work and Pensions (DWP) (2013d) *Supporting automatic enrolment: The government response to the call for evidence on the impact of the annual contribution limit and the transfer restrictions on NEST*. Available at: https://assets.publishing.service.gov.uk/government/uploads/system/uploads/attachment_data/file/211063/nest-automatic-enrolment-call-for-evidence-response.pdf (accessed 25 August 2019).

Department for Work and Pensions (DWP) (2014) *Reshaping workplace pensions for future generations: Government response to the consultation*. Available at: https://assets.publishing.service.gov.uk/government/uploads/system/uploads/attachment_data/file/322647/reshaping-workplace-pensions-for-future-generations-response.pdf (accessed 1 April 2019).

Department for Work and Pensions (DWP) (2015) *Automatic transfers: A framework for consolidating pension saving*. Available at: https://assets.publishing.service.gov.uk/government/uploads/system/uploads/attachment_data/file/402860/automatic-transfers.pdf (accessed 1 September 2019).

Department for Work and Pensions (DWP) (2018a) *Consolidation of defined benefit pension schemes: Public consultation*. Available at: https://assets.publishing.service.gov.uk/government/uploads/system/uploads/attachment_data/file/762503/consolidation-of-defined-benefit-pension-schemes.pdf (accessed 1 April 2019).

Department for Work and Pensions (DWP) (2018b) *Employers' pension provision survey 2017*. Available at: https://assets.publishing.service.gov.uk/government/uploads/system/uploads/attachment_data/file/717607/employers-pension-provision-survey-2017.pdf (accessed 1 August 2019).

Department for Work and Pensions (DWP) (2018c) *Protecting defined benefit pension schemes*. Available at: https://assets.publishing.service.gov.uk/government/uploads/system/uploads/attachment_data/file/693655/protecting-defined-benefit-pension-schemes.pdf (accessed 1 April 2019).

Department for Work and Pensions (DWP) (2019a) *Delivering collective defined contribution pension schemes*. Available at: https://assets.publishing.service.gov.uk/government/uploads/system/uploads/attachment_data/file/789051/response-delivering-collective-defined-contribution-pension-schemes.pdf (accessed 1 April 2019).

Department for Work and Pensions (DWP) (2019b) *Investment innovation and future consolidation: A consultation on the consideration of illiquid assets and the development of scale in occupational defined contribution schemes*. Available at: https://assets.publishing.service.gov.uk/government/uploads/system/uploads/attachment_data/file/776181/consultation-investment-innovation-and-future-consolidation.pdf (accessed 1 February 2020).

Department for Work and Pensions (DWP) (2019c) *Workplace pension participation and savings trends of eligible employees official statistics: 2008 to 2018*. Available at: https://assets.publishing.service.gov.uk/government/uploads/system/uploads/attachment_data/file/806513/workplace-pension-participation-and-saving-trends-2008–2018.pdf (accessed 1 August 2019).

Department for Work and Pensions (DWP) (2020) *Automatic enrolment evaluation report 2019*. Available at: https://assets.publishing.service.gov.uk/government/uploads/system/

uploads/attachment_data/file/883289/automatic-enrolment-evaluation-report-2019.pdf (accessed 1 March 2020).

Dixon, A. (2008) The rise of pension fund capitalism in Europe: An unseen revolution? *New Political Economy*, 13(3), 249–70.

Dixon, A. and Sorsa, V.-P. (2009) Institutional change and the financialisation of pensions in Europe. *Competition and Change*, 13(4), 347–67.

Dorling, D. and Gietel-Basten, S. (2017a) Life expectancy in Britain has fallen so much that a million years of life could disappear by 2058—why? *The Conversation*, 29 November. Available at: https://theconversation.com/life-expectancy-in-britain-has-fallen-so-much-that-a-million-years-of-life-could-disappear-by-2058-why-88063 (accessed 7 March 2018).

Dorling, D. and Gietel-Basten, S. (2017b) *Why demography matters*. London: Polity.

Dromey, J. (2019) Reforming the pension system to work for the many. *Prospect*, 15 February. Available at: https://www.prospectmagazine.co.uk/sponsored/reforming-the-pension-system-to-work-for-the-many (accessed 20 September 2019).

Duarte, E. (2019) Foreign investments by pension funds protect Canada's triple-A credit rating. *Bloomberg*, 23 April. Available at: https://business.financialpost.com/news/fp-street/overseas-shopping-spree-by-pension-funds-protects-canadas-aaa-rating   (accessed   6 August 2019).

Ebbinghaus, B. (ed.) (2011) *The varieties of pension governance: Pension privatization in Europe*. Oxford: Oxford University Press.

Echalier, M., Adams, J., Redwood, D., and Curry, C. (2013) *Tax relief for pension saving in the UK*. London: Pensions Policy Institute.

The Economist (2019) Canada's vast pension fund is gaining even more financial clout. 19 January. Available at: https://www.economist.com/finance-and-economics/2019/01/19/canadas-vast-pension-fund-is-gaining-even-more-financial-clout (accessed 6 August 2019).

Edmund, J. and Turner, B.S. (2005) Global generations: Social change in the twentieth century. *British Journal of Sociology*, 56(4), 559–77.

Engelen, E. (2003) The logic of funding European pension restructuring and the dangers of financialisation. *Environment and Planning A*, 35, 1357–72.

Epstein, G. (2006) Introduction: financialization and the world economy. In: *Financialization and the world economy*, ed G. Epstein. Northampton, MA: Edward Elgar, 3–31.

Espahinda, M. (2019) FCA tells 7 firms to create governance committees. *FT Adviser*, 15 April. Available at: https://www.ftadviser.com/pensions/2019/04/15/fca-tells-7-firms-to-create-governance-committees/ (accessed 1 February 2020).

Espahinda, M. (2020) FCA fined £2k for pension scheme failures. *FT Adviser*, 27 January. Available at: https://www.ftadviser.com/pensions/2020/01/27/fca-fined-2k-for-pension-scheme-failures/ (1 February 2020).

Esping-Andersen, G. (1990) *The three worlds of welfare capitalism*. Princeton, NJ: Princeton University Press.

Esposito, E. (2011) *The future of futures: The time of money in financing and society*. Cheltenham: Edward Elgar.

EU Directorate-General for Internal Policies (2014) Pension schemes. Available at: http://www.europarl.europa.eu/RegData/etudes/STUD/2014/536281/IPOL_STU(2014)536281_EN.pdf (accessed 1 November 2018).

Fastenrath, F., Schwann, M., and Trampusch, C. (2017) Where states and markets meet: The financialisation of sovereign debt management. *New Political Economy*, 22(3), 273–93.

Fernyhough, J. (2017) Britons in multiple jobs miss out on auto-enrolment. *Financial Times*, 22 February. Available at: https://www.ftadviser.com/auto-enrolment/2017/02/22/britons-in-multiple-jobs-miss-out-on-auto-enrolment/ (accessed 1 August 2019).

Fichtner, J. Heemskerk, E., and Leaver, A (2018) If this is capitalism, where are the price signals? The glacial effects of passive investment. *SPERI Comment*. Available at: http://speri.

dept.shef.ac.uk/2018/09/03/if-this-is-capitalism-where-are-the-price-signals-the-glacial-effects-of-passive-investment/ (accessed 1 February 2020).

Fichtner, J., Heemskerk, E., and Petry, J. (2020) Three financial firms could change the direction of the climate crisis—and few people have any idea. *The Conversation*, 24 February. Available at: https://theconversation.com/three-financial-firms-could-change-the-direction-of-the-climate-crisis-and-few-people-have-any-idea-131869 (accessed 25 February 2020).

Financial Conduct Authority (FCA) (2015) *Retirement income market study: Final report—confirmed findings and remedies*. Available at: https://www.fca.org.uk/publication/market-studies/ms14-03-3.pdf (accessed 1 September 2019).

Financial Conduct Authority (FCA) (2016a) *Asset management market study: Interim report*. Available at: https://www.fca.org.uk/publication/market-studies/ms15-2-2-interim-report.pdf (accessed 25 August 2019).

Financial Conduct Authority (FCA) (2016b) *Asset management market study: Interim report, annex 7—fund charges analysis*. Available at: https://www.fca.org.uk/publication/market-studies/ms15-2-2-annex-7.pdf (accessed 25 August 2019).

Financial Conduct Authority (FCA) (2018) *Data bulletin: September 2018*. Available at: https://www.fca.org.uk/publication/data/data-bulletin-issue-14.pdf (accessed 1 September 2019).

Financial Conduct Authority (FCA) (2019) *Publishing and disclosing costs and charges to workplace pension scheme members and amendments to COBS 19.8*. Available at: https://www.fca.org.uk/publication/consultation/cp19-10.pdf (accessed 1 September 2019).

Financial Conduct Authority (FCA) (2020) *Business plan 2020/21*. Available at: https://www.fca.org.uk/publication/business-plans/business-plan-2020-21.pdf (7 April 2020).

Financial Conduct Authority (FCA) and the Pensions Regulator (TPR) (2014) *Guide to the regulation of workplace defined contribution pensions*. Available at: https://www.fca.org.uk/publication/finalised-guidance/workplace-defined-contribution-pensions-guide.pdf (accessed 25 August 2019).

Financial Conduct Authority (FCA) and the Pensions Regulator (TPR) (2018) *Regulating the pensions and retirement income sector*. Available at: https://www.fca.org.uk/publication/corporate/regulating-pensions-retirement-income-sector-our-joint-regulatory-strategy.pdf (accessed 25 August 2019).

Financial Services Consumer Panel (2014) *Investment costs: More than meets the eye*. Available at: https://www.fs-cp.org.uk/sites/default/files/investment_discussion_paper_investment_cost_and_charges.pdf (accessed 25 August 2019).

Financial Times (2015) Fix UK pensions, then no longer fiddle with them. 29 July. Available at: https://www-ft-com.ezproxy.babson.edu/content/45b95806-35e0-11e5-b05b-b01debd57852 (accessed 1 September 2019).

Fink, L. (2020) A fundamental reshaping of finance. Available at: https://www.blackrock.com/uk/individual/larry-fink-ceo-letter (accessed 1 February 2020).

Finlayson, A. (2009) Financialisation, financial literacy and asset-based welfare. *British Journal of Politics and International Relations*, 11, 400–21.

Finnigan, L. (2015) Britons in the workplace: The figures that lay bare the life of an average British employee. *The Telegraph*, 4 November. Available at: https://www.telegraph.co.uk/finance/jobs/11975788/Britons-in-the-workplace-The-figures-that-lay-bare-the-life-of-an-average-British-employee.html (accessed 1 September 2019).

Flood, C. (2019) Japanese pension funds put record amounts into alternatives. *Financial Times*, 5 August. Available at: https://www.ft.com/content/802cbaf6-11c6-3152-b137-f2d58995b274 (accessed 5 August 2019).

Fordham, L. (2016) Government to reduce money purchase annual allowance. *Employee Benefits*, 23 November. Available at: https://www.employeebenefits.co.uk/issues/november-online-2016/government-to-reduce-money-purchase-annual-allowance/ (accessed 9 March 2017).

Foster, L. (2010) Towards a new political economy of pensions? The implications for women. *Critical Social Policy*, 30(1), 27–47.

Foster, L. (2017) Young people and attitudes towards pension planning. *Social Policy and Society*, 16(1), 65–80.

Foster, L. (2018) Active ageing, pensions and retirement in the UK. *Journal of Population Ageing*, 11(2), 117–32.

Foster, L. and Heneghan, M. (2017) Pensions planning in the UK: A gendered challenge. *Critical Social Policy*, 38(2), 345–66.

France, A. (2016) *Understanding youth in the global economic crisis*. Bristol: Policy Press.

Franzen, D. (2010) Managing investment risk in defined benefit pension funds. *OECD Working Papers on Insurance and Private Pensions No.38*. Available at: http://www.oecd.org/pensions/private-pensions/44899253.pdf (accessed 3 March 2017).

Frenkels Forensics (2012) Morrisons launch new auto-enrolment exempt pension scheme. 7 November. Available at: https://frenkels.com/news/morrisons-launch-new-auto-enrolment-exempt-pension-scheme/ (accessed 7 March 2017).

Froud, J., Johal, S., Leaver, A., and Williams, K. (2006) *Financialisation and strategy: Narrative and numbers*. London: Routledge.

Froud, J., Leaver, A., and Williams, K. (2007) New actors in a financialised economy and the remaking of capitalism. *New Political Economy*, 12(3), 339–47.

Furlong, A., Goodwin, J., O'Connor, H., Hadfield, S., Hall, S., Lowden, K., and Plugor, R. (2018) *Young people in the labour market: Past, present, future*. London: Routledge.

Gamble, A. (2014) Austerity as statecraft. *Parliamentary Affairs*, 68(1), 42–57.

Gardiner, L. (2016) *Stagnation generation: The case for renewing the intergenerational contract*. London: Intergenerational Commission.

Giles, C. (2015) Osborne has hit on a better pension plan. *Financial Times*, 15 July. Available at: https://www.ft.com/content/495bed92-294d-11e5-8613-e7aedbb7bdb7 (accessed 1 September 2019).

Gillion, C., Turner, J., Bailey, C., and Latulippe, D. (eds) (2000) *Social security pensions: Development and reform*. Geneva: International Labour Organisation.

Gospel, H. (1992) *Markets, firms, and the management of labour in Britain*. Oxford: Oxford University Press.

Gospel, H., Pendleton, A., and Vitols, S. (eds) (2014) *Financialization, new investment funds, and labour*. Oxford: Oxford University Press.

Gourevitch, P.A. and Shinn, J. (2007) *Political power and corporate control: The new global politics of global governance*. Princeton, NJ: Princeton University Press.

Grady, J. (2015) Gendering pensions: Making women visible. *Gender, Work and Organisation*, 22(5), 445–58.

Grady, J. (2017) The state, employment and regulation: Making work not pay. *Employee Relations*, 29(3), 274–90.

Grady, J. (2018) The USS dispute and the dynamics of industrial action. *Medium*, 3 April. Available at: https://medium.com/ussbriefs/the-uss-dispute-and-the-dynamics-of-industrial-action-85231f4382a8 (accessed 26 April 2019).

Grady, J. (2019) *A manifesto for a modern education union*. Available at: https://grady4gs.files.wordpress.com/2019/04/grady4gs-manifesto-pdf-170420191700.pdf (accessed 26 April 2019).

Grasso, M. (2016) *Generations, political participation and social change in Western Europe*. London: Routledge.

Gray, J., Griffith-Jones, S., and Sandberg, J. (2012) *No exemption: The financial transactions tax and pension funds*. London: Network for Sustainable Financial Markets. Available at: http://www.stephanygj.net/papers/No_Exemption_FTT_Pension_Funds.pdf (accessed 1 April 2020).

Green, A. (2017) *The crisis for young people: Generational inequalities in education, work, housing and welfare*. Basingstoke: Palgrave.

Gregory, A. (undated) The end of the cheapo repo. *Actuarial Post*. Available at: http://www.actuarialpost.co.uk/article/the-end-of-the-cheapo-repo-8500.htm (accessed 1 December 2019).

The Guardian (2012) Pensions: A conspiracy against the public. 7 March. Available at: https://www.theguardian.com/commentisfree/2012/mar/07/pensions-conspiracy-against-public-editorial (accessed 25 August 2019).

The Guardian (2017) New Tata Steel scheme secures pensions for 130,000 workers. 11 August. Available at: https://www.theguardian.com/business/2017/aug/11/tata-steel-set-to-unveil-new-pension-scheme-for-thousands-of-workers (accessed 1 April 2019).

Guardiancich, I. (2012) Poland: Are flexible labour markets ready for individualized pensions? In: *Labour market flexibility and pension reforms flexible today, secure tomorrow?* eds K. Hinrichs and M. Jessoula. Basingstoke: Palgrave, 93–123.

Haberly, D., MacDonald-Korth, D., Urban, M., and Wójcik, D (2019) Asset management as a digital platform industry: A global financial network perspective. *Geoforum*, 106, 167–81.

Hacker, J. (2005) Policy drift: The hidden politics of US welfare state retrenchment. In: *Beyond continuity: Institutional change in advanced political economies*, eds W. Streeck and K. Thelen. Oxford: Oxford University Press, 40–82.

Haiven, M. (2014) *Cultures of financialization: Fictitious capital in popular culture and everyday life*. London: Palgrave.

Haldane, A. (2014) *The age of asset management*. London: Bank of England. Available at: https://www.bankofengland.co.uk/-/media/boe/files/speech/2014/the-age-of-asset-management.pdf?la=en&hash=673A53E92A9EB43E5689ED7BE33628F62C4871F1 (accessed 1 April 2020).

Haldane, A., Goldin, I., Gupta, A., Breeden, S., Davies, P., Gray, R., Hyde-Harrison, M., Mayer, C., O'Neill, J., Palmer, A., Pilcher, S., and Urwin, R. (2014) *Procyclicality and structural trends in investment allocation by insurance companies and pension funds*. London: Bank of England and the Procyclicality Working Group. Available at: https://www.bankofengland.co.uk/-/media/boc/files/paper/2014/procyclicality-and-structural-trends-in-investment (accessed 1 February 2020).

Hall, P. (1993) Policy paradigms, social learning and the state: The case of economic policy-making in Britain. *Comparative Politics*, 25(3), 275–96.

Hall, P. and Soskice, D. (eds) (1999) *Varieties of capitalism: The institutional foundations of comparative advantage*. Oxford: Oxford University Press.

Hannah, L. (1986) *Inventing retirement: The development of occupational pensions in Britain*. Cambridge: Cambridge University Press.

Hanton, A. (2011) *A small number with surprisingly large consequences: Why the government choice of discount rate should interest everyone*. London: Intergenerational Foundation. Available at: http://www.if.org.uk/wp-content/uploads/2014/03/A-Small-Number-with-Surprisingly-Large-Consequences.pdf (accessed 20 September 2018).

Hassel, M., Naczyk, M., and Wiß, T. (2019) The political economy of pensions financialisation: public policy responses to the crisis. *Journal of European Public Policy*, 26(4), 483–500.

Haverland, M. (2007) When the welfare state meets the regulatory state: EU occupational pensions policy. *Journal of European Public Policy*, 14(6), 886–904.

Haves, E. (2020) Pension Schemes Bill HL Bill 5 of 2019–20. *House of Lords Library Briefing Note 2019-0140*.

Hay, C. (1998) Globalisation, welfare retrenchment and the 'logic of no alternative': Why second-best won't do. *Journal of Social Policy*, 27(4), 525–32.

Hay, C. (2006a) Constructivist institutionalism. In: *The Oxford handbook of political institutions*, eds R.A.W. Rhodes, S.A. Binder, and B.A. Rockman. Oxford: Oxford University Press, 56–74.

Hay, C. (2006b) What's globalisation got to do with it? Economic interdependence and the future of European welfare states. *Government and Opposition*, 41(1), 1–22.

Hay, C. (2013) *The failure of Anglo-liberal capitalism*. Basingstoke: Palgrave.

Hay, C. (2019) Does capitalism (still) come in varieties? *Review of International Political Economy*, DOI: 10.1080/09692290.2019.1633382.

Hay, C. and Wincott, D. (1998) Structure, agency and historical institutionalism. *Political Studies*, 46(5), 951–57.

Hay, C. and Wincott, D. (2012) *The political economy of European welfare capitalism*. Basingstoke: Palgrave Macmillan.

Hayes, G. (2019) Pensions industry making 'fat living' from charging savers, MPs claim. *The Guardian*, 5 August. Available at: https://www.theguardian.com/business/2019/aug/05/pensions-industry-making-fat-living-from-charging-savers-mps-claim?CMP=share_btn_link (accessed 1 September 2019).

Hayton, R. (2014) Conservative Party statecraft and the politics of coalition. *Parliamentary Affairs*, 67(1), 6–24.

Hazell, T. (2014) Savers could have lost £230bn in Brown's pensions raid. *FT Adviser*, 7 May. Available at: https://www.ftadviser.com/2014/05/07/opinion/tony-hazell/savers-could-have-lost-bn-in-brown-s-pensions-raid-WTQAjLW5DSRp9HUxwNZN7K/article.html (accessed 9 March 2017).

Henderson, R. (2020) BlackRock attracts record inflows as stock markets soar. *Financial Times*, 15 January. Available at: https://www.ft.com/content/1d727e02-3786-11ea-a6d3-9a26f8c3cba4 (accessed 17 February 2020).

Hennessy, A. (2014) *The Europeanization of workplace pensions: Economic interests, social protection, and credible signalling*. Cambridge: Cambridge University Press.

Hills, J. (2006) A new pensions settlement for the twenty-first century: The UK pensions commission's analysis and proposals. *Oxford Review of Economic Policy*, 22(1), 113–32.

Hinrichs, K. (2012) Germany: A flexible labour market plus pension reforms means poverty in old age. In: *Labour market flexibility and pension reforms flexible today, secure tomorrow?* eds K. Hinrichs and M. Jessoula. Basingstoke: Palgrave, 29–61.

Hinrichs, K. and Jessoula, M. (eds) (2012) *Labour market flexibility and pension reforms flexible today, secure tomorrow?* Basingstoke: Palgrave.

HM Treasury (2004) *Myners principles for institutional investment decision-making: Review of progress*. Available at: https://uksif.org/wp-content/uploads/2012/12/MYNERS-P.-2004-Myners-principles-for-institutional-Investment-Decision-making-review-of-progress.pdf (accessed 1 September 2019).

HM Treasury (2012) *Autumn Statement 2012*. Available at: https://assets.publishing.service.gov.uk/government/uploads/system/uploads/attachment_data/file/221550/autumn_statement_2012_complete.pdf (accessed 1 April 2019).

HM Treasury (2013) *The UK investment management strategy*. Available at: https://assets.publishing.service.gov.uk/government/uploads/system/uploads/attachment_data/file/258952/uk_investment_management_strategy_amended.pdf (accessed 1 September 2019).

HM Treasury (2014a) *Budget 2014: Greater choice in pensions explained*. Available at: https://assets.publishing.service.gov.uk/government/uploads/system/uploads/attachment_data/file/301563/Pensions_fact_sheet_v8.pdf (accessed 1 September 2019).

HM Treasury (2014b) *Freedom and choice in pensions*. Available at: https://assets.publishing.service.gov.uk/government/uploads/system/uploads/attachment_data/file/294795/freedom_and_choice_in_pensions_web_210314.pdf (accessed 1 September 2019).

HM Treasury (2014c) *Freedom and choice in pensions: Government response to the consultation*. Available at: https://assets.publishing.service.gov.uk/government/uploads/system/uploads/attachment_data/file/332714/pensions_response_online.pdf (accessed 1 September 2019).

HM Treasury (2015a) *Budget 2015: Policy costings.* Available at: https://assets.publishing.service.gov.uk/government/uploads/system/uploads/attachment_data/file/413895/Policy_Costings_18_00.pdf (accessed 1 September 2019).

HM Treasury (2015b) *Strengthening the incentive to save: A consultation on pensions tax relief.* Available at: https://assets.publishing.service.gov.uk/government/uploads/system/uploads/attachment_data/file/442160/Strengthening_the_incentive_to_save_consultation__web_.pdf (accessed 1 September 2019).

HM Treasury (2015c) *Strengthening the incentive to save: Summary of responses to the consultation on pensions tax relief.* Available at: https://assets.publishing.service.gov.uk/government/uploads/system/uploads/attachment_data/file/508184/summary_of_responses_to_pensions_tax_relief_consultation_final.pdf (accessed 1 September).

HM Treasury (2017a) *Financing growth in innovative firms.* Available at: https://assets.publishing.service.gov.uk/government/uploads/system/uploads/attachment_data/file/642456/financing_growth_in_innovative_firms_consultation_web.pdf (accessed 1 December 2019).

HM Treasury (2017b) *Financing growth in innovative firms: Consultation response.* Available at: https://assets.publishing.service.gov.uk/government/uploads/system/uploads/attachment_data/file/661398/Patient_Capital_Review_Consultation_response_web.pdf (accessed 1 December 2019).

HM Treasury (2017c) *The UK investment management strategy.* Available at: https://www.ft.com/content/3b681224-8a52-11e8-bf9e-8771d5404543 (accessed 1 September 2019).

HM Treasury (2017d) *Whole of government accounts: 2016/17.* Available at: https://assets.publishing.service.gov.uk/government/uploads/system/uploads/attachment_data/file/720160/WGA_2016-17-print.pdf (accessed 1 April 2019).

HM Treasury (2020) *Budget 2020: Delivering on our promises to the British people.* Available at: https://assets.publishing.service.gov.uk/government/uploads/system/uploads/attachment_data/file/871799/Budget_2020_Web_Accessible_Complete.pdf (accessed 1 February 2020).

HM Treasury and Department for Work and Pensions (2001) *Myners review: Institutional investment in the UK—government response.* Available at: https://webarchive.nationalarchives.gov.uk/20050302010905/http://www.hm-treasury.gov.uk/mediastore/otherfiles/myners_response.pdf (1 September 2019).

HM Treasury and Department for Work and Pensions (2015) *Creating a secondary annuities market.* Available at: https://assets.publishing.service.gov.uk/government/uploads/system/uploads/attachment_data/file/413764/Creating_a_secondary_annuity_market__web_file_.pdf (accessed 1 September 2019).

Holman, D., Foster, L., and Hess, M. (2018) Which women knew about state pension age changes? Inequalities in awareness and their implications. *LSE British Politics and Policy Blog*, 29 August. Available at: https://blogs.lse.ac.uk/politicsandpolicy/state-pension-age-inequalities-in-awareness/ (accessed 1 September 2019).

Holzmann, R. and Hinz, R. (2005) Old age income support in the 21st century: An international perspective on pension systems and reform. Washington, DC: World Bank. Available at: http://siteresources.worldbank.org/INTPENSIONS/Resources/Old_Age_Inc_Supp_Full_En.pdf (accessed 1 November 2018).

Hope, K. (2017) How long should you stay in one job? *BBC News*, 1 February. Available at: https://www.bbc.co.uk/news/business-38828581 (accessed 1 September 2019).

Hopkin, J. and Alexander Shaw, K. (2016) Organized combat or structural advantage? The politics of inequality and the winner-takes-all economy in the United Kingdom. *Politics and Society*, 44(3), 345–71.

Houlder, V. (2017) 'Patient capital' plan could unlock pensions savings limits. *Financial Times*, 24 November. Available at: https://www.ft.com/content/0c48f8f6-d048-11e7-9dbb-291a884dd8c6 (accessed 1 September 2019).

House of Commons Work and Pensions Committee (2016a) *Automatic Enrolment.* Available at: https://publications.parliament.uk/pa/cm201516/cmselect/cmworpen/579/579.pdf (accessed 25 August 2019).

House of Commons Work and Pensions Committee (2016b) *Defined benefit pension schemes.* Available at: https://publications.parliament.uk/pa/cm201617/cmselect/cmworpen/55/55.pdf (accessed 1 April 2019).

House of Commons Work and Pensions Committee (2018a) *Collective defined contribution pensions.* Available at: https://publications.parliament.uk/pa/cm201719/cmselect/cmworpen/580/580.pdf (accessed 1 April 2019).

House of Commons Work and Pensions Committee (2018b) Royal Mail deal could 'transform UK pensions landscape'. Available at: https://www.parliament.uk/business/committees/committees-a-z/commons-select/work-and-pensions-committee/news-parliament-2017/collective-defined-contribution-pensions-report-published17-19-/ (accessed 1 April 2019).

House of Commons Work and Pensions Committee (2019) *Pensions costs and transparency.* Available at: https://publications.parliament.uk/pa/cm201719/cmselect/cmworpen/1476/147602.htm (accessed 1 September 2019).

Hughes, E.A. (2013) NEST admits 99% of cash in default fund. *FT Adviser*, 25 July. Available at: https://www.ftadviser.com/2013/07/25/pensions/personal-pensions/nest-admits-of-cash-in-default-fund-IIQRtWeXRyIohrSDeXjfAM/article.html (accessed 1 February 2020).

Hunter, T. (2015) A turbulent history of British pensions, since 1874. *The Telegraph*, 9 April. Available at: http://www.telegraph.co.uk/finance/personalfinance/special-reports/11523196/A-turbulent-history-of-British-pensions-since-1874.html (accessed 9 March 2017).

Hutton, W. (1995) *The state we're in.* London: Random House.

Hutton, W. (2014) Osborne's pensions 'freedom' will spell long-term social disaster. *The Observer*, 22 March. Available at: https://www.theguardian.com/commentisfree/2014/mar/22/osborne-budget-annuities-decision-disaster (accessed 1 September 2019).

Hyde, D. (2014) True cost of Labour's pension tax raid (and others since seventies). *The Telegraph*, 30 April. Available at: http://www.telegraph.co.uk/finance/personalfinance/pensions/10798785/True-cost-of-Labours-pension-tax-raid-and-others-since-Seventies.html (accessed 9 March 2017).

Independent Public Service Pensions Commission (2011) *Final Report.* Available at: https://www.gov.uk/government/publications/independent-public-service-pensions-commission-final-report-by-lord-hutton (accessed 1 April 2019).

Inderst, G. (2009) Pension fund investment in infrastructure. *OECD Working Papers on Insurance and Private Pensions No.32.* Available at: https://www.oecd-ilibrary.org/finance-and-investment/pension-fund-investment-in-infrastructure_227416754242 (accessed 1 September 2019).

Inderst, G. and Croce, R.D. (2013) Pension fund investment in infrastructure: A comparison between Australia and Canada. *OECD Working Papers on Finance, Insurance and Private Pensions No.32.* Available at: https://www.oecd.org/pensions/pensionfundinfrastructureaustraliacanada2013.pdf (accessed 1 September 2019).

Inman, P. (2006) Government to back away from Turner's vision of state-sponsored scheme. *The Guardian*, 5 April. Available at: https://www.theguardian.com/business/2006/apr/05/politics.money (accessed 25 August 2019).

Institute for Government (2010) Pensions Commission policy reunion. Available at: https://www.instituteforgovernment.org.uk/sites/default/files/policy_seminar_report_pensions_commission.pdf (accessed 1 August 2019).

Institute for Government (2011) Pensions reform: The Pensions Commission (2002–06). Available at: www.instituteforgovernment.org.uk/sites/defualt/files/pension_reform.pdf (accessed 9 March 2017).

Investment Association (2019) *Investment management in the UK 2018/19.* Available at: https://www.theia.org/sites/default/files/2019-09/IMS%20full%20report%202019.pdf (accessed 1 December 2019).

Investment Management Association (2010) *Asset management in the UK 2009/10.* Available at: https://www.theia.org/sites/default/files/2019-05/20100726-imaams.pdf (accessed 1 December 2019).

Investment Management Association (2013) *Asset management in the UK 2012/13.* Available at: https://www.theia.org/sites/default/files/2019-05/20130806-IMA2012-2013AMS.pdf (accessed 1 December 2019).

Jaiswal, S. (2018) Connections and conflicts of interest: Investment consultants' recommendations. Available at: https://papers.ssrn.com/sol3/papers.cfm?abstract_id=3106528 (accessed 1 February 2020).

Jessoula, M. (2012) A risky combination in Italy: 'Selective flexibility' and defined contributions pensions'. In: *Labour market flexibility and pension reforms flexible today, secure tomorrow?* eds K. Hinrichs and M. Jessoula. Basingstoke: Palgrave, 62–92.

Johnson, B. (2014a) A citizens' wealth fund would create billions for investment. *The Telegraph,* 5 October. Available at: https://www.telegraph.co.uk/finance/personalfinance/pensions/11142293/A-Citizens-Wealth-Fund-would-create-billions-for-investment.html (accessed 1 December 2019).

Johnson, B. (2014b) The Lamborghini ride that says: Power to the people. *The Telegraph,* 23 March. Available at: https://www.telegraph.co.uk/finance/personalfinance/pensions/10717846/Budget-2014-the-Lamborghini-ride-that-says-power-to-the-people.html (accessed 1 September 2019).

Johnson, M. (2019) Tackling intergenerational inequity at its roots. *BrightBlue,* 25 February. Available at: https://brightblue.org.uk/tackling-intergenerational-inequity-at-its-roots/ (accessed 1 April 2019).

Johnson, P. (2018) Britain's taxation system is an inefficient mess. *Financial Times,* 13 August. Available at: https://www.ft.com/content/268a33d8-9ed3-11e8-b196-da9d6c239ca8 (accessed 1 September 2019).

Johnson, P., Yeandle, D., and Boulding, A. (2010) *Making Automatic Enrolment Work: A Review for the Department for Work and Pensions.* Department for Work and Pensions. Available at: https://assets.publishing.service.gov.uk/government/uploads/system/uploads/attachment_data/file/214585/cp-oct10-full-document.pdf (accessed 24 August 2020).

Jones, R. (2014) Honor Blackman to rejoin Equitable Life compensation protestors. *The Guardian,* 21 October. Available at: https://www.theguardian.com/money/2014/oct/21/honor-blackman-equitable-life-demonstrators-compensation (accessed 9 March 2017).

Jones, R. (2017) Government pension scheme begins ditching oil and gas investments. *The Guardian,* 24 February. Available at: https://www.theguardian.com/money/2017/feb/24/government-pension-scheme-ditching-oil-gas-investments-shell-exxonmobil (accessed 24 August 2020).

Joyce, M., Liu, Z., and Tonks, I. (2014) Institutional investor portfolio allocation, quantitative easing and the global financial crisis. *Bank of England Working Paper No. 510.* Available at: https://www.bankofengland.co.uk/-/media/boe/files/working-paper/2014/institutional-investor-portfolio-allocation-quantitative-easing-and-the-global-financial-crisis (accessed 1 November 2018).

Kay, J. (2012) *The Kay review of UK equity markets and long-term decision making: Final report.* London: Department for Business, Innovation and Skills. Available at: https://assets.publishing.service.gov.uk/government/uploads/system/uploads/attachment_data/file/253454/bis-12-917-kay-review-of-equity-markets-final-report.pdf (accessed 1 September 2019).

Keating, C. (2010) *Don't stop thinking about tomorrow: The future of pensions.* London: Long Finance. Available at: http://archive.longfinance.net/Publications/Future%20Of%20Pensions.pdf (accessed 1 March 2017).

Keating, C. (2011) *Don't stop believing: The state and future of UK occupational pensions*. London: Long Finance. Available at: https://www.longfinance.net/publications/long-finance-reports/dont-stop-believing-the-state-and-future-of-uk-occupational-pensions/ (accessed 1 March 2017).

Keating, C., Settergren, O., and Slater, A. (2013) *Keep your lid on: A financial analyst's view of the cost and valuation of DB pension provision*. London: Long Finance. Available at: https://www.longfinance.net/media/documents/Keep_your_lid_on_feb2013.pdf (accessed 1 March 2017).

Keeley, B. and Love, P. (2010) *From crisis to recovery: The causes, course and consequences of the great recession*. Paris: OECD Publishing. Available at: https://www.oecd-ilibrary.org/finance-and-investment/from-crisis-to-recovery_9789264077072-en (accessed 6 August 2019).

Konings, M. (2018) *Capital and time: For a new critique of neoliberal reason*. Stanford, CA: Stanford University Press.

Kopf, E.W. (1927) The early history of the annuity. *Proceedings of the Casualty Actuarial Society*, 13(27–8), 225–6. Available at: https://www.casact.org/pubs/proceed/proceed26/ (accessed 9 March 2017).

Kowske, B., Rasch, R., and Wiley, J. (2010) Millennials' (lack of) attitude problem: An empirical examination of generational effects on work attitudes. *Journal of Business and Psychology*, 25, 265–79.

KPMG (2016) Paradise postponed: Long-term impacts of the pension freedoms. Available at: https://home.kpmg.com/uk/en/home/insights/2016/01/paradise-postponed-prospects-for-the-pension-industry.html (accessed 9 March 2017).

Lain, D., Vickerstaff, S., and Loretto, W. (2013) Reforming state pension provision in 'liberal' Anglo-Saxon countries: Re-commodification, cost-containment or recalibration. *Social Policy and Society*, 12(1), 77–90.

Lamborghini Media Center (2019) Record figures take Automobili Lamborghini to a new level: 5,750 cars delivered in 2018. 10 January. Available at: https://media.lamborghini.com/english/latest-news/record-figures-take-automobili-lamborghini-to-a-new-level-5-750-cars-delivered-in-2018/s/2da49ad6-608a-4a1b-8711-370c47356528 (accessed 1 September 2019).

Lamont, D. (2020) Three charts that show how the coronavirus has hurt pension schemes. *Schroders*, 13 March. Available at: https://www.schroders.com/en/uk/pensions/insights/markets/three-charts-that-show-how-the-coronavirus-has-hurt-pension-schemes/ (accessed 1 April 2020).

Langley, P. (2004) In the eye of the 'perfect storm': The final salary pensions crisis and financialisation of Anglo-American capitalism. *New Political Economy*, 9(4), 539–58.

Langley, P. (2006) The making of investor subjects in Anglo-American pensions. *Environment and Planning Part D: Society and Space*, 24(6), 919–34.

Langley, P. (2008) *The everyday life of global finance: saving and borrowing in Anglo-America*. Oxford: Oxford University Press.

Langley, P. and Leaver, A. (2012) Remaking retirement investors: Behavioural economics and defined-contribution occupational pensions. *Journal of Cultural Economy*, 5(4), 473–88.

Langley, P. and Leyshon, A. (2017) Platform capitalism: The intermediation and capitalisation of digital economic circulation. *Finance and Society*, 3(1), 11–31.

Lapavitsas, C. (2013) The financialization of capitalism: 'Profiting without producing'. *City: Analysis of Urban Trends, Culture, Theory, Policy, Action*, 17(6), 792–805.

Lavery, S. (2019) *British capitalism after the crisis*. London: Palgrave.

The Law Commission (2012) *Fiduciary duties of investment intermediaries*. Available at: https://www.lawcom.gov.uk/project/fiduciary-duties-of-investment-intermediaries/ (accessed 1 September 2019).

LCP (2013) *Accounting for Pensions 2013*. Available at: https://www.lcp.uk.com/media/636443/lcp_afp2013_interactivepdf.pdf (accessed 1 March 2017).

LCP (2017) *Accounting for Pensions 2017*. Available at: https://www.lcp.uk.com/pensions-benefits/publications/accounting-for-pensions-2017/ (accessed 1 March 2017).

Leaver, A. (2018a) Out of time: The fragile temporality of Carillion's accumulation model. *SPERI Comment*, 17 January. Available at: http://speri.dept.shef.ac.uk/2018/01/17/out-of-time-the-fragile-temporality-of-carillions-accumulation-model/ (accessed 20 January 2018).

Leaver, A. (2018b) Outsourcing firms and the paradox of time travel. *SPERI Comment*, 12 February. Available at http://speri.dept.shef.ac.uk/2018/02/12/outsourcing-firms-and-the-paradox-of-time-travel/ (accessed 1 April 2019).

Leslie, C. and Umunna, C. (2011) Changing the culture: New rules to support British business at its best. In: *Stewardship and the stakeholder economy: Perspectives on the role of shareholder engagement in the UK economy*, ed. Pensions and Investment Research Consultants, 1–2. Available at: http://pirc.co.uk/news-and-resources2/files/Stewardship_and_the_stakeholder_economy.pdf (accessed 1 September 2018).

Lewin, C. and Sweeney, E. (2007) *Deregulatory review of private pensions: An independent report to the Department for Work and Pensions*. London: Department for Work and Pensions. Available at: https://webarchive.nationalarchives.gov.uk/20130125095551/http://dwp.gov.uk/docs/reviewpaperjuly2007.pdf (accessed 7 March 2017).

Leyshon, A. and Thrift, N. (2009) The capitalisation of almost everything: The future of finance and capitalism. *Theory, Culture and Society*, 24(7–8), 97–115.

Lindley, D. (2014) *Dashboards and jam-jars: Helping consumers with small defined contribution pension pots make decisions about retirement income*. London: Age UK.

Little, B. (ed.) (2010) *Radical future: Politics for the next generation*. London: Lawrence and Wishart.

Little, B. (2014) A growing discontent: Class and generation under neoliberalism. In: *After Neoliberalism: The Kilburn Manifesto*, eds S. Hall, D. Massey, and M. Rustin. London: Lawrence and Wishart, 27–40.

Little, B. and Winch, A. (2017a) Generation: The politics of patriarchy and social change. *Soundings*, 66, 129–44.

Little, B. and Winch, A. (2017b) Why the idea of 'generation' needs to be articulated more carefully in politics. *LSE British Politics and Policy Blog*, 10 October. Available at: http://blogs.lse.ac.uk/politicsandpolicy/generation-in-political-discourse/ (accessed 1 June 2018).

Lowe, J. (2014) *Whither UK annuities: Why lifetime annuities should still be part of good financial advice in the post-pension-liberalisation world*. Available at: https://ilcuk.org.uk/wp-content/uploads/2018/10/ILC-Whither-annuities-2.pdf (accessed 1 September 2019).

Mabbett, D. (2012) The ghost in the machine: Pension risks and regulatory responses in the United States and the United Kingdom. *Politics and Society*, 40(1), 107–29.

Mabbett, D. (2020) Reckless prudence: Financialization in UK pension scheme governance after the crisis. *Review of International Political Economy*. Available at: https://www.tandfonline.com/doi/full/10.1080/09692290.2020.1758187 (accessed 7 May 2020).

Mackenzie, G.A.(S.) (2010) *The decline of the traditional pension: A comparative study of threats to retirement security*. Cambridge: Cambridge University Press.

Macnicol, J. (2015) *Neooliberalising old age*. Cambridge: Cambridge University Press.

Maer, L. and Thurley, D. (2009) Defined benefit pension schemes. *House of Commons Library Standard Note BT/1759*. Available at: http://researchbriefings.parliament.uk/ResearchBriefing/Summary/SN01759#fullreport (accessed 9 March 2017).

Malik, S. and Howker, E. (2010) *Jilted generation: How Britain has bankrupted its youth*. London: Icon.

Mander, B. (2016) Chile pension reform comes under world spotlight. *Financial Times*, 12 September. Available at: https://www.ft.com/content/b9293586-7680-11e6-bf48-b372cdb1043a (accessed 6 August 2019).

Mannheim, K. (1952) *Essays on the sociology of knowledge*. Oxford: Oxford University Press.

Marx, K. (1852) *The eighteenth Brumaire of Louis Bonaparte*. Available at: https://www.marxists.org/archive/marx/works/download/pdf/18th-Brumaire.pdf (accessed 15 August 2018).

Marx, K. (1970 [1843]) *The German ideology*. London: Lawrence and Wishart.

McCarthy, M.A. (2014) Neoliberalism without neoliberals: evidence from the rise of 401(k) retirement plans. *MPIfG Discussion Paper 14/12*. Available at: https://www.mpifg.de/pu/mpifg_dp/dp14-12.pdf (accessed 28 August 2020).

McCarthy, M.A. (2017) *Dismantling solidarity: Capitalist politics and American pensions since the New Deal*. Ithaca, NY: Cornell University Press.

McCarthy, M.A., Sorsa, V.P., and van der Zwan, N. (2016) Investment preferences and patient capital: Financing, governance, and regulation in pension fund capitalism. *Socio-Economic Review*, 14(4), 751–69.

McClymont, G. and Tarrant, A. (2013) *Pensions at work, that work: Completing the unfinished pensions revolution*. London: Fabian Society.

Meeks, G. (2017) Understanding pension obligation figures (although your boss might not want you to). *LSE British Politics and Policy Blog*, 15 September. Available at: https://blogs.lse.ac.uk/politicsandpolicy/understanding-pension-obligation-figures/ (accessed 1 December 2019).

Meyer, T., Bridgen, P., and Riedmüller, B. (eds) (2007) *Private pensions versus social inclusion: Non-state provision for citizens at risk in Europe*. London: Edward Elgar.

Milburn, K. (2019) *Generation Left*. Cambridge: Polity.

Millar, J. (2002) Diminishing welfare: The case of the UK. In: *Diminishing welfare: A cross-national study of social provision*, eds G. Schaffer Goldberg and M. Rosenthal. New York: Praeger, 149–80.

Montgomerie, J. (2008) Bridging the critical divide: Global finance, financialisation and contemporary capitalism. *Contemporary Politics*, 14(3), 233–52.

Mooney, A. (2017) Asset managers turn against investment consultants. *Financial Times*, 26 February. Available at: https://www.ft.com/content/95bf65de-f934-11e6-bd4e-68d53499ed71 (accessed 1 December 2019).

Mooney, A. (2018) UK's investment consultants avoid forced break up. *Financial Times*, 18 July. Available at: https://www.ft.com/content/3b681224-8a52-11e8-bf9e-8771d5404543 (accessed 1 December 2019).

Moore, E. (2016) Bank of England bond-buying programme hits trouble. *Financial Times*, 9 August. Available at: https://www.ft.com/content/681cc244-5e2e-11e6-bb77-a121aa8abd95 (accessed 1 December 2019).

Moore, E. and Cumbo, J. (2016) Fears for pensions as gilt yields turn negative. *Financial Times*, 16 August. Available at: https://www.ft.com/content/c338f3c0-5ed6-11e6-a72a-bd4bf1198c63 (accessed 1 December 2019).

Moore, P.V. (2017) *The quantified self in precarity: Work, technology and what counts*. London: Routledge.

Moreolo, C.S. (2016) Liability-driven investment: Time to review LDI approaches. *Investment and Pension Europe*, June. Available at: https://www.ipe.com/reports/special-reports/liability-driven-investment/special-report-liability-driven-investment-time-to-review-ldi-approaches/10013534.article (accessed 1 December 2019).

Morris, P. and Palmer, A. (2011) *You're on your own: How policy produced Britain's pensions crisis*. London: Civitas.

Moynihan, J. (2018) The slow death of the public-sector pension. *The Spectator*, 6 January. Available at: https://www.spectator.co.uk/2018/01/the-slow-death-of-the-public-sector-pension/ (accessed 1 April 2019).

Munnell, A.H. (2018) United States. In: *Towards a new pensions settlement: The international experience* (Vol. 2), eds G. McClymont and A. Tarrant. London: Policy Network, 13–22.

Murdoch, S. and Duran, P. (2019) Australian pension funds' $168 billion 'wall of cash' may lead overseas. *Reuters*, 10 September. Available at: https://uk.reuters.com/article/us-australia-funds-pensions/australian-pension-funds-168-billion-wall-of-cash-may-lead-overseas-idUKKCN1VV07S (accessed 12 September 2019).

Murphy, R. (2010) *Making pensions work*. London: Finance for the Future. Available at: http://openaccess.city.ac.uk/id/eprint/16570/1/MakingPensionsWork.pdf (accessed 1 October 2019).

Murphy, R. (2015) Putting the fundamental pension contract at the heart of our macroeconomy. *Tax Research*, 26 August. Available at: https://www.taxresearch.org.uk/Blog/2015/08/26/putting-the-fundamental-pension-contract-at-the-heart-of-our-macroeconomy/ (accessed 25 May 2020).

Myners, P. (2001) *Institutional investment in the United Kingdom: A review*. London: HM Treasury. Available at: https://webarchive.nationalarchives.gov.uk/20010603090552/http://www.hm-treasury.gov.uk:80/pdf/2001/myners_report.pdf (accessed 1 September 2019).

Naczyk, M. (2016) Poland. In: *Towards a new pensions settlement: The international experience*, eds G. McClymont and A. Tarrant. London: Policy Network, 53–8.

Naczyk, M. and Domonkos, P. (2016) The financial crisis and varieties of pension privatization reversals in Easter Europe. *Governance*, 29(2), 167–84.

Naczyk, M. and Hassel, A. (2019) Insuring individuals...and politicians: Financial services providers, stock market risk and the politics of private pension guarantees in Germany. *Journal of European Public Policy*, 26(4), 579–98.

NAPF (2011) *Quantitative easing: The pension scheme perspective*. Available at: https://www.plsa.co.uk/portals/0/Documents/0197_Quantitative_Easing_the_pension_scheme_perspective.pdf (accessed 1 April 2019).

NAPF (2015) *Guide to responsible investment reporting in public equity*. Available at: https://www.plsa.co.uk/Policy-and-Research/Document-library/Guide-to-Responsible-Investment-reporting-in-Public-Equity-Published (accessed 1 December 2019).

NAPF, TUC, and CBI (2014) Letter to Steve Webb on Directive on Institutions for Occupational Retirement Provision. Available at: https://www.plsa.co.uk/portals/0/Documents/0386-NAPF-CBI-TUC-letter-to-Steve-Webb.pdf (accessed 3 April 2019).

Natali, D. (2011) Pensions after the financial and economic crisis: A comparative analysis of recent reforms in Europe. *ETUI Working Paper 2011/07*. Available at: https://www.etui.org/Publications2/Working-Papers/Pensions-after-the-financial-and-economic-crisis-a-comparative-analysis-of-recent-reforms-in-Europe (accessed 6 August 2019).

National Audit Office (2019) *Help to buy: Equity loan scheme—progress review*. Available at: https://www.nao.org.uk/report/help-to-buy-equity-loan-scheme-progress-review/ (accessed 1 August 2019).

Nauman, B. (2020) How passive investment dulls the green wave. *Financial Times*, 7 February. Available at: https://www.ft.com/content/abd2a946-48d5-11ea-aee2-9ddbdc86190d (accessed 17 February 2020).

Nesbitt, S. (1995) *British pensions policy making in the 1980s*. Aldershot: Avesbury.

NEST (2018) *Corporate plan 2018–2021*. London: NEST Corporation.

Newell, H. (2005) Pensions Commission issues final report. *Eurofound*, 20 December. Available at: https://www.eurofound.europa.eu/publications/article/2005/pensions-commission-issues-final-report (accessed 1 August 2019).

Ng, E., Schweitzer, L., and Lyons, S. (2010) New generation, great expectations: A field study of the millennial generation. *Journal of Business and Psychology*, 25(2), 281–92.

Nolan, P. (2018) New Zealand. In: *Towards a new pensions settlement: The international experience* (Vol. 2), eds G. McClymont and A. Tarrant. London: Policy Network, 55–62.

O'Brien, C. (2013) *Annuities: A complex market for consumers*. Nottingham: Centre for Risk, Banking and Financial Services. Available at: https://www.nottingham.ac.uk/business/businesscentres/gcbfi/documents/crbfs-reports/crbfs-paper5.pdf (accessed 1 September 2019).

O'Brien, P. and Pike, A. (2017) The financialisation and governance of infrastructure. In: *Handbook of the geographies of money and finance*, eds R. Martin and J. Pollard. Aldershot: Edward Elgar, 223–52.

O'Brien, P., O'Neill, P., and Pike, A. (2019) Funding, financing and governing urban infrastructures. *Urban Studies*, 56, 7, 1291–303.

OECD (2008) *Pension markets in focus: Issue 5*. Available at: http://www.oecd.org/daf/fin/private-pensions/41770561.pdf (accessed 1 November 2018).

OECD (2012) *Pensions Outlook 2012*. Available at: https://www.oecd-ilibrary.org/finance-and-investment/oecd-pensions-outlook-2012_9789264169401-en (accessed 1 November 2018).

OECD (2014a) *Pensions at a glance: Latin America and the Caribbean*. Available at: https://doi.org/10.1787/pension_glance-2014-en (accessed 6 August 2019).

OECD (2014b) *Review of pension systems: Ireland*. Available at: https://read.oecd-ilibrary.org/social-issues-migration-health/oecd-reviews-of-pension-systems-ireland_9789264208834-en#page3 (accessed 6 August 2019).

OECD (2016a) Pensions outlook 2016. Available at: https://www.oecd-ilibrary.org/finance-and-investment/oecd-pensions-outlook-2016_pens_outlook-2016-en (accessed 1 November 2018).

OECD (2016b) The OECD roadmap for the good design of defined contribution pension plans. Available at: https://www.oecd.org/finance/private-pensions/50582753.pdf (accessed 1 November 2018).

OECD (2017) *Pensions at a glance 2017*. Available at: http://www.oecd.org/publications/oecd-pensions-at-a-glance-19991363.htm (accessed 1 November 2018).

OECD (2018) *Pensions outlook 2018*. Available at: http://www.oecd.org/finance/oecd-pensions-outlook-23137649.htm (accessed 1 November 2018).

Office of Fair trading (2013) *Defined contribution workplace pension market study*. Available at: https://webarchive.nationalarchives.gov.uk/20131101172428/http://oft.gov.uk/shared_oft/market-studies/oft1505 (accessed 25 August 2019).

Office for National Statistics (ONS) (2013) *Pension trends: Private pensions, 2013*. Available at: https://www.ons.gov.uk/economy/investmentspensionsandtrusts/compendium/pensiontrends/2014-11-28/chapter6privatepensions2013edition#participation-in-private-pensions (accessed 1 April 2019).

Office for National Statistics (ONS) (2014) *Pension trends: Pensions scheme membership, 2014*. Available at: https://www.ons.gov.uk/economy/investmentspensionsandtrusts/compendium/pensiontrends/2014-11-28/chapter7pensionschememembership2014edition (accessed 7 March 2017).

Office for National Statistics (ONS) (2018a) *Occupational pension schemes survey 2018*. Available at: https://www.ons.gov.uk/peoplepopulationandcommunity/personalandhouseholdfinances/pensionssavingsandinvestments/datasets/occupationalpensionschemessurvey (accessed 1 April 2019).

Office for National Statistics (ONS) (2018b) *Shortcomings of the retail price index as a measure of inflation*. Available at: https://www.ons.gov.uk/economy/inflationandpriceindices/articles/shortcomingsoftheretailpricesindexasameasureofinflation/2018-03-08 (accessed 1 April 2019).

Office for National Statistics (ONS) (2018c) *Trends in self-employment in the UK*. Available at: https://www.ons.gov.uk/employmentandlabourmarket/peopleinwork/employmentandemployeetypes/articles/trendsinselfemploymentintheuk/2018-02-07 (accessed 3 April 2019).

Office for National Statistics (ONS) (2019) *Public sector employment: March 2019*. Available at: https://www.ons.gov.uk/employmentandlabourmarket/peopleinwork/publicsectorpersonnel/datasets/publicsectoremploymentreferencetable (accessed 1 April 2019).

O'Neill, P. (2013) The financialisation of infrastructure: The role of categorisation and property relations. *Cambridge Journal of Regions, Economy and Society*, 6, 3, 441–54.

Opperman, G. (2018) *Answer to written question 135025*. Available at: https://www.parliament.uk/business/publications/written-questions-answers-statements/written-question/Commons/2018-03-29/135025/ (accessed 1 September 2019).

Opperman, G. (2019a) It's your future, so don't let retirement savings go to seed. *The Sunday Times*, 15 September. Available at: https://www.thetimes.co.uk/edition/money/pensions-minister-its-your-future-so-dont-let-retirement-savings-go-to-seed-tllvvm2db (accessed 20 September 2019).

Opperman, G. (2019b) The future of pensions is easy—and fast. *The Sunday Times*, 21 July. Available at: https://www.thetimes.co.uk/article/guy-opperman-the-future-of-pensions-is-easy-and-fast-lplmvrm3g (accessed 20 September 2019).

Osborne, G. (2014) Pensions. *Written Ministerial Statement*, 21 July. Available at: https://assets.publishing.service.gov.uk/government/uploads/system/uploads/attachment_data/file/332674/21_July_pensions_final_WMS__C_.pdf (accessed 1 September 2019).

Osborne, G. (2015a) Budget speech, delivered on 8 July. Available at: https://www.gov.uk/government/speeches/chancellor-george-osbornes-summer-budget-2015-speech (accessed 1 September 2019).

Osborne, G. (2015b) It's right you have this new pension freedom—after all, it is YOUR money. *This Is Money*, 22 March. Available at: https://www.thisismoney.co.uk/money/pensionfree/article-3004305/GEORGE-OSBORNE-s-right-new-pension-freedom-money.html (accessed 1 September 2019).

Parfitt, C. (2018) Contradictions of financialised neoliberalism: The contemporary practice of responsible investment. *Journal of Sociology*, 54(1), 64–76.

Pemberton, H. (2010) 'What matters is what works': Labour's journey from 'national superannuation' to 'personal accounts'. *British Politics*, 5(1), 41–64.

Pemberton, H. (2017) The Fowler Inquiry into Provision for Retirement and the 1986 personal pensions revolution: A short summary. Paper presented at The Fowler Inquiry and the 1986 Personal Pensions Revolution, workshop held at Institute of Actuaries, London, 6 December. Available at: https://research-information.bristol.ac.uk/files/139514538/Briefing_note_short_v2.pdf (accessed 6 December 2018).

Pemberton, H. (2018) UK pensions: The making and breaking of a welfare consensus. In: *The state of welfare: Comparative studies of the welfare state at the end of the long boom 1965–1980*, eds E. Eklund, M. Oppenheimer, and J. Scott. Oxford: Peter Lang, 17–38.

Pendleton, A. and Gospel, H. (2017) Financialization, labor and pensions: The UK experience. In: *The Contradictions of Pension Fund Capitalism*, eds K. Skerrett, J. Weststar, S. Archer, and C. Roberts. Champaign, IL: Labour and Employment Research Association, 9–29.

Pension PlayPen (2016) Measures of support: How users rate workplace pension providers. Available at: https://www.pensionplaypen.com/download-file/8063d41c28f527ef12772884
07d0a402 (accessed 9 March 2017).

Pension Protection Fund (2010) *The purple book: DB pensions universe risk profile*. Available at: https://www.ppf.co.uk/sites/default/files/file-2018-11/purple_book_2010.pdf (accessed 1 April 2019).

Pension Protection Fund (2018) *The purple book: DB pensions universe risk profile*. Available at: https://www.ppf.co.uk/sites/default/files/file-2018-12/the_purple_book_web_dec_18_2.pdf (accessed 1 April 2019).

Pension Protection Fund (2019) *The purple book: DB pensions universe risk profile*. Available at: https://www.ppf.co.uk/sites/default/files/2020-01/Purple%20Book%202019.pdf (accessed 1 February 2020).

The Pensions Commission (2004) Pensions: Challenges and choice—the first report of the Pensions Commission. Available at: https://www.webarchive.org.uk/wayback/archive/20070802120000/http://www.pensionscommission.org.uk/publications/2004/annrep/index.html (accessed 9 March 2017).

The Pensions Commission (2005) A new pension settlement for the twenty-first century—the second report of the Pensions Commission. Available at: https://www.webarchive.org.uk/wayback/archive/20070802120000/http://www.pensionscommission.org.uk/publications/2005/annrep/annrep-index.html (accessed 9 March 2017).

The Pensions Commission (2006) The final report of the Pensions Commission. Available at: https://www.webarchive.org.uk/wayback/archive/20070802120000/http://www.pensionscommission.org.uk/publications/2006/final-report/index.html (accessed 9 March 2016).

Pensions Policy Institute (2016) *Defined benefits: today and tomorrow*. Available at: https://www.pensionspolicyinstitute.org.uk/media/1355/201612-bn86-db-today-and-tomorrow.pdf (accessed 24 August 2020).

Pensions Policy Institute (2019) *The DC future book: 2019 edition*. Available at: https://www.pensionspolicyinstitute.org.uk/media/3270/20190919-the-dc-future-book-2019.pdf (accessed 1 December 2019).

The Pensions Regulator (TPR) (2017a) *Protecting workplace pensions*. Available at: https://www.thepensionsregulator.gov.uk/-/media/thepensionsregulator/files/import/pdf/tpr-future-protecting-workplace-pensions.ashx (accessed 1 April 2019).

The Pensions Regulator (TPR) (2017b) *Regulatory intervention report issued under Section 89 of the Pensions Act 2004 in relation to the BHS pension schemes*. Available at: https://www.thepensionsregulator.gov.uk/-/media/thepensionsregulator/files/import/pdf/regulatory-intervention-section-89-bhs.ashx?la=en&hash=59A0380CACEFD9D193ABEF4B1FD19C EC32514E71 (accessed 1 April 2019).

The Pensions Regulator (TPR) (2018a) *Code of practice 15: Authorisation and supervision of master trusts*. Available at: https://www.thepensionsregulator.gov.uk/en/document-library/codes-of-practice/code-15-authorisation-and-supervision-of-master-trusts (accessed 25 August 2019).

The Pensions Regulator (TPR) (2018b) Guidance for DC superfunds. Available at: https://www.tpr.gov.uk/en/document-library/regulatory-guidance/db-superfunds (accessed 1 April 2019).

The Pensions Regulator (TPR) (2018c) Guidance for employers considering transferring to a DB superfund. Available at: https://www.thepensionsregulator.gov.uk/en/employers/managing-a-scheme/transfer-your-db-scheme-to-a-superfund?_ga=2.18828731.348612830.1568715415-755297763.1568715415 (accessed 1 April 2019).

The Pensions Regulator (TPR) (2018d) *Understanding DB pension scheme funding*. Available at: https://www.thepensionsregulator.gov.uk/-/media/thepensionsregulator/files/import/pdf/understanding-db-_scheme-funding.ashx (accessed 1 December 2019).

The Pensions Regulator (TPR) (2019a) *The current master trust market*. Available at: https://www.thepensionsregulator.gov.uk/-/media/thepensionsregulator/files/import/pdf/master-trust-monthly-report.ashx (accessed 19 July 2020).

The Pensions Regulator (TPR) (2019b) TPR lifts the bonnet on default investment governance. Available at: https://www.thepensionsregulator.gov.uk/en/media-hub/press-releases/tpr-lifts-the-bonnet-on-default-investment-governance (accessed 1 February 2020).

Peters, A. (2018) Insurers compete with fund managers for lucrative pension pots. *Financial Times*, 16 January. Available at: https://www.ft.com/content/db461f6e-d695-11e7-8c9a-d9c0a5c8d5c9 (accessed 3 April 2019).

Petry, J., Fichtner, J., and Heemskerk, E. (2019) Steering capital: The growing private authority of index providers in the age of passive asset management. *Review of International Political Economy*, DOI: 10.1080/09692290.2019.1699147.

Pfeuti, E. (2016) Repo revolution needed for pension funds. *Financial News London*, 7 March. Available at: https://www.fnlondon.com/articles/pension-funds-opt-for-peer-to-peer-repo-alternatives-20160307 (accessed 1 December 2019).

Phillipson, C. (2013) *Ageing*. Cambridge: Polity.

Piachaud, D., Macnicol, J., and Lewis, J. (2009) A thinkpiece on intergenerational equity. *Equality and Human Rights Commission.* Available at: http://justageing.equalityhuman-rights.com/wp-content/uploads/2009/09/Intergenerational-Equality.pdf (accessed 13 June 2018).

Pickard, J. and Cumbo, J. (2016) Treasury abandons flagship Osborne reform on pensions. *Financial Times,* 18 October. Available at: https://www.ft.com/content/b694ca06-9557-11e6-a1dc-bdf38d484582 (accessed 1 September 2019).

Pierson, P. (1994) *Dismantling the welfare state? Reagan, Thatcher, and the politics and retrenchment.* Cambridge: Cambridge University Press.

Pilcher, J. (1995) *Age and generation in modern Britain.* Oxford: Oxford University Press.

Pitt-Watson, D. and Mann, H. (2012) *Collective pensions in the UK.* RSA. Available at: https://www.thersa.org/globalassets/pdfs/reports/collective-pensions-in-the-uk.pdf (accessed 7 March 2017).

Plimmer, G. (2014) UK Cabinet Office 'nudge' team to be spun off into private group. *Financial Times,* 5 February. Available at: https://www.ft.com/content/571eef16-8d99-11e3-9dbb-00144feab7de (accessed 1 August 2019).

PLSA (2017) *DB taskforce: Opportunities for change.* Available at: https://www.plsa.co.uk/Portals/0/Documents/Policy-Documents/2017/DB-Taskforce-third-report-Opportunities-for-Change.pdf (accessed 8 October 2018).

PLSA (2018) *Master trusts: Made simple guide.* Available at: https://www.plsa.co.uk/Portals/0/Documents/Made-Simple-Guides/2018/Master%20Trusts%20Made%20Simple%202018.pdf (accessed 25 August 2019).

Pooler, M. (2018) Tata Steel's UK arm suffers deepening core losses. *Financial Times,* 23 August. Available at: https://www.ft.com/content/86e402a4-a6ee-11e8-926a-7342fe5e173f (accessed 1 April 2019).

PPF (2018) *Annual report and accounts 2017/18.* Available at: https://ppf.co.uk/sites/default/files/file-2018-11/annual_report_2017-2018_0.pdf (accessed 1 April 2019).

Price, M. (1997) *Justice between generations: The growing power of the elderly in America.* Westport, CT: Praeger.

Prosser, T. (2016) Dualization or liberalization? Investigating precarious work in eight European countries. *Work, Employment and Society,* 30(6), 949–65.

Prudential Regulatory Authority, Financial Conduct Authority, Financial Reporting Council, and The Pensions Regulator (2019) *Joint statement on climate change.* Available at: https://www.fca.org.uk/publication/documents/joint-statement-on-climate-change.pdf (accessed 1 February 2020).

Quaglia, L., Howarth, D., and Liebe, M. (2016) The political economy of European capital markets union. *Journal of Common Market Studies,* 54(s1), 185–203.

Ragin, C. (1994) A qualitative comparative analysis of pension systems. In: *The comparative political economy of the welfare state,* eds T. Janoski and A.M. Hicks. Cambridge: Cambridge University Press, 320–45.

Rajan, A. (2018) *Passive investing: Reshaping the global investment landscape.* London: Create-Research. Available at: http://www.create-research-uk.com/?p=dlreport&t=report&r=44 (accessed 1 December 2019).

Ralfe, J. (2013) 'Actuaries' magic pencil' hides UK university pension deficit. *Financial Times,* 27 October. Available at: https://www.ft.com/content/14e5b2e6-3ccd-11e3-a8c4-00144feab7de (accessed 3 April 2019).

Ralph, O. (2017) UK companies look to sell off pension liabilities. *Financial Times,* 4 January. Available at: https://www.ft.com/content/fc3fcf42-d1bb-11e6-9341-7393bb2e1b51 (accessed 1 April 2019).

Ralph, O. and Cumbo, J. (2017) Prudential to withdraw from UK annuity market. *Financial Times,* 10 February. Available at: https://www.ft.com/content/8c49099a-efb3-11e6-ba01-119a44939bb6 (accessed 1 September 2019).

Ralph, O. and Cumbo, J. (2018) Insurers raise concerns about pension superfund. *Financial Times*, 2 April. Available at: https://www.ft.com/content/1a235f3e-3371-11e8-b5bf-23cb17fd1498 (accessed 1 April 2019).

Reeve, N. (2018) Carillion schemes poised to enter PPF as company liquidated. *Investment and Pensions Europe*, 15 January. Available at: https://www.ipe.com/countries/uk/carillion-schemes-poised-to-enter-ppf-as-company-liquidated/www.ipe.com/countries/uk/carillion-schemes-poised-to-enter-ppf-as-company-liquidated/10022680.fullarticle (accessed 1 April 2019).

Reichman, C. (2018) State of the annuity market 3 years after Armageddon. *Financial Times*, 12 April. Available at: https://www.ftadviser.com/pension-freedom/2018/04/12/state-of-the-annuity-market-3-years-after-armageddon/ (accessed 1 September 2019).

Rhodes, C. (2019) Financial services: Contribution to the UK economy. *House of Commons Library Briefing Paper No. 6193*. Available at: https://researchbriefings.parliament.uk/ResearchBriefing/Summary/SN06193#fullreport (accessed 1 August 2019).

Rhodes, M. and Natali, D. (2003) Welfare regimes and pension reform agendas. Paper presented at London School of Economics and Political Science workshop *Pension Reform in Europe: Shared Problems, Sharing Solutions*, December. Available at: https://www.researchgate.net/profile/David_Natali/publication/253143208_WELFARE_REGIMES_AND_PENSION_REFORM_AGENDAS/links/54354baf0cf2dc341dafebb3/WELFARE-REGIMES-AND-PENSION-REFORM-AGENDAS.pdf (accessed 24 August 2020).

Riedmüller, B. and Willert, M. (2007) The German pension system and social inclusion. In: *Private pensions versus social inclusion: Non-state provision for citizens at risk in Europe*, eds T. Meyer, P, Bridgen, and B. Riedmüller. London: Edward Elgar, 139–67.

Royal London (2019) Group personal pension or master trust: A guide for employers. *Royal London Policy Paper No.32*. Available at: https://www.royallondon.com/siteassets/site-docs/media-centre/policy-papers/royal-london-policy-paper-32-gpps-and-mastertrusts-final.pdf (accessed 25 August 2019).

Sanchez, C., Greenall, M., and Curry, C. (2007) *The changing landscape for private sector defined benefit pension schemes*. London: Pensions Policy Institute. Available at: https://www.webarchive.org.uk/wayback/archive/20080820220734/http://www.pensionspolicyinstitute.org.uk/uploadeddocuments/PPI_Landscape_for_DB_Schemes_8_October_2007.pdf#page=27 (accessed 1 April 2019).

Sardana, S. (2019) Carney warns of climate change threat to pension funds. *Financial Times*, 30 December. Available at: https://www.ftadviser.com/investments/2019/12/30/carney-warns-of-climate-change-threat-to-pension-funds/ (accessed 24 August 2020).

Schelkle, W. (2019) EU pension policy and financialisation: Purpose without power. *Journal of European Public Policy*, 26(4), 599–616.

Scruggs, L. and Allan, J. (2006) Welfare state decommodification in 18 OECD countries: A replication and revision. *Journal of European Social Policy*, 16(1), 55–72.

Scruggs, L. and Allan, J. (2008) Social stratification and welfare regimes for the twenty-first century: Revisiting 'The Three Worlds of Welfare Capitalism'. *World Politics*, 60(4), 642–64.

Shalev, M. (ed.) (1996) *The privatization of social policy? Occupational welfare and the welfare state in America, Scandinavia and Japan*. London: Macmillan.

Sharman, L. (2017) Emerging market equity the most popular asset class with pension schemes. *Pension Funds Online*, 17 September. Available at: https://www.pensionfundsonline.co.uk/content/pension-funds-insider/investment/emerging-market-equity-most-popular-asset-class-with-pension-schemes/2559 (accessed 1 December 2019).

Sier, C. (2012) *Local authority pensions fund costs*. London: Stonefish Consulting. Available at: https://www.tuc.org.uk/sites/default/files/tucfiles/understanding_your_investment_management_costs_chris_sier.pdf (accessed 25 August 2019).

Sikka, P. (2018) Corporate governance and family-owned companies: The case of BHS. In: *Corporate governance in contention*, eds C. Driver and G. Thompson. Oxford: Oxford University Press, 86–114.

Sikka, P. (2020) Flybe employees stand to lose much more than their jobs. *LeftFootForward*, 9 March. Available at: https://leftfootforward.org/2020/03/flybe-employees-stand-to-lose-so-much-more-than-their-jobs/ (accessed 1 April 2020).

Silcock, D. (2015) Who is ineligible for automatic enrolment? *PPI Briefing Note No. 75*. Available at: https://www.pensionspolicyinstitute.org.uk/media/1343/201509-bn75-who-is-ineligible-for-automatic-enrolment.pdf (accessed 1 February 2020).

Silcock, D., Popat, S., and Pike, T. (2016) *The under-pensioned 2016*. London: Pensions Policy Institute. Available at: https://www.pensionspolicyinstitute.org.uk/media/1802/20160301-the-underpensioned-2016-report.pdf (accessed 1 February 2020).

Sinfield, A. (2000) Tax benefits in non-state pensions. *European Journal of Social Security*, 2(2), 137–67.

Sinha, T. (2018) Mexico. In: *Towards a new pensions settlement: The international experience* (Vol. 2), eds G. McClymont and A. Tarrant. London: Policy Network, 31–8.

Somerset Webb, M. (2016) Autumn statement: Hammond needs to untangle the pension mess. *Financial Times*, 18 November. Available at: https://www.ft.com/content/82013900-aca9-11e6-ba7d-76378e4fef24 (accessed 1 March 2017).

Smith, P. (2020) World's three biggest fund houses shed €28tn of assets. *Financial Times*, 15 March. Available at: https://www.ft.com/content/438854a8-63b0-11ea-a6cd-df28cc3c6a68 (accessed 1 April 2020).

Smith, S. (2020) USS to proceed with March valuation; deficit rises to £11 billion. *Pension Age*, 31 March. Available at: https://www.pensionsage.com/pa/USS-to-proceed-with-March-valuation.php (accessed 1 April 2020).

Smith Institute, Centre for Local Economic Strategies, Pensions Investment Research Consultants, and Local Authority Pension Fund Forum (2012) *Local authority pension funds: Investing for growth*. Available at: https://cles.org.uk/wp-content/uploads/2012/09/Local-authority-pension-funds-investing-for-growth.pdf (accessed 17 February 2020).

Stewart, F. (2007) Pension fund investment in hedge funds. *OECD Working Papers on Insurance and Private Pensions No.12*. Available at: http://www.oecd.org/finance/private-pensions/39368369.pdf (accessed 1 December 2019).

Streeck, W. (2011) Taking capitalism seriously: Towards an institutionalist approach to contemporary political economy. *Socio-Economic Review*, 9(1), 137–67.

Streeck, W. and Thelen, K.A. (eds) (2005) *Beyond continuity: Institutional change in advanced political economies*. Oxford: Oxford University Press.

Sullivan, M. (2003) *Understanding pensions*. London, Routledge.

Tapper, H. (2016) The pernicious effects of NEST's market distortion. *The Vision of the Pension PlayPen*, 25 October. Available at: https://henrytapper.com/2016/10/25/the-pernicious-effect-of-nests-market-distortion/ (accessed 9 March 2017).

Taylor, M. (2017) *Good work: The Taylor review of modern working practices*. London: HM Government. Available at: https://assets.publishing.service.gov.uk/government/uploads/system/uploads/attachment_data/file/627671/good-work-taylor-review-modern-working-practices-rg.pdf (accessed 3 April 2019).

Taylor-Gooby, P. (1997) In defence of second-best theory: State, class and capital in social policy. *Journal of Social Policy*, 26, 171–92.

Thaler, R. (1994) *Quasi-rational economics*. New York: Russell Sage Foundation.

Thaler, R. and Benartzi, S. (2004) Save more tomorrow™: Using behavioural economics to increase employee saving. *Journal of Political Economy*, 112(S1), S164–87.

Thaler, R. and Sunstein, C. (2008) *Nudge: Improving decisions about health, wealth and happiness*. New Haven, CT: Yale University Press.

Thomas, B., Dorling, D., and Smith, G.D. (2010) Inequalities in premature mortality in Britain: An observational study. *British Medical Journal*, 341, c3639.

Thurley, D. (2010a) Financial Assistance Scheme. *House of Commons Library Standard Note SN/BT 3085*. Available at: https://researchbriefings.parliament.uk/ResearchBriefing/Summary/SN03085 (accessed 1 April 2019).

Thurley, D. (2010b) National Employment Savings Trust: Background. *House of Commons Library Standard Note 04826*. Available at: https://researchbriefings.parliament.uk/ResearchBriefing/Summary/SN04826#fullreport (accessed 25 August 2019).

Thurley, D. (2011) Pension credit. *House of Commons Library Standard Note 1439*. Available at: researchbriefings.files.parliament.uk/documents/SN01439/SN01439.pdf (accessed 9 March 2017).

Thurley, D. (2015) Pensions: Annuities. *House of Commons Library Briefing Paper SN06552*. Available at: https://researchbriefings.parliament.uk/ResearchBriefing/Summary/SN06552 (accessed 1 September 2019).

Thurley, D. (2017) Pension scheme charges. *House of Commons Library Briefing Paper CBP-06209*. Available at: https://researchbriefings.parliament.uk/ResearchBriefing/Summary/SN06209 (accessed 1 September 2019).

Thurley, D. (2018a) Overview of the Pensions Protection Fund. *House of Commons Library Briefing Paper CBP-03917*. Available at: https://researchbriefings.parliament.uk/ResearchBriefing/Summary/SN03917 (accessed 1 April 2019).

Thurley, D. (2018b) Pension flexibilities: The 'freedom and choice' reforms. *House of Commons Library Briefing Paper CBP-6891*. Available at: https://researchbriefings.parliament.uk/ResearchBriefing/Summary/SN06891 (accessed 1 September 2019).

Thurley, D. (2020) State pension uprating. *House of Commons Library Briefing Paper CBP-5649*. Available at: http://researchbriefings.files.parliament.uk/documents/SN05649/SN05649.pdf (accessed 1 May 2020).

Thurley, D. and McInnes, R. (2019) Public service pensions provision: Facts and figures. *House of Commons Library Briefing Paper CBP-8478*. Available at: https://researchbriefings.parliament.uk/ResearchBriefing/Summary/CBP-8478 (accessed 1 April 2019).

Timms, N. (2004) Turner report will require much more hard work. *Financial Times*, 8 October. Available at: https://www.ft.com/content/3ec8c58e-1875-11d9-8963-00000e2511c8 (accessed 1 August 2019).

Tolos, H., Wang, P., Zhang, M., and Shand, R. (2014) Retirement systems and pension reform: A Malaysian perspective. *International Labour Review*, 153(3), 489–502.

Tovey, A. (2016) Multi-billion pension hurdle set to block Tata deal. *The Telegraph*, 28 April. Available at: https://www.telegraph.co.uk/business/2016/04/26/multi-billion-pension-hurdle-set-to-block-tata-steel-deal/ (accessed 1 April 2019).

Toynbee, P. (2014) Older people vote—that's why George Osborne's budget is for them. *The Guardian*, 21 March. Available at: https://www.theguardian.com/commentisfree/2014/mar/21/older-people-vote-george-osborne-budget (accessed 9 March 2017).

Trades Union Congress (TUC) (2013) Many private sector workers will be worse off under state pension reforms. Available at: https://www.tuc.org.uk/news/many-private-sector-workers-will-be-worse-under-state-pension-reforms (accessed 1 February 2020).

Trades Union Congress (TUC) (2018) *The retirement lottery*. Available at: https://www.tuc.org.uk/sites/default/files/Fixingretirementlottery.pdf (accessed 1 September 2019).

Trampusch, C. (2013) Employers and collectively negotiated occupational pensions in Sweden, Denmark and Norway: Promoters, vacillators and adversaries. *European Journal of Industrial Relations*, 19(1), 37–53.

Trampusch, C. (2015) The financialisation of sovereign debt: An institutional analysis of the reforms in German public debt management. *German Politics*, 24(2), 119–36.

Turner, J.A. and Hughes, G. (2008) Large declines in defined benefit pension plans are not inevitable: The experience of Canada, Ireland, the United Kingdom, and the United States.

Pensions Institute Discussion Paper PI-0821. Available at: https://www.pensions-institute. org/workingpapers/wp0821.pdf (accessed 3 April 2019).

Tutyens, P. (2019) Countering financial interests for social purposes: What drives state intervention in pension markets in the context of financialisation? *Journal of European Public Policy*, 26(4), 560–78.

UCU (2018) *Report of the Joint Expert Panel*. Available at: https://www.ucu.org.uk/ media/9523/JEP-report-September-2018/pdf/report-of-the-joint-expert-panel_002.pdf (accessed 26 April 2019).

USS (2018) *Reports and Accounts for the Year Ended 31 March 2018*. Available at: https://www. uss.co.uk/~/media/document-libraries/uss/how-uss-is-run/reports-and-accounts/uss-report-accounts-2018.pdf (accessed 1 April 2019).

van der Veen, R.J. and van der Brug, W. (2012) Three worlds of social insurance: On the validity of Esping-Andersen's welfare regime dimensions. *British Journal of Political Science*, 43(2), 323–43.

van der Zwan, N. (2014) Making sense of financialization. *Socio-Economic Review*, 12(1), 99–129.

van der Zwan, N. (2017) Financialisation and the pension system: Lessons from the United States and the Netherlands. *Journal of Modern European History*, 15(4), 554–84.

Walker, A. and Foster, L. (2006) Caught between virtue and ideological necessity: A century of pension policies in the UK. *Review of Political Economy*, 18(3), 427–48.

Walker, A. and Naegele, G. (1999) *The politics of old age in Europe*. Buckingham: Open University Press.

Walker, O. (2018) M&A in asset management sector climbs to 8-year high. *Financial Times*, 15 January. Available at: https://www.ft.com/content/2f1e77f2-f80c-11e7-88f7-5465a6ce1a00 (accessed 1 December 2019).

Wang, P., Zhang, M., Shand, R., and Howell, K.E. (2014) Retirement, pension systems and models of pension systems. University of Plymouth Economics Working Paper No.14/02. Available at: https://www.plymouth.ac.uk/uploads/production/document/path/8/8845/ models_of_pension_systems_wp.pdf (accessed 1 November 2018).

Watson, M. (2013) New labour's 'paradox of responsibility' and the unravelling of its macroeconomic policy. *British Journal of Politics and International Relations*, 15(1), 6–22.

Webb, S. (2004) Citizen's pension is the only way forward. Press release. Available at: http:// www.stevewebb.org.uk/news2004/news378.html (accessed 16 October 2013).

Webb, S. (2012) A new future for workplace pensions? *The Telegraph*, 8 April. Available at: https://www.telegraph.co.uk/finance/personalfinance/pensions/9193598/A-new-future-for-workplace-pensions.html (accessed 9 March 2017).

Webb, S. (2015) 'Still much to do' on pensions policy. *Retirement Planner*, 30 June. Available at: https://www.retirement-planner.co.uk/3786/steve-webb-still-much-to-do-on-pensions-policy (accessed 1 September 2019).

White, J. (2017) Climate change and the generational timescape. *The Sociological Review*, 65(4), 763–78.

Whiteside, N. and Ebbinghaus, B. (2012) Shifting responsibilities in Western European pensions systems: What future for social models. *Global Social Policy*, 12(3), 266–82.

Wigglesworth, R. (2020) The ESG revolution is widening gaps between winners and losers. *Financial Times*, 4 February. Available at: https://www.ft.com/content/12bd616e-442b-11ea-a43a-c4b328d9061c (accessed 16 February 2020).

Willets, D. (2010) *The pinch: How the baby boomers took their children's future—and why they should give it back*. London: Atlantic.

Wilson, R. (2017) Millennials likely to have 12 jobs in their working lives, research finds. *Talint International*, 20 November. Available at: https://www.recruitment-international. co.uk/blog/2017/11/millennials-likely-to-have-12-jobs-in-their-working-lives-research-finds (accessed 1 September 2019).

Wiß, T. (2019) Reinforcement of pension financialisation as a response to financial crises in Germany, the Netherlands and the United Kingdom. *Journal of European Public Policy*, 26(4), 501–20.

Wolf, S. (2019) Housing: A 'good' investment for pension funds? *Mallow Street*, 4 November. Available at: https://mallowstreet.com/Article/b45682 (accessed 17 February 2020).

Wood, A., Young, P., Körbitz, C., and Ramambason, C. (2017) *Pension scheme charges survey 2016*. Available at: https://assets.publishing.service.gov.uk/government/uploads/system/uploads/attachment_data/file/645005/pension-charges-survey-2016-charges-in-defined-contribution-pension-schemes-summary.pdf (accessed 25 August 2019).

Woods, D. (2011) High court decision on what makes a DC pension throws up questions for employers. *HR Magazine*, 28 July. Available at: http://www.hrmagazine.co.uk/article-details/high-court-decision-on-what-makes-a-dc-pension-throws-up-questions-for-employers (accessed 9 March 2017).

World Bank (1994) Averting the old age crisis: Policies to protect the old and promote growth. Available at: http://documents.worldbank.org/curated/en/973571468174557899/pdf/multi-page.pdf (accessed 1 November 2018).

Zhu, H. and Walker, A. (2018) Pension system reform in China: Who gets what pension? *Social Policy and Administration*, 52(7), 1410–24.

Index